Theology and the Experience of Disability

The Christian gospel compels humanity to embrace deeper ways of being human together that will overcome false divisions and exclusions in search of flourishing and graced communities. Presenting both short narratives emerging out of theological reflection on experience and analytical essays arising from engagement in scholarly conversations Theology and the Experience of Disability is a conscious attempt to develop theology by and with people with disabilities instead of theology about people with disabilities. A mixture of academic, professional, practical, and/or lived experience is brought to the topic in search of constructive multi-disciplinary proposals for church and society. The result is an interdisciplinary engagement with the constructive possibilities that emerge from a distinctly Christian understanding of disability as lived experience.

Myk Habets lectures at Carey Baptist College in Systematic Theology, Hermeneutics, and Ethics. He is Head of Carey Graduate School and is Editor of *Pacific Journal of Baptist Research*, Associate Editor of *Participatio: The Journal of the Thomas Torrance Theological Fellowship*, vice-President of the Thomas F. Torrance Theological Fellowship, and is on the editorial board of *Journal for Theological Interpretation*.

Andrew Picard lectures at Carey Baptist College in Applied Theology, Ecclesiology, and Theology of Culture. He is Associate Editor of *Pacific Journal of Baptist Research* and Co-President of New Zealand Baptist Research and Historical Society.

Theology and the Experience of Disability

Interdisciplinary Perspectives from Voices Down Under

Edited by
Andrew Picard and Myk Habets

LONDON AND NEW YORK

First published 2016
by Routledge
2 Park Square, Milton Park, Abingdon, Oxon OX14 4RN

and by Routledge
711 Third Avenue, New York, NY 10017

Routledge is an imprint of the Taylor & Francis Group, an informa business

© 2016 selection and editorial matter, Andrew Picard and Myk Habets; individual chapters, the contributors

The right of Andrew Picard and Myk Habets to be identified as the authors of the editorial material, and of the authors for their individual chapters, has been asserted in accordance with sections 77 and 78 of the Copyright, Designs and Patents Act 1988.

All rights reserved. No part of this book may be reprinted or reproduced or utilised in any form or by any electronic, mechanical, or other means, now known or hereafter invented, including photocopying and recording, or in any information storage or retrieval system, without permission in writing from the publishers.

Trademark notice: Product or corporate names may be trademarks or registered trademarks, and are used only for identification and explanation without intent to infringe.

British Library Cataloguing in Publication Data
A catalogue record for this book is available from the British Library

Library of Congress Cataloging-in-Publication Data
Names: Picard, Andrew, editor.
Title: Theology and the experience of disability : interdisciplinary perspectives from voices down under / edited by Andrew Picard and Myk Habets.
Description: Burlington : Ashgate, 2016. | Includes bibliographical references and index.
Identifiers: LCCN 2015038669 | ISBN 9781472458209 (hardcover : alk. paper) | ISBN 9781317011149 (ebook) | ISBN 9781317011132 (epub)
Subjects: LCSH: Church and minorities. | People with disabilities. | Disabilities—Religious aspects—Christianity. | Church work with people with disabilities.
Classification: LCC BV639.M56 T44 2016 | DDC 261.8/321—dc23
LC record available at http://lccn.loc.gov/2015038669

ISBN: 9781472458209 (hbk)
ISBN: 9781317011149 (ebk - PDF)
ISBN: 9781317011132 (ebk - ePUB)

Typeset in Bembo
by Apex CoVantage, LLC

Contents

List of Figures and Table	viii
Notes on Contributors	ix
Foreword by Marva J. Dawn	xv
Acknowledgements	xvii

Introduction: Theology and the Experience of Disability 'Down Under'   1
ANDREW PICARD AND MYK HABETS

PART I
Theology, Disability, and Being   7

1   **Disability and the Theology of 4-D Personhood**   9
SUE PATTERSON

2   **The World of Cystic Fibrosis: From Diagnosis to Dignity**   21
D. GARETH JONES

3   **Parenting a Child with Autism, and the Father-heart of God**   32
IAN WADDINGTON

4   **Disability Discrimination in the Book of Job**   41
KIRK PATSTON

5   **No Longer Strangers: Disabled Ontology and the Church as Meaningful Community in Liquid Modernity**   53
ANDREW PICARD

6 Conversations with James on Leadership: What
   Can We Learn about Leadership and Personhood
   from People with Severe Cognitive Disability?   73
   CHARLES HEWLETT

7 'He's My Mate': Cerebral Palsy, Church, and
   the Gift of Friendship   78
   MANUELE TEOFILO

PART II
Theology, Disability, and Belonging   87

8 The Silence Surrounding Psych Wards   89
   CHRISTINE WELTEN

9 Disability in the Australian Church: Results
   from the 2011 Church Life Survey   95
   JASON FORBES AND LINDSEY GALE

10 'A Person Standing in the Gap': The Deaf
   Community as a Mission Field   118
   CELIA KING

11 Banqueting and Disability in the Ancient World:
   Reconsidering the Parable of the Great Banquet
   (Luke 14:15–24)   129
   LOUISE GOSBELL

12 Mephibosheth at the Table: A High Point in
   Davidic Kingship – 2 Samuel 9:1–13   145
   ROD THOMPSON

13 Welcoming and Including People with Intellectual
   Disability: A Report on a Study of Five Churches   152
   CAROL FEARON

14 From Inclusion to Belonging: Why 'Disabled' Bodies
   are Necessary for the Faithfulness of the Church   171
   JOHN SWINTON

PART III
Theology, Disability, and Becoming 183

15 **Unseen Disability in the Australian Pentecostal Church: Australian Christian Churches, the Four-fold Gospel, and Challenges for the Mentally Ill** 185
GRETA E.C. WELLS

16 **Beyond Charity: How can Society have a High Value of Disabled People?** 199
EVAN CLULEE

17 **Disability and Divinization: Eschatological Parables and Allegations** 212
MYK HABETS

18 **Hope in the 'Mountain Manifesto': The Beatitudes' Alternative to the Social Model's Hope** 235
IMMANUEL KOKS

19 **Disability and the Renewal of Theological Education: Beyond Ableism** 250
AMOS YONG

20 **The Trouble with Normal: What Difference Does a Theology of Disability Make?** 264
RHONDA SWENSON AND MARY CAYGILL

Author/Subject Index 273
Biblical References Index 279

Figures and Table

Figures

9.1	NCLS 2011 findings	98
9.2	Disability in church and society	99
9.3	Disability in the denominations	100
9.4	Families living with disability in church and society	101
9.5	People working/volunteering in the disability sector	102
9.6	Achieving an active culture of disability inclusion in churches	107
9.7	Public church statements on disability inclusion	107
9.8	Congregational education on disability inclusion	108
9.9	Overall performance of church accessibility	109
9.10	Perceptions of attendees regarding church performance on disability inclusion	109
9.11	Frequency of church attendance for people who live with disabilities compared to people with no disability	111
9.12	Frequency of devotional practice for people who live with disabilities compared to people with no disability	112
9.13	Churches that connect with disability	113
11.1	Black-figure Laconian *kantharos* with *komast*, fifth century BCE, from the Louvre, Paris	142
20.1	The disproportionate cross	265
20.2	Mosaic butterfly	268

Table

12.1	Sequence of chapters in 2 Samuel 8–10	146

Notes on Contributors

Mary Caygill is an ordained Methodist minister working in an inner-city parish in Christchurch, one of the city churches that were destroyed by the earthquakes of September 2010 and February 2011. Prior to taking up this appointment she was a lecturer in Practical Theology at the School of Theology, University of Auckland, and Principal of Trinity Methodist Theological College in Auckland. Her postgraduate studies have been in the area of Practical Theology, looking at Theology and Practice of Hope in the context of ecclesial and cultural 'death'. In recent years her research interests have been in the area of Body Theology, and in particular the interface between Disability Studies and Disability Theology and the intersection with Feminist, Post-colonial and Queer Theologies and the respective offerings that can be made to an emerging Theological Anthropology that is more liberative in the area of Disability Theology.

Evan Clulee is a disabled person who advocates and educates for the full inclusion of disabled people in society. He is passionate about seeing justice for people with disabilities and promoting their ability to live full and good lives. At the same time he wishes to see a society that fully accepts and includes every member of society – including disabled people. Evan is CEO/Community Leader at Mt Tabor Trust, a non-profit organization and intentional Christian community supporting people with intellectual disabilities. This community is run on L'Arche principles, with disabled people at the core. Evan completed a Bachelor of Applied Theology at Carey Baptist College as well as prior training at Faith Bible College. Evan works hard to ensure that his theological study and Christian faith deeply inform his practice. Evan and his family reside in the Rodney district of Auckland City.

Carol Fearon, after finishing a BSc. in Environmental Science, married and had four children, she and her family moved to New Zealand in 1988. Shortly after arriving in New Zealand, her third child, Rachel, developed epilepsy and developmental delays. Carol spent many years raising her family and running her own business. Carol has recently completed a Master of Applied Theology at Carey Graduate School, Carey Baptist College. Chapter 13 is based on her thesis, 'Welcoming and Including People with Intellectual Disability: A Study of Five Churches'. Now that her children are grown and Rachel is living independently, Carol is hoping to do further research about the church and disability.

Jason Forbes is a minister in the Presbyterian Church of Australia. He has cerebral palsy, which affects his speech, mobility and fine motor control, yet maintains an independent lifestyle. Jason works for New South Wales Presbyterian Social Services as the Disability Advocate to the New South Wales Presbyterian Church. This involves raising awareness of disability and equipping the church to respond to the needs of people who have disabilities. Jason graduated from Presbyterian Theological Centre in 2012 with a BTh. and a PG Dip. in Advanced Theology, and wrote his exit thesis on 'The Work of the Holy Spirit in a Person with a Disability and Their Relationship with the Church'. He has a keen interest in biblical languages, and would like to extend his academic work in theology and disability in the future.

Lindsey Gale is an occupational therapist, currently working for CBM Australia as Resource Co-ordinator for the Luke 14 programme, an initiative that educates and equips the church on disability inclusion. Additional post-graduate qualifications in theology and twenty years of involvement in Anglican ministry alongside her husband Phil have enabled the development of a range of practical ministry resources for churches on this topic. These include bible studies, access guides, interactive workshops and the Australian College of Theology intensive course 'Disability and Normality'.

Louise Gosbell is a PhD candidate at Macquarie University in Sydney, Australia. Her dissertation, 'The Poor, the Crippled, the Blind and the Lame: Physical and Sensory Impairment in the Gospels of the New Testament', addresses the social and cultic aspects of impairments attested in the Gospels in light of their Greco-Roman context. Louise also works in a voluntary capacity as the Sydney Co-ordinator for CBM's Luke 14 programme, which aims to help churches become more inclusive and welcoming of people with disability and their families. In these combined roles Louise has not only met with various church representatives, but has also preached in churches, presented at various conferences and lectured in theological institutes on the issues of disability and inclusion. Louise is married to Mark, a special educator, and they have three beautiful daughters.

Myk Habets lectures in Systematic Theology and Ethics at Carey Baptist College. He is Head of Carey Graduate School and Editor of the *Pacific Journal of Baptist Research*, Associate Editor of *Participatio: The Journal of the Thomas Torrance Theological Fellowship*, Co-Vice-President of the Thomas F. Torrance

Theological Fellowship, and is on the editorial board of the *Journal for Theological Interpretation*. Myk is also on the steering committee of the Theological Interpretation of Scripture Seminar at the Society of Biblical Literature. He has published articles on constructive systematic theology in international journals and is the author of *Theosis in the Theology of Thomas Torrance*; *The Anointed Son*, and *Theology in Transposition*, in addition to editing over five books. Myk and his family preach and worship in a Baptist church in Auckland.

Charles Hewlett is Principal of Carey Baptist College, where he also lectures in Leadership and Applied Theology. Charles is married to Joanne, and they have three children. Janelle died from cancer in 2005 aged 13 years. James, aged 21 years, has severe intellectual disabilities. Their third child, Jessica, is seven years old. In 2011 they co-authored the book *Hurting Hope: What Parents Feel when Their Children Suffer*. Charles and Joanne speak widely in New Zealand churches and Christian organizations on the topic of theology and disability. Charles's research interests include how those with severe intellectual disability participate in the mission of God.

D. Gareth Jones is an Emeritus Professor at the University of Otago, where he is a Professor of Anatomy. He has also been Director of the Bioethics Centre, and Deputy Vice-Chancellor (Academic and International) at Otago. He has written extensively at the interface of the biomedical sciences, ethics and faith, especially as regards the human body and reproductive technologies. While some of his writings are directed at academic audiences, others have a Christian focus and are aimed at more general readerships. His latest books range from *Speaking for the Dead: The Human Body in Biology and Medicine* and *The Peril and Promise of Medical Technology* to *Designers of the Future* and two edited volumes on *Medicine and Theology in Dialogue*. Gareth has a grandson with cystic fibrosis.

Celia King, a Deaf Christian, is a trained teacher of Deaf and hearing-impaired students in the Auckland metropolitan area. In 2013 she was seconded to the Ministry of Education to develop tools to support the curriculum in the inclusion of special needs students in mainstream classrooms. Along with teaching, she holds a Master of Counselling degree with Honours and offers counselling to Deaf people and their families as well as supervision of Deaf professionals working in the area of mental health. She was previously a Chaplain for the Deaf, and is currently a chaplain for St Johns in West Auckland, advising on matters of faith relating to the services they provide. A strong interest in mission sees her travel overseas regularly to meet and work with other Deaf Christians.

Immanuel Koks lectures in Biblical Theology at Laidlaw College in Auckland. He also guest-teaches disability-related topics at the college. He has recently completed his MTh. from Regent College, Vancouver. Immanuel's thesis examined the way Jürgen Moltmann's understanding of God impacts his theology of hope. As a person with cerebral palsy, Immanuel is drawn to the study of hope because he wants to know how the gospel gives hope to those with disabilities, while not minimizing all the good arising from rich lives experienced in diverse embodiment.

Kirk Patston lectures in the Old Testament at Sydney Missionary and Bible College, with a focus on the book of Isaiah and the Old Testament Wisdom Literature. He has recently completed a PhD through the University of Sydney on how otherness in Job contributes to a Christian understanding of disability. His connections to disability include previous work as a speech pathologist and being the father of a young man with intellectual impairment and autism. He is a Presbyterian minister involved in preaching at conventions and his local church. He sits on the Ethics Committee of the Cerebral Palsy Alliance.

Sue Patterson returned to New Zealand in 2010 to take up the post of Senior Lecturer at Bishopdale Theological College in Nelson following a decade of pastoral ministry in the (Anglican) Church of Ireland. Prior to that she lectured at Trinity College, Bristol and was a Fulbright Scholar at the Center of Theological Inquiry, Princeton. Her first book, *Christian Realist Theology in a Postmodern Age*, was published in 1999, and her second, *Word, Words and World*, in 2013. She is currently writing a book on conversion and personhood. Her research explores the interface between theology, philosophy, psychology, and ethics. Her interest in theological and medical ethics has arisen out of the experience of caring and advocating for her tetraplegic daughter, who sadly passed away in October 2014 aged 37.

Andrew Picard lectures in Applied Theology at Carey Baptist College. His research and teaching interests are at the intersection of Christian Doctrine, Culture, and Ecclesiology. Along with teaching, Andrew is pursuing a PhD through the University of Otago which engages Colin Gunton's Trinitarian theology and Zygmunt Bauman's social theory in order to develop a Trinitarian ecclesiology in the context of Liquid Modernity. Andrew is Co-President of New Zealand Baptist Research and Historical Society and an Associate Editor of the *Pacific Journal of Baptist Research*. Andrew is a Baptist minister who attends Titirangi Baptist Church, where his family enjoy journeying together with Deaf friends.

Rhonda Swenson is a self-taught artist and poet who lives with multiple disabilities. She is interested in disability advocacy at both systemic and individual levels. Rhonda's art and poetry provokes and encourages discussion around the intersection of issues related to spirituality and the social norms of disability.

Notes on Contributors   xiii

John Swinton holds the chair in Practical Theology and Pastoral Care at the University of Aberdeen, Scotland. He is also an honorary Professor at Aberdeen's Centre for Advanced Studies in Nursing. John is an ordained minister of the Presbyterian Church of Scotland who for more than a decade worked as a registered nurse specializing in psychiatry and learning disabilities. He also worked for a number of years as a hospital chaplain. His areas of research include the relationship between theology and health, and the theology of disability. He has published widely on the theology of disability, including *Dementia: Living in the Memories of God* and a new reader in disability and theology, *Disability in the Christian Tradition: A Reader*, which he co-edited with Brian Brock. He founded the Centre for Spirituality, Health and Disability at the University of Aberdeen, which recently won a major research award for a two-year project exploring the spiritual needs of people with profound and complex learning disabilities. He is an ordained minister of the Church of Scotland with a strong commitment to supporting the work of the church.

Manuele Teofilo is a young man with a cerebral palsy condition. He was born in Samoa, a South Pacific Island, and grew up in New Zealand. His Christian faith began later in his childhood, in an English-speaking Baptist church. Youth group, church events and his Christian surroundings have had a pronounced influence on his views and attitudes towards disability in general as well as his own disability. Manuele credits his Christian faith for teaching him how to be persistent and positive in life. This has planted a desire in him to pursue a life which displays a 'can-do' regardless of the narrow expectations of society. He graduated with a Certificate in Applied Theology from Carey Baptist College, and he is now studying for a Bachelor of Human Services at the University of Auckland.

Rod Thompson is currently the National Principal/CEO of Laidlaw College in Auckland. He and his wife Rosanne live on the college campus, though their family, including four grown-up children and five grandchildren, live in Sydney. Rod has lived in Australia for most of his life, coming to New Zealand in 2004 after he had completed his doctoral studies in education at Macquarie University in Sydney. He joined the staff of Laidlaw College in 2008, becoming Principal towards the end of 2010. Since beginning this role, Rod has initiated a Disability Reference Group at Laidlaw College in order to help form it as a community where people with disabilities belong and flourish. Rod's areas of particular interest include biblical theology and worldview studies.

Ian Waddington is the Co-ordinator of the Certificate of Christian Studies programme at Laidlaw College, Auckland. In this programme he lectures on the New Testament, Old Testament, biblical theology, discipleship and church history, as well as academic writing, research and study skills. He is also involved with the assessment of college applicants for language ability, and academic support for students on campus, with a particular focus on students of other cultures. He completed his MTh. in Biblical Studies in 2014, looking at aspects of service, servanthood, and slavery as narrative themes in the Gospel of Mark. Ian is also a member of the Laidlaw College Disability Reference Group, and worked for five years in the disability sector with Riding for the Disabled.

Greta E.C. Wells lectures in Pastoral Ministry at Alphacrucis College, Sydney. Her research interests reflect the broad range of tertiary studies she has undertaken, which include architecture, journalism, sociology, biblical studies and pastoral theology. Greta is engaged in research on the perceptions of mental illness within the Pentecostal church, the impact of postmodernity on ministry and spirituality practices, and the rhetorical role of architecture in shaping spaces of communal worship. She completed her MTh. (Pastoral Studies) at Excelsia College in June 2013, with her dissertation exploring the attitudes of Australian Christian Churches pastors towards anxiety disorders. More recently, her research has focused on the implications of Pentecostal-Charismatic spirituality for ageing Australians.

Christine Welten graduated from Laidlaw College in 2014 with a Master of Theology degree. Her research interests are focused in practical theology and exploring culture and mental health through the lens of theology. Christine works as a freelance journalist and is a small business owner. She speaks about mental health and community in churches throughout New Zealand and mentors at-risk youth. Christine has published in the area of theology and mental health, and she hopes to pursue a PhD in the area of theology and psychosis.

Amos Yong is Professor of Theology and Mission and Director of the Center for Missiological Research at Fuller Theological Seminary, Pasadena, California. He writes widely on Pentecostal Theology, Systematic Theology and the Theology of Disability. He is a former President of the Society for Pentecostal Studies (2008–9) and the founding Co-chair for the Pentecostal-Charismatic Movements Group for the American Academy of Religion (2006–11). Amos is co-editor of four book series: *Pentecostal Manifestos*, *CHARIS: Christianity and Renewal – Interdisciplinary Studies*, *Missiological Engagements: Church, Theology, and Culture in Global Contexts*, and *Studies in Religion, Theology and Disability*. He has published widely in the area of theology and disability, including his important book *Theology and Down Syndrome*, and his recently published *The Bible, Disability, and the Church*. He is married with three children, and is a licensed minister in the Assemblies of God churches.

Foreword

It is doubly ironic (as well as a double blessing) that after I had agreed to write this foreword – and just before I had a chance to start reading the contributions that comprise the book – I fell off my walker because my feet stumbled, and I broke my arm. Now three limbs out of four were useless: one leg crippled because of a doctor's misdiagnosis and encased in a toe-to-knee brace, one leg amputated and imitated by a well-crafted prosthesis, and one arm now immobilized in a hot-pink cast.

One reason why I call it ironic is that I was already disabled and did not think I needed more troubles to make me sympathetic. The blessing is that I did discover a deeper compassion, especially for those folk with disabilities who wrote first-person articles, who encountered various difficulties to engage in the symposium and writing that this book represents.

The second irony is that I have never before experienced strain in reading (except with my vision affliction), and this time it was the difficulty of turning and holding stapled pages in a manuscript (each chapter as a separate document) with one hand. The blessing that accompanied this adversity was the ponderous slowness that enabled me to contemplate each writer's perspective more carefully. The result was to connect more thoroughly, for example, with the dissimilar descriptions for how to care for people with distinct kinds of disabilities, whereas previously I had treated their needs more generally.

What comes through clearly in this assortment of articles is that each person should be cared for individually. That, of course, is common sense, but the gift of this volume is that each voice speaks out with unique deviations. That necessitates indispensable conversations in the initiation of our friendships, but it also provides a practical approach for kindling a more insightful relationship that truly encompasses the genuine needs of each exceptional personality.

The originality of each character is manifested in the brilliance of the disparate styles in these chapters. I am grateful that there are several more scholarly monographs because they furnish numerous morsels of precise knowledge that were lacking in my (and, I am sure, many other persons') comprehension of plentiful sets of limitations.

On the other hand, but equally significant, several chapters in this collection strike more heartfelt notes and empower all of us to participate in some of the emotional burdens that persons with disabilities often quietly bear. This reminds me of one of the most consequential lessons I ever learned in a hospital many years ago – that I am not an 'amputee', but an individual with an amputation. In other words, all of us with copious impairments are not defined by those disablements. We have them, but they do not make us who we are. We especially need to teach this to doctors, who often say such things as 'the diabetic in Room 104' instead of 'the lady in Room 104 who has diabetes'. Do you see how important this lesson is in connection with partaking in each person's own unparalleled emotional jolts?

I commend the planners of the original symposium on which this book is based for including a wide selection of types of affliction in the gathering – not only to ensure a range of perspectives in the initial conversations, but also to enlarge the vision of readers of this subsequent publication. We all lack sufficient awareness of how many objects and attitudes in our society build obstacles and barriers for men and women of divergent abilities. This is a typical problem for religious communities. That is why I am so grateful that this book was written from a faith perspective – to invite us all to make sure that care for those with limitations is a greater concern for our devout fellowships, to establish more friendships across the scale of believers and abilities, to multiply the numbers of those with needs that are being met by the church, to make individual congregations more hospitable to a superior breadth of the population.

I *love* this book. It feeds our souls, our hearts, and our minds. It remains for me to plead with you: after you read this, please put its many gifts into your actions and attitudes and affections.

Marva J. Dawn
Ascension Day, 2015

Acknowledgements

The genesis of this volume arose out of a unique conference on the difference a theology of disability makes which was co-sponsored by Carey Baptist College and Laidlaw College. Both colleges are committed to journeying together with people with disabilities in a way that bears witness to the rich diversity that is the body of Christ.

To that end, we acknowledge the leadership of both principals, Charles Hewlett and Rod Thompson, who in their respective ways have a long and deep commitment to people with disabilities. We thank the various authors for their profound contributions to this volume, especially those for whom academic publishing is not their vocation. We thank two Sarahs: Sarah Lloyd for having the foresight to commission this volume, and Sarah Snell for formatting the work.

Finally, we thank those families, churches, and communities who fostered the passion, dedication, and ability for this research to find fruition. It is out of these families, churches, and communities that a conversation like this can be had.

Introduction

Theology and the Experience of Disability 'Down Under'

Andrew Picard and Myk Habets

Humans come in a dizzying array of sizes, shapes, colours, personalities, and temperaments. We are physically, emotionally, geographically, genetically, and psychologically different from each other; we are individuals. Yet the 'we', the 'human' spoken of and identified here, suggests commonality, continuity, and consistency. Being human and human being is thus a constant and a variable. Various anthropologies have sought to account for these constant-variables; none, however, have found universal acceptance. This is especially so amidst the conditions of late modernity, where people are often treated as commodities. Theological anthropology has its own contribution to defining what it is to be human. While contested, the dominant definition of the human amongst Christian theology is that we are created in the image of God to image God, and it is this imaging of God that most clearly defines who we are.

But what of those amongst us who either do not clearly exhibit certain forms of being human (such as discursive reason, personal relationality, and purposive action) or whose personhood is characterized by difference from the established (ableist) assumptions of what it means to be human (blindness, deafness, Down syndrome, and so forth)? John Swinton asks, precisely what is it that holds together such diverse human experiences as autism, schizophrenia, paraplegia, Alzheimer's, attention deficit hyperactivity disorder, multiple sclerosis, cystic fibrosis, and Down syndrome, and defines them all as disabilities? What binds these radically diverse, and in many ways unconnected, human experiences and gives them commonality? He rightly contends that the answer, of course, is nothing at all, other than that, for a variety of reasons, people have chosen to place them together under the general term 'disability'. People might choose to do this for many reasons – some good, some bad. The point is that the modern notion of disability considers all disabilities as a socially constructed category rather than naturally occurring phenomena.[1] The social model of disability argues that disability is not about

---

1 John Swinton, 'From Inclusion to Belonging: A Practical Theology of Community, Disability and Humanness', *Journal of Religion, Disability and Health* 15 (2012): 173–74.

individual impairments, but the shared experience of oppression and injustice by people who are considered to be different. As Swinton states:

> It is society's negative response to human impairment and difference that holds together the disparate group of experiences that come under the banner of disability. 'You may be blind and I might have Down's syndrome, but we are melded together in our shared oppression; to be disabled is to be oppressed.'[2]

Awareness of the socially constructed nature of disability does not imply we are not all different, and some of those differences can be classified and distinguished from other groups. The early diagnosis of those with schizophrenia, for instance, allows for the loving care of those in our midst who struggle in areas of life. It affords the opportunity for medication which can significantly assist in flourishing where people would otherwise flounder, and to provide counselling, support, and services which enable them to remain within their communities and networks of relationships. Nonetheless, defining such groupings is not neutral, and the definitions often assume stable and fixed identities by employing stereotyped narratives to distinguish 'disability' from 'normativity'.[3] Human difference and diversity can be unsettling, especially for those who are used to the assumed forms and structures of society. The contributors to this volume view the richness, plurality, and intersubjectivity of human difference and otherness as a gift to be received rather than a problem to be overcome. In Christ, the gospel offers us a renewed understanding of what it means to be human which challenges our established assumptions and creates fissures in our disabling narratives and schemas.

This volume emerged from a 2013 conference, *Theology, Disability, and the People of God*, co-sponsored by Carey Baptist College and Laidlaw College in Auckland, New Zealand. As islands in the South Pacific, in the Southern Hemisphere, New Zealand and Australia are affectionately referred to as being 'down under'. Given what it means to be human, with our shared impairments, disabilities, and idiosyncrasies, what difference does a theology of disability make 'down under'? The emphasis on 'down under' highlights the unique South Pacific perspective where the conversation took place and the context from which the contributions emerge and seek to serve. Of course, we are only 'down' and 'under' from the perspective of those who assume themselves to be 'up' and 'over'. When people from the South Pacific use the term of themselves, they are accepting an identity constructed for them by and in relation to others. Perhaps this makes 'down under' a particularly appropriate location within which to explore the experience of those construed by others as dis-abled. The title also plays on the experience of being 'down' and 'under' that people with disabilities continue to face. This book emerges from the conviction that the gospel compels us to embrace deeper ways of being human together that will overcome false divisions and exclusions in search of

---

2 John Swinton, 'From Inclusion to Belonging', 175.
3 For a particularly incisive and constructive counter-narrative, see Louise Lawrence, *Sense and Stigma in the Gospels: Depictions of Sensory-disabled Characters* (Oxford: Oxford University Press, 2013).

flourishing, graced communities. In doing so, we seek to equip one another for participation in communities restored to God, one another, and all creation.

The conference drew together local and international people with academic, professional, practical, and/or lived experience across a wide array of disability studies, all focused on the task of examining the difference a theology of disability can make for the church and society. Whilst some of the authors are engaging with a theology of disability as experts in the field of disability studies, most are not. This book does not engage with a theology of disability in order to renew disability studies, but in the belief that a theology of disability has the capacity to renew theology, church, and society. As John Swinton has highlighted, whilst disability theology is rich with possibilities for practical theology, its richness has drawn engagement from across the theological disciplines: 'It seems that when we think about issues of disability the obvious fact that all theology is practical and intended to enable the church to practice faithfully becomes apparent. To distort Karl Rahner a little, when it comes to disability, we are all anonymous practical theologians!'[4] A theology of disability serves as a prescient reminder of theology's integrative task. Its wide reach of implications calls into service all the resources of Christian faith, scholarship, and reflection so that the church may faithfully embody and perform the gospel in society. What unites the wide array of contributors together is the hope that walking together into one conversation on the difference that a theology of disability makes might contribute to renewing the church and society.

A theology of disability challenges the mythologies that are rooted in Modernity's attempts to order and purify society according to imposed norms and settled discourses. These mythologies are embedded in dehumanizing discourses that ontologize disability as a pathology and create systems which exclude and oppress people with disabilities. Unfortunately the church has often colluded with these mythologies and allowed them to define the reception people with disabilities receive in ecclesial communities. Their reception is, as Manuele Teofilo (Chapter 7) and Evan Clulee (Chapter 16) account, too often that of passive objects of able-bodied pity or benevolence rather than active persons who participate in communities of love where we are persons in relationship. A theology of disability calls forth renewed ways of knowing, being, and practising Christian faith because it opens up new vistas on God, church, and being human together. These new vistas challenge the entrenched assumptions of ableism by exposing settled categories (for example, ability/disability, normal/abnormal, and academic/practical/personal) as false binaries which conflate the rich diversity of human experience into universalized and essentialized categories. A theology of disability demands more faithful and creative embodiments of the gospel in church and society than the reductions of ableism recommend or require.

---

4 John Swinton, 'Who is the God We Worship? Theologies of Disability; Challenges and New Possibilities', *International Journal of Practical Theology* 14 (2011): 274.

Before detailing the parts of the book, it is worth considering how the conference has affected what is written and how the book is structured. This was not an ordinary academic conference, by design and providence. By design, academics, practitioners, and people with disabilities were invited to participate in dialogue and learn together, as papers were presented, questions were discussed, and meals were shared together. By providence, it was the actions of one of the hearing dogs which set the mood for what was to follow as she chewed through a video projector cable just as a keynote address was to be given. With the colour drained from the projected images, as well as the faces of the conference organizers, the quick scurry of activity was drowned out by the humour, grace, and imperturbability of the attendees. This willingness to embrace vulnerability and limitation with gentleness and courage characterized our time together, and called forth a way of being together that blurred traditional boundaries between academics, practitioners, and people with lived experience. Such categories as ability/disability, normal/abnormal, and academic/practical/personal could not contain the nature of the conversation which developed during our time together. As a result, these categories were subverted, and the gift of walking together into one conversation, with a wide variety of sometimes conflicting perspectives, produced fresh possibilities for faithful gospel embodiment and performance. The richness of the interaction emerged from the gift of being together in all our brokenness, limitation, gentleness, and courage.

The conference proceeded along different lines than a typical academic gathering, and that required us to think carefully about how to capture and translate this difference into written form. Jacques Derrida reminds us that hospitality is often based upon the assumed mastery of the sovereign host filtering guests in such a way that conditional hospitality enforces dependent relationships.[5] As we walked together into one conversation the established roles of hosting and guesting were destabilized by the gospel in which Christ comes to us as guest to host us in a new community of friends. This subversion of traditional categories of hosting and guesting offered us much deeper conversations and more creative insights and connections. It is this subversion of traditional categories and the renewed possibilities that a theology of disability creates that is the guiding motif of this book and its organizing structure.

This book is written by people with disabilities, parents of children with disabilities, and friends of people with disabilities. We want to try, as best as possible, to speak *as* and *with* people with disabilities, instead of speaking *for* people with disabilities, in the hope that we might 'get an "insider" view of complex personal identities and shared rich sub-cultural heritages'.[6] As such, we are attempting to employ the 'minority group' model to empower the personhood and

---

5 Jacques Derrida, *Of Hospitality: Anne Dufourmantelle Invites Jacques Derrida to Respond*, trans. Rachel Bowlby (Stanford, CA: Stanford University Press, 2000), 55. For a theological account of the need to transform the paradigms of sovereign host and guest, see Swinton, 'Who is the God We Worship?', 287.
6 Lawrence, *Sense and Stigma in the Gospels*, 4–5.

voice of people with disabilities and immerse ourselves in their experience for the renewal of church and society. A theology of disability offers the church the chance to render its life anew to the contours of the gospel, and it offers new possibilities to comprehend and embody the divine love of the Creator for the creature.

The contributions which follow contain a mixture of academic, professional, practical, and/or lived experience which is brought to the topic in search of constructive multi-disciplinary proposals for church and society. A number of the chapters are short narratives, and emerge out of theological reflection on experience; others are written in the scholarly genre, and emerge from engagement in academic conversations, and still others are a mixture of both genres. It is important to note that these distinctions are neither fixed, decisive, nor evaluative. Each of the chapters, regardless of genre, emerges from reflection on lived experience in the hope of renewed gospel action in the world. Each chapter, whether laden with narrative stories or academic referencing, is regarded as a constructive contribution to an integrative theology of disability. Readers will misunderstand our intentions, and the integrating impulse that a theology of disability gifts us, if it is assumed that one genre is regarded as more significant than another or that the didactic work fills out the narrative contributions. In Scripture, narrative forms are not interruptions from the fundamentally didactic pericopae. Instead, the narrative and the didactic combine in the one task of revealing God's work in history. Similarly, in this volume narrative and didactic enhance the task of exploring the difference a theology of disability can make to the church and society. We have actively sought to avoid the false divisions that can occur in forms of what Mary McClintock Fulkerson describes as 'trickle-down theology'. 'Trickle-down theology' does theology in abstraction from lived experience, and then, as a second step, 'applies' the insights to contemporary settings.[7] This volume is engaged in understanding God's purposes for the church and society more generally through a theology of disability, in order that the church's embodiment and performance of the gospel faithfully reflects the nature and purposes of God's mission in the world.[8] These integrative possibilities emerge from a theology of disability and its ability to integrate traditionally disparate disciplines and *loci* in search of the holism which the gospel offers. Integration is at the heart of a theology of disability as we understand it, and it is at the heart of this volume. The various contributors are committed to walking together into *one* conversation where each person offers their best gifts in order to explore the difference a theology of disability can make for church and society.

The book is structured as broad parts which focus on a central theme – being, belonging, and becoming. The chapters in each part are ordered to move

---

7 Mary McClintock Fulkerson, 'Interpreting a Situation: When is "Empirical" also "Theological"?', in *Perspectives on Ecclesiology and Ethnography*, ed. Pete Ward (Grand Rapids, MI: Eerdmans, 2012), 128.
8 Ray S. Anderson, *The Shape of Practical Theology: Empowering Ministry with Theological Praxis* (Downers Grove, IL: InterVarsity Press, 2001), 22.

from action to reflection to renewed action. Part I, 'Theology, Disability, and Being', focuses on the possibilities that emerge from a theology of disability with regard to what it means to be human. Part II, 'Theology, Disability, and Belonging', focuses on the possibilities that emerge when churches move from being places where people with disabilities are included to places where people with disabilities belong (a theme developed from Swinton's work which became the leitmotif of the conference). Part III, 'Theology, Disability, and Becoming', focuses on the possibilities that emerge when a theology of disability is engaged from an eschatological perspective and allowed to reshape our current ways of thinking, being, and practising.

While we are each walking together into one conversation, our unity is not uniformity. Given the reality of our plural and multifarious lives, some chapters stand in juxtaposition to others within the book, but each is seeking to answer the question of what difference a theology of disability makes for the church and society in order that the church might faithfully embody and perform the gospel.

Part I
Theology, Disability, and Being

1 Disability and the Theology of 4-D Personhood

Sue Patterson

Introduction

On 1 April 1984 our daughter Felicity, aged seven, broke her neck in a fall, spent some months on life-support and altogether twenty months in hospital. During those months my husband John and I fought and won battles with two doctors who wanted to let her die. The first one, a young registrar anaesthetist, advanced a quality of life argument. Felicity, still in a coma, was breathing with her accessory muscles and would sooner or later become too exhausted to continue. When that happened, wouldn't it be better to not put her on life support? Would we want her to have a life in which she would never be able to go skiing? Later on, Felicity recovered enough to move to the children's ward from intensive care, but had ongoing breathing difficulties. One night she stopped breathing and was resuscitated by the night nurse. The consultant anaesthetist wanted our permission not to put her back on a ventilator. He advanced a combination of moral and economic arguments. It was obscene, he suggested, to be spending so much government money keeping Felicity alive when the same amount of money could benefit a large number of other children.[1]

It is possible to extract two propositions in relation to personhood from this story: first, viable personhood is to be defined in terms of *quality of life*, which is dependent on individual autonomy; second, what our life is worth is subject to cost-benefit factors, and is therefore an economic issue. I suggest that these propositions are indicators of two models of personhood that are inextricably linked: personhood as autonomous individuality and personal worth as economically quantifiable.

The Values Behind the Values

If being a person means being autonomous – that is, being a self-mastering and self-responsible individual – individuals with disabilities that preclude autonomy

---

1 The consultant capitulated when we called in our minister at 3 a.m. on Sunday. Felicity lived for another thirty years as a ventilated incomplete tetraplegic, running her own household from age 20, later marrying and entering paid employment as a school resource worker helping children with reading recovery, before succumbing to liver cancer in October 2014, just short of her 38th birthday.

do not qualify. There are two reasons why autonomy is seen as inseparable from personhood. First, the view of the person as a self-determining, self-mastering, even self-creating individual is deeply entrenched at all levels in our society. It has become the water we swim in. Enlightenment individualism – understanding of the self and personhood in terms of individual autonomy – has generated a view of society as composed of individuals.[2] An emphasis on personal autonomy has led to a devaluing of relationships of mutual interdependence, and the duty of care toward adults who are not able to be independent has shifted to governments and their agencies, and others to whom they delegate this duty.

Second, autonomy underpins the notion of personal worth as quantifiable. Autonomy is self-sufficient. It makes no demands on others, therefore it has economic worth. It underpins the commodification of society,[3] in which members become economic units such as customers, consumers, and earners.[4] In this way, autonomy as a primary value enables certain economic ends such as control of health budgets. This has profound consequences for those suffering from disabilities.

The Ethical and Moral Consequences

A system is only as good as its weakest point. If principles of justice and fairness for all are employed, the test of adequacy of any system which undertakes a duty of care will be the worst-case scenario: the person with severe disabilities. Our response to the consultant anaesthetist might have been: Why should one needy person be sacrificed to benefit other needy persons? Why not increase the pot to address the real level of need?[5] Yet it is obvious from his statement that such a test of adequacy does not obtain here. Instead, things operate in

---

2 In his book *The One, the Three and the Many* (Cambridge: Cambridge University Press, 1993) Colin Gunton explores this whole scenario and its consequences.
3 Words such as 'care', 'respect', 'dignity', and 'social inclusion' and other language related to dignity and rights featured on government websites and leaflets mask the operating values of atomistic individualism and utility. The word 'independent' is the give-away that links the words with the underlying values they hide.
4 We note that Work and Income New Zealand (a government department) clients and Hospital Board patients have become 'customers', with the implied economic profit baggage that carries.
5 John Rawles (writing from Aberdeen in Scotland about the National Health Service) observes that most doctors at the coalface of need do in fact operate with a needs-based approach, but are frustrated by (and implicitly in conflict with) the economic model of the government health services provider: 'A surgeon may have more demands on him than he is able to meet, due to limited operating time or numbers of beds. He rations care by means of a waiting list. People with potentially fatal conditions are generally given the highest priority. Amongst the others, those who are most disabled will tend to be seen quicker than those less disabled, or those distressed but with no disability. The surgeon will therefore give priority according to the perceived degree of suffering, with overriding priority being given to those at risk of loss of life. The principle describing his actions is "to each according to his need", where need is seen as both relief of suffering and prolongation of life. If facilities are totally inadequate he may indulge in shroud-waving, i.e. announcing publicly that unless resources are increased patients will suffer and die unnecessarily. His opinion may well be right. He has, after all,

reverse: adequacy is used as a test of the individual case rather than as a test of the system, which is not held accountable to the principles of justice and fairness for all.[6] It is adequacy in terms of personal autonomy or projected quality of life that is required to qualify for the support that makes living possible. The corollary is that those human beings who fail to achieve this threshold are likely to be treated as less than persons because their lives are not worth investing in to the point that will make them viable as understood in terms of profit to society. This is the more so where investment of the same money elsewhere would be more profitable; hence the cost-benefit analysis of the consultant anaesthetist.

The true determiner of a decision that appears to be based on viability or sustainability of life or health may therefore be economic. This is apparent in the use of various calculation systems to work out the economic value of an individual's life year ratio – that is, the person's projected productive utility – in order to assess the cost-effectiveness of medical treatment or intervention.[7] Viewed theologically, the use of such models as economic calculators of medical entitlement, however pragmatically necessary they might seem,[8] are indicators of 'structural sin'.[9] The reductionist model of personhood they represent has arisen from deeply entrenched values endemic in our worldview which are antagonistic to complete human personhood. In other words, their very necessity is generated by a deeper problem that affects the whole of society: the turning from a relational 'I–thou' to an instrumental 'I–it'[10] which has led to the

---

spent his professional life assessing his patients' distress and disability and the risk to their lives posed by disease'; John Rawles, 'Castigating QALYs', *Journal of Medical Ethics* 15 (1989): 147.

6 However, Nicholas Wolterstorff argues that God holds all of us accountable for how we treat one another in terms of basic human rights – that is, for the delivery of natural justice. See Nicholas Wolterstorff, *Justice: Rights and Wrongs* (Princeton, NJ: Princeton University Press, 2010), 393.

7 These include QALYs (Quality Adjusted Life Years) and the more recent DALYs (Disability Adjusted Life Years) as a measure of overall disease burden, expressed as the number of years lost due to ill health, disability, or early death. The logic goes like this: 'If we can determine the exchange rate then disability and distress can be considered in a common currency, the quality of life', when mapped over a projected life expectancy, and then one traded off against another. John Rawles exposes the dangerous fallacies behind such systems: 'Illness causes disability and it causes distress, but to what extent are we prepared to trade one for the other? If we can determine the exchange rate then disability and distress can be considered in a common currency, the quality of life ... the best value for money of all is offered by turning off the life-support machine of an unconscious patient, enhancing his quality of life by 1, at a saving of hundreds of pounds per day.' However, 'The value of life is not the same as the absence of suffering ... although the matrix merely demonstrates the equivalence of disability and distress as forms of suffering that detract from the quality of life, it is used to put a valuation on life itself ... life and years may not be completely interchangeable in our calculations'; Rawles, 'Castigating QALYs', 144, 146. See also Jagadish Guria, 'Fix Flawed Values', *NZIER Insight* 16 (June 2010) [accessed November 2015]. Online: http://nzier.org.nz/publication/fix-flawed-values-of-statistical-life-and-life-years-to-get-better-policy-outcomes.

8 In fact, they are counter-productive because ultimately they contribute to increased morbidity with later medical intervention, which imposes a greater cost on the system.

9 That is, sin that is entrenched and perpetuated at societal level. See Marjorie Hewitt Suchocki, *The Fall to Violence: Original Sin in Relational Theology* (New York: Continuum, 1999).

10 These are Martin Buber's terms. See his *I and Thou*, 2nd edn (New York: Scribner, 1958).

commodification of persons[11] and which – along with and related to another model, person as consumer – is an ideological legacy of modern capitalism, although its roots are far more ancient.

So, in a circular way, the ethic of economic utility is justified according to the axioms of the model of person-as-individual-as-economic-unit it reinforces; however, the model of personhood is itself challengeable on the basis of adequacy: it does not describe the reality of human personhood as we live it.

Personhood

I need to acknowledge at this point that personhood is a notoriously slippery concept that has been tossed around by philosophers and theologians for millennia, as have the equally slippery and related concepts of 'mind' and 'soul'.[12] Whatever the difficulties with the concept of personhood that dispose philosophers and scientists to argue about it or throw it out,[13] there are theological reasons why we should talk about human beings as persons rather than selves. Theologically, 'person' is a category which includes, but is not exhausted by, 'human', as it includes both divine and human personhood. It is also more than the equivalent of 'individual'. Relational social models of personhood challenge the coherence of the prevalent worldview of persons as individuals in society. Philosophers such as Buber, Macmurray, and Gillett and theologians such as Gunton, Zizioulas, Grenz, and Alan Torrance demonstrate that personhood is characterized by inextricable connectivity or relationality.[14]

---

11 See Thomas E. Reynolds, *Vulnerable Communion: A Theology of Disability and Hospitality* (Grand Rapids, MI: Brazos Press, 2008), 73.

12 While today those metaphysicians called Physicalists would begin by defining a human person as a particular kind of animal and maintain that the body is where human personhood begins and ends, and while there are few these days outside spiritualist circles that would argue for disembodied minds or souls as persons (although the notion is alive and well in popular thinking about life after death), Cartesian mind–body dualism remains in currency today as an unexamined assumption of much modern and post-modern thinking. Stanley Grenz observes that the Enlightenment 'world-mastering rational self' was a development of Boethius' definition of 'person' as 'the individual substance of a rational nature'. In this, the 'essence of personal existence lies in its connection to reason'. Locke equated self and personal identity with consciousness – which is 'what leads human beings to consider themselves a self'. This in effect reduces personal identity to self-consciousness. Stanley J. Grenz, *The Social God and the Relational Self: A Trinitarian Theology of the Imago Dei* (Louisville, KY: Westminster John Knox Press, 2001), 67, 72, 74.

13 For instance, Grant Gillett develops a non-dualistic model, although he is reluctant to tread the 'person' minefield, preferring to talk of selves and subjectivity. He rehabilitates the concept of 'soul', which he relates to the Aristotelian concept of 'form'. Human selves take the form of a soul that comprises the essence of self, but in an inextricably embodied way. Therefore, we *are* souls, but we do not *have* souls. Grant Gillett, *Subjectivity and Being Somebody* (Exeter: Imprint Academic, 2008), 11.

14 See Buber, *I and Thou*; John Macmurray, *The Self as Agent: The Form of the Personal* (Atlantic Highlands, NJ: Humanities Press International, 1957); Gillett, *Subjectivity and Being Somebody*; Gunton, *The One, the Three and the Many*; John Zizioulas, *Being as Communion: Studies in Personhood and the Church* (Crestwood, NY: St. Vladimir's Seminary Press, 1985); Grenz, *The Social God and the Relational Self*;

Personhood consists of reciprocal being in relation as a member of family and community, which means that social being is constitutive of personhood and subsumes individual being. As this relationality is dynamic and ongoing, human beings live out their lives as persons-in-relation in time.[15] This is the fourth (and overarching) dimension of personhood.

4-D – four-dimensional – social models of personhood have a narrative quality because social continuity of personhood is maintained through a dialogue between personal and social recalling. Inherent to relationality is the sense-making of lives – the articulation of their meaning as they develop, and their projection beyond the present into a future that is both personal and communal. My story is told from conception to beyond the grave, and the storied-ness of my personhood is reciprocal with the storied-ness of my family and other communities, so that my own narrative of personhood takes place within the narratives of these communities just as theirs are expressed in part through mine.

The Ethics of 4-D Personhood

Understanding personhood as both relationally and socially constituted *and* four-dimensional entails levelling the playing field, because at any one time the burden of disability is communally shared, and furthermore, in a four-dimensional view, all members of society lack able-bodiedness at some time in their lives.[16] The neglected principles of justice and fairness[17] that might have been used to test the adequacy of the care offered by society may be seen to rest on a relational model of personhood in which entitlement cannot be compartmentalized according to economic calculators. The web of relationality does not allow any of its components or moments to be isolated into atomistic units. As adequacy is set by the hardest case, this rules out an ethic of utility in

---

Alan J. Torrance, *Persons in Communion: Trinitarian Participation and Human Description* (Edinburgh: T&T Clark, 1996).

15 Of course, any discussion of personal continuity over time immediately begs the question 'When does (or should) personhood begin and end?' How we decide on what is the span of human personhood will be determined by what we take to be the bottom line of personhood. So this again is a circular argument, in which the starting point determines where we end up. For instance, if one defines personhood in terms of biological life, then biology will determine the span of personhood; if one defines it in terms of cognitive (thinking) being, then cognitive function will determine the span. Physicalists may take the span to be that of bodily, biological being. Yet there is no agreement on when the span of biological human life begins and ends. Cognitive viability determined by brain function may yield brain death as the point at which it could be argued that those attributes that confer and maintain personhood have ceased to operate. However, it is less easy to determine the point at which cognitive viability (once we have defined what that is) is present at the beginning of life. And again it comes down to how we define 'person'.

16 Even those who die suddenly while in good health before old age lack autonomy and various capacities in infancy.

17 Their foundation is in fact the divine–human relationship. See Wolterstorff, *Justice*, 381.

which the disabled person is assessed according to his or her benefit or cost to society. Instead, the ethic is the principled one of justice and fairness expressed in the meeting of personal need, responsibility for which in a relational society is shared by all. Grant Gillett sees personhood in terms of membership in a moral community, and the potentiality of personhood as existing socially as part of the moral community of family and community from the moment of intended conception onward. In the process of personal development, the role of the community is shown to be more than recognition and respect; it is also a mutual embrace which promotes growth, enriches, and helps fulfil personhood.[18]

Our daughter Felicity's personhood was not hers alone; it was (and remains) inseparable from the continuity of the communities of which she was a member – her family, friends, church, and the school where she worked. Her disability was shared by these communities, and she shared in the wholeness of their history, which in the case of family has included a time of potential and anticipated wholeness before disability that is held in the family memory. Her disability remains the possession of the community. The relational nature of personhood means that whatever is done to one is done to all. Her neglect or exclusion would diminish the whole: 'When one part of the body suffers, all suffer. When one part rejoices, all rejoice' (1 Cor 12:26). Yet while the realization of her capacity was also at the hands of her communities, with the encouragement and addition of resources that enabled her to function and bear fruit in her various roles and gifts (in the family, we always had a saying: 'Add more resources until the thing can be done'), her presence also enriched and extended the family and communities to make them more than they could have been without her, and continues to do so.

The life-trajectory comes to include the disability, however and whenever it is acquired, as part of its *telos*. To regard it as *telos* is not, however, to be deterministic (as in DNA determinism[19]) or to suggest that the disability-including trajectory is divinely predestined. It is to suggest that the trajectory of our lives may include a disability which will deliver, paradoxically, a wholeness and good which otherwise would not be that may challenge human considerations as to what is whole and good, and by implication, how we understand God's

---

18 'Personal identity is never a private reality, but has a communal element; it is shaped by the community of which the person is a participant. Such a community contributes to the formation of the "self" by mediating the communal transcendent narrative necessary for personal identity formation . . . . In the same way, the paradigmatic narrative in accordance with which those who are in Christ find their identity is a shared story, a communal narrative, even though its application may be individual in focus'; Grenz, *The Social God and the Relational Self*, 331.
19 Origins are more than DNA. It is not possible to determine from DNA what the developmental path of an embryo will be: 'The early human embryo has an indeterminate status in that its formation is an extended event with significant epigenetic influences rather than a "row of dominoes" based on DNA alone. Any given embryo may be a human-being-in-the-process-of-becoming (and therefore potentially a member of our moral community)'; Gillett, *Subjectivity and Being Somebody*, 13.

goodness.[20] Therefore, Felicity's shared story concerns 'the issue of [her] place relative to the good ... within a social-cultural context'.[21] So when she became incompetent as she neared death[22] to articulate and/or live out the potential trajectory of her story, that story nevertheless had, and continues to have, its place in, and must be told by, the community or communities in which she was placed, as relative to their good because her disability was, and continues to be, related to the overall good of those communities of which she is a part, and as such enriches their moral life. Thus, paradoxically, the negative of dis-ability becomes a moral positive.

Theological 4-D Personhood

Through grace, weakness becomes strength (2 Cor 12:9) as a gift to community. The christological paradox of strength being revealed in weakness to deliver a wholeness which otherwise would not be challenges and transcends human notions of weakness and wholeness as God works all things together for good (Rom 8:28).[23] It follows that the involvement of the community is not focused solely on the enabling of life and prayer for healing, but also includes a re-envisioning of disability as a unique contribution to community which confers aspects of personhood which would otherwise not be a part of the community, the purpose of which lies beyond our world and our comprehension. The corollary of this is that if fulfilment of personhood is seen to require an endpoint in a new creation for some, then that endpoint is not merely reserved for those who cannot find earthly fulfilment.

Felicity's story cannot tell the whole of her because it cannot take in the future, the *telos*, of her personhood. It may tell of her potential and its degree of realization in this life, but it cannot tell of its ultimate purpose and realization. A 4-D theory of personhood-in-relation requires a telos of fulfilment[24] which obtains in every case, not simply in most cases, and which has true continuity because it includes all of our personhood, including the most defective or damaged bodily parts, as necessary to the whole (1 Cor 12:22), and therefore does not shed these for a disembodied afterlife. As Colin Gunton has said: 'for

---

20 Or even what is normal. See Reynolds, *Vulnerable Communion*, 105.
21 Charles Taylor, *Sources of the Self: The Making of the Modern Identity* (New York: Cambridge University Press, 1989), 41, 48, quoted in Gillett, *Subjectivity and Being Somebody*, 227.
22 See footnote 1.
23 See Reynolds, *Vulnerable Communion*, 117.
24 Stanley Grenz argues that for a self-constituted in relation, fulfilment in Christ is narrative and teleological: 'The Spirit places humans "in Christ" and thereby bestows on them personal identity *extra se in Christo* insofar as the Spirit incorporates them into a transcending narrative – the Jesus story, the narrative of God acting in the crucified and resurrected Messiah .... Being "in Christ" ... involves retelling one's own narrative, and hence making sense out of one's life, by means of the plot of the Jesus narrative'; Grenz, *The Social God and the Relational Self*, 329.

the Christian there is no "cheap hope" for true fulfilment lies the other side of suffering and death'.[25]

Such a view of personhood is radically opposed to those that begin with human beings as self-conscious and self-determining individuals. Ray Anderson argues along with Barth that 'we are subjects because God has addressed us as such'. Our subjectivity as persons is a response to being addressed by God as subjects.

We do not first of all know ourselves, and then search for a divine, transcendent Word to know and grasp. We are first of all grasped and known; then follows knowledge of ourselves. Paul expresses this in his hymn of love: 'Now I know in part; then I shall understand fully, even as I have been fully understood' (1 Cor 13:12).[26]

In other words, it all begins and is realized by our being known by God.

In his commentary on the Psalms, John Goldingay describes Psalm 139 as affirming 'the nature of YHWH's involvement [in a person's life] from the earliest beginning of life . . . in the context of a personal relationship' in which the other is always present and all is laid bare.[27] As such, it describes the 4-D narrative of divine–human relationality that overarches life and death. The psalm tells two stories simultaneously: the story of the reality of that divine–human relationality as embracing the whole of human life, and the story of the denial of that reality as flight or escape which proves futile. The psalmist's epiphany occurs as he understands his personhood as constituted in being known by God. This reality, 'confessed in adoration', acknowledges the enveloping 'I–thou relationship' in which 'the outline of a person's life, the days that will unfold for them, is written into their origins'.[28] The decisions about our beginnings and endings are God's decisions, which is not to say that our lives are predestined, but 'simply' that his purpose is the framework within which our destiny is worked out.[29] Psalm 139 might be described as an anticipatory 'exegesis' (if there is such a thing) of 1 Cor 13:12, for it describes the divinely encompassed travelling and conclusion of a human journey that includes our 'least' moments,

---

25 Colin Gunton, 'Dogmatic Theses on Eschatology', in *The Future as God's Gift*, ed. D. Ferson and M. Sarot (Edinburgh: T&T Clark, 2000), 140, quoted by John Polkinghorne in *The God of Hope and the End of the World* (New Haven, CT: Yale University Press, 2002), 87.
26 Karl Barth, *Church Dogmatics*, ed. and trans. G.W. Bromiley and T.F. Torrance, 2nd rev. edn (Edinburgh: T&T Clark, 1975 and 1977), vol. III/2, 195, cited in Ray S. Anderson, *On Being Human: Essays in Theological Anthropology* (Pasadena, CA: Fuller Seminary Press, 1982), 56.
27 John Goldingay, *Psalms 90–150, Baker Commentary on the Old Testament Wisdom and Psalms*, ed. Tremper Longman III (Grand Rapids, MI: Baker Academic, 2008), 626. Cf. Barth (re Ps 139:1–12): 'For the man whom God has created and with whom He covenants, there is no corner in which he does not exist for God, in which he is not enclosed by the hand of God behind and before. There is no heaven or hell in which he is out of the reach of God's Spirit or away from His countenance'; Barth, *Church Dogmatics* IV/1, 482.
28 Ibid., 627, 633. Gillett's gloss on such a statement is that this does not necessarily imply DNA determinism. See footnote 19.
29 Goldingay, *Psalms 90–150*, 635 (re vv. 17–18, with cross-reference to Job 14:5).

whether through weakness or incapacity, or through sin. If God knows how our lives will unfold from their earliest point in the womb, this includes knowledge of our disabilities, genetic and acquired, physical, mental, and moral.[30]

Ethically, this knowledge redefines human rights in terms of worth divinely bestowed through relationship. Nicholas Wolterstorff comments that while '[o]ur Judaic and Christian heritage neither denies nor overlooks the flaws of humankind ... it nonetheless declares that all of us have great and equal worth: the worth of being made in the image of God and of being loved redemptively by God'.[31] Being a human person is about being known by God, who confers on us, through that knowledge, the great and equal worth of humanness irrespective of the earthly sum and definition of our capacity and incapacity.

This worth is revealed incarnationally in God's becoming one of us. Barth refers to Ps 139 in his discussion of Jesus as the true human being and Lord of Time.[32] The christological conclusion that Ps 139 points towards is that through incarnation, God's intimate personal knowledge of us is at the same time a redeeming embrace – a reconciling re-creation of all that is human in Christ. As T.F. Torrance explains:

> God has not come in Jesus Christ to operate above the world or over our heads, even when acting savingly on our behalf; he has entered into our human and physical existence in order to operate within its limits and measures, within its created order and intelligibility, and there to establish relations with us in an intimate reciprocity in which he communicates himself to us and takes us into communion with himself ....[33]

Ray Anderson observes that reading Ps 139 in connection with Rom 8:29 ('For those whom he foreknew he also predestined to be conformed to the image of

---

30 Ibid., 640.
31 'It adds that God holds us accountable for how we treat each other – and for how we treat God. It is this framework of conviction that gave rise to our moral subculture of rights. If this framework erodes, I think we must expect that our moral subculture of rights will also eventually erode and that we will slide back into our tribalisms'; Wolterstorff, *Justice*, 393.
32 'The being of man in all its independence and particularity, in all its difference from the being of God, is the being which is acted upon in this action of God, ruled in this rule of God and drawn into this history inaugurated and controlled by God. It thus concerns all men and every man that in the man Jesus God Himself is man, and therefore acts and rules and makes history. It is to be noted that this fact concerns man precisely in his independence and particularity, in his own being as distinct from God. It concerns man himself. For in the presence of God he cannot retreat into himself and thus remain inviolate. It is he himself who is fleeted when God invades his sphere. Nor can he find shelter from God behind another being outside himself and connected with himself: his naturalness or rationality, earth or heaven. He might wish to do so. But in the sphere to which Jesus as man also belongs he is reached and pierced by God however much he may wriggle. He is reached and pierced by God even when he becomes guilty of ontological impossibility, of godlessness. The well-known words of Ps 139:5–12 may be recalled in this connexion ...'; Barth, *Church Dogmatics* III/2, 141.
33 Thomas F. Torrance, *Space, Time and Resurrection*, 2nd edn (Edinburgh: T&T Clark, 1998), 178.

his Son, in order that he might be the firstborn within a large family') reveals the eschatological horizon to personhood. The events of our whole existence are embraced in Christ in his redemptive purpose. This life is explained by way of the next life – the new creation. Christ's incarnation is 'the hermeneutical horizon for authentic personhood. All answers to questions about the nature of the human in terms of what it means to be a person must be derived from this event.'[34] Christ is the one who in his incarnation reveals personhood to be both divine and human, and in his resurrection is the bridge between divine and human personhood which enables the *telos* of 4-D personhood to be fulfilled through human participation in the trinitarian personhood of God. It follows that the resurrection of the body, as christologically inaugurated and fulfilled, is the bridge of bodily continuity yet discontinuity – that is, bodily transformation from old to new creation – which connects human personhood in this world with human personhood in the next. Socially, this continuity yet discontinuity is expressed in the communion of saints.[35]

Ecclesial 4-D Personhood

The church must neither buy into society's reductionist utilitarian values and models of personhood nor be squeezed into their mould. As a contrast community (Bonhoeffer's term[36]), the church witnesses to the true character of human society, and it does so in the face of the prevailing individualist and utilitarian models of personhood in our society. The presence of its disabled members from before cradle to grave witnesses to this social personhood-in-relation as fully embracing of all human beings at all stages of their lives. This reveals the ethical principle and character of Christian community as expressed in Jesus' teaching in relation to 'the least of these' and in the practice of the church as described in Acts.[37] It is also described by Paul in 1 Cor. 12 as the living out of an incarnational 4-D model of personhood as the Body of Christ in which each member is unique and indispensable, where all suffer and rejoice together. The contrast (and therefore the witness) is in the quality of sacrificial love demonstrated by the Christian community.

This witness needs to be proclaimed as well as lived for it to be clear that the Christian community includes those members who may not be visible to outsiders, as may be the case with people who are severely disabled, and those who may not even be visible to the community itself, such as those not yet born.

---

34 Anderson, *On Being Human*, 199.
35 Thus it all ends in eschatology, which begins with inaugurated eschatology because 4-D personhood in Christ, through the agency of the Spirit, bridges 'the eschatological tension between the now already and not yet'. As John Polkinghorne comments: 'It is the Spirit of God who bridges the eschatological tension between the now already and not yet'; Polkinghorne, *The God of Hope and the End of the World*, 84.
36 See Dietrich Bonhoeffer, *The Cost of Discipleship* (New York: Touchstone, 1959).
37 See Matt 25:39–46, Luke 9:47–9, Acts 2: 44–5, Acts 4:32–7.

This means that the contrast is likely to lie in situations where the groundswell of opinion in the wider society might regard abortion or euthanasia as merciful relief of suffering, or where the entrenched value of personal autonomy's 'my body, my life' meets the contrast of costly witness of trust in God through all stages and situations in life. Love is not to be confused with kindness; it is cruciform. It does not avoid suffering, but joins with it to transform it.

However, this witness extends through sacrificial love to the enrichment of the Christian community through its disabled members. Through the costly grace of God, the weakness of disability becomes strength (2 Cor. 12:9), and a gift to community that confers a wholeness which would otherwise be lacking – a wholeness that transcends human notions of wholeness as God works all things together for good (Rom 8:28). The re-envisioning of disability as conferring a greater good of personal and communal wholeness is in powerful contrast to our autonomy- and utility-obsessed society's view of disability as unmitigatedly 'ungood'. While the witness of this counter-societal vision will be apparent in the way the Christian community lives its life, the witness will need a proclamatory component to explain how and why what appears un-whole, even tragic and wasteful, can nevertheless, without denying the reality of suffering, be an agent of wholeness in ways that human beings can only begin to fathom, but which empowers hope. If the *telos* of ultimate fulfilment lies beyond our world, we have not had God's last word on evil. In the paradox of disability as transformative of community, we receive an anticipatory glimpse of how all that seems evil, and may indeed be evil, in relation to our world will be made to participate in God's purpose in that ultimate transformation which is the new creation.

The witness of this trajectory of hope as the *telos* of Christian community is a witness that defies reality as the world sees it. It converts – turns around – that view of reality to show that all human hope hangs on what needs to happen for the ones Jesus calls 'the least of these our brothers and sisters'. It witnesses to Christ as the one who embraces the depths of 'least-ness' along with the entire span of human personhood and draws it into the new creation to come.[38] To embrace this hope is to read our lives from the end backwards, because their complete meaning may be understood only in terms of their *telos*, as T.F. Torrance points out.[39] It is this *telos* read back which inaugurates the eschatological fulfilment of personhood in the stark witness to hope of a Christian community constituted as 'disability in relation'.[40] As centred in Christ, such hope is cruciform; conversely, 'least-ness' enables us to glimpse the depths of Christology.

---

38 Rom 8:18–38 is the theological underpinning of all this.
39 See his *Space, Time and Resurrection*.
40 'Although participation in the divine life – and hence the advent of the ecclesial self in its fullness – is ultimately eschatological, the deification that constitutes the self in community is proleptically present in the here and now'; Grenz, *The Social God and the Relational Self*, 334.

Reading back fulfilment from a future the other side of the grave is in sharp contrast to the anxiety of the ageing human being that capacity, and therefore hope of fulfilment, are slipping away towards death with each day that passes. Popular vague beliefs about heaven as some sort of disembodied afterlife, or notions of personal survival in the memory of family and friends (as expressed in many funeral services) fail to address the deep human fear of loss of self. The witness to hope in the resurrection of the dead needs to be proclaimed as well as enacted to counter a spiritualizing reading of the hope of resurrection that would see the healing of disability in the next life in terms of the removal of physical disability, along with all bodily impediment, rather than its transformation.

Conclusion

This chapter began with a discussion of the failure of a utilitarian ethic to meet the needs of disabled persons in our society. While the move to a principled ethic of justice and fairness for all might indeed deliver on these needs, such rights, however relationally they are understood, have no foundation unless justice is understood to be grounded in the grace of a divine conferral of worth which is summed up christologically. Yet the matter goes beyond justice and the meeting of needs. The hardest case of severe disability points up that models of personhood as four-dimensional need a teleological trajectory that reaches beyond this world for the realization of personhood in all its fullness, but far more than this, that the fulfilment of our Christian life in community and its witness to the world depends on the ones Jesus calls 'the least of these our brothers and sisters'.

2 The World of Cystic Fibrosis
From Diagnosis to Dignity

D. Gareth Jones

The World of Cystic Fibrosis

The following appeared in a June 2012 news item from the UK:

> A brave music student battling a terminal disease has achieved his dream of graduating from Cambridge University – after refusing to be treated in hospital during his finals. Music prodigy Alex Stobbs, 22, suffers from a virulent form of cystic fibrosis and became dangerously ill during his exams – even losing one-and-a-half stone. His lung capacity is just 38 per cent – a level at which doctors usually recommend a lung transplant – and he has to take 50 tablets a day and oxygen at night to survive. But against all the odds Alex managed to complete his music degree and has now graduated with an impressive 2:1.[1]

'I'm very pleased and proud to have got my degree,' Alex said.

Alexander Stobbs is one of the most high-profile people with cystic fibrosis (CF), as a result of a 2008 UK TV documentary on him entitled 'A Boy Called Alex'.[2] This was followed by his 2009 book *A Passion for Living*.[3] As a choral scholar at Kings College Cambridge, he sang in the choir a few times each week on top of his normal studies, and then topped this off by conducting a performance of Bach's *St Matthew Passion* in his first year. Previously, while still at school, he had conducted Bach's *Magnificat*. Alex Stobbs is exceptional on two counts: in musical ability, and in his determination to live life to the full in the face of a life-threatening condition.

He has a severe form of CF, caused by a recessive gene that manifests itself when both parents are carriers (the defective gene was identified in 1989). Around 1 in 25 people in the population are carriers, although most have no idea

---

[1] Jo Riley, 'Brave Music Prodigy Battling Terminal Disease Graduates from Cambridge with 2.1' [accessed 4 September 2013]. Online: http://www.dailymail.co.uk/health/article-2165943/Music-prodigy-battling-terminal-disease-graduates-Cambridge-2–1.html.
[2] 'A Boy Called Alex', Channel 4 *Cutting Edge* documentary (2008) [accessed 4 September 2013]. Online: http://www.imdb.com/title/tt1177981.
[3] Alexander Stobbs, *A Passion for Living* (London: Hodder and Stoughton, 2009).

this is the case. When both parents are carriers, the chance of having a child with CF is 25 per cent. It is caused by a mutation in the gene for the protein that regulates the components of sweat, digestive fluids, and mucus. As a result, CF affects a number of organs in the body by clogging them with thick, sticky mucus. In the lungs this can cause shortness of breath, a chronic cough, and repeated chest infections. If the blockages affect the pancreas, this will reduce or prevent enzymes from being released into the gastrointestinal tract to digest food, causing problems with poor weight gain and malnutrition due to malabsorption.[4]

Approximately 70,000 individuals worldwide have CF, a condition that is more common in Caucasians of European descent. There is no cure, and affected individuals have chronic ill health. Over the past few decades there has been considerable progress in treatments to reduce morbidity and increase life expectancy, with the first drug developed specifically for CF receiving approval in 1993. When the genetic disorder was first discovered in the 1930s, 80 per cent of children born with CF died before the age of one. By 1970, life expectancy was around 12 years. Today, the median life expectancy of people with CF is the late thirties, although this varies considerably from one country to another.

Treatment is intensive and ongoing, and is directed towards:

1   preventing and controlling lung infections;
2   loosening and removing thick, sticky mucus from the lungs;
3   preventing or treating blockages in the intestines;
4   providing enough nutrition;
5   preventing dehydration.

More extreme measures include the insertion of a feeding tube directly into the stomach to provide nutrition overnight, while lung transplants are relatively common. From shortly after birth, affected individuals take numerous medications each day (including intensive antibiotic therapy and aerosols) and receive constant physiotherapy. They eat extra food and exercise vigorously. As the individual with CF gets older, the disease advances, so hospitalizations increase in frequency. A major thrust of therapy is to delay, for as long as possible, damage to the lungs.

Approaches to CF take us into a world of vigorous research, as attempts are made to devise increasingly effective therapies. These are aimed at (1) circumventing CF-related ion transport defects pharmacologically, (2) finding ways of correcting the basic defect in cells in what is known as a chloride channel (CFTR, the CF transmembrane conductance regulator), and (3) using gene therapy to insert a normal copy of the CF gene into affected cells.[5]

---

4   James R. Yankaskas et al., 'Cystic Fibrosis Adult Care: Consensus Conference Report', *Chest* 125 (2004): 1S–39S. See also Pamela B. Davis, 'Cystic Fibrosis Since 1938', *American Journal of Respiratory and Critical Care Medicine* 173 (2006): 475–82.
5   Ibid.

In my view, this clinical and research background is essential to an understanding of the challenges facing those with CF, and even more so by their families.

Is the Individual with CF Disabled?

There can be no doubt that the individual has a chronic illness, and has never experienced a period of wellness, stability, or perceived normality. Interestingly, though, children and young people with CF tend to say: 'I've never not had it so I don't really know what it's like not to.'[6]

They are not blind, they do not have an intellectual disability, they are not in a wheelchair, they can communicate normally, and they probably do not look much different from anyone else. And yet they exist on an intensive medical regime, their lifespan is much less than that of their contemporaries, and they will experience hospitalization far more than most other people. While the severity of CF varies considerably, the activities of many of them are restricted; they are disadvantaged in life. For most of them there will be annual hospitalizations for one or two weeks (in some cases, far more), the daily treatment regime is invasive, the dietary regime is intense, and the prospect of lung transplants in their teens or twenties is high. They may miss a considerable amount of school, and so get behind in their studies. The pressure placed on family and siblings is unending, with immense strain on all involved. And yet there is considerable ambiguity about whether it is classed as a disability.

It is a condition that is relatively hidden, and about which something can be done, even if there is nothing like a cure and much of the treatment is essentially palliative. Is it these glimmers of hope that separate it from the conventional notion of what constitutes a disability? In the USA disability support is provided when certain criteria are met:

1. a chronic infection of the lungs in which symptoms surface at least once every six months and which is severe enough to require intravenous or nebulizer administration of antibacterial medications;
2. chronic bronchitis, pneumonia or respiratory failure, which requires physician intervention or hospitalization at least six times per year or once every two months;
3. test results in the Forced Expiratory Volume (FEV1) exam that meet certain specified criteria.[7]

In New Zealand it is accepted that inherited conditions like cystic fibrosis (which is classified as a metabolic disorder) are often associated with various

---

6 Brian Williams et al., 'I've Never Not Had It So I Don't Really Know What It's Like Not To: Non-difference and Biographical Disruption among Children and Young People with Cystic Fibrosis', *Qualitative Health Research* 19 (2009): 1,443–55.
7 'Respiratory System Disorders and Social Security' [accessed 6 September 2013]. Online: http://www.disability-benefits-help.org/disabling-conditions/cystic-fibrosis.

degrees of functional disability among children.[8] This is in line with the World Health Organization definition of disability: 'a long-lasting physical, sensory, intellectual, or developmental difficulty that restricts a person's ability to perform activities considered to be within the normal range for human beings'. This definition focuses on functional outcomes rather than the causes of disability.

The disability criteria are therefore determined by the severity of certain manifestations of CF, and not by the presence of CF itself. No matter how we may react to this, what we have here is a challenge to the Christian community to know how best to address the needs and challenges of these individuals, as well as those of their parents and caregivers. And this is not the only condition in this category. Responding to disabilities is a far-ranging task demanding of us multi-faceted answers.

Clinical and Ethical Options

Imagine this scenario. Two babies were born on the same day in the same hospital. One was a girl, who we will call Joy, to represent the joy she immediately brought to her parents. The birth was straight forward; the resulting baby was as 'perfect' as one could expect. All was happiness and light. A gorgeous little girl had entered the world. For her Christian parents there was no question whatsoever that she was a 'gift of God'. She gave the appearance of being everything they could ever have hoped for. That was four years ago, and she has gone on developing and growing with little help from the medical profession. Of course there have been infections and coughs, and bouts of sickness, but nothing more than expected, and nothing to particularly worry her parents.

The other baby was a little boy, Neil, who seemed to be fine for 24 hours or so, before it became apparent that all was not well. He had a blockage of the intestines that necessitated an emergency operation about 36 hours after birth. This immediately suggested the diagnosis of CF, a diagnosis confirmed by genetic analysis a couple of weeks later. The treatment he received at the time and has subsequently received has been state-of-the-art, and his progress has been as good as could be expected. But how are his Christian parents to respond?

The easy answer is to say that they do their best and get on with looking after him as best they possibly can. There is no doubt they love him and want to do all they can for him – all within the bounds of their abilities and strength. In this sense they love Neil as much as the other parents love Joy. Both parents are devoted to their respective children. And yet there is a difference. While Joy grows and develops with only limited assistance from the health care system

---

8 Ministry of Health, 'Children with Disabilities' [accessed 6 September 2013]. Online: http://www.moh.govt.nz/moh.nsf/Files/Chapter4/$file/Chapter4.pdf.

(beyond vaccinations, and visits to the health care nurse and GP), it is a different story with Neil. He requires close supervision, numerous visits to paediatricians, dieticians, and physiotherapists, let alone GPs. In fact, hardly a week passes without a visit to one professional or another. His parents regard him as a 'gift of God', yet if they are honest, they often think it is a tarnished gift. Perhaps this represents their lack of faith, but there is no concealing the easy ecstasy in the one household and the joy mingled with sadness in the other.

This points to the contrast between an ongoing trajectory of natural growth and development in the one case versus intense, therapy-dependent growth and development in the other. It is the contrast between normal/healthy development and artificial or artificially supported development. This contrast has nothing to do with the nature of the treatment that may or may not be administered. Neil is intimately dependent for his daily needs upon a very high level of technological expertise. If the facilities had not been available, he would have died within a week of birth, and if only some had been available, he would have died by the age of two or three; his future lifespan depends largely upon continuation of state-of-the-art treatment, some of which is still experimental.

The resources necessary to save the life of a child like this, and hopefully provide him with an ongoing good quality of life, are expensive and essential. There can be no escape from sophisticated science and technology in this case; in the absence of this assistance there will be no ongoing life, since illness and premature death will intervene.

Research is central to the treatment of CF, and therefore to the well-being of those with CF. The life expectancy of those with this genetic condition has been transformed over the past 20 or 30 years. Inevitably, this has profound implications for patients and family alike, since they impact directly on the life hopes and aspirations of a real human being.

Neil is these parents' first child, to whom they are utterly devoted, but they now begin to think about having a second child. This is where the relatively 'simple' situation begins to take on added dimensions. The future is beginning to intrude into their lives. What does it hold for them if they have a second child? They know the chance of having a second child with CF is 1 in 4, and this is far from statistically remote. They have to face up to it as a possible outcome. Can they adequately look after two children with CF; can they love both sufficiently, and would they regard another child with CF as a 'gift of God'? They don't want to devalue Neil; they love him, and they care for him unstintingly. But are they up to it? Will their faith in the goodness of God be strong enough to support them?

As they think in these terms, they know they are faced with theological questions they have never confronted – and these are far too practical for their liking. They are not sitting in armchairs pontificating; they are sitting in their lounge asking whether they have the faith and daily strength for what could be the task ahead. They have to be honest; they would prefer not to have another child with this condition because the demands on them, let alone on Neil, are immense. They have four options:[9]

- Option 1 – They could decide against having another child; the 1 in 4 prospects of another child with CF are more than they can bear. Neither do they want to bring into the world another individual with a debilitating condition like CF.
- Option 2 – They could take a chance and proceed with a pregnancy as normal. They know that their next child has a 1 in 4 chance of having CF, but they hope it will be unaffected. Whatever eventuates, they will continue with the pregnancy even if it means having a second child with CF. As Christians, they might argue that the welfare of their next child is in God's hands regardless of the outcome.
- Option 3 – They could take a chance, knowing that they can have an abortion if the foetus, when tested at nine to ten weeks' gestation using chorionic villus biopsy, turns out to be affected. They would only go down this path as a very last resort. They might feel that to abort a foetus with CF would be to demean their little boy, who they love very much.
- Option 4 – They could go in the direction of IVF (in vitro fertilization) and PGD (pre-implantation genetic diagnosis). If this dual procedure is carried out and shows that an embryo at the four- or eight-cell stage does not have the CF gene, it will be transferred to the woman in the normal way. On the other hand, if the CF gene is present in an embryo, that embryo will be discarded and the same procedure will be carried out on a second embryo, and so on until an embryo lacking this gene is found. The couple are prepared to consider this as a possible way forward, but feel they are treading a very delicate and uncertain path spiritually.

What emerges from a cursory glance at these options is that for a couple in this situation there is no escape from the reality of CF, and its profound effects on any children they bring into existence. No matter what path they opt to take, even if it apparently is a path of not wanting to make a decision, they will have made a decision. They will have staked their colours to a mast, and in effect made a theological statement. They will have to live with the consequences and repercussions of their position.

Depending on the direction they take, they could decide to have no further children, they may end up with a child with CF or a child without CF, and they may generate embryos or foetuses that will be discarded as embryos or aborted as foetuses. These are invidious choices, but there is no escape for a couple in this situation.

---

9 I have sketched these options in a couple of other publications: D. Gareth Jones, 'Conclusion: The Necessity of Dialogue', in *A Glass Darkly: Medicine and Theology in Further Dialogue*, ed. D. Gareth Jones and R. John Elford (Oxford: Peter Lang, 2010), 211–38; D. Gareth Jones, *The Peril and Promise of Medical Technology* (Oxford: Peter Lang, 2013), 18–26.

When faced with such a personal and taxing dilemma as this, one has to sympathize with those who feel that it taxes their Christian convictions almost to breaking point. The competing forces at work within the dilemma pit one life against another, and one set of values against another set. And where does the Bible enter the picture for these Christians grappling with a forbidding dilemma?

Of What Relevance is Scripture?

In attempting to answer this question in a situation like this one, there are in my estimation three categories:

1. The Bible alone provides a complete guide to ways in which Christian decision-making should be framed, making scientific input irrelevant.
2. The Bible is one of a number of sources of concepts and information, but is the major determinant whenever there is conflict or confusion.
3. The Bible is one of a number of sources of concepts and information, and helps to inform decision-making, but may not be the major source.[10]

Category 1 cannot apply in this case because the diagnosis, prognosis and treatment are all bound up in an understanding of a particular genetic condition. There is no getting away from a welter of scientific input that demands responses.

Categories 2 and 3 are far more plausible, with their stress on the Bible as one of a number of sources of concepts and information. The driving force then becomes the balance between biblical and scientific inputs, and the extent of any biblical input. The way this science is used will stem from the attitudes and aspirations of the parents, and this is where the Christian character of the decision-making will come to the fore.

What, then, of the four options open to this young family?

Option 1, deciding against having another child, raises issues associated with self-inflicted childlessness – albeit for extremely well-intentioned reasons. Is this an acknowledgement that God is in charge, or are these human beings taking too much control into their own hands?

Option 2, proceeding with another pregnancy and accepting the outcome, means there is a 1 in 4 chance of having another child with CF. This, I believe, is an acceptable way forward for Christians, with its explicit recognition that God can use both illness and ongoing limitations for good. It has many merits, but is it automatically the only, or even the ideal, way for Christians?

Rejecting some of the possibilities opened up by scientific advance means being prepared to allow into the world an individual with a well-recognized disease. While the rights and wrongs of such a way of acting are hotly contested, there is no explicit scriptural warrant for undertaking it.

---

10 D. Gareth Jones, 'Responses to the Human Embryo and Embryonic Stem Cells: Scientific and Theological Assessments', *Science and Christian Belief* 17 (2005): 199–221.

Option 3, to proceed with a pregnancy and have an abortion in the face of a positive diagnosis of CF, will be the most problematic for most Christians, on the grounds of the willingness to abort a foetus with CF. It may also have severe negative repercussions for the parents, especially the mother. It also gives the appearance of being life-denying.

This option revolves around the ethical and theological legitimacy or otherwise of induced abortion. Any decision needs to take account of the interests of each member of the family in light of the picture presented by the New Testament writers of the body of Christ.

What then of Option 4, with its dependence upon IVF and PGD? Quite apart from the financial costs involved, it is invasive and involves the selection of embryos. Many Christians reject this possibility, with its reliance upon choosing one embryo over another and inevitably destroying embryos. The debate so often comes down to the value placed upon embryos, to the neglect of the other participants, including the future child.

Integral to the scientific milieu in which we live are techniques like IVF and PGD, and their availability has to be taken into consideration in deciding how best God is glorified in specific situations like the one here. What resources do Christians possess to assist them in this invidious position? Before attempting to answer this question, let us remind ourselves of some of the general theological principles previously encountered.

Theological Perspectives

As they contemplate the options, the parents will need to take account of injunctions:

- to protect the defenceless and disenfranchised;
- to stress the importance of human flourishing;
- to realize that their ultimate dependence is upon God.

They will be aware that Jesus came to proclaim good news to the oppressed, and that human life is not devoid of meaning simply because it is physically flawed.[11]

Alongside this, they will be reminded of the transformative power of the physical and spiritual healing that Jesus brought and that can be experienced today in the midst of Christian community. They will also be grateful for the manner in which human creativity manifested in medical achievements brings hope and new prospects in the midst of illness. However, uncertainty and

---

11 Allen Verhey has written most helpfully in these areas, and has provided a valuable backdrop to the direction of my own thinking. See Allen Verhey, *Reading the Bible in the Strange World of Medicine* (Grand Rapids, MI: Eerdmans, 2003); Allen Verhey, *Remembering Jesus: Christian Community, Scripture, and the Moral Life* (Grand Rapids, MI: Eerdmans, 2002).

ambiguity are never far from the surface, and the limited nature of human powers should never be downplayed.[12]

Considerations like these do not lead inevitably to any one knock-down conclusion, but they do form the framework within which decision-making should occur. They need to be worked out in terms of what is in the best interests of the family as a whole, the existing child with CF, any future children who may exist with or without CF, and possibly any embryos. The weight placed on each of these will depend on many factors, and the balance achieved between these often conflicting interests should reflect the diverse relationships that characterize the family, the human community, and the church community.

Any decision the parents take will be fraught and uncertain – something that applies in differing measures to all four options. If they go down the IVF and PGD route, they will be agreeing to dispose of the affected embryos. This is not inevitable, and they could decide it is a step too far. That is perfectly acceptable, as long as they do not hope to remain ignorant by refusing to think about it. In my view, remaining ignorant is not an easy option they should take. This is because technology makes certain things possible; so does genetic knowledge, and with this knowledge comes a host of inevitable ethical (and theological) choices.

This raises an important question for Christians. Is there a biblical mandate for remaining ignorant? Is freely chosen ignorance a Christian virtue, or is it a denial of the biblical mandate to be creative, to fill the Earth and replenish it, and to be stewards of God's good creation?

Is ignorance a moral virtue? If it is, then a couple like this one should go ahead and accept whatever comes. If ignorance is not a moral virtue, then Option 2 may not be the ideal way forward. Few would consider ignorance to be a virtue when confronted by malaria, tuberculosis, or dysentery, let alone by measles or smallpox, about which something can be done in all these cases. Failure to act in these circumstances is an evil that blights our world. While genetic advances in my scenario are not precisely the same as in these infectious diseases, it is increasingly forcing us to confront and then make hard choices, and this is where these parents find themselves.

Any Further Biblical Clues?

In considering the four options and considering the pros and cons in each case, no single option stands out as being clearly the one and only acceptable one (to me anyway). This will undoubtedly sound unsatisfactory, so it is important to go further and see whether there might be additional biblical directives, ones I have not already touched on. In thinking about this, I have turned to the New Testament letters to see how Paul coped with some of the applied

---

12 Allen Verhey, 'What Makes Christian Bioethics Christian? Bible, Story and Communal Discernment', *Christian Bioethics* 11 (2005): 297–315.

ethical issues facing him and the early church. Eating food sacrificed to idols is one example (1 Cor 8). What were these early Christians to do? There were arguments on both sides, in favour and against, and different groups responded in one or other way.

In addressing his issue, Paul drew a distinction between knowledge and love: 'knowledge puffs up, while love builds up'. Their knowledge, of course, was incomplete, and they could all too readily become too assured that they had the correct answer. Having come to this conclusion, they may then be tempted to foist it onto others. So they had to exercise care and discernment, within a context provided by love and concern for others – especially for those who adopted the opposite perspective.

With this in mind, I have concluded that we should be exceedingly wary about relying excessively on a technological solution to the exclusion of other considerations. Technological knowledge may puff us up and make us too dependent upon ourselves and our projects. This is not inevitable, and I do not think we should conclude from this that any technological solution is dangerous. After all, individuals with CF have a far enhanced quality of life today than they would have had 20 or 30 years ago, almost entirely on account of technological skills and increasing scientific know-how. So, in terms of the options open to parents in the predicament of those in my scenario, the use of IVF/PGD should not be viewed as out of bounds for the Christian believer. However, this approach should be resorted to only when the parents have assured themselves that at the most fundamental level they are depending upon God, and that they are trusting him no matter what the eventual outcome.

Consequently, such parents should only resort to a technological solution after very considerable reflection and after viewing it within a broad human and divine framework. Conversely, ignorance by itself is not as virtuous as sometimes assumed. If not accompanied by trust in the goodness of God, and a commitment to the purposes of God, it may reveal a disturbing lack of faith. While a technological direction as an end in itself may well end in dehumanization, ignorance as an end in itself may amount to little more than fatalism. Either way, in Christian terms, the end result may lead to isolating the decision-makers from God as they trust in themselves and their own solutions.

Science and faith are inextricably linked. In my view, not one of the various options put forward is untenable, as long as each is adopted within a framework governed by prayer and a realistic assessment of the technology involved and its alternatives.

Learning from Cystic Fibrosis

Of the many lessons that emerge from acquaintance with CF, there are three I wish to highlight. The first is that any definition of disability should be broad enough to encompass conditions that at times are far from obvious to outsiders. The need for constant support is sufficient to warrant use of the term, and should not be reserved simply for those occasions when there is hospitalization or particularly intensive therapy.

The second is that a disabling condition may be alleviated by the application of cutting-edge, innovative therapies. These are to be welcomed by people of faith since they are directed towards improving the lot of individuals who are made in the image of God. Inevitably, though, the technologies used may have different ends – improving the quality of life of existing individuals, and indicating which embryos continue to develop and which do not. In both cases, the intended result is the same, although the means of achieving this come with different ethical, and possibly theological, baggage.

The third lesson suggests that we should not view disabilities in a homogeneous manner. There is no one single stance on dealing with disabilities or dealing with those who are disabled. There are substantial differences between cystic fibrosis on the one hand and Down syndrome on the other, so social attitudes towards the two display many different features. These may spill over into ethical issues, such as the validity of employing pre-natal diagnostic tests. They may also have implications for the role of treatment in alleviating the worst effects of the condition. While these may be welcomed in CF, they may not be as positively received by some advocating for those with Down syndrome.

Underlying these three lessons are theological challenges, to the way in which Christians contribute towards helping those with disabling conditions – albeit relatively hidden in some instances – towards social and health policy debates, and towards the conflicting attitudes encountered in connection with diverse disabilities. The array of scriptural and theological considerations brought to bear on the decision-making of parents in the CF arena have far broader relevance than sometimes imagined, and it is my hope that their relevance within the disability context will come to be recognized.

3   Parenting a Child with Autism, and the Father-heart of God

Ian Waddington

Let me tell you a little about myself. I spend most Friday afternoons in the Cameron Pool and Leisure Centre kids' pool with my youngest son and a swimming teacher. I swim alongside them, modelling the instructions – how to kick, how to stroke, how to hold your arms by your ears – when I've known how to swim for years. I negotiate with McDonald's staff over what toy they are putting in the Happy Meal this time. I get T-shirts printed with the characters of kids' movies, because they don't make them in a size big enough for my 11-year-old, who won't wear anything else. I am divorced, amicably, and still spend the afternoons Monday to Friday looking after the kids at their place. I cry when I watch the movie *Mercury Rising*, or when I see YouTube clips of people being nice to disabled kids. I have to explain sometimes to parents at parks why the big boy in the sandpit has just borrowed their five-year-old's toy. And sometimes I have to stand in the girls' toy aisle at The Warehouse with that same boy as he happily plays with the Barbie Dreamhouses, the My Littlest Petshop toys, and other 'girls' toys, while seven-year-old girls in pigtails look at him and me and wonder what on earth we are doing there. I am the father of a child with autism.

Autism

What is autism? Let me give you a layman's view of this complex disorder, as a background to my observations of my son, James, his brothers' interactions with him, and some reflections on God.

Autism, or ASD (autism spectrum disorder), is generally now seen not as a behavioural or social disorder, but as a 'group of brain-based whole-body disorders with organic causes'.[1] It is much more likely to be found in boys (approximately 80 per cent of ASD children are male). It is a global problem with the way the brain is 'wired' – some sections of the brain are over-sized

---

1   Sue X. Ming, 'When Your Child is Diagnosed with an Autism Spectrum Disorder', in *Navigating the Medical Maze with a Child with Autism Spectrum Disorder*, ed. Sue X. Ming and Beth A. Pletcher (London: Jessica Kingsley, 2014), 14.

(such as the frontal lobes, the amygdala, the hippocampus, and the cerebellum), some are under-sized (such as the corpus collosum, the link between the left and right sides of the brain), and the individual neuron connections of the brain are closer and 'clumped', yet not well-networked across other areas of the brain. The overall effect of this is that someone with ASD has a greater awareness of input than normal, but a poor ability to co-ordinate it or process it in a global manner.[2] Autism is diagnosed by the 'triad of impairments' – impairment of communication, social interaction, and imagination. Communication may be lower than normal, and is often very literal or may involve echolalia (the repetition of others' words). Social interaction is often perceived of as aloof, passive, or conversely, active, but inappropriate. Imagination and flexibility is generally lacking, and there is a rigidity of thoughts and interests. There may be difficulty in integrating related activities or in generalizing from one activity or context to another, and there are often obsessive interests in particular activities.

This triad is accompanied by a difference in sensory sensitivity from the norm. ASD may exhibit as hypersensitivity (they may cover their ears, or seek to escape loud noises) or as hyposensitivity (a seeking of over-stimulation – a fascination with more and complex noises, or with intricate or changing sights such as twirling ribbons, falling dust, or flowing water). James definitely exhibits the latter, and would spend long periods when he was young watching flowing water or picking up fine dust to see how it drifted away in a breeze. The classic ASD behaviours have now been attributed to this sensitivity to sensory input. Spinning, flapping of the hands, banging the head, and phrase repetition are all evidence of increasing or reducing sensory input. Similarly, many of the patterning behaviours of those with ASD – a fascination with maps, music, mathematics, groups and sets, patterns, or detailed illustration – are seen as their coping with the 'chaos' of their input world by imposing a sense of order upon it. An example of this was when, as parents of children with ASD, we attended a Hanen Communication course. We were asked to write down seven words the lecturer would read out. We were given floppy paper, nothing to rest it on, and as the lecturer read the words out, the following things happened: the lights were flicked on and off, someone danced around between us and sprayed perfume, and a CD player was turned on and off intermittently in a random pattern. Needless to say, we struggled with getting the words down! This was an illustration of what the sensory input is like for someone with autism – they experience 'everything', all the time. In *The Curious Incident of the Dog in the Night-time*, Mark Haddon narrates from the point of view of Christopher, a 15-year-old boy with ASD, and describes looking at a field like this: 'But most people are lazy. They never look at everything. They do what is called *glancing*, . . . and the information in their head is really simple.' He then lists six general observations about looking at a field full of cows. These include that there are cows, that it's sunny, that there is grass with flowers, that there

---

2 Claudia Wallis, 'Inside the Autistic Mind', *Time* (15 May 2006): 46–7.

is a village in the distance, and that the field is fenced. In contrast, the autistic Christopher remembers the exact date when he saw the field, the number of houses in the village, the 'ridge and furrow' nature of the field, that 'there is an old plastic bag from Asda in the hedge, and a squashed Coca-Cola can with a snail on it, and a long piece of orange string', the orientation of the field, the numbers of different types of grasses and flowers, the orientation of most of the cows, and the pattern of markings of each individual cow.[3]

This is an excellent illustration of the totality of experience for someone with ASD, but also of their inability to globally process information, and to assign importance or appropriateness or relevance to a particular situation in a meaningful way.

One final thought on autism: in contrast to some Hollywood portrayals, there are few autistic savants – people with autism who are geniuses at maths or music, or who can crack super-codes merely by looking at them. Less than 1 in 10 are likely to have some type of gifted ability along with their ASD. Most children with autism will have some sort of struggle to integrate into society as adults, and compensating 'giftedness' is rare.

James

Having looked at autism spectrum disorder, let me give a brief snapshot of James and what autism has looked like in one family. James was born in 2002, the youngest of three boys. At age three, delayed speech, limited concentration span, and lots of playing alone led to us seeking a paediatric consultation. The paediatrician struggled to get James's attention, to get close to him, or to interest him for long with toys. A diagnosis was made of his having behaviour 'suggestive of ASD'.

For us, what that meant was that James was able to keep good eye contact with people, but had only a few stock phrases – 'Hi, guys' and 'Look at this.' He had his own vocalization, a kind of 'zigga-zigga-zigga' sound that seemed like words, but wasn't. He echoed lines from the *Thunderbirds* TV series (which we had on DVD), and spent limited time playing with his brothers. If he wanted something he couldn't reach, he would drag one of us by the hand and look at what he wanted; at this stage he did not even point, let alone speak. He would also communicate by demonstration – if he wanted to leave somewhere, he would start putting on his jacket and bag to show he was ready to leave. When he went to the playground, he was often more interested in the bark and the dust it made than in the play equipment. He was picky with his food, drinking only milk, and not interested in fruits, vegetables, or most meats. There was concern at one stage that James was not getting enough iron and other vitamins in his diet. We went to a nutritionist, who recommended less milk, more water,

---

3 Mark Haddon, *The Curious Incident of the Dog in the Night-time* (Oxford: David Fickling Books, 2010), 174–6.

and a supplement. James hated the water, and wouldn't touch the supplement. After a week of near tantrums on both fronts, we arrived at a solution – we discovered that as long as it was white and in a bottle, he thought it was 'milk'. So we created 'James's milk', a foul brew of watered-down milk and Floradix iron and vitamin tonic that he drank quite happily. However, it made little difference to his diet. This concoction, Vegemite sandwiches, and apricot Fruit Sticks were as close as he got to vitamins and minerals.

Having said this, he was generally happy, and coped remarkably well at home. Although he coped less well at day-care, where the lack of structure, the numbers of children surrounding him, and some of the expectations around learning goals and toileting stressed him. By the time he was preparing to go to school, as well as communication, behavioural, and dietary issues, he was not yet toilet-trained, was unpredictable in traffic, got himself lost in malls on a regular basis, and was finding a busy day-care environment increasingly stressful, despite now having a teacher aide on a regular basis.

With relief, we got him ORRS (Ongoing and Reviewable Resourcing Schemes) funding, which opened the door to his being able to have special education, with experienced staff, small classes, and a securely fenced facility. This was attached to Glenavon Primary School and under the auspices of Oaklynn Special School. The ORRS application finally gave him a confirmed diagnosis of high-needs autism, something we had known about for nearly two years by this stage.

James has now just turned 11, and has good friends in his school environment. He continues to be a picky eater. Despite years of 'experience-sharing' games at school which are designed to promote coping mechanisms to deal with the unexpected, he still has a range of inflexible behaviours concerning the order in which he puts on his clothes or watches his DVDs, what he expects to buy at the shops, and other regular weekly routines. Despite these problems, however, he has come a long way. He is more flexible with unexpected events, and has coped with experiences like riding on a horse, flying in an aeroplane, meeting new people, and sleeping in a strange bed in a way that was unthinkable even a few years ago. He became toilet-trained soon after starting school, has become well co-ordinated in most physical activities, and is careful about where he goes and the safety considerations around water and in traffic. He is even – slowly – learning to swim.

What the future holds for James, we are not certain. Though divorced, Christine, my 'ex', and I both still have significant roles in his life. And we both hope that James will be able to develop skills to live independently in the future, although that seems a long way off right now. What insight, though, can this boy give us into the parenting heart of God?

God's Care for the Poor and Powerless

The first thing I have noticed about being a father to James is this: James is the youngest of three boys, currently aged 17, 13, and 11. As a father, I love all my boys equally, and appreciate their different gifts and abilities, their different characters and natures. I love them all equally, but paradoxically, I love James just that little bit more, just because for him life is harder. I think that God has a similar care for the poor and the powerless, and for a similar reason. Consider God's compassion in the Old Testament for the poor, the widow, the orphan, and the foreigner (Ps 68:5; Amos 2:6), or in the New Testament, Jesus' concern for the poor, the disabled, the marginalized, the sinner, and the unclean. Many of those groups remain, to a large extent, to this day, and there are strong overlaps between them.

Those who have compassion towards James are rare, and I treasure every one. The man at the swimming pool cafe who kindly speaks to him each week to give him his change (James loves his ice creams!). The young guy who has volunteered to teach him to swim, out of interest and thoughtfulness. The couple at his church who write him postcards when they go on holiday. God, too, seems prepared to go out of his way for those of his 'children' who are less able to care for themselves. Does God's heart go out to his people in the same way that mine does when I see James trying to make friends with strangers (and failing), for example? At Muriwai, when we were camping, he tried to get kids to play with him by throwing a ball and getting them to chase it. He'd just been watching the movie *Up*, and the dogs in it seemed to enjoy chasing the ball – why wouldn't it work with kids? The kids left him there alone, and I wanted to weep. I wonder how often God wants to do the same at our insensitivities to each other?

In Exod 22:21–3 God prohibits the abuse of foreigners, widows, and orphans. If they are abused, he will become angry ('my wrath will burn') and he will arise on their behalf (cf. Deut 24:17; Prov 15:25; Isa 10:1–4; Mal 3:5). He provides for them (Deut 14:29) and includes them in the festivals (Deut 16:11, 14). In short, 'the LORD watches over the strangers; he upholds the orphan and the widow' (Ps 146:9). Sounds just like most of the parents of disabled children I've known!

Similarly, in the gospels Jesus has a ministry to the poor and the oppressed (Luke 4:18), and corrects the understanding that disability came from sin and uncleanness (John 9:1–3; cf. Mark 2:1–12). In the balance of the New Testament, the better treatment of widows seems to have sparked new growth in the church (Acts 6:1–7; cf. the good treatment of the needy in Acts 2:44–5, 4:34–5). Paul is charged by the 'pillars' James, Peter, and John to 'remember the poor', which he was already 'eager to do' (Gal 2:10). And James's comment in his epistle is that pure religion consists of two things – keeping 'oneself unstained by the world' and 'car[ing] for orphans and widows in their distress' (Jas 1:27). These texts orient us to God's concern for the most vulnerable in our society, and the demand for the centre to be defined by the (assumed) margins.

Partnering with God in Service

The second thing that has become clear over time, is that working with God in the service of others almost always builds character and maturity. The Mental

Health Foundation puts out regular information sheets on disabilities, and one from 2001 on autism noted that the other children in the family of an ASD child may have to put up with constant disruptions to their life, or deal with the discomfort of having a 'different' sibling in public situations. Certainly, Nick and Liam, James's older brothers, have had their share of this. They have had to help find James when he went walkabout in the mall, have had their toys broken, have had to explain to other kids, and even adults, their brother's condition – why he 'talks funny'. Liam has slept in the same room as James all his life, and has had to listen to him talking to himself, found toys 'taken over', and even had James sleep in the same bed from time to time.

The mental health information sheet then went on to make the observation that siblings may choose either to take on more responsibility than normal, almost 'parenting' the child, or they may withdraw and become resentful of their sibling's intrusions. In a sense, they must choose whether to partner with their parents, or withdraw and work against them. Thankfully, our boys have taken the first course, and what we've seen is a maturity beyond their years that may not have developed without James. For example, Nick, the oldest, is involved in robotics competitions. A couple of years ago this boy, who was then around 14, was explaining about a problem in the group that he was leading. He had a group of five, and there was one kid, he said, 'and everyone hates him 'cos he talks too much'. His solution? 'I think I'll break the team into two groups. I'll have this kid, and the others can go together.'

Then there's Liam, my middle son, the nurturer and carer of the family, who can make friends with complete strangers and who helps other parents with their children. We were at Muriwai camping one year, and we had a family move into the campsite next to us: a dad and two young boys, about six and four years of age. Dad sounded as though he'd just been in a very messy break-up: he was loud, he was angry, and he was drinking a lot. He ignored his boys. The boys took a soccer ball out to the field, and the older boy threw the ball at his brother and made him cry, then left him by himself. So Liam went out there. He began by playing soccer with the younger boy, kicking the ball, encouraging him, having a great time. The older boy soon joined them, and then, unbelievably, so did the dad. Liam eventually had the entire family having a good time for nearly an hour.

I think God offers us the same opportunity, and we have to constantly choose whether working with him, the cosmic Parent, will be an embarrassment or something to resent, or whether we can allow it to mature us. Once again, it is helpful to note the biblical stress upon character-formation through difficult or unusual circumstances. Consider these passages below:

> For we are what God made us, created in Christ Jesus for good works, which he prepared beforehand to be our way of life. (Eph 2:10)
> And not only that, but we also boast in our sufferings, knowing that suffering produces endurance, and endurance produces character, and character produces hope, and hope does not disappoint us, because God's love has

> been poured into our hearts through the Holy Spirit that has been given to us. (Rom 5:3–4)
>
> My brothers and sisters, whenever you face trials of any kind, consider it nothing but joy, because you know that the testing of your faith produces endurance; and let endurance have its full effect, so that you may be mature and complete, lacking in nothing. (Jas 1:2–4)

I so admire my older children for taking this path, and a part of me hopes that they will continue to be blessed for doing so. They certainly deserve it. It is difficult to compare what they are like today with what they might have been like without an ASD brother. But as I've told them a number of times, I feel very privileged to have had the sons I do – more like having won a competition than raised children. And in this there seems to be the hand of God.

God's Wisdom and Love in Discipline

Discipline with an ASD kid is interesting, to say the least. We were very fortunate to have had two children before James. We kind of knew it wasn't our parenting style or decisions. But this boy just *did not listen*! Inevitably, as with most children with ASD, he had his hearing checked, and as expected, it was diagnosed as being fine. I remember bringing James home from day-care one day, and he got a couple of metres ahead of me. He also missed where the car was in the parking lot. So I called him, and called him, and called him. In the end, I called him six times. He just didn't hear me in the rush of data that was his world. I have often reflected since then on how I 'lose' God's voice in the rush of appointments, needless worries, pointless speculations, and other 'data' that make up my world.

Generally, children with autism won't tend to bother you. They like their world and their routines. I have often said to friends that despite appearances, James is our most obedient child; it's just that sometimes it takes him a while to figure out what it is that you want. Sometimes, however, routines become obsessions or fixed expectations. At the moment James is a huge fan of Kinder Surprise eggs. They combine three of his favourite things: chocolate, building stuff, and movie tie-ins. And he expects that every trip to the supermarket will result in a Kinder Surprise egg. As parents, what is our response to this behaviour? Sometimes he has to go to the supermarket or elsewhere and *not* get a Kinder Surprise egg. Do we do this because we like to see him cry (and he does too; he wells up with big fat tears of absolute desolation)? No, it's because life is varied, and we must encourage him to be strong enough to take the variety of life as it is.

The writer to the Hebrews said the same thing to his flock, who were undergoing persecution:

> Endure trials for the sake of discipline. God is treating you as children; for what child is there whom a parent does not discipline? If you do not have

that discipline in which all children share, then you are illegitimate and not his children. Moreover, we had human parents to discipline us, and we respected them. Should we not be even more willing to be subject to the Father of spirits and live? For they disciplined us for a short time as seemed best to them, but he disciplines us for our good, in order that we may share his holiness. Now, discipline always seems painful rather than pleasant at the time, but later it yields the peaceful fruit of righteousness to those who have been trained by it. (Heb 12:7–11)

Our God, in the same way as an earthly father, disciplines in ways that are sometimes confusing and painful in order to instil flexibility, strength, good character, and, yes, *peace* in his children – a reality we often struggle with and often forget.

James's Hope for the Future

I am fascinated by Paul's description in 1 Cor 15:35–49 of what will happen to our bodies on the Last Day. And I find myself wondering what James will look like on that day. Paul offers three picture comparisons, and we will look at each in turn.

First, the resurrection body is different from our current one in both time and nature. A seed must die before it becomes a plant, and so must our bodies, after which the resurrection body will be experienced (15:36). Different seeds then make different plants, with the plant also being different from the seed. We might therefore expect that each resurrection body will be different from others, and that all will be different from what they have been (15:36–8). So will the 'seed' James become a different boy or man on the Last Day? Will his essentially sweet and willing nature be enabled in a new way? 1 Cor 15:38 says that God will choose his body for him. Has this choice already been made, in who he now is? Or might there be some kind of reversal, as God loved to do through the Scriptures? For example, the prisoner Joseph is made Pharaoh's assistant; the exile Daniel is made into the courtier and interpreter of dreams; the crucified and apparent failure Jesus is made into the glorified Lord of all creation. Will the limited boy be granted great new powers and wisdom in the new heaven and earth? Or will he be the same boy on the Last Day? As a seed leads to a plant, Paul says, we will become a resurrection body, suggesting continuity of our 'self', our personality (15:42–9).

Secondly, the resurrection flesh will differ from ours both in consistency and 'glory' (15:39–42). James's new flesh will be as different from his old as animal flesh is different from human, or that of birds from fish. It will also be of a greater glory, as far above his current body as the sun or moon or stars are above the earth (although again, there is a difference in levels of glory). Will James's brain therefore be a new brain that enables holistic processing function? Will he become 'normal', as indeed some children with ASD have become as they have grown older?

Thirdly, the relationship of human difference and redemption is not obvious to our fallen human minds. The resurrection body will be immortal (15:42, 52–3), powerful and glorious (15:43), motivated not by the fleshly sinful desires, but only by those of the Holy Spirit – 'a body wholly vitalized and transformed by the Spirit of the risen Christ' (15:44, 56).[4] What would a Spirit-filled James look like? Would he be exactly the same? And would we perhaps be granted vision instead of what his view of the world was? Would there be things he might teach me? Or would he be able to explain the ways in which I assumed I was helping him, but was wrong? Regardless, I look forward to the Last Day. I have a sneaking suspicion that James will be similar in almost every respect, except perhaps communication. And if that is the case, I'm looking forward to a good long chat!

Why does James have autism? I don't know. I know he makes life interesting. I can't imagine a world without him in it. But despite the challenges, he has already given me and the others of our family (and some further afield) a gift in helping us to learn about God – a God of compassion for those who find it tough; a God who invites us to partner with him in difficult things and who gives maturity as a reward; a God who calls for our attention, and who disciplines us to give us flexibility and strength, and finally a God who gives us hope, not just of a resurrection body, but of a world where everything now wrong – whatever that happens to end up being – is made right.

---

4 R.J. Bauckham, 'Eschatology', in *New Bible Dictionary*, 2nd. edn, ed. J.D. Douglas (Leicester: InterVarsity Press, 1982), 345.

4 Disability Discrimination in the Book of Job

Kirk Patston

'Why are the Criminal Insane incarcerated in special institutions for their care and custody, while the Criminal Feebleminded, though sporadically imprisoned, are allowed opportunity to roam, rob and rape? . . . "Feeblemindedness is the mother of Crime, Pauperism, and Degeneracy."'[1] Thus wrote Frank C. Richmond in the early decades of the twentieth century in an article in which he also concurred with the opinion that '"Not all criminals are feebleminded, but all feebleminded are potential criminals."'[2] In 1916 two anatomists made notes on the autopsies of the feeble-minded and used these kinds of descriptions: 'The brain of this microcephalic idiot, of the mental age estimated less than one year, has somewhat the suggestion of the brain of an ape.'[3] Another was described as 'a good case of the so-called old demented imbecile found in almshouses'.[4] Another patient was described as 'a moron, . . . a subnormal . . . [who] perhaps belongs in the delinquent group'.[5]

There is a long history of forming links between disability, criminality, and being viewed as subhuman. Centuries before the anatomists and criminologists published their views, a wealthy man who was facing verbal abuse dismissed his mockers because they were wandering vagrants, economically unproductive, and comparable to animals. He complained:

> But now they make sport of me, those who are younger than I, whose fathers I would have disdained to set with the dogs of my flock. They are driven out from society; they are delinquents who live among rocks and bushes and nettles. They are a senseless, disreputable brood, who have been whipped out of the land.

---

1 Frank C. Richmond, 'The Criminal Feebleminded', *Journal of the American Institute of Criminal Law and Criminology* 21 (1931): 537.
2 Ibid. Richmond quoted this opinion from Lewis M. Terman, *The Measurement of Intelligence* (Boston, MA: Houghton Mifflin, 1916).
3 E.E. Southard and Annie E. Taft, 'Clinical, Anatomical and Brief Histological Descriptions of Ten Cases of Feeble-mindedness', *Memoirs of the American Academy of Arts and Sciences* n.s. 14 (1918): 105.
4 Ibid., 106.
5 Ibid., 107.

The wealthy man is, of course, Job. These arresting words come from his speech in Job 30. It is a troubling passage for what it displays of the way societies practise discrimination. The passage seems to be an important, but often overlooked, element in grasping how the book of Job may contribute to a biblical and Christian understanding of disability.

A growing number of studies of disability address the book of Job. The main approach is to view the man Job as evidencing illness and, perhaps, disability, and to discuss the ways that Job or the author of Job chose to respond to this. Some attempt to come up with a medical diagnosis for Job's physical suffering. Jewish tradition has described Job's skin as discoloured, ulcerated, lacerated, and filled with worms and evidencing leprosy.[6] David Clines has catalogued other dermatological symptoms: pustules in Job 7:5 and blackened, peeling skin in Job 30:30.[7] He notes that leprosy, elephantiasis, and psychosomatic dermatitis have been discussed. However, modern medical analysis of ancient texts is always tentative, and Clines is right that it is best 'to admit our ignorance of the precise malady'.[8] Recently Jeremy Schipper has pointed out that at the end of the book of Job there is no mention of his skin disease being healed, leaving interesting questions about the nature of Job's restoration.[9]

We might also note that Job reports general wasting (19:20), fever (30:30b), sleep disturbances (7:4, 14), and aching or rotting bones (30:17, 30), but these may be general descriptions of illness, or metaphors for Job's emotional state.[10] Indeed, some commentators would consider Job's condition to be psychiatric.[11] Dan Merkur's survey of the literature reveals discussions of Job as a masochistic devotee of an abusive God, as a man struggling with guilt and conscience, as an obsessional personality with a psychosomatic illness, and so on.

Rachel Magdalene has come at the issue through the lens of ancient legal status, and proposes that the book of Job is like a trial in the Neo-Babylonian period, in which disability would be seen as a legal punishment.[12] This seems to be how Job's friends understand his condition. Another most promising thread of study is that begun by Rebecca Raphael and picked up recently by Amos Yong, that the monsters in the book of Job are a rhetorical trope that allow us to access the author's view on disability.[13]

---

6 Lynn A. Holden, *Forms of Deformity* (Sheffield: JSOT Press, 1991), 71,75,78,77, 62, respectively.
7 David J.A. Clines, *Job 1–20*, Word Biblical Commentary, vol. 17, ed. Robert L. Hubbard Jr (Dallas, TX: Word, 1989), 49. Clines thinks reference to maggots in Job's sores is a way of describing pus.
8 Ibid., 48.
9 Jeremy Schipper, 'Healing and Silence in the Epilogue of Job', *Word and World* 30 (2010): 18–22.
10 Clines, *Job 1–20*, 49.
11 Dan Merkur, 'Psychotherapeutic Change in the Book of Job', in *Psychology and the Bible: A New Way to Read the Scriptures*, ed. J. Harold Ellens and Wayne G. Rollins (Westport, CT: Praeger, 2004), 129–31.
12 F. Rachel Magdalene, *On the Scales of Righteousness: Neo-Babylonian Trial Law and the Book of Job* (Providence, RI: Brown Judaic Studies, 2007).
13 Rebecca Raphael, 'Things Too Wonderful: A Disabled Reading of Job', *Perspectives in Religious Studies* 31 (2004): 399–424; Rebecca Raphael, *Biblical Corpora: Representations of Disability in Hebrew*

Basically, these studies situate disability in the medical, psychiatric, legal, or rhetorical perception of Job's own body or illness. But Job is not the only person with a disability in the book of Job. In Job 29 and 30 Job speaks about his relationship with people with disabilities, and his talk reveals a social and moral context in which one can make some sense of disability in Job's world. This accords with the recent work of Carol Newsom, who has made the valuable suggestion that the book of Job is a contest of moral imaginations.[14] The narrator, the friends, the various perspectives on Job are all windows into moral possibilities, and as the reader ponders the dialogue, the book does its work of moral formation.

This chapter explores the moral visions of Job and Yahweh to see where disability may exist for each of them. This moral imaginations approach is appealing because it moves the conversation away from Job's itchy skin or troubled mind into the domain of social relationships, consistent with the way that disability is more than a medical impairment, and is developed and maintained by social and political relationships.

Job's final speech in Job 29 and 30, and sections of the speeches of Yahweh at the end of the book, contain material relevant to the issue of disability discrimination. What may at first appear to be incidental comments about people with disabilities actually provide a most revealing portrait of the man Job that is deeply relevant to the book's main concerns. Moreover, Job's choice of imagery to describe people on the margins of his society seems to significantly influence Yahweh's speeches to Job. What is surprising is how discriminatory Job is – even the blameless and upright Job. In contrast, God's creative grace shockingly undermines such disability discrimination. Yahweh's grand description of creation contains pointed tropes that are redolent with disability imagery in a way that rebuffs the stance of charity or contempt and replaces it with wonder, reciprocity, and laughter as ways of being in the presence of disability.

People with disabilities are explicitly mentioned in Job 29:15, among Job's account of his own righteousness:

> 14 'I put on righteousness, and it clothed me;
> my justice was like a robe and a turban.
> 15 I was eyes to the blind,
> and feet to the lame.
> 16 I was a father to the needy,
> and I championed the cause of the stranger.' (NRSV)

The words come from a meditative soliloquy of Job in his final long speech. Job is remembering his former life, lamenting its passing, positioning himself to present God with an oath of innocence.

Biblical Literature (London: T&T Clark International, 2008); Amos Yong, *The Bible, Disability, and the Church : A New Vision of the People of God* (Grand Rapids, MI: Eerdmans, 2011).
14 Carol A. Newsom, *The Book of Job: A Contest of Moral Imaginations* (New York: Oxford University Press, 2003).

It is not hard to find commentators who applaud the exemplary conduct of Job.[15]

If we consider Job's self-presentation of his religious and moral life in Job 29 and 31, he addresses topics of sexual ethics, justice and social obligation, land ethics, and his ultimate allegiance to God.[16] He has conducted himself with purity, and has made sure he has not exploited power. He has worked for the good of the community. Importantly, he is concerned not only with behaviours, but with underlying attitudes of the heart, in a way that has attracted comments comparing this section of Job with the high moral vision of the Sermon on the Mount.[17]

There is reason to think, then, that the author of the book of Job is implicitly commending Job's treatment of people with disabilities. Along with other needy people like widows, orphans, and the dying, people with disabilities received the overflow of Job's largesse, and their lives were better for it. These powerless ones provided Job with their gratitude, and the onlooking society afforded Job honour for his works of charity. Job's disability ethics and practice are part of the reason he is described as a blameless, upright, God-fearing servant of God.

There are reasons, however, why one should not rush to endorse Job's behaviour. Saul Olyan notes that it is all too common for the Old Testament to link people with disabilities with the needy, so that texts that seem to commend the fair treatment of people with disabilities perpetuate a patronizing stance toward them.[18] The disability theorist and activist Bill Hughes has noted that pity depends on the conceptualization of disability as tragedy and the ways that life with a disability is a life of darkness and ontological invalidity.[19] The person who offers money, say, may seem to be doing good to the person with a disability, but perhaps he or she is engaged in a hierarchical rite that is also, or even dominantly, about the bolstering of their view of themselves as powerful and good.

The generosity embodied in the charitable gift or donation is an attempt to ameliorate the personal and the socio-political deficits of the 'unfortunates'. In the act of giving, the non-disabled person converts pity into social capital and

---

15 Francis I. Andersen, *Job: An Introduction and Commentary*, ed. C.B.E. Wiseman (Leicester: InterVarsity Press, 1976); John Hartley, *The Book of Job* (Grand Rapids, MI: Eerdmans, 1988). More nuanced but approving comments are offered by John H. Walton, *Job, The NIV Application Commentary*, ed. Terry Muck (Grand Rapids, MI: Zondervan, 2012); J.A. Wharton, *Job*, ed. P.D. Miller and D.L. Bartlett (Louisville, KY: Westminster John Knox Press, 1999).
16 Samuel E. Balentine, *Job, Smyth and Helwys Bible Commentary*, ed. Keith Gammons (Macon, GA: Smyth and Helwys, 2006), 476. He is following Newsom.
17 Karl Barth, *Church Dogmatics*, ed. and trans. G.W. Bromiley and T.F. Torrance, 2nd rev. edn (Edinburgh: T&T Clark, 1975 and 1977), vol. IV/3.2, sections 70–71, 17.
18 Saul M. Olyan, *Disability in the Hebrew Bible: Interpreting Mental and Physical Differences* (Cambridge: Cambridge University Press, 2008), 6–7.
19 Bill Hughes, 'Fear, Pity and Disgust: Emotions and the Non-disabled Imaginary', in *The Routledge Handbook of Disability Studies*, ed. Nick Watson, Alan Roulstone, and Carol Thomas (New York: Routledge, 2012), 72. Not surprisingly, there is a disability rights slogan 'Piss on pity.'

confirms his or her status as a benevolent person-citizen who is independent and authentic. There is no reciprocation in the charitable gift: it is a pure act of 'othering'.[20]

Hughes understandably fears that pity may be thinly veiled contempt.[21] Is this what is happening in Job 29?

Given that Job is a righteous man, it is worth considering whether Job is really guilty of such othering. Maybe Job's words are an ancient description of empowerment. He did not just give people with disabilities money, but he was *feet* to the lame and *eyes* to the blind. Could it be that Job somehow resourced people with mobility and visual impairments so that they could function in society? However, this feels like a reading into the text of categories from another time and place.[22]

Questions about how to read Job 29 are illuminated by the fact that Job 29 is followed by Job 30. Job 30 gives us reasons to come to the text with some reservation. There is no doubt that Job's former life was morally good and generated benefits for many. However, there is a pattern in Job's self-presentation. He is always the one in a position of power. Once that power is removed, other aspects of Job's attitudes become apparent.

In Job 29 he is lamenting his former life, and then in Job 30 he protests about his current experience. He is deeply troubled that he has become the object of mocking. He imagines that his detractors are from the lowest ranks of his society, and this makes their derision of him all the more abhorrent:

1 But now they make sport of me, those who are younger than I, whose fathers I would have disdained to set with the dogs of my flock.
2 What could I gain from the strength of their hands? All their vigour is gone.
3 Through want and hard hunger they gnaw the dry and desolate ground,
4 they pick mallow and the leaves of bushes, and to warm themselves the roots of broom.
5 They are driven out from society; people shout after them as after a thief.
6 In the gullies of wadis they must live, in holes in the ground, and in the rocks.
7 Among the bushes they bray; under the nettles they huddle together.
8 A senseless, disreputable brood, they have been whipped out of the land.
9 And now they mock me in song; I am a byword to them.
10 They abhor me, they keep aloof from me; they do not hesitate to spit at the sight of me.

---

20 Ibid., 71.
21 Empirical evidence of the complex attitudes that are present in acts of kindness towards people with disabilities can be found in Irwin Katz, *Stigma: A Social Psychological Analysis* (Hillsdale, NJ: L. Erlbaum Associates, 1981).
22 Of course, adopting the suspicious, postmodern insistence that the ancient man Job describe his relationship to people with disabilities in today's acceptable language is also to impose something potentially foreign to the text.

In Job 30:1 Job speaks of young ones who are mocking, and he disparages them by describing their fathers. Then in vv. 2ff. he talks about 'them' – and it is not possible to be sure whether the rest of Job's description is of the mockers themselves or their fathers. It is likely to be their fathers because in v. 2 they seem like older people who have lost their strength. This would mean that Job is thinking in terms of patriarchal representation and clans, associating his young mockers with a whole social group.

But who is this social group? They are clearly marginalized, but it is not completely clear why. The people are homeless and marginalized, scavenging on the outskirts of civilization. Many commentators assume they are criminal, but Job *compares* them to criminals, suggesting that they are not really criminals. There is a real possibility that these are people with a disability. In v. 2 Job maligns the mockers or their fathers because their vigour is gone. For whatever reason, the physical incapacity of these people makes them unattractive to an employer. They may be physically disabled. They may be elderly and frail. They may be so hungry that their strength is gone. In v. 8 Job calls them senseless which is the Hebrew בְּנֵי־נָבָל 'sons of a fool'. There is an understandable tradition to see the fool as a moral description in books like Proverbs. Job was scared that his wife was sounding like a fool for advising him to curse God, so the book of Job resonates with a theological view of foolishness. However, Clines wonders in this context whether the term may also include people with intellectual disability or mental illness.[23]

It is interesting that Job, and most of the commentaries on Job, easily enter into a way of viewing people that takes their impoverished way of living as a reason to make all kinds of assumptions about them. Job values the old, those who are able to work, and those who live in the centre of things. If you lack these things, it seems a small step in Job's mind to associate you with criminality and being subhuman. Job assigns these people a status less than that of a sheepdog. His image of them possibly braying furthers the sense that these people are like animals. In Job 30:8 he dismisses these people's value and status by calling them 'disreputable', which is literally בְּנֵי בְלִי־שֵׁם 'the sons of those without a name'. Job sounds like a social commentator who is making a facile association between feeble-mindedness, criminal deviance, and the assumption that you will spend your life without purpose in an alms-house.

Biblical commentators easily follow Job in making associations between weakness, homelessness, and immorality. John Hartley writes of the people in Job 30 as rabble, deplorable, despicable, riffraff, repulsive outcasts who 'continually manifest their incorrigible folly'.[24] John Gray assumes they are criminals. They hide among the thistles and mutter plans to each other, sounding like

---

23 The attribution of physical rather than mental impairment seems more convincing; however, Clines's observation creates an important question for further disability-sensitive research.

24 Hartley, *The Book of Job*, 397–8.

animals, before they attack.²⁵ John Walton describes them as 'disreputable predators' who are 'the dregs of society'.²⁶ David Clines, with his characteristically canny eye, has noted how easily commentators collude with Job's rhetoric in a way that does not befit their status as religious experts, or how they go beyond what is in the text. He writes: 'Well-fed commentators rarely recognize that being homeless is not a moral fault. What are described in these verses are not wicked people but desperately poor people for whom there is no place in regular human society.'²⁷

Clines does not think that Job maligns the morality of these people, since the word 'fool' may be to do with mental, not moral, state. But many commentators do make moral and theological judgements, so Clines comments that 'the venom of the commentators against the outcasts is astonishing'.²⁸ It is important to see how powerful Job's rhetoric is here, and how easily readers move into ways of thinking that are embarrassingly discriminatory. The words of Job and their reception evidence an all too familiar process. A homeless man at a railway station is easily viewed as a criminal threat. Of course, he may have schizophrenia or intellectual impairment and just want to belong.

The writer of Job is cleverly creating a moral dilemma for the reader of the book. In Newsom's terms, what moral imagination will the reader choose? Job 30 is a signal that all was not or is not right in Job's world. Suspicions about Job's acts of charity are not just some fashionable, postmodern reading against the grain. The ancient author of Job included difficult information about the man Job that calls into question a straightforward reading of Job's impressive self-presentation in Job 29 and 31.

Psychological explanations of Job's vitriolic words are of some help, and of some relevance to disability studies. There is good evidence that there is a projection here. The intensity of Job's hatred for the marginal other is really Job's hatred of his own beleaguered state.²⁹ Job imagines that the fathers of the mockers are weak, hungry, live away from others, and are like animals. Job has said of himself that his own strength is failing, that his appetite has gone, and that no one seems to notice him while he is sitting among the ashes. Job compares the ancestors of his mockers to animals, and Job has himself wondered whether God sees him as a monstrous beast. Job reports that the jackal is his only friend. Job's self-contempt turns to contempt for the other.

---

25 John Gray, *The Book of Job*, *The Text of the Hebrew Bible*, vol. 1, ed. David J.A. Clines (Sheffield: Sheffield Phoenix, 2010), 368.
26 Walton, *Job*, 317.
27 David J.A. Clines, *Job 21–37*, *Word Biblical Commentary*, vol. 18A, ed Bruce M. Metzger (Nashville, TN: Thomas Nelson, 2006), 1,001.
28 Ibid.
29 Allan G. Frankland, *The Little Psychotherapy Book: Object Relations in Practice* (New York: Oxford University Press, 2010), 180.

Job may be evidencing the paranoid-schizoid position.[30] Under psychological threat, Job retreats to an immature stage where he can see others only in black-and-white terms. The other must be all good or all bad, so a homeless person who laughs at Job becomes in his mind an evil, criminal threat.

Job is also trying to achieve something in terms of social identification. Sociologists and social psychologists have explored ways that human beings set up distinctions between themselves and others. People like to think of themselves as belonging to an in-group and not belonging to an out-group for a variety of reasons.[31] In social identity theory, individuals need to enhance their self-esteem, or at least not diminish it, and so define themselves as belonging to a group that has favourable associations. It may be that Job feels so utterly humiliated that he has to convince his three friends that at least he does not belong to the very worst of groups. In his sermons on Job, John Calvin suggests that in Job 30 Job is not saying what he really thinks, but simply articulating the commonly held assessment of the lowly mockers.[32] This may be a polemical attempt by Job to persuade his friends to place him back in the in-group.

More broadly, Job may be buying into the symbolic system of his culture, a symbolic system created to make the world seem more patterned and manageable. A famous anthropological study of this phenomenon is Mary Douglas's work on purity and danger.[33] With reference to so-called primitive religion, food laws in Leviticus, and practices from Hinduism and Christianity, Douglas proposes that humans tend to classify things as belonging in a particular place and can categorize things as belonging or not belonging to a particular class. Certain people can be designated as inferior or even dangerous as they manifest characteristics that violate the search for order. Job seems to be doing this by trying to cast his detractors as animals of the wilderness.

Erving Goffman has also noted the way symbolic systems can be part of the mechanism of otherness and discrimination. His work on stigma points out that a person may have a characteristic that is interpreted by others in a way that spoils identity.[34] In ancient Greece a person who was a slave, a criminal, or a traitor had a sign cut or burnt into the body. These were like an advertisement that the person was to be avoided. Today, the sign may not be so crude, but physical

---

30 Moran uses this psychological category for a discussion of racial discrimination. See Anthony Moran, 'The Psychodynamics of Australian Settler-nationalism: Assimilating or Reconciling with the Aborigines?', *Political Psychology* 23 (2002): 667–701.

31 Dora Capozza et al., 'A Comparison of Motivational Theories of Identification', in *Social Identities: Motivational, Emotional and Cultural Influences*, ed. Rupert Brown and Dora Capozza (New York: Psychology Press, 2006), 52–3.

32 John Calvin, *Sermons on Job: Facsimile of 1574 Edition* (Edinburgh: The Banner of Truth Trust, 1993), 511. Wharton also hopes that Job's words are more rhetorical than indicative of his true attitudes to people; see Wharton, *Job*.

33 Mary Douglas, *Purity and Danger: An Analysis of Concept of Pollution and Taboo* (London: Routledge, 2003).

34 Erving Goffman, *Stigma: Notes on the Management of Spoiled Identity* (Englewood Cliffs, NJ: Prentice-Hall, 1986). The idea of stigma is applied to the Hebrew Bible in Olyan, *Disability in the Hebrew Bible*.

disfigurement, skin colour, disability, or sexual orientation may be interpreted in a way that reduces the person who carries them. Goffman suggests that there are always people who are viewed as tainted, discounted, or discredited.[35] Job discriminates and discredits people on the basis of age, economic productivity, and place of residence.

Goffman's study has produced decades of research and writing, mainly within the field of social psychology. Bruce Link and Jo Phelan have reviewed this literature and suggest that it could be enhanced through more sociological analysis.[36] They propose that stigma is a phenomenon that occurs when several components come together. First, a person's differences must be distinguished and labelled. These differences must then be associated with negative attributes. People then form a distinction between 'them' and 'us'. The social consequences of these cognitive and affective behaviours play out in terms of status loss and discrimination. These processes are complex because the status loss may be believed by both the 'us' and the 'them'. Further, the discrimination may be entrenched in social structures and be perpetuated beyond the choices of individuals. Finally, Link and Phelan argue that the process of stigmatization can only occur with an exercise of power. It does seem that Job has, or had, such power, and his final speech is a desperate attempt to get the world to return to its familiar patterns of relationships, even if this means there will be a group of despised outsiders. In a way, all that matters to Job is that he escapes identification with or humiliation by the marginalized group.

In their studies of the book of Job, Carol Newsom and Samuel Balentine have helpfully schematized the vision Job has of his society and how his morality works itself out in Job 29–31. In Job 29 Job describes a world in which everybody has a place. Job's world can be schematized as a series of concentric circles with himself and God at the centre;[37] then there is his household (Job 29:2–6); then the city gate (Job 29:7–11) where Job was honoured and his opinion desired and respected; next is the circle of the socially marginalized: the poor and needy (Job 29:12–17). These are the people Job helps. But then Job 30 takes us to another realm: the place of the foolish and no-names. They are the others, the despicable, the ones to whom nothing is owed.

Newsom notes that such a vision of society brings some moral problems with it:

> I can find little indication that the ancient biblical culture was troubled by its depiction of its moral world. Modern critics, however, stand sufficiently outside of it to be disturbed. What is troubling is that Job's identity as a

---

35 Goffman, *Stigma*, 3.
36 Bruce G. Link and Jo C. Phelan, 'Conceptualizing Stigma', *Annual Review of Sociology* 27 (2001): 363–85.
37 Balentine, *Job*, 458; Carol A. Newsom, 'The Moral Sense of Nature: Ethics in the Light of God's Speech to Job', *Princeton Seminary Bulletin* 15 (1994): 9–27.

person of righteousness and justice is inextricably bound up with the logic of inequality. There is a binary relationship of donor/recipient, dominant/subordinate that undergirds the moral thinking of such relationships. As we know, the paternalism of such a moral vision can encompass amelioration of suffering but not transformation of the structures that generate the inequalities that produce suffering.[38]

Newsom perceptively argues that Job lives in a culture of honour and shame.[39] For all of his life Job has lived on the good side of this arrangement. He has only known honour. But cultures that create honour also create shame and contempt. And now Job has had a radical change of category. It is the contemptible who treat him with contempt.

Job himself seems to long for a return to normal. If his innocence were endorsed by God, then he can return to his honoured status and everyone can resume their familiar relationships.

Psychosocial readings that find the man Job to be wanting in Job 30 raise important questions about how to read the book of Job overall. Could it be that his blamelessness and uprightness is not all that can be said about this man? Many commentators are now offering suspicious readings of the prologue that make Job's characterization more complex. But even without these, the man Job does testify at the end of the book that he has grown through his experience – from a knowledge of God that was like hearing, to a knowledge of God that is more like seeing. This raises another question: Why does a blameless and upright person need to change? What is going on?

Considering the large movements of the book of Job, it is possible that while the *purpose* of Job's suffering was not to educate Job, nevertheless the *result* is that the suffering did educate him. He grew in wisdom. Before his suffering, Job responded to what he knew of God with impressive action and true sincerity. When he encountered a nice person with a bit of a limp or a blind beggar who would say 'Thank you,' he was generous and helpful. This is what his culture taught him to do. And Job probably imagined that he was being like his God, who was nice to nice people and judged wicked people. So, to Job, it would have made sense that his moral obligations did not really extend to those scary people who lived out of town. Weren't they criminals out there?

God always blessed Job's piety, so he had no reason to think there was anything wrong with his moral life. Then along came the most devastating suffering, and with profound impact on Job, Job was assigned a place with the animals and criminals. Even the riffraff could laugh at him. Job becomes a victim of othering, and he begins to discover that he was actually a participant himself in the processes of othering.

---

38 Ibid., 12.
39 Similarly, Walton, *Job*.

Yahweh graciously speaks challenging words to Job and offers something much richer: a vision that transcends and critiques the moral universe that Job has been inhabiting.

In Yahweh's speeches the concentric circles of Job's society are exposed as irrelevant. When Yahweh speaks to Job he makes mention of a menagerie of the margins that undermines the way Job had been viewing life.

God's speech offers a new way of thinking about space. In Job's mind, some people lived in a place that was undesirable. There was a wasteland where you would be sent against your will and where you would be in danger of starving. God speaks about the very same place, and presents it in completely different terms:

> Who has let the wild ass go free?
> Who has loosed the bonds of the swift ass,
> to which I have given the steppe for its home,
> the saltland for its dwelling place?
> It scorns the tumult of the city;
> it does not hear the shouts of the driver.
> It ranges the mountains as its pasture,
> and it searches after every green thing. (Job 39:5–8)

Yahweh assigns associations and value to places of residence that are the opposite of Job's understanding. Who would want to live in the centre of the city? The saltland can be your place of freedom. It can be your home. It can be the place that God is pleased to give you. God's speech is full of ways in which he is actually present in the wasteland. He sends rain on the wasteland even if there is no human being there, so that grass grows. Out there in the wilds God is helping the lion find food and the eagle swoop down on its prey. The wasteland is a place of God's presence and provision. Job was imagining the concentric circles of the world wrongly.

God's speech presents a new way of viewing life as an animal. In Job's rhetorical world, dogs and jackals and ostriches are terms of belittling and disgust. But God describes wild animals as strong, fast, courageous, and wise. Even if the ostrich lacks wisdom and maternal instincts, God seems mighty impressed with its speed when it runs. Importantly, the animals have agency. In Job's world, the centre of the circle moves to the outer groups with either charity or contempt. But God says the donkey can look back at the city and treat it with contempt. Power relationships are more two-sided and complex in the creation that God governs and loves.

Both Job and Yahweh use the word 'laughter', but the sense of it is different. There may be something very important for disability theology here. In Job 30:1, where the NRSV says that 'now they make sport of me', the Hebrew is 'they laugh against me' (שָׂחֲקוּ עָלָי). Many of the animals in Yahweh's speech also laugh, but the verb is always followed by a different preposition; the animals laugh to/for/about things. The English differentiation of laughing *at* and laughing *with* may have a Hebrew equivalent. The donkey 'scorns the tumult of the city; it does not hear the shouts of the driver' (Job 39:7). So, too, the ostrich. When it spreads its plumes aloft, it laughs at the horse and its rider (Job 39:18). The warhorse 'laughs at fear, and is not dismayed' (Job 39:22). Leviathan 'laughs at the rattle of javelins' (Job 41:29).

As part of giving animals agency and value and making their home seem desirable, Yahweh emphasizes that the animals laugh. While the animals' laughter involves their mocking an opponent, the whole tone of Yahweh's speech is one of wonder. This makes the laughter of the animals seem more like sport or play rather than contempt.

In Hebrew, 'laugh' is an important word in the practice of discrimination and otherness. It comes from recognizing that a pattern has been broken. If sin is found where righteousness should be, then one might laugh in the sense of judgemental scoffing (Ps 2:4). It might carry a sense of disdain or disgust. But it can also be used when there is an unexpected blessing and one is delightfully surprised, captured in Abraham and Sarah naming their surprising baby with the name Isaac, 'laughter'. It can also carry a playful sense, and has been translated with the word 'frolic' (Ps 104:24 NIV), 'dance' (2 Sam 6:5) or 'merrymaking' (Jer 31:4). Through repetition of the word 'laughter', God is further inviting Job to a new vision of the world. It can be a place where a deviation from a pattern is not greeted with contempt or disdain, but playful, celebratory wonder.

One reason why Job despises his distractors is that they are of no use to him: 'What could I gain from the strength of their hands? All their vigour is gone' (Job 30:1). His comment about gain takes Job into the dynamics of the question that actually makes the book of Job happen: 'Does Job fear God for nothing?' Whatever the exact motives of the satan in Job 1, his question is one of great value to Job's growth in moral wisdom. God has created a world of donkeys, ostriches, and horses where value is not always judged in economic productivity or social status.

Job thought that Yahweh was with him, but not with the nameless brood who lived on the margins of Job's world and who deserved no help from him, only contempt. But that marginal world is God's world. He is there. It is a place where freedom, provision, and laughter may be present in ways that Job could barely imagine. Job would grow in moral wisdom as his world of concentric circles and status collapsed so that people with disabilities became more than objects of discrimination through charity or contempt. This ancient text offers a moral vision that leaves discriminatory ways, replacing the laughter that scoffs with laughter that rejoices in a world of difference.

5 No Longer Strangers
Disabled Ontology and the Church as Meaningful Community in Liquid Modernity

Andrew Picard

People with disabilities have faced relentless exclusion and injustices in society. Unfortunately, they have also faced exclusion and injustice within the church too. The church has often colluded with the ableist hegemonies of the surrounding culture to exculturate people with disabilities from its midst as aliens and strangers. When the church colludes with ableist hegemonies, it not only betrays the gospel, it betrays its own calling to be God's new community of reconciliation. This chapter explores the unique set of injustices and forms of exclusion that people with disabilities face, both in society and the church, as the collateral casualties of consumerism. Drawing from Zygmunt Bauman's analysis of Solid Modernity and Liquid Modernity, the first section will contrast the differing forms of exclusion and injustice that people with disabilities face with the shift from Solid to Liquid Modernity. In Liquid Modernity, many consumer communities are, according to Bauman, empty spaces. Empty spaces are primarily empty of *meaning* because the particularities of identity are left at the door upon entry so that the entrants can enjoy civilized togetherness. The church often fits the hallmarks of Bauman's empty spaces which celebrate the kaleidoscopic diversity of consumer culture whilst silently silencing the particularities of otherness. In these meaning-resistant spaces people with disabilities have the particularity of their personhood 'silently silenced' for the sake of faux togetherness. As John Swinton has cogently suggested, the church is often a place of inclusion but not belonging for people with disabilities.[1] This chapter argues that, in contrast to consumerism's empty spaces, the church is called to be a meaningful community where the particularities of disabled ontology loom large in the church's reconciled community. Indeed, the particularities of disabled ontology offer the church an opportunity to render its life to the contours of the gospel and the personal action of the triune God of grace. As such, a Hauerwasian question lingers over this chapter:[2] What kind of

---

1 John Swinton, 'From Inclusion to Belonging: A Practical Theology of Community, Disability and Humanness', *Journal of Religion, Disability and Health* 15 (2012): 172–90.
2 Stanley Hauerwas, with regard to the church and disabled children, asks: 'what kind of families and communities should we be so we could welcome retarded [sic] children into our midst regardless of the happy or unhappy consequences they may bring'; Stanley Hauerwas, 'Having and Learning to

community should the church be in order for people with disabilities to belong in the church in their full particularity, regardless of the happy or unhappy consequences?

From Solid Modernity to Liquid Modernity

Zygmunt Bauman, a leading Polish sociologist, argues that Western culture has undergone a significant shift from being a society of producers to a society of consumers. This shift has resulted in major changes for personhood and community which have affected the way in which we relate to one another and construct our lives. In Solid Modernity, personhood and identity were defined by large social structures and human collectives such as citizenship, the state, trade unions, and class. Men were defined by what they produced on the battlefield and in the workplace, and women by what they produced at home in terms of children and domesticity.[3] The time horizons of Solid Modernity were long-term, and identity was formed through the large social structures and human collectives. Personhood and identity unfolded in the context of a reliable, orderly, and time-resistant setting, and any individuation was to help fit into the niche one was allocated.[4] However, these sacreds of Solid Modernity have been profaned as the search for individual freedom and autonomy has developed into the consumerist rendition of life. The solids of the producer society have been melted through deregulation, privatization, and commodification as Solid Modernity has given way to Liquid Modernity and the relentlessly fluid and changing culture of consumerism.[5]

The rise of globalized consumer capitalism has recast everything in the image of the consumer market as commodities to be bought and sold in a market-mediated world. It is not merely goods which have been recast into the mould of the market, but the status of the consumer has also been raised to that of a sellable commodity.[6] Now the burden of pattern-weaving and meaning-making is no longer found in solid structures or large human collectives, but falls upon the shoulders of individuals and their life-politics.[7] Each emancipated individual is responsible for their own social acceptability by creating desire and demand for themselves. Bauman suggests that the Liquid Modern version of the Cartesian *cogito* is 'I am seen, therefore I am,' and the more I am seen, the more I am.[8] Identities are projects in need of constant attention, and the

---

Care for Retarded Children', in *Critical Reflections on Stanley Hauerwas' Theology of Disability: Disabling Society, Enabling Theology*, ed. John Swinton (Binghamton, NY: Harworth Pastoral Press, 2004), 150.

3 Zygmunt Bauman, *Consuming Life* (Cambridge: Polity Press, 2007), 54–5.
4 Zygmunt Bauman, *Liquid Modernity* (Cambridge: Polity Press, 2000), 33.
5 Ibid., 6–7. 'Liquid Modernity' is the term Bauman uses to describe the contemporary phase of Modernity.
6 Bauman, *Consuming Life*, 57.
7 Bauman, *Liquid Modernity*, 3–8.
8 Zygmunt Bauman and Leonidas Donskis, *Moral Blindness: The Loss of Sensitivity in Liquid Modernity* (Cambridge: Polity Press, 2013), 28.

relentless rate of change ensures that remaining a desirable product is a sentence to hard labour and insecurity.[9] Those who fail to keep pace and continually recast themselves as desirable products risk exclusion, stigmatization, and social estrangement. This commodification of personhood on market-mediated terms creates new forms of exclusion and estrangement for people with disabilities than that which existed in Solid Modernity.

In the following sections we will examine the distinct approaches towards the disabled stranger in Solid Modernity and Liquid Modernity. These will not provide a thorough examination of their strengths and weaknesses. Instead, they will aim to show how shifts in culture have developed shifts in society's treatment of people with disabilities. Importantly, we will see that the differing treatments result in differing forms of exclusion and estrangement.

Strangers in Solid Modernity

In Solid Modernity, otherness, difference, and strangeness were regarded as a threat to the vision of purity and order-building. Progression in the ordered society required freedom from the stranger who threatened 'to poison the comfort of order with suspicion of chaos'.[10] Difference and otherness needed to be corrected, ordered, and assimilated, or else excluded, banished, and hidden from view. In Solid Modernity the disabled stranger was met with prejudice and resentment which was embedded in the medicalization of disability. The processes of disablement that developed in Solid Modernity reflected the assumptions of Solid Modernity to control and order society through heavy systemic structures. In Solid Modernity's 'great confinement'[11] the disabled stranger was incarcerated in large institutions which were built with the thickest of stone walls to exorcize otherness, difference, and the stranger from the orderly society. In the New Zealand context this was the age of the institution which saw the proliferation of lunatic asylums and deaf and dumb institutes that housed those regarded as lunatic, idiotic, deaf, dumb, blind, or infirm. Governments passed a variety of acts, such as the 1882 Imbecile Passengers Act and the 1911 Mental Defective Act, which sought to screen undesirable immigrants out of the country or keep undesirable residents out of sight.[12] This violent system of order-building laid the disabled stranger to rest in 'a state of suspended extinction'.[13]

In the ordered society, disability was not merely rendered invisible, it was pathologized and subjected to cruel rehabilitative strategies such as sterilization, shock

---

9 Bauman, *Consuming Life*, 110–11.
10 Zygmunt Bauman, *Modernity and Ambivalence* (Cambridge: Polity Press, 1991), 56.
11 Bill Hughes, 'Bauman's Strangers: Impairment and the Invalidation of Disabled People in Modern and Post-modern Cultures', *Disability & Society* 17 (2002): 575.
12 Hilary Stace, 'The Long Unfinished Journey Towards Human Rights for Disabled People in Aotearoa New Zealand', *Human Rights Research* 5 (2007): 4.
13 Zygmunt Bauman, *Postmodernity and Its Discontents* (Cambridge: Polity Press, 1997), 19. See also Hughes, 'Bauman's Strangers', 575.

therapies, and psychosurgery in the war against otherness, difference, and alterity. As Bill Hughes, a disability scholar, writes: '[the] science of rehabilitation was the bourgeois solution to the demon of imperfection. If the demon could be exorcized then the "cleansed" individual could be returned to the orderly world. If not, then she was confined forever in the invisible spaces behind the high walls where the "others" lived.'[14] With the liquification of Solid Modernity, the era of solid institutions and their solid forms of care have come to an end. Liquid Modernity presents a changed social environment where strangeness has been normalized and the demons of order-building have been cast out. However, whilst the room has been swept clean of the demons of purification, new forms of exclusion and oppression, arising from consumer society, have rushed to fill the void.

Strangers in Liquid Modernity

The shift from Solid Modernity to Liquid Modernity has created a very different relationship to strangeness. The rise of globalization has meant that otherness, difference, and strangeness have been normalized and the clearly defined order of Solid Modernity has been melted into Liquid Modern flux, flow, and change. Globalization has seen the rise of the global free-market economy, mass communication, technology, accessibility of global travel, and the development of the global village. Consequently, there has been a drastic increase in human mobility, with an attendant loss of cartographic boundaries, the despatialization of time, mass migration, and the compression of the world. With the melting of solid human collectives such as society, citizenship, and 'community', settled categories of 'us' and 'them' have been disturbed. Chris Rumford suggests that it is not merely the rise of strangers but the development of the universal condition of strangeness that marks out Liquid Modern life.[15] Whilst the forms of amelioration of the stranger have changed, many of the impulses towards the stranger appear in new guises.

Social responses to the rise of otherness have seen the development of gated communities, the rise of a surveillance society, and 'ethno-burbs' (racially segregated ethnic precincts)[16] as the condition of strangeness has made one's neighbour the closest potential stranger.[17] Living in a community of strangeness means living with a sense of disorientation and the reality that strangers are no longer the exception, but the norm. The impact is that the stranger has moved from invisibility to visibility and we are faced with the new situation of the unexcludability of the strange-other.[18] In the New Zealand context the growth of

---

14 Ibid., 575–76.
15 Chris Rumford, *The Globalization of Strangeness* (New York: Palgrave Macmillan, 2013), 10–21.
16 Paul Spoonley and Richard Bedford, *Welcome to Our World? Immigration and the Reshaping of New Zealand* (Auckland: Dunmore, 2012), 236–43.
17 Rumford, *The Globalization of Strangeness*, 80.
18 Ulrich Beck, 'Ulrich Beck: The Necessity for a Cosmopolitan Outlook' [accessed 12 November 2015]. Online: https://euroalter.com/2015/ulrich-beck-the-necessity-of-a-cosmopolitan-outlook.

diversity and otherness has been rapid. James Belich suggests that through the domestic process of decolonization (1960–2000) there was both the 'coming in' of new influences and migrations and the 'coming out' of diversity, otherness, and dissent as the settled myths of colonial discourse were challenged and repealed.[19] The shift from Solid Modernity to Liquid Modernity has seen the decarceration of people with disabilities from total institutions. Difference, otherness, and strangeness have moved from being an aberration in need of purification to the new norm in a world of globalized strangeness. As a result, impairment has been brought into the lives of all people; able and disabled: 'The "other" comes out into the world and shows herself and will not go away.'[20]

Care for people with disabilities has liquefied from the solid forms of total institutions as inmates have been decarcerated and given the freedom to assert their identity and make their own decisions. Care for people with disabilities has been liquefied and remade to fit the consumer rendition of life. In consumer markets the consumer is defined first and foremost as *Homo eligens* ('the chooser').[21] Freedom is defined as the freedom to choose consumer products which are placed in the role of the fully docile obedient Cartesian object whilst the consumer is raised to the ego-boosting rank of the emancipated sovereign subject.[22] This sovereignty of the unencumbered subject is interpreted in consumer culture as the individual's right to free choice. Consumer freedom is manifest in new forms of support for people with disabilities such as individualized funding. People with disabilities, and their closest support networks, now access care through consumer choice and dexterity rather than Solid Modern institutions. Whilst the merits of individualized funding are beyond the scope of this chapter, it highlights the shift from Solid Modern to Liquid Modern forms of care.

Consumer Freedom and its Collateral Casualties

Lurking among the shadows of consumerism is what Bauman calls the collateral casualties of consumerism – the unintended consequences of consumer culture. The collateral casualties of consumerism are the uncommoditized men and women ('flawed consumers') who, through poor choices, sloth, or lack of skill, fail to capitalize on their freedom and make the most of their life chances.[23] The collateral casualties of consumerism face the worst kind of death in a society that is based on individual desirability – invisibility.[24] In a society based

---

19 James Belich, *Paradise Reforged: A History of the New Zealanders From the 1880s to the Year 2000* (Auckland: Penguin, 2001), 465.
20 Hughes, 'Bauman's Strangers', 579.
21 Bauman, *Consuming Life*, 61.
22 Ibid., 16–17.
23 Zygmunt Bauman, *Collateral Damage: Social Inequalities in a Global Age* (Cambridge: Polity Press, 2011), 8.
24 Ibid., 18.

upon individual freedom, defined as the freedom to act on the right to choose, it is the chooser who bears the responsibility of their choices, and bears them personally and individually. Bauman's flawed consumers are those individuals who, through sloth, sin, or neglect, have failed to exercise their rights as a consumer and now must lick their individual wounds alone and in private.[25] Whereas Solid Modernity still viewed the poor and the disabled as part of society and the state's responsibility, the highly individualized environment of consumerism demands individual responsibility. Bauman writes:

> Recast as collateral casualties of *consumerism*, the poor are now and for the first time in recorded history purely and simply a worry and a nuisance. They have no merits to relieve, let alone redeem, their vices. They have nothing to offer in exchange for the taxpayers' outlays. Money transferred to them is a bad investment, unlikely to be repaid, let alone to bring profit .... The poor are not *needed*, and so they are *unwanted*.[26]

Whilst consumerism offers each individual the – supposedly equal – right to sovereign self-assertion through choosing, not every individual can act equally on that right. Those who cannot act, or refuse to act, on their right to free choice become the collateral casualties of consumerism.[27]

In consumerism, people with disabilities must also recast themselves as desirable, commodified products for a market-mediated world. Hughes draws upon Bauman's work to highlight the reality that people with disabilities will only be included in Liquid Modernity's idealized community by their ability and willingness to consume.[28] However, the ability of people with disabilities to recast themselves as desirable products in a competitive consumer culture is severely limited. In their report to the World Health Organization Alana Officer and Tom Shakespeare highlight the fact that disability and poverty are deeply linked in a way that inhibits people with disabilities from having the economic wherewithal to act on their right to self-assertion in a market-mediated world. Disability is both a cause and a consequence of poverty.[29] People with disabilities face widespread environmental barriers such as stigmatization, discrimination, lack of adequate healthcare and rehabilitation services, inaccessible information, and lack of participation in decisions which directly affect them. Due to these barriers, people with disabilities experience poorer health, lower educational achievements, fewer economic opportunities, and higher rates of poverty than

---

25 Ibid., 151–6.
26 Bauman, *Consuming Life*, 126.
27 Ibid., 64–7.
28 Hughes, 'Bauman's Strangers', 580.
29 Department for International Development, 'Disability, Poverty and Development', DFID Issues Paper (London: UK Department for International Development) [accessed 5 July 2013]. Online: http://hpod.org/pdf/Disability-poverty-and-development.pdf.

people without disabilities.[30] Whilst consumerism may offer the formal freedom for each individual to create themselves as a desirable product for others to 'friend', 'follow', or 'tag', some are freer than others. The result is that people with disabilities are often among the collateral casualties of consumerism and face the exclusion and stigmatization that comes with being a source of unfreedom and burden in a highly individualized consumer society.

In the past, the misery of those excluded or stigmatized was treated as a collectively caused problem that needed to be cured by collective means such as total institutions. However, in the highly individualized society of consumerism individuals must find biographical solutions to systemic problems. There is no common cause or solid cure such as state, unions, institutions, or church to which they can connect. Freedom in the Liquid Modern version of life is freedom *from* the other and any of the demands they might make upon the individual's treasured freedom. It is the other who bears the cost of the individual's freedom: 'The collateral victim of the leap to the consumerist rendition of freedom prevalent in the "liquid" phase of modernity is the Other as the prime object of ethical responsibility and moral concern.'[31]

The idealized community in Liquid Modernity offers freedom and security together in the right doses – the security of holding hands and the freedom to let go.[32] Idealized community offers the individual freedom to move and explore, but also security from any burden-creating, space-reducing, or guilt-inducing other who limits the freedom, flexibility, and independence of the individual. In the society of consumers, relationships are 'pure relations' that are offered on market-mediated terms with 'no strings attached'.[33] Liquid Modern consumers are taught to enjoy life, not to suffer it. The sovereign individual has the ability to 'block', 'unfriend', or 'hide' any space invaders who threaten to burden their marvellous freedom. Solid Modernity's desire for friendship as 'a friend in need is a friend indeed' has morphed in our consumer culture into 'a friend *without* need is a friend indeed'. Responsibility for the other is recast as responsibility to oneself. Liquid Modern life, shorn of Solid Modernity's human collectives, only conceives of solo performances, and remaining on the stage of public attention requires keeping other people off it.[34]

In a society of consumers all ties and bonds have to follow the pattern of the relationship between buyer and commodities bought: commodities are not expected to outstay their welcome, and must leave the stage of life once they start

---

30 Alana Officer and Tom Shakespeare, 'The World Report on Disability and People With Intellectual Disabilities', *Journal of Policy and Practice in Intellectual Disabilities* 10 (2013): 86.
31 Zygmunt Bauman, *The Art of Life* (Cambridge: Polity Press, 2008), 108.
32 Zygmunt Bauman, *Community: Seeking Safety in an Insecure World* (Cambridge: Polity Press, 2001), 19–20. See also Zygmunt Bauman, *Culture in a Liquid Modern World* (Cambridge: Polity Press, 2011), 20–21.
33 Bauman and Donskis, *Moral Blindness*, 14.
34 Zygmunt Bauman, *Does Ethics Have a Chance in a World of Consumers?* (Cambridge, MA: Harvard University Press, 2008), 54.

to clutter it up. At the same time, buyers are neither expected nor willing to swear eternal loyalty to their purchases or grant them permanent rights of residence. Relationships of the consumerist type are, from the start, 'until further notice'.[35]

Demand to care for the other in the society of consumers is measured by the level of unfreedom that such care would create, and adiaphorization provides the 'relief from responsibility' that Liquid Modern freedom desires. Adiaphorization places many moral acts or omitted acts outside the sphere of ethical evaluation. They are exempted by social consent (universal or local) from ethical evaluation and freed from conscience or moral stigma.[36] In the nowist time horizons of Liquid Modernity, it is the one-off disasters, such as earthquakes or floods, that are more likely to spur us into action than the daily doses of humiliation and indignity that the new poor face.[37] Bauman is surely correct when he states that whilst a 'consumerist attitude may lubricate the wheels of the economy; it sprinkles sand into the bearings of morality'.[38]

A recent example of such adiaphoria was the amendment the New Zealand government made to the New Zealand Public Health and Disability Act. These changes produced outrage amongst the disabled community and their supporters. The amendment sought to address the decision by the Human Rights Tribunal, subsequently upheld by the High Court and the Court of Appeal, that the government was discriminating against family members who cared for disabled adults by not paying them as caregivers.[39] The bill was passed under urgency, on the same day debate commenced on it, and capped funding at NZ$24 million. The bill also limited the number of people who can be paid for caring for disabled family members, and offered the minimum wage to carers of disabled adult family members who are assessed as having high or very high needs. Chief Human Rights Commissioner David Rutherford noted that official advice from the Health Ministry was heavily censored, thus prohibiting access by the public and other parliamentarians to the relevant information, and the bill prohibited any possibility of legal recourse through the Human Rights Review Tribunal.[40] Jonathan Boston, Professor of Public Policy at Victoria University, outlines the removal of recourse to the Human Rights Commission and its protections, stating: 'the ease with which our elected officials can disregard important and long-standing constitutional safeguards is surely concerning'.[41]

---

35 Bauman, *The Art of Life*, 15.
36 Bauman and Donskis, *Moral Blindness*, 41.
37 Ibid., 43.
38 Ibid., 15.
39 'New Zealand Public Health and Disability Amendment Bill (No 2)' [accessed 5 July 2013]. Online: http://www.legislation.govt.nz/bill/government/2013/0118/latest/whole.html#DLM5205123.
40 'Editorial: Disability Bill Demonstrates Contempt for Due Process', *New Zealand Herald* [accessed 5 July 2013]. Online: http://www.nzherald.co.nz/nz/news/article.cfm?c_id=1&objectid=10884930.
41 Jonathan Boston, 'Why New Zealand Needs Constitutional Reform' [accessed 5 July 2013]. Online: http://igps.victoria.ac.nz/documents/Why_New_Zealand_needs_constitutional_reform_Oct2013.pdf.

Leaders from within the disability community said families felt ambushed by the bill, which was passed in a single day, as they had no warning the law was going to change and no opportunity for public input through select committee hearings.[42] Professor Andrew Geddis, a constitutional law expert, accused the government of breaking constitutional order: 'It [the Government] did it because it thought it could get away with treating the disabled community and carers in this way because [they] are relatively weak and don't have a strong political voice.'[43] In his work on the injustices of consumerism Bauman adopts the phrase 'silent silencing' from the work of Thomas Mathiesen. Silent silencing describes the process whereby dissent and protest are quietly, and without notice, subordinated and acquiesced into the prevailing system by being dissipated and dissolved.[44] In the passing of this bill, people with disabilities were silently silenced by the New Zealand government and they became its collateral casualties.

Consumer Communities as Empty Space

In the ruggedly individualized setting of Liquid Modernity, community is formed to uphold freedom and security in the right doses, on consumerist terms. Bauman states that consumer community spaces are designed so that strangers interact with one another as strangers, through mis-meetings. Mis-meetings are one-off chance interactions which have no past, offer no future, and are most certainly 'not to be continued'.[45] Malls, cinemas, cafes, tourist resorts, and airport lounges are examples of shared public spaces where strangers meet. Bauman calls these spaces 'empty places' or 'non-space', and they are marked by the culture of civility. Whilst encounters are unavoidable, empty spaces ensure that they are brief and shallow. Empty spaces are secure, purified places which are well protected from any meddlers, loiterers, beggars, or intruders who would interfere with the consumer's splendid isolation.[46] Attendees are secure in the knowledge that no person's particularity will be allowed to impinge upon their prized freedom: 'Shopping/consuming places offer what no "real reality" outside may deliver: the near-perfect balance between freedom and security.'[47] However, empty spaces are

---

42 'Editorial: Disability Bill Demonstrates Contempt for Due Process'. See also Boston, 'Why New Zealand Needs Constitutional Reform'.
43 Issac Davison, 'Trust Lost, Disability Advocates Warn Govt', *New Zealand Herald* [accessed 5 July 2013]. Online: http://www.nzherald.co.nz/nz/news/article.cfm?c_id=1&objectid=10911611. See also Professor Geddis's blog post that accuses the government of breaking constitutional order: Andrew Geddis, 'I Think National Just Broke Our Constitution' [accessed 5 July 2013]. Online: http://pundit.co.nz/content/i-think-national-just-broke-our-constitution.
44 See Bauman, *Consuming Life*, 48. See also Zygmunt Bauman, *Liquid Fear* (Cambridge, Polity Press, 2006), 6–7.
45 Bauman, *Liquid Modernity*, 95–6.
46 Ibid., 97–8.
47 Ibid., 99.

not cleansed of alterity, otherness, and difference. On the contrary, empty spaces are appealing because colour, variety, and difference are kaleidoscopic whilst ensuring that the differences are tamed, sanitized, and purified. Empty spaces are primarily empty of *meaning*, so that the particularities of the individual's identity are left at the door upon entry. As a result, one is unlikely to face protests about the Treaty of Waitangi, the treatment of asylum seekers, or the barriers to inclusion that people with disabilities relentlessly face: 'If meeting strangers cannot be averted, one can at least try to avoid the dealings.'[48] Empty spaces welcome all forms of diversity and otherness at the same time as purifying their particularities so that the impact of the stranger is mollified and diluted.[49] Such purification is more subtle than its Solid Modern forebear, but no less radical.

Where diversity was confined for the sake of an ordered society in Solid Modernity, diversity is celebrated for the sake of kaleidoscopic community in Liquid Modernity. However, the love of diversity in Liquid Modernity is not a sign that the strangeness of the stranger is welcome. In her important work on the commodification of desire for the other in consumer society, bell hooks argues that minority cultures are depersonalized, instrumentalized, commodified, and consumed as part of the identity construction of majority culture. This process of 'eating the other' objectifies otherness and difference as a consumptive product that, from an African American perspective, adds spice to the dull dish of mainstream white culture.[50] Far from being empowered in their particularity, the difference and otherness of minority cultures are kitschified for celebration and their particularities are rendered invisible by consumerism's violent process of silent silencing. In the society of consumers, otherness is celebrated, but it is also neutered of its particularity and meaning to make it palatable to the majority culture.

Hughes, in an important article on disabled ontology, draws on hooks's work for disability studies and disabled ontology. Hughes argues that disabled ontology remains pathologized within contemporary culture as the other which is not 'eaten' nor desired (other than misappropriating their car parks): '[Non-disabled] people do not desire a "bit of the disabled other" and impairment is seldom, if ever, constructed or represented as exotic.'[51] The flagships of disabled ontology, frailty, and vulnerability are not desired by the dominant ableist culture, and in fact constitute risk to their sense of ontological security. As Hughes contends, the hallmarks of disabled ontology, vulnerability, limitation, and dependency are the stuff of Kierkegaardian dread in an ableist consumer society.[52] Whilst the disabled other has come out into the open and shown herself and will not go

---

48 Ibid., 105.
49 Ibid., 103.
50 bell hooks, *Black Looks: Race and Representation* (Boston, MA: South End Press, 1992), 21.
51 Bill Hughes, 'Being Disabled: Towards a Critical Social Ontology for Disability Studies', *Disability and Society* 22 (2007): 680.
52 Ibid.

away, she is neither desired nor desirable in a market-mediated world. Disabled ontology throws into question the consumerist ideals of autonomous freedom and self-determination from which empty spaces emerge. The church herself has often failed to receive the gift of disabled ontology because she too has colluded with the assumptions of consumerism and become an empty space.

The Church as an Empty Space

With the shift to Liquid Modernity, exclusion and oppression take on new forms. Diversity and otherness are un-excludable and churches have been reawakened to the gospel's demand for communities of difference which are united in Christ. Nonetheless, in the midst of this desire for cultural diversity lurk many dangers of silent silencing. Many contemporary church contexts are typified by the culture of civility that characterizes empty spaces. The church as empty space is primarily empty of meaning because the particularities of personhood have been left at the door to ensure a neutered and neutral zone for worship – an empty space. In his recent work on moving the church from inclusion to belonging John Swinton captures many of the issues facing the church as a non-space. Churches often welcome the presence of people with disabilities to add to their kaleidoscopic diversity, but they also ensure that the particularity of their disabled ontology does not spoil the happy balance of freedom and security for the individual worshipper. Swinton recounts the story of Elaine, an elderly woman with intellectual disabilities. Elaine's experience of church is for ninety minutes on a Sunday and no more. She experiences thin inclusion, and is not invited into the homes of her religious friends, despite desiring this. Swinton argues that Elaine is included, but she does not belong. Her co-worshippers have little desire 'to thicken their understanding of her or to invite her to *belong* with them and [to] them'.[53] Such stories are common – too common.[54] The thin inclusion which Elaine experienced is indicative of the church as an empty space. The church as empty space ensures that she is included through the culture of civility that pervades after-church coffee, but it also ensures that she does not belong in the fullness of her disabled particularity.

Churches are often happy to celebrate diversity and multiculturalism whilst purifying the painful particularities of minority cultures to ensure a sense of togetherness. Bauman critiques the language of multiculturalism as a socially conservative term used in bourgeois discourse to transform discussions regarding the unjust systems of social inequality into politically neutral celebrations of cultural diversity.[55] When the church encourages minority cultures to display

---

53 Swinton, 'From Inclusion to Belonging', 181.
54 Thomas Reynolds shares the story of his disabled son being asked not to return to Sunday school because he was a 'problem child' who modelled 'bad behaviour'. See Thomas E. Reynolds, *Vulnerable Communion: A Theology of Disability and Hospitality* (Grand Rapids, MI: Brazos, 2008), 11.
55 Bauman, *Culture in a Liquid Modern World*, 46.

their otherness in a celebration of the kaleidoscopic and colourful without addressing the hegemonic powers of the majority culture, the church has become an empty space.

Towards the Church as Meaningful Community

In response to the church as an empty space, I want to explore the possibilities of disabled ontology contributing to the church as a meaningful community in the midst of consumer society. The meaninglessness of empty spaces is because identity and particularity are sanitized and neutered. In order to develop a theology of church as a community of meaning, identity and particularity must bulk large. The particularity of disabled ontology offers a gift to the church to render its true identity to the gospel rather than that of consumer culture. In this final section, I will explore some of the work disability theologians have done with regard to disabled ontology and its contribution to the church as a vulnerable community. I will then develop this work further through Colin Gunton's trinitarian theology of personhood that places particularity at the heart of the Spirit's work in the world and in the church. Finally, I will outline the cosmic ecclesiology of Ephesians and the church's role in displaying God's wisdom to the cosmos through its 'rich variety' of persons reconciled into one new community, and conclude with possibilities for the church as a community of meaning.

Disabled Ontology and Vulnerability

Many disability scholars and theologians have rightly argued that the 'cult of normalcy' is based upon Modernity's assumptions about human personhood and ontology.[56] In Modernity human personhood and ontology were defined by autonomy, self-assertion, choice, cognition, and independence. As a result, personhood was defined by one's ability to 'to live one's life, develop one's potential and live out a purposeful life-course without any necessary reference to others'.[57] However, Modernity's vision of ontology confuses the categories of creator and created, and disabled ontology underlines the reality of created being as inherently limited, dependent, vulnerable, and in need of relationship to constitute our being. Stanley Hauerwas reminds us that the fact that people with disability are constituted by narratives which they do not choose reveals the true character of creaturely being.[58]

---

56 Reynolds, *Vulnerable Communion*, 55.
57 John Swinton, 'Who is the God We Worship? Theologies of Disability; Challenges and New Possibilities', *International Journal of Practical Theology* 14 (2011): 295.
58 Stanley Hauerwas, 'Timeful Friends: Living with the Handicapped', in *Critical Reflections on Stanley Hauerwas' Theology of Disability: Disabling Society, Enabling Theology*, ed. John Swinton (Binghamton, NY: Harworth Pastoral Press, 2004), 16.

In response to 'the cult of normalcy', Thomas Reynolds develops a vision of human ontology that normalizes vulnerability as the hallmark of not only disabled human personhood, but all forms of human personhood.[59] Far from being problems to overcome, or flaws to be hidden, the hallmarks of disabled ontology, vulnerability, dependency, and limitation, are the starting point of our shared finite humanity. There is no clear dualism between ability and disability, but only a nexus of reciprocity through shared vulnerability.[60] As a consequence, disabled personhood and ontology are neither abnormal nor flawed, but part of the human experience of vulnerable personhood. Indeed, our fear of vulnerability and weakness often cuts ourselves off from God, others, and the life of meaning we desire. As Hughes states: 'the refusal to recognise – and, indeed, celebrate – frailty and imperfection makes each of us a stranger to ourselves'.[61] Such protective mechanisms not only dehumanize the other, they dehumanize us from the life of relational meaning for which we are created.

Reynolds's work on vulnerability leads to important implications for human personhood, ontology, and church. In Reynolds's account, vulnerability is normal for humanity, church *and* God.[62] Whatever the merits of Reynolds's open view of God,[63] his normalizing of vulnerability for human personhood, ontology, and ecclesiology offer an alternative theological ontology to the Kierkegaardian dread of disability that pervades many contemporary churches. Reynolds's work draws upon wider work within disability studies that argues for the normalizing of difference and vulnerability. However, as Hughes highlights, whilst normalizing vulnerability is crucial to human personhood and ontology, it offers a fairly hollow scholastic victory for disabled personhood. Whilst impairment and limitation is the experience and destination of all humanity, the shared experience of exclusion, prejudice, and disablement that people with disabilities face are not.[64] Vulnerable ontology may have taken the negativity out of the categories of impairment and disability, but it does not negate the negativity of the unjust lived experience of disability.[65] Universalizing vulnerability, limitation, and impairment can departicularize disabled ontology and strip it of the political teeth needed to address the continued injustice, prejudice, and exclusion that many people with disabilities unnecessarily face. There is a need to uphold the politics of disability whilst embracing vulnerable ontology, otherwise the

---

59 Reynolds, *Vulnerable Communion*, 13–14.
60 Ibid., 14.
61 Hughes, 'Bauman's Strangers', 581.
62 Reynolds, *Vulnerable Communion*, 197.
63 There are significant critiques of such open views of God. See Colin E. Gunton, *Christ and Creation* (Milton Keynes: Paternoster, 1992), 81–9; Thomas G. Weinandy, *Does God Suffer?* (Notre Dame, IN: University of Notre Dame Press, 2000), and the essays contained in James F. Keating and Thomas Joseph White, ed., *Divine Impassibility and the Mystery of Human Suffering* (Grand Rapids, MI: Eerdmans, 2009).
64 Hughes, 'Being Disabled', 678–9.
65 Ibid., 680.

injustices that people with disabilities face are subsumed under a false universal, and oppressive ableist assumptions remain unchallenged.

Vulnerability not only risks subsuming disabled politics into a false universal, there is also a tendency to idealize people with intellectual disabilities.[66] It is undoubted that vulnerable ontology offers an important gift to able-bodied confusion regarding personhood, but it is also true that some are more vulnerable than others.[67] Wayne Morris reminds us that vulnerability is not simply a rose garden of discovery about personhood, but a scary, tough, and painful place for disabled and able-bodied alike. Vulnerability can lead to hurt and harm where some, through their vulnerability, can inflict pain and violence on themselves and others.[68] What is needed is a form of community where the particularity of people with disabilities looms large in all its graced complexities, and we are drawn into one new humanity in which we find our being in relationship with God and one another.

Colin Gunton's Trinitarian Ontology

Christoph Schwöbel has suggested that if we still followed the ancient custom of venerating the great doctors of the church by giving them a particular title, Colin Gunton would be the Doctor of Particularity.[69] Gunton's theological project was developed in conscious engagement with Western culture and the concern that the homogenizing forces of Modernity suppress otherness and deny particularity. In Gunton's analysis, the drive towards individualism in modern culture does not give rise to a 'rich variety' of diversity, but the superficiality of homogenized being that exists in our herd society: 'The heart of the paradox of the modern condition is that a quest for the freedom of the many has eventuated in new forms of slavery to the one.'[70] In response, Gunton sought to develop a Christian ontology where particularity bulks large, as it is personal being that is at stake in the modern world. It is the eschatological work of the Spirit to perfect created beings by establishing them in their substantiality and otherness and drawing them into personal relationship with God and others, through Christ, to be who we uniquely are in relationship.[71]

---

66 Wayne Morris, 'Transforming Able-bodied Normativity: The Wounded Christ and Human Vulnerability', *Irish Theological Quarterly* 78 (2013): 241–2.
67 See Charles and Joanne Hewlett, *Hurting Hope: What Parents Feel When Their Children Suffer* (Carlisle: Piquant Editions, 2011), 25–28.
68 Morris, 'Transforming Able-bodied Normativity', 242.
69 Christoph Schwöbel, 'A Tribute to Colin Gunton', in *The Person of Christ*, ed. Stephen R. Holmes and Murray A. Rae (London: T&T Clark, 2005), 14.
70 Colin E. Gunton, *The One, the Three and the Many: God, Creation and the Culture of Modernity* (Cambridge: Cambridge University Press, 1993), 34.
71 Colin E. Gunton, 'The Forgotten Trinity', in *Father, Son, and Holy Spirit: Toward a Fully Trinitarian Theology* (London: T&T Clark, 2003), 13–15.

For Gunton, the Holy Spirit is the perfecting cause of creation who liberates created beings to be what God created them to be in their particularity. The Spirit does this by bringing them into relationship with the Son who is the Lord and mediator of creation. It is the distinctive eschatological work of the Holy Spirit to orient persons to otherness and the perfection of their particularity in relationship with God and one another through Christ.[72] The Spirit sets the creation free to be what God intended it to be, which is redeemed and reconciled to the fullness of their unity under Christ: 'This does not happen in a general way, but takes place as particular parts of creation are set free through Christ and enabled to be themselves, and so anticipations of the universal redemption in the age to come.'[73] These anticipations of the age to come are displayed in the reconciliation of particular persons into relationship with God through Christ to be who they are in relationship with God and one another. Thus, freedom in Gunton's work is a relational category. To be free in the biblical tradition is to be set free by the redeeming work of the Son in the power of the Spirit, and to be unfree is to be out of true communion with the divine and human other.[74] Freedom is not the Liquid Modern freedom *from* God, others, and the world; freedom is to be set free *in* and *for* relationship with God, others, and the world. This stands in direct challenge to Liquid Modern adiaphoria, and asserts that the other, through Christ and by the Spirit, is the source of our freedom and true human being. True human being is being-in-relationship with God, one another, and all else.

This true human being is anticipated in the church, the community of those who Christ has set free to be God's eschatological community by the Spirit's power. It is in Christ, the second Adam, and his body that we find our true humanity restored as otherness-in-relationship. As an eschatological witness, the church is to have its life ordered by the triune God in such a way that it is a school of personal being, 'a place where, among other things, we learn to be with, from and for one another'.[75] The church offers up from within the creation a way of being in relationship that is an anticipation of the renewal of all things in Christ. Life in communion with God, one another, and all else is creation's gift and *telos* which God gives through his Son and in the Spirit.[76] Gunton suggests that the church now lives by a kind of skill – a way of being towards God and in the world which renders praise to its maker and healing to our culture.[77] As God's eschatological community, the church is drawn by the Spirit to participate in Christ's self-offering of the first fruits of the liberated creation back to the Father. This offering of redeemed creation back to the Father, through

---

72 Colin E. Gunton, *Act and Being* (London: SCM, 2002), 120.
73 Colin E. Gunton, 'God the Holy Spirit: Augustine and His Successors', in *Theology Through the Theologians: Selected Essays, 1972–1995* (London: T&T Clark, 1996), 121.
74 Gunton, *Act and Being*, 105.
75 Gunton, 'The Forgotten Trinity', 17.
76 Ibid.
77 Gunton, 'The Forgotten Trinity', 18.

Christ, is a sacrifice of praise given in worship of the Father's wise purposes in the beginning – deep and lasting relationship with God and others.[78] The church as God's eschatological community offers significant possibilities for disabled ontology to assist the church to become what God has made her to be – a meaningful community of particular persons who are reconciled to God and one another in transformative relationship. As such, the church, by its very being, gives witness to God's promised restoration of all things through Christ by the power of the Spirit.

Disabled Particularity and the Church as Mission

N.T. Wright has recently insisted upon the centrality of ecclesiology to Paul's theology. In his magnum opus on Pauline theology Wright laments the way Western Protestantism often relegates the scandalous unity of the *ekklesia* in Paul's theology to secondary or tertiary significance in favour of focusing upon sin and salvation.[79] The unity of God's people is central to Paul's thought, and Wright argues, 'if it gives way, everything comes crashing down'.[80] Having reviewed the importance of unity across the undisputed Pauline letters, Wright concludes that what is found to be central in the undisputed letters of Paul turns out to be summarized in Eph 2:11–3:21.[81] Following Wright's suggestion, we will examine Eph 2:11–3:21 and its call to the church to welcome difference and otherness as part of God's wise purposes for the church and the world. In what follows we will explore Ephesians's celebration of God's reconciliation of a rich variety into one body, which prefigures God's mysterious plan to bring all things in heaven and on earth together in Christ. This has important implications for the church's mission to display the wisdom of God to the entire cosmos, and it places the welcome and belonging of people with disabilities, in their distinct particularity, at the heart of the church's being and mission.

In Ephesians, Paul develops a cosmic image of the church where the wisdom of God and the mystery of his will to reconcile all things in Christ are now revealed in and through the church. The reconciling work of Christ finds expression in the reconciliation of Jew and Gentile, two formerly hostile and disparate people, into one new community. The church in its scandalous unity displays the wisdom of God in its 'rich variety' (3:10) and reveals to the cosmos the eternal plan of God to reconcile all things in Christ. Paul stresses the newness of this revelation, and argues that it was not known to former generations (3:5). Commentators highlight the paradox of this statement given Paul's

---

78 Gunton, *The One, the Three and the Many*, 230–31.
79 N.T. Wright, *Paul and the Faithfulness of God* (Minneapolis, MN: Fortress Press, 2013), 385.
80 Ibid., 396.
81 Ibid., 402, 1,514–15. It is beyond the scope of this chapter to evaluate the merits of Wright's work for renewing scholarly assumptions on Pauline authorship. This chapter uses 'Paul' to refer to the author of the letter, whether the Apostle Paul or a later writer, as it is the name the author chose to use.

intertextual echoes of Isaiah's vision of Gentile inclusion in the eschatological people of God in 2:11–22 (Isa 52:7; 57:19) and note that it 'raises some sharp questions'.[82] How can the former generations have no knowledge of this reconciling mystery when Paul relies upon Isaiah's vision to describe it? Frank Thielman suggests that the focus upon the discontinuity of Isaiah's vision of the eschatological people of God with Paul's new vision is based on the specific nature of the unity Paul envisions. Whilst texts from the Old Testament and the Second Temple period spoke of the inclusion of the Gentiles, it is not clear from these texts that Gentiles would occupy a place of equal importance as Jews.[83] Thielman contends that this is not merely a vision for the assimilation of Gentiles into Jewish dominance, but the belonging of Gentiles in their full particularity *as Gentiles*.[84] In order to describe the significance of the changed status of the Gentiles in the radical unity of the church, Paul piles words compounded by the Greek preposition *syn* ('with') together into one sentence: fellow heirs (*sygklēronoma*), fellow members of one body (*syssōma*), and fellow sharers (*symmetocha*).[85] The stress of these compounded words, often lost in English translations,[86] is upon the equal participation of the Gentiles *as Gentiles* in the eschatological people of God. In Paul's vision of church unity, the otherness and particularity of the Gentiles is not subsumed into Jewish particularity for the sake of a generalized togetherness. Instead the Gentiles are no longer strangers or aliens, but fellow heirs, fellow members of one body, and fellow sharers in the promises in Jesus Christ *as Gentiles*. Their reconciliation in their full particularity is the very thing that displays God's wisdom in its rich variety to the powers and principalities.[87] Paul's vision of the church has substantial import for disabled ontology to reshape the church as a meaningful community in consumerism.

As many contributors to this volume note, people with disabilities desire to no longer be aliens or strangers in the empty space of an ableist church. People with disabilities desire to belong in churches which welcome them and allow

---

82 Stephen E. Fowl, *Ephesians: A Commentary* (Louisville, KY: Westminster John Knox Press, 2012), 108. See also Ernest Best, *A Critical and Exegetical Commentary on Ephesians* (London: T&T Clark, 1998), 304–6; Andrew T. Lincoln, *Ephesians* (Dallas, TX: Word, 1990), 177–8, and Margaret Y. MacDonald, *Colossians and Ephesians* (Collegeville, MN: Liturgical Press, 2000), 262–3.
83 Frank S. Thielman, 'Ephesians', in *Commentary on the New Testament Use of the Old Testament*, ed. G.K. Beale and D.A. Carson (Grand Rapids, MI: Apollos, 2007), 819.
84 Thielman, 'Ephesians', 819.
85 For translations of these words, see W. Arndt, F.W. Danker, and W. Bauer, *A Greek–English Lexicon of the New Testament and Other Early Christian Literature* (3rd edn; Chicago, IL: Chicago University Press, 2000): συγκληρονόμα, 952; σύσσωμα, 978; συμμέτοχα, 958.
86 A more direct translation would be: 'the Gentiles are fellow heirs [*sygklēronoma*] and fellow members of one body [*syssōma*] and fellow sharers [*symmetocha*] in the promise in Christ Jesus'. See MacDonald, *Colossians and Ephesians*, 263.
87 Whilst Ephesians uses broad categories of Jew and Gentile, it is clear that behind these broad categories were a wide variety of people from a variety of positions in the social strata (for example, *paterfamilias*, slaves, and children). See Wright, *Paul and the Faithfulness of God*, 397.

their particularity to shape and enrich the church rather than being accommodated into ableist assumptions. Ephesians places this desire at the heart of the church's faithful embodiment of the gospel as it displays the reconciling power of the gospel in its rich variety. Swinton rightly argues that the call to shift from an ecclesiology of inclusion for people with disabilities to an ecclesiology of belonging is not because it is morally or politically expedient, but because it is faithful.[88] The scandalous unity of the church is of primary importance to the church's faithfulness to the gospel, and as such it is not an optional extra that will be given some focus once other, more important, work is completed.

The church is not called to merely proclaim the gospel of all things made new through Christ, it is called to embody it as a foretaste of God's intentions to renew all creation.[89] This means that questions of justice, power, and accessibility for people with disabilities in the church are organically linked to questions about the faithfulness and integrity of the church. Attending to the issues of ableism in the church and its embodiment of the gospel is a difficult call to faithfulness so that the church can be the promised new community that anticipates the reconciliation of all things in Christ. As Hauerwas continually reminds us, the task of the church is to be the church in order to help the world understand itself as the world. This is not a proclamation of sectarianism, but a call to be God's faithful community who display God's purposes to the world.[90] Embodying God's purposes for people with disabilities to belong in the church as fellow heirs, fellow members, and fellow sharers will create substantial demands for change upon the church.

Nancy Eiesland, in her important book *The Disabled God*, asks the church to consider its body language – the meanings that are consciously or unconsciously embedded in the rituals, practices, structures, and traditions of the church: 'In the church, the body practices are the physical discourse of inclusion and exclusion. These practices reveal the hidden "membership roll", those whose bodies matter in the shaping of liturgies and services.'[91] Eiesland pronounces the church to be a 'city on a hill' which is totally inaccessible for many people with disabilities. She describes her experience of sharing the Eucharist as a dreaded and humiliating remembrance.[92] If the church is to move from accommodating and including people with disabilities to being a place of belonging, it is going to have to face its own collusion in systems and structures that oppress people with

---

88 Swinton, 'From Inclusion to Belonging', 187.
89 Andrew Picard, 'Be the Community: Baptist Ecclesiology in the Context of Missional Church', *Pacific Journal of Baptist Research* 5 (2009): 31–5. See also Murray Rae, 'The Liturgical Shape of Christian Life' [accessed 7 February 2013]. Online: http://knoxcentre.ac.nz/wp-content/uploads/2012/11/The-Liturgical-Shape-of-Christian-Life.pdf.
90 Stanley Hauerwas, 'The Servant Community: Christian Social Ethics', in *The Hauerwas Reader*, ed. John Berkman and Michael Cartwright (Durham, NC: Duke University Press, 2001), 375.
91 Nancy L. Eiesland, *The Disabled God: Toward a Liberatory Theology of Disability* (Nashville, TN: Abingdon, 1994), 112.
92 Nancy L. Eiesland, 'Encountering the Disabled God', *PMLA* 120 (2005): 584.

disabilities. It will have to allow the gospel to slay the church and make it alive again in Christ to be his scandalous community of united persons by the Spirit. For this to occur, the church will need to reconsider its assimilation of people with disabilities into ableist assumptions. It is not easy to break out of the power imbalances which are embedded in the categories of oppressor and oppressed. It is more difficult for those with privilege to realize its reach. Privilege is like having the wind at your back when you are riding a bicycle: you do not realize you have it until you have to turn around and bike into the wind.[93]

Privilege is exercised in the sedimented practices of domination that infuse daily living, and the first step for the church is to begin to recognize these practices. In her excellent article on the Pākehā[94] assertion of colonial dominance over Māori, Ani Mikaere suggests that the first step is for those with privilege to give up control of decision-making and entrust minorities to lead through their own personal agency. Without such trust the minority group is forced to submit to the terms of the majority and the patriarchal relationship continues.[95] In the church setting this will mean that power is given over to disabled brothers and sisters to lead the church in a process towards greater gospel faithfulness which able-bodied people do not control. It may mean the ceasing of assumed forms of worship, traditions, practices, and rituals, and the development of forms which are totally foreign to able-bodied experience, but completely 'normal' to people with disabilities. It is unlikely that the normativity of settled worship practices carry much meaning to people with disabilities as it is often exclusive and oppressive. Possibilities may emerge in developing new forms of church communication and interaction with people with severe learning difficulties, such as intensive interaction, which do not negativize their non-verbal communications.[96] As such, people with severe learning difficulties would take the lead in communication whilst others imitate and weave interactive games around their stereotyped behaviour: 'Thus interactive sessions might involve rocking together in blended rhythms, interrupting the flicking of the pages of a book in a playful burst–pause pattern or imitating hand-clapping with exaggerated and occasionally altered movements'.[97] Such refusals to default to conformity, listening to unfamiliar voices, and celebrating difference

---

93 Robin Ryle, *Questioning Gender: A Sociological Exploration* (Thousand Oaks, CA: Pine Forge Press, 2012), 19.
94 'Pākehā' refers to a New Zealander of European descent – probably originally applied to English-speaking Europeans living in Aotearoa/New Zealand; 'Pākehā', *Māori Dictionary* [accessed 5 July 2013]. Online: http://www.maoridictionary.co.nz/search?idiom=&phrase=&proverb=&loan=&keywords=p%C4%81keh%C4%81&search=.
95 Ani Mikaere, 'Are We All New Zealanders Now? A Māori Response to the Pākehā Quest for Indigeneity', in *Colonising Myths – Māori Realities: He Rukuruku Whakaaro* (Wellington: Huia, 2011), 117.
96 Melanie Nind and Mary Kellett, 'Responding to Individuals with Severe Learning Difficulties and Stereotyped Behaviour: Challenges for an Inclusive Age', *European Journal of Special Needs Education* 17 (2002): 265–82. I am grateful to Charles Hewlett for alerting me to the possibilities of intensive interaction for renewing church practices.
97 Ibid., 271.

in dignified ways were characteristic of Jesus' ministry. Intensive interaction is but one example of how people with disabilities could help the church to be present to God, one another, and ourselves in new and deeper ways. The possibilities which could emerge from able-bodied people giving up power are vast and untapped. However, as Mikaere states in regards to Pākehā dominance, it will take a leap of faith or else the minority will, once again, be assimilated into the status quo. Within the church this leap of faith is not only trusting people with disabilities to lead with their own personal agency, it is also a leap of faith in the God who has called us together into one body, in our rich variety, to be his people and display his reconciling purposes to all the world. If churches collude with the culture of consumerism that silently silences minorities, we will not only continue to oppress people with disabilities, we will not seek repentance, receive forgiveness, or be the promised new community of reconciled persons in relationship with God and one another.

The church is called, in Christ and by the Spirit, to anticipate a different way of being human together, a way which is the antithesis of empty spaces. The church is called to be a community of meaning where people with disabilities are no longer strangers or aliens, but fellow heirs, fellow members of one body, and fellow sharers in the promise in Christ Jesus. As the church learns to be God's community of particular persons in relationship, it will be a community of meaning in regards to human particularities, but also, and more significantly, with regard to the gospel itself. The church will anticipate another way of being human together: God's intended way. And it will offer to God, in Christ and by the Spirit, the sacrifice of praise that is the due human response to his wise purposes in the beginning – to bring all things in heaven and on earth into unity in Christ by the Spirit's power.

6   Conversations with James on Leadership

What Can We Learn about Leadership and Personhood from People with Severe Cognitive Disability?

Charles Hewlett

This is the transcript of a conversation I had with my son, James. James is a 21-year-old man who has profound intellectual disabilities. James has the cognitive ability of a six-month-old, and depends on us to meet all his needs. However, this does not mean that James is merely a passive recipient of care. James is a person, and he is an active contributor to our family life. This conversation is a conscious attempt to recognize the contributions James has made to me, and my understanding of leadership, and to take his non-verbal communication seriously. In this conversation I offer five things I have learnt from James about leadership and their significance for Christian leadership.

Introduction

James, it's really nice to have you here with me – I am so proud of you, son. There are some important people here in this room today. These men and women have the responsibility for spiritually managing and directing an awful lot of people. As principal of Carey Baptist College, I was invited to come along and speak to them. And I thought they might benefit from listening to me and you having a conversation about leadership. I appreciate that you are only 21 years of age, with the cognitive ability of a six-month-old baby, but James, you have taught me more about being a leader than anyone else I know. Son, I would not be the leader I am today without the way you have ministered to me. I reckon that you might be able to help these people too, in their desire to love and serve God.

Stop Pretending

One of the reasons I like spending time with you, James, is because I can't impress you. Well, unless I was holding a big piece of cake! I mean, it is so different being your dad from being the leader of a theological college. Often being a leader is so much about performance, charisma, being able to motivate, and cast impressive visions. It's about being able to speak the right words, blog the right thoughts, read the right books, and network with the right people. It's about rubbing shoulders with academics, keeping up with the competition, and maintaining a glossy, well-run, machine.

I remember when I was pastoring in the local church: the pressure to keep up with that city church everyone talked about; the need to perform in the pulpit like that pastor down the road; having elders who wanted me to have the solution to every problem. And then the young people – they wanted me to be 'wicked'!

But it's so not like that with you, James! These things mean nothing to you. My leadership skills don't impress you at all. And it's so freeing. It's so liberating. When we hang out, I don't have to perform for you or pretend that I can. You don't love me because of what I can do, you love me because I'm here, and that's enough. I appreciate that a lot of these things are just part of being in charge, but James, you have taught me that sometimes these things can take over – and my whole job becomes driven by performance, the need to impress, and to look good. And my motivation can so easily get skewed; decisions become pragmatic and shallow, and looks become more important than depth and transparency. James, thank you for loving me simply for who I am. Thank you for challenging me to rethink the importance I place on performance, and for the encouragement to stop pretending.

Enjoy the Broken

Well, James, you really are broken, aren't you? I remember that little rhyme I'd say when I was a boy: 'When God passed out brains, I thought he said trains, and I missed mine.' Well, James, you really did miss yours! We've laughed together a lot over the years about this, haven't we? Remember the time you got stuck under the coffee table and couldn't work out a way to get out – and we just had to laugh. I remember the time we were pushing the trolley around Palmer's Garden Nursery together and I wondered why you were moving so slow – I thought you must have been tired. After a while I looked, to see that both your trousers and your nappies had come down and they were caught around your ankles. James, you were walking around the garden centre in the starkers! We joked all the way home about how those pretty young assistants were taking more notice of us than usual!

Son, I like things that are broken, that can't be fixed – things like you. Ha, we seem to live in a world that is very preoccupied with things being just right, and we struggle to cope with things that are somehow flawed. I get sick of being the leader who has to fix things all the time. There's so much pressure: 'What are we going to do about this Charles?' 'What ideas have you got to make us more successful?' 'Present your solution to us at the next board meeting.' And if I can't fix it, then maybe I'm a lousy leader.

I love the fact that you are broken and I don't have to fix you. There is nothing that can be done about your disability, and I have to accept it. You have made me realize that instead of resenting your brokenness, instead of wishing you were different, I can enjoy you and live in all the richness that your brokenness brings. It is through your disabilities that I have learnt the most about myself, about life, about living, and about God. Thank you for reminding me not to be sucked in by perfection and all of its glossiness and superficiality. You've helped me understand that there might not be a quick fix for that family struggling with marriage issues. You've helped me appreciate that there might be value in having that eccentric person as part of our team. You've helped me see that it doesn't matter that the woman with mental health issues keeps interrupting the worship service. You've helped me realize that it doesn't matter that the church foyer is looking a bit tired – in fact, it's quite quirky (apparently it's retro!). And it doesn't matter that our worship leader doesn't look like a model. James, you have helped me to appreciate the ordinary, the different, and to accept things and people the way they are.

Slow Down

You love your cuddles, don't you? Even now, as a big 21-year-old, you still love to sit on my knee and snuggle into me. You'd happily do that for hours. James, I think we need to talk to these leaders about slowing down a bit.

Now, I appreciate you can't talk to me, that we can't have a spoken conversation, watch sports together, or discuss politics. But I guess that's your whole point, James, isn't it? With you, it's not about doing things, it's just about being. In fact, time doesn't mean anything to you. It stretches out between meals and snacks, and one hour blurs happily into the next. For a leader, time can mean everything. We get so busy, James. Rushing from meeting to meeting, hurrying from problem to problem, from person to person. Phone calls, emails, organizing, planning, sermons. James – we simply run out of time, and the quality of what happens in each hour gets diluted. We become driven and task-focused. Our big purpose even gets overrun by the nuts and bolts. We're so busy perfecting the song progression that we forget to see God. We're so busy trying to fix the mistakes of Christendom that we miss out on enjoying the richness of the body of Christ that we are part of. We're so busy trying to get the sermon finished on time that we miss the very wonder of God's Word itself. And we're so busy developing the plan to reach the whole community that we miss the opportunity to share the gospel with our next-door neighbour.

James, you have taught me to slow down and become less task-focused. You've helped me to remember what really matters, to take a step back and to revisit the big picture, to pause and catch glimpses of beauty in the small things. James, you have taught me so much.

Get Excited

You're very quiet today, James. Sometimes you can get pretty loud – and it gets us in a bit of trouble. I love it when we're out in public and you unexpectedly give out a big yell, and it makes people jump. We get some stares – but they don't understand that it's your way of showing us how excited you are. You flap your arms and yell out as loud as you possibly can. That's one of the reasons I love visiting your school – Oaklynn Special School. You and your friends are crazy – in a nice way. You're so easily excited with no inhibitions. If you want to do something, you just do it. If you feel like dancing, you get up and dance. If you feel like yelling, you yell. And you're so rude – belching and farting in the middle of the graduation ceremony.

It makes me laugh when your mates come up and stare at me. They hold my hand, give me a hug, or ask me a question, it doesn't seem to matter that I don't know them. You're young adults, but in many ways just little kids, little preschoolers. So trusting, so accepting, so naïve, so spontaneous, so honest. So easily excited, with no hang-ups or embarrassments or self-consciousness. James, I love these things about you.

It's so easy to lose excitement when you're a leader. You come into the job as a young pastor, ready to change the world – a risk-taker, a pioneer, an adventurer. You're energetic, fired up, and excited. And then you slowly change. You get wiser, you take a few knocks, criticism comes your way, you learn to pace yourself, you learn about self-preservation. We become self-aware, self-contained, and self-conscious. But I don't want to be like that, James, I want to be more like you. I want to be a leader who is less careful, less politically correct, and less cautious. Thank you for reminding me that in my apathy and safeness I might just be missing out on the exciting things God has in mind for me.

Chill Out

People often compliment me and your mum on our patience in dealing with you and your disabilities. I wonder if they ever stop to think how patient you must be? I often try to imagine what it must be like not being able to communicate, not being able to easily express how you feel, what you need, and what you're thinking. What's it like to be constantly misunderstood? It must get pretty frustrating at times. I know I'm pretty thick sometimes, aren't I? You push the drink away, and I keep offering it to you, just in case you change your mind. I bet you want to say, 'Dad, I've already said no, OK!' We try to make you eat more food, but you're pushing the spoon away and closing your mouth tight. You're saying no the best you can, but we keep trying to shove it in.

Then there's this ongoing saga with your walking. That cast that went from your toes to your groin – those long months recovering in respite care, just lying on your back in bed. And now the weekly trips to Middlemore Hospital each Monday morning with Mum to have a new, slightly adjusted cast put on. You're such a patient man, James. In all this, you don't grizzle and grump, you don't throw a paddy or give up. I seem to get so impatient when things aren't going my way: 'The elders, they just don't understand me!' 'Why won't they provide me with the resources I need to get the job done?' And the way I complain to Mum when my mates in secular work upgrade their cars, move into a bigger house, and tell us about their planned overseas trip. Well, it's not fair, James! James, I have watched the way you respond to the challenges, and I have learnt so much.

Thanks, too, for the reminder to listen well, that I need to take the time to listen properly instead of hearing what I think is being said. You have taught me to look deeper, below the surface stuff, and be more discerning, more insightful.

Conclusion

Well, James, I think we've run out of time. That wasn't so bad after all. I wonder why we got so nervous? But these are the things you want to say to us as leaders: *Stop pretending, enjoy the broken, slow down, get excited, and chill out.*

> But God chose the foolish things of the world to shame the wise; God chose the weak things of the world to shame the strong. (1 Cor 1:27)
>
> And He has said to me, 'My grace is sufficient for you, for power is perfected in weakness.' Most gladly, therefore, I will rather boast about my weaknesses, so that the power of Christ may dwell in me. Therefore I am well content with weaknesses, with insults, with distresses, with persecutions, with difficulties, for Christ's sake; for when I am weak, then I am strong. (2 Cor 12:9–10)

7 'He's My Mate'
Cerebral Palsy, Church, and the Gift of Friendship

Manuele Teofilo

My name is Manuele Teofilo, and I am a Samoan living with cerebral palsy. My cerebral palsy impairs me physically, restricting movement from below my neck. This requires the use of an electric wheelchair and means that I must rely on others for basic needs. I also have unclear speech, which makes communication difficult. My experience of living with my cerebral palsy has been like a rollercoaster: filled with twists and turns, both miserable and memorable; throughout it all I have recognized God's presence and will in my life.

My physical impairment has been the defining factor in my upbringing. I was born in Samoa, and at the age of three migrated with my mother to New Zealand in search of a better opportunity in life. My grandparents recognized that I would not be able to live well in Samoa, so decided to invite my mother and I to live with them in Auckland. As a little toddler, my family found it easy to take care of me because carrying me around was not too strenuous. Getting around home was effortless, because I was either in a walker or crawling. My family happily took me to church, other homes, and various places. Being little allowed my *aiga*[1] and others to take me to places without much bother, which gave us a deep sense of pleasure.

My grandparents enrolled me in Carlson School in Epsom, a cerebral palsy school. This was a new era in my childhood. Carlson School was not only a place of academic learning, but also a place that nurtured the achievement of children with cerebral palsy. At this school I received opportunities to begin journeys in both academic and social capacities.

The friends I made in school were my closest peers; we bonded during our school days and loved each other's company. My friendships grew tight, and I wished I could see them all the time. I did not really have anyone to talk to at home. I appreciated everything that happened in school, although I found classroom share time difficult for several reasons. First, listening to what my peers did outside of the classroom made me envy their exciting lives. Secondly, most of the time I did not have much to share. So, every so often, I would

---

1 *Aiga* is the Samoan word for 'family'. For more information, see 'Aiga', *Samoan Dictionary* [accessed 14 October 2013]. Online: http://nzetc.victoria.ac.nz/tm/scholarly/tei-PraDict-c3–1.html.

be creative and share a childish made-up story. I think my peers and teachers enjoyed my stories.

The staff at Carlson School filled my life with joy and excitement. School taught me many things, but ultimately it taught me to have a positive attitude. Self-confidence grew within me through a mixture of academic learning, physiotherapy sessions, and other therapies and activities. Carlson allowed me to grow in my abilities and taught me that I was able to do anything despite my disability. I remember one teacher-aid who sacrificed a lot to give me the best childhood experience. He would be practical, helping me attempt things, from jumping up and down to climbing a large playground net. This gave me the courage to believe that I was capable of attempting anything in life. The decision made by my grandparents to send me to Carlson School was crucial in my development. More importantly, certain teachers at this school were the key people on my journey towards Jesus Christ.

Meanwhile, life at home was heading downhill. As I grew older, I became heavier and less mobile. Consequently, my family's ability to take me to places lessened. If I wasn't at school, I was at home on my knuckles and knees finding some activity to keep myself entertained, like scribbling on a piece of cardboard or watching television. These things kept me busy after school and in the weekends. Unfortunately, my grandparents never had the financial means to buy a mobility vehicle to transport me around. Not being able to go anywhere with my family also meant that I could not be taken to church. I remember every Sunday morning watching my family getting dressed to go to their Samoan congregational church. This left my mother and me at home.

Other than school, the only time I got to go out was to doctor appointments. Then, if I was lucky, a teacher from school would kindly offer to come and take me out. When I think back now, I wonder, 'Why did my grandparent's church not do more to help me?' They could have helped me connect with the church, but as far as I knew, they had not considered alternatives. To me there was a lack of communication and connection between the pastors and my family in terms of encouraging my attendance at church. This was my earliest experience of the church; and as far as I can recall, it remained this way for some time.

After the first few years at Carlson they began to integrate me into classes at Three Kings School. Going into a mainstream classroom was an unfamiliar experience for me. It was the first time I had to mix with non-disabled students. I only knew how to interact with Carlson students. The transition between the two groups affected me profoundly. I liken this to a migration, much like my own from Samoa to New Zealand. This journey introduced me to a long road of understanding disability in the reality of wider society. Up until this point my family and school sheltered me. I had to do this journey by myself. This new world strongly formed my identity, and continues to do so today. It took me a couple of years to learn to relate adequately with my able-bodied peers. Carlson gradually increased my time in Three Kings School, from attending one afternoon class to a few classes, and eventually letting me and my classmates into their school during intervals. I thank Carlson for the way they encouraged me to integrate with my able-bodied peers.

Church was still a non-existent part of my life. If I was lucky, my family took me to a Christmas midnight mass. My primary school teacher for five years, Joslyn Christians, recalls me asking questions several times about church and God. So, in year six, Joslyn invited me to come to her church, Papatoetoe Baptist Church. At the time there was a missionary team from America who were interested in helping with special needs. Joslyn arranged for the American missionary team to give me a ride to and from church every Sunday. Going to church was exciting because not only did I get to learn about God, it was another place I could go to.

Many people in the congregation made me feel welcomed. Although I was welcomed by all, I was still very much unaccustomed to interacting with those the same age as me. Despite this, I gladly joined the church's Sunday school. Joslyn ended up being my Sunday school teacher! It took me a few months to participate in Sunday school activities. Gradually through the year I formed bonds with the leaders and some of the kids. Later that year, when a close schoolmate with cerebral palsy started coming to church, I began to feel more comfortable in Sunday school, although this took away my focus from getting to know other kids from Sunday school for a little while. Whilst others from Sunday school bonded with me, these friendships were still not the same as the friendships I had formed with my friends with cerebral palsy.

The church did everything they could to help me participate in church events. This included providing transport to church when I had none, providing carers for camps, looking out for me when I was at church; I felt like my cerebral palsy didn't contribute to how I was seen as a person. As I started to spend more time in mainstream schooling and the intermediate-aged youth group, I became less sheltered and more aware that my cerebral palsy is intrinsically linked to my place, role, status, and identity. I was not aware that society could treat me as an outcast for having cerebral palsy until this point in my life. I did year seven twice, and was falling behind my friends, who were all starting high school while I was still in intermediate.

Whilst school held me back, youth group gave me an opportunity to grow with others of the same age, and this left me feeling less disabled. As I became more aware of these things, I had the desire to move on to high school with some of my church friends. If I had not been part of the intermediate-aged youth group at this time, I would not have realized that my school was holding me back. I thank God for showing himself to me at this time of my life.

Meanwhile, my family situation was also changing, for the better. My parents had applied for a Lottery grant for a mobility vehicle, and gained approval. It was a huge milestone to have a mobility vehicle because it gave me that ability to go out with my family and be more involved at church. The church has played a big role in shaping how I understand my place in wider society as a person with cerebral palsy.

What Can Churches Learn from People with Cerebral Palsy?

Living with my disability has taught me several lessons about life. Over the years attending church, many experiences have highlighted different areas I need to speak about as a person with special needs. These experiences have formed convictions which I have close to my heart. These are my observations and suggestions for the church.

Many people within churches are given a role according to the skills they have to fulfil that role. Yet I feel that the church has not given me, and others with special needs, proper attention in this area. I have been included in church activities and church events, but I am still yearning for a full sense of belonging in the community of believers. Some people have not respected me as a person. I hear people talk about the word 'normal' as a category, and people with special needs do not belong to this category.

Find Out Our Abilities and Use Them

Generally, the church has looked at me and asked, 'How can I help you?' What I see in both secular and religious circles is this sense of obligation and paternalism. These paternalistic forms of relationship do not allow me to contribute back. Consequently, the church can often view me and others with special needs as 'charity cases'. But what does this perspective do to the individual – *what does this do to me*? It disempowers me, stripping me of my *mana*.[2] I feel that I have no role in society other than being helped. This makes me feel worthless. My abilities are seen to be limited, and as a result I am exempt from some groups such as music, sports, and the tech team. Indeed, this has been a rising issue for me at church. I see all my friends serving in the church in a variety of ways – music, tech crew, or youth leading. But, I am left wondering, 'How am I serving?' It has been a challenge trying to find the right area for me to serve in. It has been encouraging to hear people say that my faith in God and my outpouring of wise words are inspiring. I have only recently learnt that this is one way of serving – to inspire others.

People with disabilities, like the non-disabled, are gifted with different abilities. We can be used, though often we're excluded from doing so. I once asked a pastoral leader if I could help out on the computers during church services using my head wand. He agreed, and set up a training session for me. After this conversation he never got back to me, despite my efforts to continue training. It seemed to me that I was not a priority, that I was put in the 'too hard' basket

---

2 *Mana* is a Māori word that is difficult to translate accurately, but in this context it refers to the inherent dignity, power, or authority of an individual, as gifted by God. For more information, see 'Mana', *Māori Dictionary* [accessed 14 October 2013]. Online: http://www.maoridictionary.co.nz/search?idiom=&phrase=&proverb=&loan=&keywords=mana.

because of my impairment. Sadly, for those of us with special needs in the Christian community this is an all too familiar story. This leaves me with many questions for the church and how she sees me. Why don't people take the time to commit to partnering with me? Why do I always have to go out of my way to establish connection? Does the church see value and worth in me? Can the church see me and others like me as being able to contribute, or not? In my own story many abilities have been identified, but few people have been willing to engage with me so that these qualities could be nurtured and used within the church. The Pauline image of the Body of Christ in 1 Cor 12 speaks about the different parts of the body being united in their diversity, as God has arranged it. Paul warns against forms of church which leave some members believing that because they are not like the dominant group, they do not belong: 'If the foot would say, "Because I am not a hand, I do not belong to the body," that would not make it any less a part of the body' (1 Cor 12:15). Paul goes on to remind us that *God* has arranged the members of the church as he chose (v. 18). Every part of the body contributes, from the least to the most honourable, as we grow into the fullness of Christ. There is no room in the body of Christ for those who, in their sense of superiority, would say to others they deem inferior, 'I have no need of you' (1 Cor 12:21). Identifying, nurturing, and utilizing the different gifts amongst God's people, including those with special needs, is essential to living out the implications of the gospel.

Create Places of Belonging

Churches need to be places of belonging, both socially and structurally.

Social

The cerebral palsy I live with is a restraining factor of my living, but I have learnt to pursue and fight to get the best of life. This restraint particularly affects me socially, and I feel that the social aspect has a big impact in creating a place of belonging. My inspiration to achieve the best of life despite my restraints comes from John 10:10, 'The thief comes only to steal and kill and destroy; I have come that they may have life, and have it to the full.' Trusting in the Lord gives me the confidence to seek and find a true sense of belonging in Christ.

I feel less disabled thanks to my family's support and how my church has treated me as just another person. Church became the greatest support during my time at high school and my teenage years. I pursued and learnt many things through my teenage struggles. Church felt like the safest place that I could be honest and open up about my struggles and find support in my distress. The high school youth group was a place of comfort where I could express my thoughts and passions. It also allowed me to be myself as just a regular teenage Christian. It was easy to socialize at youth group as the church building was accessible and it was the common meeting place of my Christian friends.

How does my cerebral palsy impair me today? Despite my church including me in common church activities, it has been a long process to involve me in the lives of others. Often I feel let down because I don't get to be a part of some of my peers' social outings, groups, and other events. When I can't do things or can't participate in events, my cerebral palsy screams at me. I feel that my friends do not ask me out sometimes because of the complications of arranging to go out with me. I understand that they want to have me present, but practically it is difficult. This makes me wonder about what could assist society to become more willing to invite their friends with special needs to casual outings? Gradually my friends from church and school have become more comfortable with going out with me. An essential conviction in my faith is that God is relational. Scripture speaks to us of a relational God and the centrality of relationships to being human: from Adam and Eve, Jesus and his twelve disciples to 'the gathered church' – people are doing life together with God and one another, day in and day out. I would like to ask the church to consider encouraging people to welcome others more into their lives, including people like me who are impaired.

Structural

To create a place of belonging, the structural framework must also be examined. Humans create structures purposed for community and a sense of belonging. Ironically, many of these structures prevent genuine belonging due to various factors. For example, the special needs centre at my high school was located outside the main campus. This allowed for ideal transportation and specialized learning and community to take place in one location. The focus has been on both the practical and academic nature of supporting those with special needs. However, the inevitable by-product of this has been segregation, a 'ghettoization' of the disabled community. The more I see this segregation, the more it frustrates me. To fight this I have grown fond of spending time with friends without special needs. During my senior high school years my friends have shown me that they were being genuine mates by treating me like 'one of the boys'. I also managed to join a group of mainstream students with some church mates. As I got to know more of the group individually I noticed that they were also showing genuine friendships. Some of these friendships continued when we left school. My connection with people without special needs was broadening, and continues to do so.

Church needs a structure which allows for everyone to feel that they belong. I despise the idea of creating a specialized group for the so-called 'disabled'. My recommendation to the church is to avoid coming to this conclusion and to focus on adopting unique individuals into the life of the church. Churches need to create a church structure that allows all members to be involved and feel indispensable to the church. I see two positive outcomes from this preferable approach. First, people with special needs will feel worthy having a significant place in their church community. Secondly, this will create more genuine relationships between special needs and non-special needs people through their common roles which they fulfil together. People with special needs despite their difficulties have considerable determination and persistence to live full and enjoyable lives. This demonstrates a thankful attitude as well as a positive attitude about life to non-special needs people. As special needs and non-special needs people share their experiences with each other, it will certainly break the unnoticed barrier between special needs people and wider society.

The unnoticed barrier between special needs people and the wider society is broken within my network of people, close relatives and close friends from church, school, and the local community. But when I go out into the wider society I am confronted with the disabling barrier that still exists. With my friends and family I forget about my cerebral palsy. However, out in public I begin to remember my label as 'disabled' by the way people treat me. Society provides accessible buildings, vans, and public spaces, and society also provides other means to aid a variety of impairments. This makes life easier for people with special needs, and it is making a difference. But these physical changes need to be met with attitudinal changes in society so that people with special needs are treated with respect and dignity, just as all people are treated with respect and dignity. Practically, society is becoming more accommodating, but there remain adverse attitudes towards visible impairment.

I get annoyed when I engage with the wider society because some people assume that I am a dumb kid. This is mostly because they don't understand what I say or misinterpret my words for something childish. John 10:10 gives me the courage to push through this painful reality and continue to be a light in this dark alley. Like they say, if you want to make a difference in the world, then be that difference. Every time I spend time with friends without special needs I feel that I am breaking the barrier between special needs people and wider society. I would like to see the barrier fully broken within the church, because the gospel tells us that Jesus Christ has broken the dividing wall (Eph. 2:14). If this can be achieved, the church can be an example to the whole world. If believers can learn how to have the right attitude to people with special needs, and learn to live together in mutually flourishing relationships, they can influence the wider society. When this barrier is broken or lessens, people with special needs will have a genuine sense of belonging in churches and wider society.

Embrace Difference

The world has an idea that things can be 'normal' and 'not normal'. As a person with cerebral palsy, people tend to place me and others like me in the 'not normal' box. What is normal? Is everybody meant to be exactly the same? Doesn't the gospel offer us a vision of God's wisdom being displayed through the church's rich variety with each unique person (Eph 3:10)? I find this idea of normalcy an utter fraud; as Thomas Reynolds states, it is 'the cult of normalcy'.[3]

---

3 Thomas E. Reynolds, *Vulnerable Communion: A Theology of Disability and Hospitality* (Grand Rapids, MI: Brazos Press, 2008), 59–63.

If we are to build a connection between people with special needs and a 'normal' person, we must drop all assumptions we may have about the other person. We must all play a part in making a world of difference. Maybe it would be a life-changing experience to get to know someone that seems really different to you.

Churches should consider becoming places that embrace difference and are less judgemental. A recent incident displays the pervasiveness of 'the cult of normalcy'. I was with my Christian friends at a local burger bar when a lady interrupted us as we were about to leave. She asked my friend, who is like a brother, 'Are you his caregiver, or family?' To which he replied, 'He's my mate.' Not receiving the answer she expected from him, she repeated the question. He then looked her dead in the eye and said with steely determination, '*He's my mate!*' I sensed the impact these words had on her, changing her perspective about me. Astonishingly, she turned around and spoke directly to me from then onwards. Why did she now speak to *me*? Because when she heard that I was just another 'mate', she saw past the apparent impairments and saw the human being that I am.

The wider church community needs education in how to interact with people who have special needs. If people were more aware that people with special needs are just as human as anyone else, it would be less disabling and give me and others like me a greater sense of belonging as a person. This is a struggle without end, but with the support of friends, family, and God, I am able to go on in the struggle. Church is a place where I don't want to face this struggle. Instead, I want church to be an enriching place of mutual support and flourishing. The best way for the church to acknowledge people with special needs is to embrace us. Do not try to 'fix' things for us, or just simply put up with us. Instead, love us, welcome us, and journey with us, just like we do with you. All I ask is for the church to be our mates. We want mates who will love us and journey with us, and we will love you and journey with you.

Finally, I ask the church to be different. The church needs to learn to be the church, and stop being like society, where people have negative assumptions towards people with special needs. We are not the church's charity cases who 'need help' so that Christians can feel better about themselves. Negativizing our disabilities creates paternalistic relationships of dependency where people with special needs feel worthless and able-bodied people assume that there is nothing they can learn from us. Being someone's patient or project gives people with special needs a sense of worthlessness. The church should be the opposite of this. The church is a place where we are all called to learn, grow, and change together to become more like Christ. We are called to see people differently, through the assumptions of the gospel, and learn to love one another in our treasured differences that God has given. I long for a church where people will say, 'He's my mate!'

Part II
Theology, Disability, and Belonging

8 The Silence Surrounding Psych Wards

Christine Welten

Ten years ago I was diagnosed with early onset schizophrenia, an illness that usually besets someone in their thirties that I started experiencing at age 12. The diagnosis was given when I was 19, just after I was married. By this time I had faced seven years of mental health issues with little help or understanding. For all my teenage years I had struggled with extreme depression, self-harming, eating disorders, and audible and visual hallucinations. In some ways it was a relief to finally be told what was wrong with me, and in other ways it felt like a death sentence. I had been labelled as incurable. For five years after my diagnosis I was placed on medication after medication, I was kept in psych wards for varying lengths of time, and my every action was viewed through the symptoms of my illness. I was told the damage in my brain was irreversible, would get worse as I aged, and I would be a permanent mental health patient. There was no hope for me, my family, or my new marriage.

As a young woman in her twenties living in the wards, I was exposed to people and behaviours for which I was completely unprepared. I watched a heavily pregnant woman attack staff and have a fire hose turned on her in an effort to control her. I heard the same lady describe her unborn child as a demon, only to find out in reality that it was her father's child. I listened to a woman talk for hours about how the skin on her face was falling off. I met a 17-year-old boy who was dropped off by his parents for suicidal behaviour – he remained there for a week with no visitors. I was verbally abused by a man who thought I was his mother, and I was confronted by nurses who were in equal measure compassionate and careworn. When I was not in the psych ward I was a daily visitor at the day ward with other mental health patients in the community. Though this was a much more pleasant environment, I was surrounded by people who were usually much older than me, who I did not know, and who were cared for by understaffed and overworked community workers.

Eventually my illness took its toll on my loved ones, and my marriage fell apart three years after it had started. My mother had to quit her job to become my full-time carer. She would wake me up, make me shower, take me for walks, and make all my food so that I ate well. We were all told that this would be a lifelong sentence and there was no hope for recovery. Despite my mother's care, my mental health continued to deteriorate and I lived only for my chance to die. My family describe me at that time as a zombie with no purpose or care for my life.

I find that when I speak of my experiences with mental illness I am met with one of four reactions by the listeners. The first reaction is ambivalence. These listeners cannot relate, or don't know how to relate, and are quick to change the subject because they are uncomfortable discussing a topic of which they have no understanding. They may think that mental illness is 'all in your head' and something that can be changed by willpower, or they may simply have no interest in the matter. The second reaction is nervousness and confusion. These listeners mean well, but simply do not comprehend what mental illness is or how to respond to it. They may look at you like you are about to pull out a gun and start a rampage, or they may ask to pray for you to release you from the demonic stronghold over your life. However, once they begin praying they often end up lost for words as they become confused about how they should pray. They often spiritualize your experience in order to bring the conversation into a language that they understand. The third reaction is unhealthy curiosity, and it is perhaps the most interesting of them all. They are the group that leans forward, with eyes shining, lapping up every word. When you have finished speaking they will say things like 'That is so cool,' and ask questions like 'So you could actually see people that weren't there? Was that freaky?' and 'What did they look like?' They are curiously excited by what is being said, and can ask insensitive questions about experiences in the psych wards. They will also be the ones most likely to call people with mental illness 'crazy' or 'psycho'. They also tend to be young. The fourth reaction is attentive listening, and it is the minority. They are the listeners who will find you alone later, share their own experiences, cry and pray with you. They usually have had an experience with mental illness and have genuine compassion for what you have been through. But these listeners are few and far between.

Unfortunately, mental illnesses have stigmas attached to them that cause reactions of fear, disinterest, and wariness. People buy into the stigmatization of schizophrenics, and other mental health patients, and assume the rhetoric that mental health patients are worthless, dirty, insincere, delicate, slow, tense, weak, foolish, incompetent, irresponsible, dangerous, violent, or unpredictable. It is my experience that this stigmatization is found just as much within the church as from without. However, the sting in the church's tail is the additional stigmatizations that mental health patients lack faith, are demon-possessed, and are being punished by God. Ultimately, mental health patients are regarded as sinful. With these labels it is easy to understand why mental health patients find it hard to contribute to society in a world where the stigmatization of your illness is often worse than the illness itself. It is also easy to understand why mental health patients often talk of feeling isolated and rejected by their communities and churches. The simple fact of the matter is that people do not know how to respond to mental illness.

'Mental illness' are two words that create a lot of confusion as they encompass a plethora of issues, from emotional depression through to psychosis that requires full-time care. There are also very few mental illnesses that are truly understood, even by the medical profession, and this leads to misunderstanding, fear, and isolation within families and communities. Diagnosis of a mental illness can create greater issues for the patient than suffering the illness alone, as diagnosis locates the illness entirely with the individual, apart from their family and environment. It claims that there is something 'wrong' with the person that defines them as outside the acceptable 'norm'. This reduces hope of recovery, creates stigma through labelling, and turns a person into a category.

In New Zealand today it is estimated that 1 in 4 people will suffer from a mental illness at some point in their lives. It is estimated that 38 per cent of Europeans, 62 per cent of Māori, 59 per cent of Asians, and 59 per cent of Pacific Islanders will be diagnosed with a psychotic disorder, such as schizophrenia, in their lifetime.[1] Despite a quarter of the population having experienced mental illness, it seems to be a common issue that we cannot comprehend or relate to a form of suffering that cannot be physically manifested. People will react out of fear and amusement, but very rarely out of genuine compassion. And this is true of the church as well.

I was healed six years ago. Some ladies from the prayer group at church answered my mother's cry for help and started a chain of events that means I am now able to speak for those who often have no voice. In the last six years I have had to re-learn social cues and behaviours, get used to being on my own with no other voices to keep me company, try to discern which of my memories were true events and which were hallucinations, and to survive on my own outside my family's care. Perhaps one of the most difficult things I have had to experience is grieving the passing of visually hallucinated people who were my friends and companions for many years. When I was healed it felt like some of the people who had kept my constant company had died. My grief was real and yet very much a solitary act, because grieving for those who never existed is incomprehensible to most people.

I carry with me always the memories of people who have not been as fortunate as I have been. The haunted eyes of the lady who believed the baby in her womb was a demon. The dead eyes of the man who received shock therapy at age eight and has been institutionalized ever since. The fear in the eyes of the lady who believed the skin on her face was melting off. The sadness in the eyes of the young teenager with suicidal tendencies. I remember the sadness, fear, anger, and hatred in the eyes of my ex-husband, who received no support and who lost all hope. I hold in my heart the conversations I had with the other patients about being forgotten, rejected, or hated by our communities. I remember the questions I received from other patients when they learnt I was a Christian. They wanted to know why no one in my church came to visit me

---

1 A. Wheeler, E. Robinson, and G. Robinson, 'Admissions to Acute Psychiatric Inpatient Services in Auckland, New Zealand: A Demographic and Diagnostic Review', *New Zealand Medical Journal* 118 (2005): 38.

in the ward. I remember the loneliness each one of us had wrapped around us like a blanket. Yet I believe with all my heart that Jesus is a friend to the broken.

It is difficult to befriend a person who doesn't speak sense, who may not even notice your existence while you sit with them, and who can act in a way that seems barely human sometimes. Yet Jesus is a friend to *these* broken. Often these people who hear and see things very differently from us do not suffer because of their own psychosis. They suffer at the hands of people who tell them that they are abnormal, strange, ill, and crazy. They suffer from the side effects of medication and from the isolation and loneliness. They suffer from feelings of guilt as they are told how much of a burden they are. They suffer because of *us*.

I know a couple who met in the psych ward, fell in love, and, against the wishes of their families, got married. Everyone expected them to spiral out of control mentally and end up back in the state's care. To everyone's surprise, they found a house, moved in, and, when I met them, had been happily married for ten years. Their love and care for each other meant that they reminded each other to take medication and see the doctor. The most profound thing the wife said to me was, 'He makes me feel human, he doesn't care about my labels.' They had discovered in each other a person who saw and loved the intrinsic value that the other contained in *simply being human*. It was through this love and acceptance that they were able to move back into the wider community and form relationships there. Their mental illnesses didn't disappear or even get much better, but in being treated as *human* rather than as an *illness* they have been able to find wholeness and healing. It was in their example that I saw a vision of what the church could be.

Loving the broken is more than praying for their cure. It is more than listening to their stories. It is more than asking questions about experiences. It is teaching the church as a whole to view people as human rather than as broken. To value the humanness of a person is to see past the brokenness, the medical labels, the sad stories, the strange behaviour, and to see the heart of a person who longs only to be treated as worthy of attention. It is treating people like they *belong* rather than to merely include them. It is to participate in Jesus' continuing mission to all who are difficult to relate to, and it is understanding and welcoming them back into a community where they belong.

In my experience I have seen this love of my humanness a handful of times. I saw it in my next-door neighbour who would come over for coffee every day and sit and listen to me ramble, help me clean my house, tell me off if I did something silly, and give me advice on my struggles. I saw it in a fellow student who discovered that I had difficulty in picking up social cues and developed a system of signals to tell me when I was doing something wrong. I saw it in one of my lecturers who let me break down in his office when things were getting on top of me. I saw it in my new parents-in-law who accepted my history and embraced me for it. I see it every day in the love my husband shows to me and his acceptance of my many continuing emotional issues. These people listened, heard the issues, accepted them, and worked with me rather than trying to change things. For me, they are the church being lived out.

I still don't know how this love for the humanness of people works in churches. There is not a simple five-step programme about reintegrating the mentally ill back into the congregation. However, in a country where at least one million people will be diagnosed with a mental illness at some point in their lives, there needs to be a beginning of a conversation. And it is a conversation that *includes* those whom it is about. They may be unwell, but they will be very aware of what they feel is missing, what they do not like, and how they want to be treated. We need to start asking ourselves and our congregations some deep, searching questions about how we treat the mentally ill, and start listening to the answers from those who live with these illnesses.

I would love to say I am totally free of all mental illness. I am not. I still suffer from chronic anxiety issues, depressive episodes, and intense migraines (which I have been told may be a side effect from my years of taking medication). I have had to take time out of my study to deal with these issues, and I thank God daily for my husband, who is a steady rock in my life and reminds me to breathe slowly when I start to feel overwhelmed. I would also love to say that I now run a ministry within psych wards. To be honest, I have found the very idea of stepping back into that environment so terrifying that I have not been able to face it yet. I am scared that if I walk in the doors, I will never be allowed to leave again. It has been six years, but the scars on my heart are still healing. However, I do what I can to show people with mental illnesses that they are worth my time and effort.

A few years ago I spent an evening sitting with my next-door neighbours' mother after she arrived at their house while they were out. I found her yelling at the fence after not taking her medication for three days. I sat with her all night as she told me about the things only she could see. In that seemingly meaningless rambling I heard her fear of being alone and her joy at being able to talk to others and share what she was seeing. I saw her love for me as she told me I was smarter than Einstein and had the faith and feet of Aborigines in the desert. I heard her concern for me as she asked me about my imagined Māori husband 'Steve' and why he was angry at me. She talked about things that weren't physically true, but in it she cared and she loved in the only way she was capable. I loved her back by simply listening. I do not know if my actions made an impact on her or if she even realized who I was, or if I even really existed. However, I remain in contact with her daughter and her daughter's partner, who have embraced the good news that the love of God shown in Jesus Christ embraces them and their broken mother.

Our congregations should have people with mental illness in them. That churches often do not have people with mental illness in them reflects the fact that we have not questioned the way we practise church. What would it look like to have mental health patients not just tolerated in our worship meetings, but celebrated and embraced as family? What does it mean to learn from the broken, rather than to teach them? What would it look like to seek friendship with the friendless, not to appease our need to act charitably, but because they are human and have something to offer? What would it look like, as Swinton suggests (Chapter 14), to stop acting as the host or hostess, and instead *receive* hospitality from people with mental health issues? What does it mean to act towards the least of these as we would Jesus? People with mental illness are a gift to the church, and allow the church the opportunity to once again render its life to the contours of God's extravagant love that is revealed in Jesus Christ.

9 Disability in the Australian Church

Results from the 2011 Church Life Survey

Jason Forbes and Lindsey Gale

Gail[1] backs down the driveway, waves goodbye to her family, and heads to Sunday morning mass. She and her husband take church-going in turns – their two boys have autism, and don't manage the environment of church well.

'When there's sensory overload, one of them clings to me, and the other one bolts,' Gail explains. 'I can't manage them both, and if they're with me, none of us get much from the service. It's easier to take it in turns, though it makes me sad. I don't think my church even knows I'm married, let alone that I have two children.'

Introduction

In 2011 the fifth Australian National Church Life Survey (NCLS) was conducted – a five-yearly co-operative church venture, begun in 1991, that tracks the life and health of Australian churches.[2] It consists of a suite of surveys conducted in the same year as the National Census, engaging hundreds of thousands of attendees in 7,000 churches and 22 Christian denominations – the largest survey of its type in the world.

For the 2011 survey CBM Australia[3] commissioned a set of five questions to uncover the presence of disability in the church, and the extent and quality of church accessibility and inclusiveness. These disability questions were placed into two different national poll surveys, and distributed randomly among all survey participants to ensure maximum representativeness throughout the total sample.[4] The two surveys in question were the Attender Survey for church attendees and the Operations Survey for church leaders.[5]

---

1 Name changed.
2 See NCLS Research: http://www.ncls.org.au.
3 CBM Australia is an international Christian development non-governmental organization working to end the cycle of poverty and disability in the world's poorest countries. See http://www.cbm.org.au.
4 The size of the random sample was almost 1,500, ensuring high reliability rates, similar to those in national polls used to estimate election outcomes. In addition to this, the known sizes of denominations and regions were used to weight national results, and compensate for the variation in participation by denominations in the national survey. In addition to the random sampling and high sample size, such weighting gives a truer representation of actual national figures.
5 See Appendices 1 and 2.

Analysis of this data has yielded interesting and useful results, which this chapter will unpack and reflect upon, including offering suggestions for improving and extending subsequent surveys. In addition, it will highlight features of a biblically informed and practical response to the issue of disability inclusion in the church, using the insights and proposals of a 2012 paper by Jason Forbes, 'The Work of the Holy Spirit in a Person with a Disability and Their Relationship with the Church'.[6] Bringing these two sets of insights together, this chapter proposes to cover the following: first, a comparison of biblical and current understandings of disability, as the context for discussion of the NCLS results relating to the presence of disability in the church; second, biblical input on the nature of the church and the ways Christ by his Spirit creates and sustains his church, as context for discussing the NCLS results relating to church access, and finally, an exploration of the indispensability of the 'seemingly weaker members' in the body of Christ, as the context for discussion of the NCLS results for the most effective means to bring about inclusion.

A Comparison of Biblical and Contemporary Understandings of Disability as Context for Discussing the NCLS Results about Presence of Disability in the Church

The Current Definition

According to the Convention on the Rights of Persons with Disabilities, disabilities are 'long-term physical, mental (psychiatric), intellectual or sensory impairments, which, in interaction with various barriers, hinder full and effective participation in society on an equal basis with others'.[7] This definition captures the interplay of factors within and external to the person that makes up disability, and is consistent with, while extending, the current impairment-focused Australian definition:

> a sensory, physical, intellectual or neurological impairment, or developmental delay or acquired brain injury, or any combination thereof, which is, or is likely to be, permanent; and causes a substantially reduced capacity in at least one of the areas of self-care, self-management, mobility or

---

6 Jason P. Forbes, 'The Work of the Holy Spirit in a Person with a Disability and Their Relationship with the Church', (Sydney: Presbyterian Theological Centre, 2012). Forbes is an ordained Presbyterian minister with cerebral palsy, and this was the final paper for his theological degree.
7 Quotation in William C. Simpson, Jr., 'John Wesley and Pentecostal power', *Living Pulpit* 13 (2004): 5. Full text: *Convention on the Rights of Persons with Disabilities and Optional Protocol* [accessed 12 November 2015]. Online: http://www.un.org/disabilities/documents/convention/convoptprot-e.pdf.

communication; and requires significant ongoing or long term episodic support; and is not related to ageing.[8]

The NCLS questions made use of both of these definitions.[9]

Biblical Perspectives on Disability

In the Old Testament mention is made of blindness, muteness, lameness, and deafness (Exod 4:11; Lev 19:14; 21:18.), yet there is no overarching term similar to the modern concept of disability. The terms used can refer to experiences other than disability, such as poverty and injustice, and disability appears alongside these other disadvantaged groups (Lev 19:11–16).

In the New Testament a similar fluidity can be observed, with no definitive term matching the modern concept. Of the terms used to mean 'disabled' and 'crippled', of particular importance is the term 'weakness' (*asthenia*), which in the context of Paul's letters to the Corinthians simply means weakness in terms of one's social status, and does not necessarily carry any notion of physical or intellectual impairment (1 Cor 1:27; 12:22; 2 Cor 12:9–10).

Comparison

Our culture's answer to the question 'What are people for?' is typically given the reply: 'for autonomy and control, health and beauty, and performance and productivity'. 'Core activities of life' are the capacities that enable those goals. It is no surprise, therefore, that our definition of disability prioritizes and makes problematical the lack of 'self-care, self-management, mobility and communication'. In the Bible independence is not paramount, and 'core activities of life' are defined in relation to God. Specifically, there are three main dynamics of Christian living: worship and prayer, living and learning in community, and ministry: speech, action, and suffering for justice, peace, goodness, and truth.[10]

---

8 Australian Disability Discrimination Act, 2006 [accessed 10 June 2013]. Online: http://www.dhs.vic.gov.au/__data/assets/pdf_file/0004/598711/disabilityact2006_guideforserviceproviders_pdf_081106.pdf.

9 The church leaders Operations Survey focus was on the expression 'various barriers' in the United Nations definition, specifically asking about provisions in place to overcome barriers. For the Attender Survey, the definition enabled people with a disability within the congregation to self-identify according to the accepted types of 'long-term physical, mental (psychiatric), intellectual or sensory impairments'. People were to tick all that applied. Personal impact was defined in relation to independence and degree of support need. The focus was on measurable requirements for support in core life tasks.

10 David Ford, *Self and Salvation: Being Transformed* (Cambridge: Cambridge University Press, 1999), 5.

A radically different group of people are disabled according to this definition. In addition, biblically, disability is part of a wider grouping of marginalized people that includes strangers, foreigners and dependent aliens. These are to be welcomed and shown hospitality in a spirit of identification, for they represent 'the true soul of the Israelite' and 'what all Christians are in the world' – citizens of heaven, foreigners, scattered across the Earth as sojourners, journeying homeward, but on Earth never fully at home (1 Peter 1:17).[11]

The modern concept has in common with the Bible that disability includes experiences of social stigma. Considering disability from this point of view helps us bring the two worlds together, and enables us to critique charity motivations in the church that fall short of the spirit of identification characterizing the biblical picture.

In 2 Cor 5 Paul no longer regards anyone from a worldly point of view (v. 16). Anyone who is in Christ is to be regarded as a 'new creation' (v. 17). Just as the scandal and shame of crucifixion becomes the symbol of hope for the believer, so the believer's view of others ought to be radically transformed. We are not to regard others by externals (literally 'the face'; Gk: *prosōpon*, v. 12), but according to the dignity of being equally beloved members of God's family. With that leveller in mind, we turn to the results of the NCLS to see whether the externals of disability are jeopardizing participation in the body of Christ (see Figure 9.1).

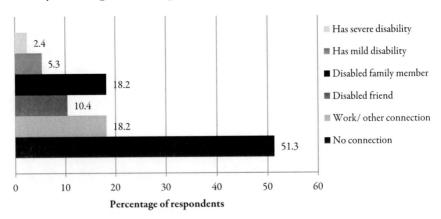

Figure 9.1 NCLS 2011 findings

Source: Author.

11 Frances M. Young, *Face to Face: A Narrative Essay in the Theology of Suffering* (Edinburgh: T&T Clark, 1990), 184.

General Findings

According to the survey, the Australian church has less than half the proportion of people with a disability compared the population as a whole – 7.7 per cent, compared to 18.5 per cent (see Figure 9.2).[12]

However, since the NCLS form is not yet accessible to people with print disabilities, this figure is likely an underestimate of the number of people with a disability in church. It may, however, illustrate their marginalization – that there is at least an 8 per cent representation, but because of various barriers the presence is less obvious.

Denominational Breakdown

The NCLS has provided further analysis of the data at a denominational level, showing a low in the Pentecostal church of just above 0 per cent, to 10 per cent amongst Anglicans and Catholics (see Figure 9.3).

There are possible reasons why the Pentecostal denomination scores lower: a younger demographic statistically includes fewer people with disabilities; teaching on physical healing as a sign of God's blessing may be problematic; acquiring a disability may critique prior theological views and cause a person to leave; a church focus on physical healing may be wearing to people who are untroubled by their disability and want to move on from a focus on it.

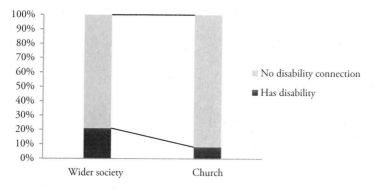

Figure 9.2 Disability in church and society
Source: Author.

12 There are no statistics of prevalence under age 15, as the NCLS is only beginning to survey this age group, but it is significant that profound/severe disability does not figure at all in the 15–29 age group of the NCLS, and the presence of young people with mild disability is only 2 per cent. In the wider society 9 per cent of children aged 5–14 have a disability, and 7.5 per cent of those aged 15–29. Disability in this age group in the church is a quarter of what it is in the wider society. Clearly, absence at church of families with children with significant disability should register as a concern.

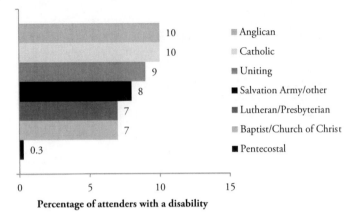

Figure 9.3 Disability in the denominations
Source: Author.

Family Members

'Secondary consumers' – parents, grandparents, children, and siblings – need to be included in the number of people impacted by disability. Of the almost 1 in 5 Australians living with disability, four million are personally affected, and (conservatively) 600,000 family members provide their daily and often lifelong care. A 2007 Australian survey of the well-being of caregivers in Australia found that it is the lowest of any group, with 56 per cent being depressed, compared to 6 per cent of the general population. Siblings, who will have the longest relationship with the person with a disability, also can find life additionally complicated by their own unmet needs.[13]

In the church, families living with disability are more prevalent than in the wider society – while they make up 8 per cent of society, they make up 18 per cent of the church (see Figure 9.4).

Presumably, church life, with its major focus on care and compassion, provides good affirmation and support to people involved in the long-term care of family members with a disability, and this would facilitate their attendance. It is likely this figure also indicates that the number of people with a disability in the church is higher than 8 per cent. We know of situations where family members filled in one form stating their connection to disability, but not a separate form for their family member, therefore this statistic may be a more reliable indication of prevalence than the number of people with a disability who self-identified.[14]

---

13 Siblings Australia Inc.: http://www.siblingsaustralia.org.au.
14 Other helpful information might include type of disability, age, and relationship to the respondent.

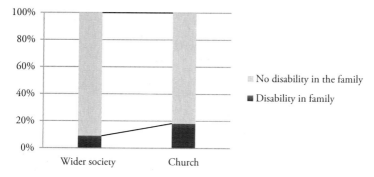

Figure 9.4 Families living with disability in church and society
Source: Author.

Workers/volunteers in the Disability Sector

In relation to the number working or volunteering in the disability sector, the findings are more pronounced again. In the wider society the figure is 2–6 per cent, whereas in the church the proportion is again around 18 per cent (see Figure 9.5).[15]

We can conclude that we have a group of people knowledgeable about disability in the church, and this should encourage church pastors to provide input on the topic of disability, as it is both a prevalent theme in the Bible and an experience to which many in the church are connected. Pastors should also develop an understanding of their congregation members' work connections to disability, to help them explore how they might use these connections and capacities to increase the disability-inclusiveness of the church.[16]

---

15 In 2006 548,384 people were employed in health occupations, comprising 6 per cent of all employed persons in Australia; see '2006 Census of Population and Housing – Fact Sheets, 2006' [accessed 24 November 2015]. Online: http://www.abs.gov.au/AUSSTATS/abs@.nsf/DetailsPage/2914.0 2006?OpenDocument. For a more detailed examination of disability services, see Bill Martin and Josh Healy, 'Who Works in Community Services? A Profile of Australian Workforces in Child Protection, Juvenile Justice, Disability Services and General Community Services' (National Institute of Labour Studies, Flinders University, Adelaide, August 2010), 109–22 [accessed 24 November 2015]. Online: http://www.flinders.edu.au/sabs/nils-files/reports/2010%20CDSMAC%20 Final%20Report.pdf.

16 'It is not too much to ask a gifted professional to extend his or her knowledge to working for the love and acceptance of individuals with disabilities within his or her own church. If the professional who knows and understands people with disabilities will not recruit them, bring them into the church and support and be with them, then who will?'; Jeff McNair and Abigail Schindler, 'A Secular Case for Religious Inclusion', in *Disability and Religious Diversity: Cross-cultural and Interreligious Perspectives*, ed. Darla Schumm and Michael Stoltzfus (New York: Palgrave Macmillan, 2011), 23.

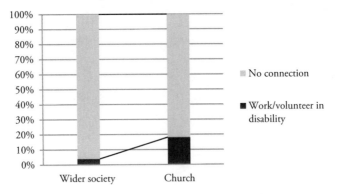

Figure 9.5 People working/volunteering in the disability sector
Source: Author.

Friendship

'Friendship is essential to quality of life.'[17] People with intellectual disability rarely have friendships outside services and professionals and reliance on volunteers. Friendships of people with intellectual disability with people without disability are 'unlikely alliances'.[18] Most friendships are with members of the mother's networks, 85 per cent being with women.[19] People with a disability in general can experience negative judgements and avoidance because of the way they look, and curiosity contributes to stigma. The irony is that while friendship reduces prejudice, prejudice is preventing the formation of friendships.[20] Therefore, the fact that in the NCLS 10 per cent of church attendees nominated a connection with disability through friendship is potentially significant and worth exploring. Who is nominating this? What do respondents mean by 'friendship'? Are these relationships predominantly with women from the mother's network? Are they reciprocal?

Finally, a study of successful long-term friendships between persons with and without an intellectual disability in L'Arche communities highlighted the

---

17 Peggy Hutchison, 'A Qualitative Study of the Friendships of People with Disabilities' (Kitchener, Ontario: Centre for Research and Education in Human Services, 1990) [accessed 26 August 2012]. Online: http://lin.ca/sites/default/files/attachments/CCLR6-12.pdf.
18 Zana Marie Lutfiyya, *Affectionate Bonds: What We Can Learn by Listening to Friends* (Syracuse, NY: Center on Human Policy, 1990) [accessed 12 November 2015]. Online: http://files.eric.ed.gov/fulltext/ED336923.pdf; John Sumarah, *Personal Relationships and Social Networks: Facilitating the Participation of Individuals with Disabilities in Community Life* (Syracuse, NY: Center on Human Policy, 1991); Colin Pottie and John Sumarah, 'Friendships Between Persons With and Without Developmental Disabilities', *Mental Retardation* 42 (2004): 55–66.
19 Wendy Taormina-Weiss, 'Literature, Gender, Disability and Friendship', *Disabled World* (2012) [accessed 2 September 2013]. Online: http://www.disabled-world.com/editorials/friends.php.
20 Mark Deal, 'Disabled People's Attitudes Toward Other Impairment Groups: A Hierarchy of Impairments', *Disability & Society* 18 (2003): 897–910.

importance to long-term friendship of maintenance behaviours, and that it was often the person with the intellectual disability who did this best – telephoning, extending dinner invitations, praying for the other, asking assistance, remembering important occasions, and offering support.[21] Such friendship-tending behaviour is vital to the relational well-being of church congregations, and highlights an asset of disability in community.

The NCLS Results and Church Access

'[F]rom the beginning to the end of the world, and from among the whole human race, the Son of God, by his Spirit and his Word, gathers, protects and preserves for himself, in the unity of the true faith, a congregation chosen for eternal life.'[22] So states the Heidelberg Catechism. It is Jesus Christ who by prophetic revelation, priestly reconciliation, and kingly rule brings the church into being, restores it to fellowship with God, and keeps it under God's governance. In the Old and New Testaments it is his Holy Spirit who establishes and sustains God's community and empowers people for the benefit of the community.[23] To sustain the community of Israel in the Old Testament, the Holy Spirit enabled people to do extraordinary work (Exod 31:3; Deut 34:9; Num 24:2–9; Judges 3:10; 14:19; 15:14; 1 Sam 1:10; 16:13; 2 Chr 20:14–17, 24:20–22). Similarly, the church is formed by the Holy Spirit (Acts 2:4, 38), who is involved in the empowerment of individuals by giving spiritual gifts (Rom 12:6–8; 1 Cor 12:7–11). 'Christ uses the ministry of men to declare openly his will ... as a sort of delegated work ... "Christ ascended on high, and gave gifts to men, that he might fill all things."'[24]

The gifts Christ gives his church by his Spirit are 'events of relation' rather than 'manipulable possessions'.[25] Church history remains an 'account of the history of Christ's acts',[26] and life by the Spirit an empowering by Christ, which cannot be frustrated, including by impairment. This is true in relation to the main forms by which faith is created and sustained.

The Work of the Holy Spirit in the Creation of Faith

The preaching and comprehension of the Word are identified by Scripture as the way people come to faith, as seen, for example, in the following: 'Faith

---

21 Pottie and Sumarah, 'Friendships Between Persons With and Without Developmental Disabilities'.
22 'Heidelberg Catechism', answer to question 52 [accessed 26 October 2013]. Online: https://www.ccel.org/creeds/heidelberg-cat.html.
23 Wayne A. Grudem, *Systematic Theology: An Introduction to Biblical Doctrine* (Leicester: InterVarsity Press; Grand Rapids, MI: Zondervan, 1994), 867–8.
24 John Calvin, *Institutes of the Christian Religion*, Library of Christian Classics, vol. 21, ed. John T. McNeill, trans. Ford Lewis Battles (Philadelphia, PA: Westminster Press, 1960), 4.3.1., 1,053–4.
25 John B. Webster, *Word and Church: Essays in Christian Dogmatics* (Edinburgh: T&T Clark, 2001), 199.
26 Jürgen Moltmann, *The Church in the Power of the Spirit: A Contribution to Messianic Ecclesiology* (Minneapolis, MN: SCM Press, 1992), 69.

comes from hearing, and hearing through the word of Christ' (Rom 10:13–14, 17; cf. Eph 1:13; Col 1:5–7; 1 Thess 2:13; 2 Tim 2:1–2; Heb 2:1; 1 John 1:3, 24). This is due to the centrality and exclusivity of the person and work of Jesus in salvation, which must be available to all believers if the gospel is genuine.

Orthodox confessions of faith assume both that the act of effectual calling is the 'outward proclamation and presentation of the gospel' and that the elect include people who are 'incapable of being called by the outward preaching of the Word'.[27] This invites inquiry: how is the gospel received by people incapable of being called by the preaching of the Word?

A presumption that a certain level of cognitive ability is required to enjoy regenerative grace runs counter both to the reality of God's gracious provision for every need in Christ and to contemporary experiences of communicating the gospel to people with intellectual disability.[28] A closer inspection of the Bible reveals that the verbal proclamation of the Word is only part of the witness to the gospel, which is to be complemented by the conduct of believers.[29] So while a person may not be able to respond to the verbal proclamation of the Word, the ongoing witness to that Word through the conduct of believers (Rom 11:11; 1 Cor 7:14, 16; 1 Peter 2:12; 3:1–2) and the person's participation in the believing community are also means by which the Holy Spirit creates faith.

The Work of the Holy Spirit in Sustaining Faith

The work of the Holy Spirit continues to grow believers into the image of Christ, using several chief means (John 17:17; Rom 8:29)[30] which are not only readily applicable, but necessary for the spiritual nourishment of believers with intellectual impairment also.

Word

Sanctification needs to be founded on the Word.[31] Paul commends the Ephesian elders to the Word that they may accept and obey it, be built up in faith and love, and have assurance of sanctification (Acts 20:32).

There is a common assumption that people with intellectual disability either cannot learn about faith or have such different learning needs that these must be accommodated in separate groups. Rather, on the basis of the diversity of the

---

27 Robert L. Reymond, *A New Systematic Theology of the Christian Faith* (Nashville, TN: Thomas Nelson, 1998), 713.
28 Lewis B. Smedes, 'Can God Reach the Mentally Disabled?', *Christianity Today* 45 (2001) [accessed 13 March 2013]. Online: http://www.christianitytoday.com/ct/2001/march5/31.94.html.
29 Grudem, *Systematic Theology*, 867–8.
30 Reymond, *A New Systematic Theology*, 780.
31 Leon Morris, *The Gospel According to John*, New International Commentary on the New Testament (Grand Rapids, MI: Eerdmans, 1995), 647; Andreas J. Kostenberger, *John*, Baker Exegetical Commentary on the New Testament (Grand Rapids, MI: Baker Academic, 2004), 495–6; F.F. Bruce, *The Book of the Acts* (Grand Rapids, MI: Eerdmans, 1988), 394.

body of Christ, and because the core business of the church is faith development that is not exclusively knowledge-based, the church should be a model of 'Universal Design'.

The six principles of Universal Design in Learning provide 'a commonsense [sic] approach to making everything usable by everyone to the greatest extent possible',[32] and the benefits of utilizing these are clearly seen in their creation of learning environments where: (1) diversity is celebrated, (2) the teaching utilizes a variety of different styles,[33] (3) there is a clear main point and life application, (4) a gracious, relaxed atmosphere encourages deep questions and thought, (5) we are encouraged to discuss and ask questions as part of our learning, and (6) we are expected to think hard and stretch as we grow in our understanding of God.

Sacraments

Sacraments are outward signs of spiritual realities – 'communication aids' of the gospel, which should not be denied to any believer out of concern that they cannot comprehend their meaning, but rather seen as having the potential to aid understanding. This doesn't mean discernment is not needed, but that individual intellectual understanding should not be the criterion governing who participates in the sacraments and who does not.[34]

Prayer

Prayer is an act of faith, a surrendering to God in all things. The act of making requests known to God acknowledges a person's total dependence upon him.[35] In fact, a person's impairment can increase awareness of their dependency on God, and contribute to a strong prayer life and the capacity to intercede faithfully for others.

Fellowship

Christian fellowship refers to our gathering together to receive from Christ through Word, sacrament, and prayer.[36] This is how we help one another draw near and stay near to God (Eph 4:25, 32; 1 John 1:3; Heb 10:24). Fellowship

---

32 'Principles of Universal Design', *Institute for Human Centered Design* [accessed 12 June 2014]. Online: http://www.humancentereddesign.org/universal-design/principles-universal-design.
33 Through creatively engaging 'multiple intelligences', all kinds of learners can learn. See Special Touch Ministry, *Compel Them to Come In: Reaching People with Disabilities Through the Local Church* (Bloomington, IN: AuthorHouse, 2010), 58; John D. Bransford et al., eds., *How People Learn: Brain, Mind, Experience, and School: Expanded Edition* (Washington DC: National Academy Press, 2000), 101; G. Reid, *Learning Styles and Inclusion* (London: Sage, 2005), 115.
34 Grudem, *Systematic Theology*, 996.
35 Peter T. O'Brien, *The Epistle to the Philippians: A Commentary on the Greek Text* (Grand Rapids, MI: Eerdmans, 1991), 439.
36 From the beginnings of the New Testament church the gathering of believers has involved teaching, observance of the Lord's Supper, and prayer (Acts 2:42).

has an inseparable vertical and horizontal dimension, involving dependence on God and mutual interdependence with one another as we share life together. Two reasons why our churches are often lacking in true fellowship are our commitment to self-sufficiency and our tendency to exclude those who are unlike us, or who lack the gifts we value.[37] In considering this lack of fellowship we can see one possible reason why Jesus does not consider his body complete or healthy without the inclusion of people with disabilities (Luke 14:23).

In addition, interdependence that includes people with a disability speaks of more than a one-way relationship, but of a mutual working together for the sake of the health and unity of the body. This unity is paramount for Paul, and undergirds his use of body imagery for the church. The point to note in his letters to the Corinthians is that it is precisely through the active inclusion of the 'seemingly weaker' members that unity is achieved – 'unity in the church [is] preserved precisely through protecting the existence of the weak'.[38]

NCLS 2011 Findings

Having seen how Scripture allows us to speak of disability as one of a number of 'seeming weaknesses' and how that is integral to the unity of the church, we turn to the NCLS results to further discuss how accessible the church is to those with a disability.

Accessibility of buildings, activities and cultural 'space'

Churches are doing well in terms of major physical facilities (ramps, parking spaces, and toilets), reasonably well with minor physical facilities (hearing loops, large-print alternatives, and alternative seating arrangements), but significantly less well in terms of adapting programmes to needs and achieving an active culture of inclusion (see Figure 9.6). A not insignificant 11 per cent of churches do none of these.

Church statement

In relation to the presence of a public statement on inclusion, 18 per cent of churches provide this – around half as part of their denomination (see Figure 9.7).

---

37 Churches are among the places where we can make cross-cutting ties outside our social sphere. According to Deepan Naryan of the World Bank, a key factor of social capital is ties between people who are different; across generation, gender, ethnicity, ability, education, and so on. This is one of the real strengths of the church. P. Hughes, A. Black, and P. Kaldor, *Building Stronger Communities* (Sydney: University of New South Wales Press, 2007), 43.

38 John K. Chow, *Patronage and Power: A Study of Social Networks in Corinth*, Journal for the Study of the New Testament Supplement Series 75 (Sheffield: Sheffield Academic Press, 1992), 478–9.

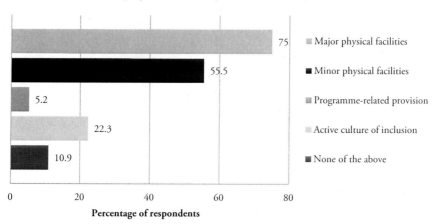

Figure 9.6 Achieving an active culture of disability inclusion in churches
Source: Author.

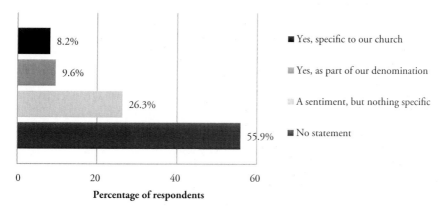

Figure 9.7 Public church statements on disability inclusion
Source: Author.

Church education

The availability of education on disability inclusion to church staff and volunteers is an unusual thought for most congregations. Of the 14 per cent who provide some sort of education, most do so at a denominational level rather than specific to the needs of the congregation.

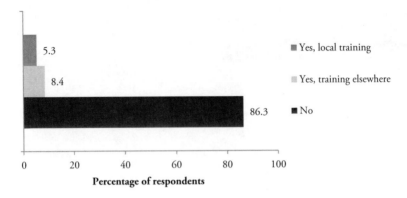

Figure 9.8 Congregational education on disability inclusion
Source: Author.

Overall performance

Responses are summarized in Figure 9.9. Denominationally, all churches are very similar.[39]

Apart from having in place the main infrastructure provisions required by law, more work needs to be done, particularly in relation to developing a welcoming culture, an intentional commitment, provision of relevant education, and programme responsiveness that accommodates for different needs. The need for education is particularly important, given the current perceptions of attendees as to how well the church is currently doing (see Figure 9.10).[40]

One result that needs to change is the level of approval for the way things currently are. Perhaps the process of education about inclusion will result first in informed dissatisfaction that then becomes proactive for change. Certainly, it would be good to change things for the 5 per cent who say the church is not adequate, but who have not left it.

---

39 The expression 'culture of inclusion' relates to the welcoming nature of the teaching and practices of the church, and is similar to 'hospitality'. In the Old and New Testaments we are called to welcome the stranger as we have been welcomed by God, which is stronger than simply recognizing equal right to the space; we recognize that we are the same, that we need each other, and that we are all the poorer without each other.

40 We expected there would be differences in the responses from people with a disability about the accessibility of the church, and that they would be more aware of inadequacies and oversights. In fact, responses were similar. It is important to note this similar finding, to counter the tendency of research to focus on differences between people with and without disabilities in order to publish noteworthy findings which serve to mask the extent of similarities between the two.

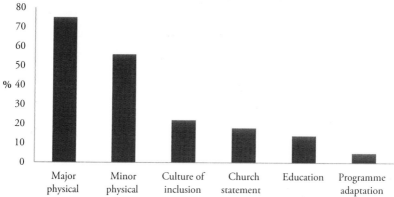

Figure 9.9 Overall performance of church accessibility
Source: Author.

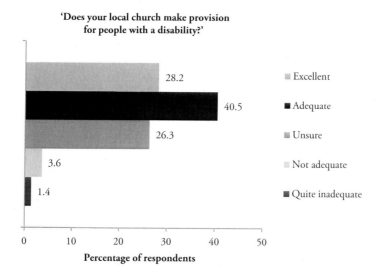

Figure 9.10 Perception of attendees regarding church performance on disability inclusion
Source: Author.

The NCLS, the 'Seemingly Weaker Members' in the Body of Christ, and Inclusion

Strength and Weakness in the Body of Christ According to 1 and 2 Corinthians

In 1 Cor 12 Paul identifies the church as the body of Christ, made up by different members with different abilities, and takes issue with the culture of status and self-promotion,[41] whereby preference was being given to those claiming 'super-spiritual experiences' of ecstatic phenomena as most perfectly displaying God's divine power, and therefore most necessary to the church. Paul counters that it is actually the weaker members who are indispensable (v. 22). To perceive who these weaker members were, and why they were indispensable, Paul's meaning of 'weak' needs to be understood, along with Paul's perception of the role weakness had in his own life.

In 1 Cor 12:27 Paul identifies the 'weak' as having been chosen by God. These were those lacking wisdom, power, or nobility – attributes important for establishing the socioeconomic divisions and status quo of the Corinthian community (1 Cor 3:3; 11:27–34).[42] Without recognized status, these believers were regarded as unnecessary and excluded from full participation (1 Cor 12:21–3; 11:18–21). When Paul speaks of 'weakness' in the Corinthian context, it is this group of low-status people to whom he is referring.

The reason for Paul's regard for these 'weaker members' comes from his own experience, where God's power became reality in the midst of weakness (2 Cor 11:23–33; 12:9).[43] This was the antithesis of the triumphalism of the Corinthian Christians, who were embarrassed by the weakness that Paul's experiences represented (1 Cor 4:8; 6:1–7). Paul's discovery was that personal weakness promoted God's grace and power – 'grace apprehended in the awareness of our weakness'[44] – thus he came to see weakness as essential for fulfilling apostolic service, and the only 'capacity' worthy of boasting (1 Cor 15:10; 2 Cor 4:7; 6:7; 13:4).[45] In this he saw a parallel between Christ's weakness and the demonstration of God's power, and his own, as Black paraphrases: 'My weakness is Christ's weakness, the only legitimate representation of the crucified Messiah and his gospel, the assurance that God is now manifesting his Son in and through my life, and the promise that one day I will fully participate in the resurrection's glory, power and incorruptibility.'[46]

As previously stated by Black, 'the limitation of our human existence is the necessary presupposition for the operation of the power of God, which is made perfect in weakness'.[47] This is why weaker members are 'indispensable' to the body (1 Cor 12:22). Being 'indispensable' denotes 'necessity' in a given situation.[48] Even though these believers appear not to be providing weight or power in

---

41 Anthony C. Thiselton, *The First Epistle to the Corinthians: A Commentary on the Greek Text* (Grand Rapids, MI: Eerdmans, 2000), 12–13.
42 Gordon D. Fee, *The First Epistle to the Corinthians* (Grand Rapids, MI: Eerdmans, 1987), 5.
43 Paul W. Barnett, *The Second Epistle to the Corinthians* (Grand Rapids, MI: Eerdmans, 1997), 275.
44 Paul W. Barnett, *The Message of 2 Corinthians* (Leicester: InterVarsity Press, 1988), 179.
45 Murray J. Harris, *The Second Epistle to the Corinthians: A Commentary on the Greek Text* (Grand Rapids: Eerdmans, 2005), 864.
46 David A. Black, *Paul, Apostle of Weakness: Astheneia and Its Cognates in the Pauline Literature*, rev. edn (Eugene, OR: Pickwick Publications, 2012), 86.
47 Ibid., 82.
48 Walter Grundmann, 'ἀναγκάζω, ἀναγκαῖος, ἀνάγκη', in *Theological Dictionary of the New Testament*, vol. 1, ed. Gerhard Kittel, Geoffrey W. Bromiley, and Gerhard Friedrich (Grand Rapids, MI: Eerdmans, 1964), 344–7.

the church's mission, they are in fact an essential part.[49] This being true, a response is required contrary to that being expressed: namely, that the honour and respect being paid to the more 'gifted' is to be given to those lacking these attributes, and to a greater measure. 'It is the weak who are needy, and know of their need, who make up the essence of the church, rather than those "on display".'[50] One practical outcome of this is members sharing one another's joys and sorrows rather than seeking ways of promoting their own position. In ways such as this – precisely through including the weaker members – the unity of the church is preserved.[51]

Thus the inclusion of people with disabilities is not an optional extra, but integral to the identity and mission of the church. As we come to our third set of NCLS findings, we find resonances to this insight of Paul's.

Strengths in Disability According to the NCLS

The NCLS asks all attendees questions about their faith, two regarding frequency of church attendance and private devotional practice. These are general questions, so we commissioned the NCLS to uncover the experiences of people with a disability within the overall responses. In the process of this we discovered some interesting results that shed further light on the gift of disability to the church (see Figures 9.11 and 9.12).

While the finding is clearer in relation to family members than people with a disability themselves, there is evidence that those with a personal connection to disability are more regular in church attendance and in the regularity

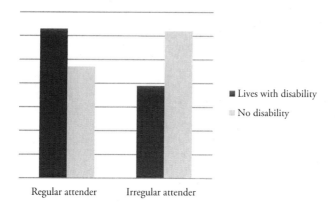

Figure 9.11 Frequency of church attendance for people who live with disabilities compared to people with no disability

Source: Author.

---

49 Thiselton, *The First Epistle to the Corinthians*, 1,007.
50 Ibid., 1,009.
51 Chow, *Patronage and Power*, 178–9.

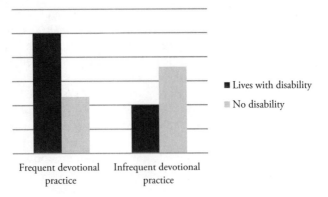

Figure 9.12 Frequency of devotional practice for people who live with disabilities compared to people with no disability

Source: Author.

of their private devotional life than those with no such connection. Possible reasons for this include: people cling to God more when in need; suffering drives people to God with their questions; more time is available to devote to prayer and church, and desire and need for meeting together would result in greater frequency.

Thus, in our congregations there are people living with disability who have gained maturity in their faith and who can be sources of wise counsel for others who are also going through trials. These are people who know how to pray, and do so regularly, and so can intercede for others, and who have experienced God's comfort in the midst of difficulty, and so can encourage others, bringing to them the comfort they have first received from God (2 Cor 1:3–4; 13:11).

Further contributions to the well-being of the church come through the experiences and contributions of people with intellectual disability: embodying a 'true humanity' that is dependent upon God and interdependent with others, they can enable a 'movement towards a radically new value system'.[52] True spirituality is found in weakness, not in status, giftedness, or spiritual experiences; ignoring social barriers which keep people separated, they can capture something that Paul desired for the Corinthians: that they would care for one another regardless of social status (1 Cor 12:25–6).

We need to learn from this, and move from the idea of serving and helping people with a disability to ministry with and alongside members with a disability, drawing on the gifts of all. This is how the church is built up: when every member works together.

---

52 John Swinton, 'The Body of Christ Has Down's Syndrome: Theological Reflections on Vulnerability, Disability, and Graceful Communities', *Journal of Pastoral Theology* 13 (2003): 67.

Disability in the Australian Church 113

Qualities of Churches that Include People with a Disability Well

NCLS asks all churches for details of the ways they connect and serve within their local communities, including whether they provide support for people with a disability. Not many do, but of those, we were interested to know what features of accessibility were aiding this (see Figure 9.13).

What we found is that there is a correlation that is stronger with all aspects of access provision except for physical access. In other words, a church's physical accessibility, while important, does not commit it to reaching out to people in the community, and the presence of ramps and toilets, or even hearing loops and seating alternatives, do not distinguish disability-engaged churches from those with no such connection. Compliance with legislation is not the area where churches need to do the most work, or the first work necessarily, and it is certainly not where churches should stop, though we know that most do.

Far more important than the building are the other contributors to accessibility: a culture that says 'Welcome!' We must work to grow this statistic from its current 22 per cent. A welcoming culture is more than a smile and social chat on a Sunday, but needs to include commitments to building ongoing friendships and sharing burdens as they arise. Welcome that does not include sharing some of the burden is not likely to ring true. Second, including a biblically informed commitment to inclusion in the public mission statement of the church and putting it on the website is a great way to communicate this commitment to the wider community. This might seem unnecessary, but people with a disability access church websites before they turn up to a new church. In addition, we often we find that churches have a very uneven record in terms of inclusiveness – things fluctuate with changing ministers and congregation members. If there is a commitment in the mission statement, this is something they can talk about with each new

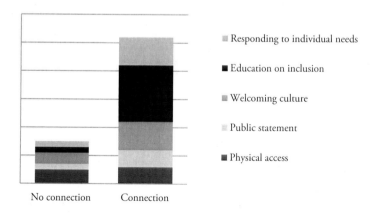

Figure 9.13 Churches that connect with disability
Source: Author.

minister that arrives, and the statement will help to keep them committed to the work of inclusion over the long haul. In some instances these statements begin with denominational commitments, such as the motions at church government levels, but the results show that these need to be translated into commitments at local level if we are going to see significant change.

A third contributor to accessibility is responsiveness to individual needs. Inclusion grows best one at a time, as this prevents the development of power imbalances where people believe they know best for others. Individual stories are also best at promoting the ideal of inclusion. Fourth, education that reduces attitudinal barriers is required, understanding that much experience of disability is constructed by poor attitudes and ignorance, and so is unnecessary and can be eliminated. We need to create meeting opportunities where the topic of disability surfaces and is explored. This has informed the Luke14 strategy, which seeks to provide education in the context of meeting. Luke14 events are always co-presented: people with and without a disability present and educate together. If people with a disability present alone, those without a disability will be confirmed in their view that disability is only for those personally affected. If people without a disability present alone, the education is theoretical, and a power imbalance can be confirmed: that people with a disability need help from altruistic others. Neither of these will bring about the change we are seeking.

Conclusions

We have seen how churches contribute to the ongoing marginalization of people with a disability by:

1. assuming disability is an optional issue for the church to focus on;
2. imitating the wider society in individualistic strivings for the externals of bodily perfection, self-actualization, and human recognition;
3. developing ministries characterized by charity motivations that fall short of identification and cast people in the role of eternal needy recipients;
4. regarding one another in terms of externals rather than who we are in Christ;
5. marginalizing people through barriers – whether physical or of communication or attitude;
6. focusing on present healing in such a way that people feel they are lesser Christians because they live with disability;
7. disability and health professionals leaving their skills at the door of the church;
8. allowing prejudice and ignorance to prevent friendships from forming;
9. pastors and leaders assuming that a certain cognitive ability is required for faith or for participating in the sacraments;
10. removing people to separate groups in the mistaken belief that some needs are better met apart and that the church doesn't need everybody;

11 churches/home groups being characterized by uniformity which quashes inclusive culture;
12 church members not being provided with education to help break down attitudinal barriers;
13 failing to prioritize and proactively welcome and include people;
14 allowing 'family rules' about how things should be done to continue harmful practices;
15 boasting of personal strengths and elevating the more gifted;
16 restricting measures to focusing on physical access, and assuming anyone can come if they want to.

We have seen the strengths of disability in community as:

1 potential for greater wisdom and deepened faith borne from many experiences of clinging to God and finding him faithful;
2 greater commitment to church attendance and personal devotion;
3 compassion and empathy for the needs of others;
4 time availability and the capacity to focus and intercede for others;
5 comfortableness with needing help – not prizing independence;
6 ignoring and able to cross social barriers;
7 commitment to friendships and the ongoing actions that maintain them.

We recommend the following improvements and additions to the next survey:

1 In order to ensure that every church attendee with a disability has an opportunity to complete the survey, make available in alternative formats. These would include an Easy English version and digital formats accessible by screen reading software, similar to the provision of the Australian Bureau of Statistics, which provides people with a number to key in online to proceed through the form.
2 In recognition of the tendency to marginalize disability, develop questions to uncover this impact – for example: How accessible are the church pulpit and stage? How accessible are the homes where small groups are run? To what extent are people with a disability being included in leadership roles? What access do people with a disability have to discipling and training opportunities?
3 In order to ascertain possible causes for low numbers in church, develop a question in the Operations Survey asking for this detail; for example:

> In what ways has the issue of disability been addressed over the last year?
>
> a   presentation from church members about living with disability, or visit by outside speakers/groups;
> b   small group bible studies;
> c   sermon topic or series (church or church camp);

d   provision made for individual members to ensure their ability to access services/programmes;
   e   renovation of the church building to make it more accessible.

4 Elicit attitudes towards disability in the Attender Survey, for example by asking for true true/false responses to the following statements:
   a   Disability is an indicator of lack of blessing or God's disciplining.
   b   God wills all people to be healed and free from suffering and disability.
   c   Prayer for healing, when accompanied by faith, restores a person to health.
   d   People with intellectual disability are unable to learn spiritual truths within the congregation, and require a separate setting.

5 Inquire further as to the nature and types of friendships identified in the survey.

Appendix 1

Attender Survey

Do you have personal experience or connection with disability? (Mark *all* that apply.)

- Yes, I have a profound/severe disability (requiring significant support in self-care, self-management, mobility, or communication).
- Yes, I have a mild disability (requiring minimal support in self-care, self-management, mobility, or communication).
- Yes, I have a close family member with a disability.
- Yes, I have a friend with a disability.
- Yes, I have experience with disability from a work or other connection.
- No, I don't have such a connection.

In terms of both facilities and being inclusive, does your local church make provision for people with a disability (whether physical, sensory, intellectual or psychiatric)?

- Yes, this church makes excellent provision.
- Yes, the church makes adequate provision.
- Unsure/don't know.
- No, the church does not make adequate provision.
- No, the church is quite inadequate in this area.

Appendix 2

Operations Survey

Does this congregation have a written, public statement expressing a commitment to welcoming and including people and families living with a disability?

- ☐ Yes, a statement specific to our church.
- ☐ Yes, a statement as part of our denomination.
- ☐ We have a sentiment of inclusion in our written statements, but nothing specific for disability.
- ☐ No, we have no such statement.

Does this congregation provide specific education on disability inclusion to your church staff and volunteers?

- ☐ Yes, by training offered locally.
- ☐ Yes, by training offered elsewhere (for example, denominational).
- ☐ No.

What provisions does your church have for the needs of people with a disability? (Mark *all* that apply.)

- ☐ major physical facilities (for example, ramps/lifts, disabled toilet, reserved parking);
- ☐ minor physical facilities (for example, hearing/induction loop, wheelchair space convenient for services, large-print alternatives to written materials);
- ☐ programme-related provision (for example, intellectual impairment adapted Bible studies, social support, education to congregation);
- ☐ an active culture of inclusion (for example, in teaching and practice of the church, adapting curriculum for children, special needs catered for);
- ☐ none of the above.

10 'A Person Standing in the Gap'

The Deaf Community as a Mission Field

Celia King

Between Two Worlds

At the age of six I wrote in my school composition book, 'When I grow up I want to be a mishrany.' At the age of 12 my deafness was diagnosed and God began weaving my call and my disability into ways to serve him. For many years I tried to cope in the hearing world, with lip-reading, hearing aids, and a lot of bluff and cunning. A sudden total hearing loss in middle age left me profoundly deaf, and was the impetus for me to learn NZSL (New Zealand Sign Language) and move into the Deaf community. As a person living 'between two worlds', I became like Ezekiel, a 'person to stand in the gap' between hearing and Deaf, and Deaf and God. Chaplaincy, counselling, teaching, mentoring, and advocacy have become ways to fulfil God's call in my childhood to be a 'mishrany'. What follows is based on my experiences as I have journeyed in and out of the hearing and Deaf worlds, and examines how the church might more effectively minister to the Deaf and support those ministering to the Deaf.

When I was around ten years old I read an autobiography by C.T. Studd about his missionary experiences in the Congo. I was inspired and wanted to go overseas to share my faith, so when my parents sought my opinion five years later on their decision to go to Nepal with the Leprosy Mission, I answered 'yes' immediately.

Although we were supported financially with money and food parcels from our small church in Masterton, New Zealand, it was another church in Ellerslie, Auckland that took a special interest in me as an MK (missionaries' kid). One of the elders there talked with me at length about mission before we left, and he and others wrote encouraging letters to me and prayed for me all the time I was overseas. I was so grateful that they shared their godly wisdom with me.

In Nepal I was able to see how missionaries operated – how they reacted when under pressure, how they handled conflict, how they managed without the comforts and conveniences of their home countries, how different cultures, nationalities, and denominations found ways of working together. I attended hospital roof church services, visited patients in the wards, and made friends with the village children, quickly picking up some Nepali.

My brother and I were sent to school in India, where Caucasians were in the minority. We were the subject of teasing and bullying because we were of a different culture with different accents and perspectives. I developed resilience, made some good friends, and adapted to different ways of doing things – once even sleeping in an Indian family bed with them all while the mother was in labour with another child!

I enjoyed my time in Nepal and India because I felt that it was preparing me for something in the future, and in part fulfilling my call to be a missionary.

However, this was a critical time in my education, and after a year at boarding school in India I had to return to New Zealand – still with the yearning to minister to people of a different culture. It was also a time when the impact of my deafness became more pronounced. I needed to sit at the front of classes, friends took notes for me in lectures, I struggled with group work, but I resisted wearing hearing aids that made me 'different'. I contemplated giving up my study to become a teacher, as at that time I could see no future for a teacher who was Deaf. Despondency settled around me as I thought that no mission committee would accept me with a hearing loss. My vision to reach a people of another culture for Christ began to fade.

Marriage, raising three lovely boys, and making a home became my priorities, and I continued to push the boundaries my deafness imposed by teaching night classes, leading Bible studies, teaching in Sunday school, speaking at women's meetings, and being a deaconess. I hid my deafness as much as possible, and developed strategies that enabled me to cope (or so I thought!).

It wasn't until my sudden hearing loss, when my self-sufficiency was withdrawn, that God got my attention again and renewed his call for me to be a missionary to people of another culture. For years I had minimized my hearing loss, but when I was suddenly plunged into total deafness overnight, I asked for prayer for healing. God graciously restored some of my hearing, but the greatest miracle was how he changed my attitude to deafness. Instead of being ashamed to be Deaf, I accepted that God has a plan for me just how I am. Instead of resisting wearing hearing aids, I accepted that they allowed me to still function to a degree in the hearing world – to enjoy music, to hear my children, husband, and friends. However, I realized that without hearing aids I was 'lost' and could not make sense of conversations, hear sounds in the environment, or enjoy an active social life.

Along with a further loss of hearing, I also lost confidence and began to withdraw. Church became a challenge as I could not hear people's testimonies or the sermon, even with hearing aids. I felt disconnected, with no real fellowship. People tried, but soon gave up repeating themselves and moved on to others they could communicate with easily. Home groups that I had previously loved became impossible because it was just too exhausting trying to lip-read, remind people to keep their heads up when they prayed, and ask for things to be written down. Eventually I stopped going. I longed for someone to do as Jesus did when he met a Deaf man and take me away from background noise and distraction, look at me when they were speaking, and use words that were easy to lip-read.

It was while I was recovering from the side effects of the drugs used to restore my hearing after the sudden hearing loss that I read an advertisement for a chaplain for the Deaf in Auckland. I had started learning NZSL and mixing a little bit with the Deaf community. God reminded me of my calling, and that Jesus said, 'You will be my witnesses in Jerusalem, all Judea and Samaria, and to the ends of the earth' (Acts 1:8). While we are to take the gospel into the whole world, I felt Jesus was saying, 'Start where you are, there's a whole mission opportunity right on your doorstep!'

Further in his mandate in Matt 28:19, Jesus commands us to 'make disciples' (people who learn how to follow God themselves) and 'baptize them' as a public declaration of their faith. Then he adds 'teach them', which means keep on teaching and making disciples of them. Teaching is what I was trained to do, and I had a passion to teach others about God.

So, in obedience to God's call and due to my own experience of deafness with the isolation and oppression it brings, I accepted a three-year term to be a chaplain to the Deaf. Although my heart was in the right place, it was a huge learning curve for me. An interdenominational committee overseeing the work was made up of members who all had their own ideas of how things should be done, and it was difficult to get consensus and even more difficult to get financial support as the denominations did not recognize the Deaf ministry as being one of 'theirs'. None of them had experience of deafness, were prepared to learn about Deaf culture, or learn NZSL. Some leaders of another Deaf Christian fellowship thought I was taking away their people and their interpreters. I felt there was opposition from the very people who could have been offering support and encouragement.

However, I did receive support from the Catholic Chaplain for Deaf at the time. She and I met regularly to discuss our work and pray for each other. Two or three times a year we would hold combined services. I also received support and encouragement from the people I ministered to, who were grateful for a chaplain who could communicate in their language, embrace Deaf culture, and involve them in the services and ministry. I loved visiting Deaf people in hospital, prison, and mental institutions, and they in turn appreciated my visits and ministry.

Towards the end of my term my husband and I were dealing with some tough problems with one of our sons and, coupled with church politics, I decided not to renew my chaplaincy and returned to our home church full-time.

Unlike mission organizations, there was no re-orientation programme or debriefing for me. I was expected to change from Deaf culture ways of doing church back to hearing ways. I found the adjustment hard. The challenges to access sermons and testimonies and enjoy fellowship returned. People told me it encouraged them to see me at church, and that they loved watching me sign the songs because it was my 'heart language' and really expressed my worship.

However, on reflection I was experiencing burnout from all that was happening in my life at the time, along with the renewed challenges, and my attendance at church became erratic. Very few people enquired why I was not there. I felt that not only was my disability invisible, I became invisible too!

So when I heard of another church nearby setting up a Deaf ministry, I became excited. With an interpreter, I was finally able to access the sermons, testimonies, and any other spoken information. I was able to have fellowship with other Deaf Christians after the service. With my keenness to once again minister to a people group I loved, along with my knowledge and experience in Deaf education, I was soon offering to adapt study materials, suggest how Deaf people could be included in the service, and be a role model in sharing my testimonies and ideas in NZSL in front of the whole congregation.

Sadly, my zeal was not appreciated. Unfortunately, the leaders of the Deaf ministry turned down my offers of support. The wider church leadership had little experience of Deaf culture, and in some ways seemed to think that deafness was something to be fixed rather than an identity and culture of a people group. Even though I was an adviser to the Ministry of Education on a project dealing with inclusion and offered to run workshops about Deaf culture and inclusion of Deaf, they were not interested. The best approach seemed to be influencing change one-on-one or in small groups of people. I got involved in the organization of various church events – the Light Party, the Christmas Eve dinner, and a Stations of the Cross display. In this way I was able to be the 'person in the gap' in explaining what needed to be done to include the Deaf and make the events Deaf-friendly. Over time, the Deaf became involved. I set up a sign singing group with young and older Deaf – mainly non-Christians – and we performed at the Light Party. Another Deaf lady joined me in teaching NZSL at the church camp, and a group of Deaf people helped me make up Christmas goodie bags and distribute these at the Christmas Eve dinner, to which I had invited non-church-going Deaf people.

Also, I started a Deaf Christian training group in my home to disciple Deaf Christians and give them opportunities for leadership and sharing in their own language and culture. This was well attended, and it was such a delight to see Deaf confident to lead in prayer, share and memorize Scripture, explain concepts, and grow in their faith. It impressed on me the need for Deaf to have their own church instead of being an 'add-on' ministry in a hearing church. I was blessed to be able to lead a Deaf sharing time once when there was no interpreter for the service and the Deaf people sat in a corner down the back. Another time, I shared the leadership of a similar group with two other Deaf people. It was incredibly encouraging to see the engagement and active participation of our 'congregation'. It was great working as a team, and I suggested that 'Deaf Church' should be a regular event, perhaps monthly.

More and more I felt God calling me back into active ministry such as I enjoyed as a chaplain. He spoke to me through missionary books that I was reading as well as the responses of the Deaf people I had ministered to. I was especially burdened for Deaf youth, with whom I have a good relationship as I have taught many of them. I also wanted to visit Deaf in prison, as they are cut off from communication and often do not understand what is happening – leading to further clashes with the law. I wanted to be a missionary, reaching out to Deaf who were not involved in churches, and I shared this sense of calling at a 'Dream Service' the church conducted to share what God was laying on people's hearts as the direction the church should take. Several people approached me afterwards with offers of practical and prayer support.

So it was a real surprise when meeting with the pastor to be told that the Deaf people did not want me in this ministry. I felt betrayed. These were people I'd encouraged, visited, and supported for the past eight years. It seemed that there was a misunderstanding in attempts to communicate between the two languages and cultures. The pastor thought he was doing the right thing by listening to some of the Deaf, but I was left feeling hurt and disappointed. I took time out from church to deal with my disappointment, and continued to seek God's guidance. He reminded me of his grace and mercy, and encouraged me to forgive those who had hurt me. I confided my confusion in a few Christians whom I trusted to give me wise counsel and pray with me. In the meantime my husband had found another church where he was happy, and it seemed best for me to join him there.

Unfortunately, I find myself in another church that has no experience or understanding of deafness. Again I struggle to access spoken communication and to enjoy fellowship. While it is a delight to be with Christian people, it is a challenge just to be there and to educate them about how they can be more inclusive so that I feel comfortable inviting Deaf people along. Perhaps that is the ministry God wants me to have – just being a 'person standing in the gap'.

This leads me to encourage those without direct experience with people with hearing loss or difficulties to learn more about Deaf culture and how to minister effectively to Deaf people, and encourage those who are ministering to Deaf people.

The Deaf Community – What You Need to Know

The Deaf community has its own language. As with any other sign language, New Zealand Sign Language is a visual-gestural language using hands, the body, facial expressions, and lip patterns to express meaning and the eyes to perceive meaning. NZSL has its own grammatical structures and does not follow English word order; no voice is used, and many ideas can be expressed simultaneously by using space. Signed English is not the natural language of the Deaf, nor is Makaton. Ministry to and with the Deaf community is ineffective without proficiency in NZSL.

Just as the Deaf community has its own language, it also has its own culture, and one must be prepared to comprehensively embrace Deaf culture if mission and ministry are to be effective. Deaf people love to be together! Deaf clubs are the meeting places for most Deaf people, and they include fishing clubs, outdoor clubs, senior citizen groups, mother and babies groups, youth groups, craft groups, and so forth. These special interest groups provide ample opportunities for meeting people of all ages and interests. Celebrations of different events and social activities are important features in a Deaf calendar.

As Deaf people are strongly visual, they learn best when concepts are presented through pictures in a *PowerPoint* presentation, mime, and drama (without much dialogue), and sign language – either direct or through interpreters. Because Deaf people are visual, they remember details of things they have seen. Drama and mime come naturally, and storytelling is a big part of Deaf culture. Deaf culture is also reflected in their art. Many Deaf people are good artists, and they include detail and portray things differently from hearing artists.

Due to heightened visual senses, Deaf people pick up on body language, attitudes, habits, and actions more than hearing people. While this can be a good thing, it can also lead to misunderstandings and misinterpretations in the same way that hearing people may misinterpret a Deaf person's behaviour. It is important to be aware of each other's perspectives rather than viewing situations through your own cultural lens. Inhabiting Deaf culture takes time, as does any enculturation process, but it is worth it.

The Deaf community, as with other minority groups, has a history of oppression. Ninety per cent of Deaf children are born to hearing parents and live in hearing families. So right from the start they are the minority culture. Many hearing parents do not learn NZSL or are not fluent enough to be able to carry on normal, everyday conversations, so the Deaf child misses out on incidental learning. Often the family will leave the house and the Deaf child will only be told that they are going out – not where or what for. Everyday activities like supermarket shopping or cooking a meal are opportunities for learning language, but if the parents are not competent in NZSL, Deaf children struggle to learn. State schools banned sign language for many years, depriving Deaf children of a natural means of communication and restricting access to the curriculum. Few Deaf students gained qualifications, and most ended up in 'manual trades', becoming machinists, builders, cabinetmakers, and so on. Educational expectations were low, and the resulting low literacy levels have been a barrier to improving qualifications or pursuing further study. Fortunately, expectations are higher now, and many young Deaf people go on to tertiary study.

Many Deaf were sent to residential schools from a young age and suffered physical, emotional, and sexual abuse there. Due to problems in communication, many of these cases went unreported. Even in families, perpetrators of abuse were able to continue because their 'secret' was safe with a Deaf child unable to express what was going on. The effect of this abuse is long-lasting, affecting relationships with hearing people and the perception that Deaf people have of themselves.

Deaf people may become resigned to the fact that they are a minority group and that 'hearing know best', with the result that they tend either to be passive and accept this as their fate, or become angry and perceived as aggressive. Many Deaf are reluctant to challenge the status quo, and would rather leave leadership to hearing people. Even though they may have the necessary skills and qualifications, it is rare to see Deaf in leadership or managerial positions in hearing organizations.

Deaf people experience isolation in their families, mainstream schools, workplaces, community organizations, and sadly even in churches, yet they have much to offer, and society as a whole is the poorer for not realizing this.

Implications for Ministry to the Deaf

There is an opportunity on our doorstep to do mission in another culture in New Zealand (the situation is largely the same elsewhere, of course). If all the Deaf people in the world were gathered together, they would be the largest unreached population group for Christ. Only 2 per cent of the Deaf community world-wide call themselves 'Christian'. Aotearoa New Zealand has 9,000 culturally Deaf people.[1] Statistically, this means there are 180 Deaf Christians in New Zealand, although in reality there are probably only about 70, and not all of those attend church or are growing in Christ.

As pointed out above, communication is the biggest barrier to reaching the Deaf community with the gospel. Knowing NZSL and participating meaningfully in Deaf culture will enable the evangelist to explain concepts, ideas, and spiritual truths in simple and understandable ways. Just as our Lord used parables and word pictures the people were familiar with, so missionaries use local culture and the environment to connect to their communities. The Christian worker for the Deaf must be prepared to use Deaf idiom, storytelling, drama, role-play, and visuals to teach Deaf communities about the Good News, otherwise communication is not being made and our witness to Christ will be ineffective.

Traditional Christian language used by preachers and Bible teachers can be problematic for Deaf people. Christians have their own religious or church jargon and use the hearing way of expressing things, but for Deaf people, none of that is transferable. Puns and word plays literally 'fall on deaf ears' – they are just not funny or even understandable to Deaf people. Many things go right over their heads!

Many people might think that having interpreters solves the communication problems. While interpreters are vital and without them Deaf people would get nothing, an interpreter is trained to sign what is spoken. Without the time to break down the spoken language or explain concepts, often such interpreted messages also 'fall on deaf ears'. It is exhausting work for interpreters to listen, think how to translate, sign – and keep listening. That is why interpreters normally work for 20-minute stretches before another takes over. It is also hard work for Deaf people to watch interpreters, as they do not get breaks every 20 minutes to rest their eyes. If you want to get an idea of how hard Deaf people have to work to access communication, try watching the news on TV with the sound and subtitles switched off.

Having made this point, I do not want to be misunderstood: interpreters are crucial. I personally stopped going to church for a time because there were no

---

1 See K. Anne Greville, 'Hearing Impaired and Deaf People in New Zealand: An Update on Population Numbers and Characteristics' [accessed 6 June 2013]. Online: http://www.grevilleconsulting.co.nz/HearingimpaireddeafpeopleNZMar05a.pdf. This publication is based on the 2001 disability survey conducted by Statistics New Zealand, 'New Zealand Disability Survey Snapshot 6: Sensory Disabilities' [accessed 6 June 2013]. Online: http://www2.stats.govt.nz/domino/external/pasfull/pasfull.nsf/web/Media+Release+2001+New+Zealand+Disability+Survey+Snapshot+6+Sensory+Disabilities.

interpreters. It is a sad fact that Deaf people are limited in the choice of church they can attend due to the dearth of interpreters willing or competent to sign in churches.

I asked some of my Deaf Christian friends for their comments on interpreters in church. Here is what they told me: 'Interpreters need to study and be highly qualified. They have to have a high level of skill, otherwise we miss out.' 'Interpreters might want the job (some churches pay interpreters), but they have no Christian experience. They need to be a Christian and have a deep love for Deaf so that they can support Deaf. They need to have their own relationship with God.' 'Interpreters need support, otherwise they will burn out!' The last comment highlights another problem in using interpreters. Most hearing people cannot communicate well with Deaf, so they ask the interpreter things they want to know about Deaf people or Deaf ministry events. An interpreter with good ethical boundaries, instead of speaking for the Deaf, will say, 'Let's ask the Deaf,' and will switch back into the interpreter role while the hearing person communicates directly with the Deaf person. This models humility and affirms Deaf people. It also helps the hearing people to become confident in interacting directly with the Deaf.

Just because Deaf cannot communicate in spoken English, this does not mean they have nothing to say! An interpreter can contribute to the oppression and dependency of the Deaf if they continue to 'speak for' the Deaf, make all the decisions, give all the prayer requests, write all the reports, and so on. It is easy for interpreters working voluntarily in a church setting to forget that they are part of a team – or part of the body. The result for the interpreter is possible burnout, and for the hearing and Deaf Christians, missed opportunities to learn from each other and serve together.

Some Deaf people have told me that as children they wanted to learn about God, so their parents sent them to Sunday school. While that is common in non-Christian families, a hearing child can pick up the concepts. However, a Deaf child with restricted access to communication is not going to learn very much. It is no wonder that churches became places of alienation rather than a community of belonging and learning.

Deaf attending a church will sit together – mainly because they need to see the interpreter, but also for the sense of belonging they feel in community with other Deaf friends. After the service the Deaf can be seen chatting and enjoying fellowship long after most of the hearing people have left. However, there is a danger that because Deaf sit together, usually at one side of the main congregation, they can become 'side-streamed' – they are 'there', but not involved or included. There is a risk that the small number of Deaf people in a dominant mainstream church culture means they will be marginalized.

Deaf people side-lined in a mainstream church may seem passive and uninterested. Many of them fall asleep because they cannot follow what is going on, but get a group of Deaf people together and they become vibrant, animated participants in whatever is happening!

Due to the difference in communication and cultural styles of learning, many Deaf prefer their own cell groups or home groups to hearing church services, where they can learn at their own pace in their own way. Deaf often like interaction with a Deaf preacher or teacher more than learning through an interpreter.

When Deaf people come to a hearing church they not only have to cope with a hearing culture, but they have to fit in with a 'church culture'. Each denomination has particular styles of worship, traditions and customs, language, celebrations, and dress codes. It can be quite daunting to learn and follow the rules of a culture within a culture: 'Attempts to "fit" Deaf people into the ways and practices of the hearing church that do not take the culture and life experience of Deaf persons into account will be largely ineffectual, if not counterproductive.'[2]

As Deaf people are visual learners, they learn best by watching and doing. Church services which incorporate visual or active worship will be more Deaf-friendly. It takes a bit of thought to change from sound-based ways of doing things, but it leads to inclusion and acceptance. One example is a church that had a competition reciting the Books of the Bible. The Deaf could not take part because there are no signs for many of the books and they would need fingerspelling, but if the Books of the Bible had been written on cards to put in order, the Deaf could have competed on equal terms (and perhaps even won!).

Due to the historical oppression of sign language and the low literacy of many Deaf, they find reading the Bible hard, therefore it is difficult for them to grow in their faith. A Deaf friend commented: 'I couldn't understand the Bible, the language was too hard. I had to learn English better first.'

As Deaf love to be together, some will attend church if they know there is going to be an afternoon tea or a lunch which provides a relaxed time to chat with other Deaf. Rapport with strangers or Deaf people from overseas using a different sign language is quickly and easily established. There is an immediate and universal bonding with other Deaf people.

If Deaf are just 'attending' church, then they are not being included. Most churches have at least one or two pastors, children's workers, youth leaders, and elders/deacons/pastoral workers, but how many of these are Deaf? Are the discourses of oppression and dominant culture perhaps being perpetuated in churches?

There is a complacency that suggests it is easier to communicate with a hearing person and that the effort needed to exchange information with a Deaf person is just too onerous and fraught with difficulty to invite them to be part of a leadership team. However, a leadership team comprising of both Deaf and hearing members models equality, partnership, and respect for diversity. To use Paul's analogy, all parts of the body can work and function together for the common good.

Another reason given for not having a Deaf pastor or a Deaf person in the leadership team is that most churches only have between four and ten Deaf

---

2 William Key, Sr, A. Albrecht, and T. Coughlin, *Eye Centred: A Study on the Spirituality of Deaf People with Implications for Pastoral Ministry* (Silver Spring, MD: National Catholic Office for the Deaf, 1992), 62.

people attending in a congregation of 200–300 people, and it is not regarded as being financially viable to employ someone for so few people. Yet how will a Deaf ministry grow if it has no cultural leader?

Many Deaf people have told me that more Deaf people would come to church if there was a Deaf pastor. Deaf people would really like to have their own Deaf church, but in New Zealand there may not be enough Deaf Christians in the same area to support this. They also need the financial support from hearing churches that see Deaf ministry as a valid mission field for this to happen.

Deaf Ministry and Inclusion

There is a lot of talk about inclusion these days. We ask the question, 'What would an inclusive church look like?' Here are some suggestions as to how a church might include Deaf people:

1. An inclusive church would have Deaf people or people fluent in NZSL at the door to welcome worshippers. The greeting would be given in NZSL, with full eye contact and a hug. There would be time to exchange information important to the people.
2. If the Deaf person was coming to the church for the first time, they would be taken to the area where the Deaf were sitting. The front two or three rows of that area would be reserved for Deaf – not for interpreter students or other interested hearing people wanting to learn NZSL. This is because Deaf people need a clear line of vision to the interpreter and the things happening on the stage, and also because hearing people can be visually distracting as they react to spoken messages and sounds around them.
3. There would be a screen with the interpreter projected onto it, so that Deaf people could see the interpreter easily. This would mean that Deaf people could sit where they want, or Deaf parents with babies who might need to be at the back of the congregation could still see the interpreter.
4. The songs would have a good rhythm and simple lyrics that told a story rather than expressing abstract concepts and jargon. The worship team would include a person signing the songs. Deaf choirs or sign singers would perform regularly.
5. The announcements would be video clips in drama or mime, or they could be recorded in NZSL with captions in English to enable hearing people to follow.
6. There would be a time for touching, hugging, and interacting briefly with others. Many churches already incorporate an informal time for greeting each other during the service.
7. The Bible reading would sometimes be done by a Deaf person in NZSL with a transcript on the screen for people to read. Alternatively, a clip from the NZSL version of the Jesus video could be used, allowing the Deaf to make meaning of the culture and traditions surrounding the text.

8 Deaf people would be on a roster to take up the offering, distribute communion, and serve morning tea. These acts of service do not require any special skills, and if Deaf and hearing provided the service together, there would be opportunity for learning from each other and sharing a task equally.
9 If the church had two services, the sermon in one would be interpreted, and in the other Deaf people could go to another area of the building to explore the sermon in NZSL at their own pace and in a visual way with a Deaf leader. This would provide an opportunity to check understanding and ask questions. Deaf would also have the choice of which service to attend if they only wanted to attend one. Or if the church only had one service or a small number of Deaf, then once a month there could be Deaf church, at a different time to the normal church service if necessary, followed by a lunch or dinner. This service would be run by Deaf people and be in full sign language. Deaf and hearing could mix freely and enjoy fellowship afterwards over the meal.
10 There would be enough interpreters – paid if necessary – so that Deaf could go to all the church events, such as women's events, men's breakfasts, youth groups, and special services.
11 People would be made aware that Deaf have their own culture, and would strive to understand Deaf perspectives rather than viewing situations through the hearing cultural lens. Misunderstandings and differences of opinion would be handled maturely with plenty of dialogue, to gain understanding of all the issues and with the goal of restoration and acceptance.
12 Deaf ministry and Deaf people would receive the same prayer, spiritual, and practical support as any other ministry in the church. People would be alert to the things going on in each other's lives that might cause them to burn out or stop attending church, and would show their concern by keeping a sense of connection and support going. People would actively listen to each other, encourage the sharing of dreams, and persevere to find ways to make them work and to keep the dream alive.

In this way, armed with knowledge of the way the Deaf community operates and the humility to embrace Deaf cultural ways of doing things, churches could move beyond needing a 'person standing in the gap', and become models of inclusion and belonging instead.

11 Banqueting and Disability in the Ancient World

Reconsidering the Parable of the Great Banquet (Luke 14:15–24)

Louise Gosbell

While there are deviations in interpretation, the traditional, and most widely accepted approach to the Parable of the Great Banquet (Luke 14:15–24)[1] is that it is an eschatological parable used by the author of Luke's gospel to emphasize to his first-century Gentile community the salvation and inclusion of Gentile Christians into the community of God.[2] In this sense, the banquet meal here

---

1 Recent scholarship on this passage has focused on the redactional history of the passage and which version of the parable (Luke 14:16–24/Matt 22:1–14/Gospel of Thomas 64) represents the earliest Jesus tradition. While this scholarship is significant, it is outside of the scope of this investigation. For a summary of the scholarship regarding the redaction of Luke 14:15–24, see G.E. Sterling, '"Where Two or Three are Gathered": The Tradition History of the Parable of the Banquet (Matt 22:1–14/ Luke 14:16–24/Gos.Thom. 64", in *Das Thomasevangelium im Kontext der frühchristlichen und spätantiken Literatur- und Religionsgeschichte*, BZNW 157, ed. J. Schröter, J. Frey, and E.E. Popkes (Berlin: Walter de Gruyter, 2008), 95–121, and Ernest van Eck, 'When Patrons are Patrons: A Social-scientific and Realistic Reading of the Parable of the Feast (Lk 14:16b–23)', *HTS Teologiese Studies / Theological Studies* 69 (2013): 1–14. Art. 1,375. Van Eck's article also features a helpful summary of the history of the social scientific approach to this parable which has also been a keen area of interest in recent parable scholarship; ibid., 6–9.

2 Allegorical interpretation of this parable has its roots in the writings of the early church. Augustine, Origen, Bede, and Thomas Aquinas all interpreted this parable allegorically, emphasizing God's act of including the Gentiles in his call to salvation. Allegorical interpretation of this parable does not solely lie with the church fathers, however, with numerous modern scholars continuing to describe this parable in terms of Gentile inclusion. Martens, for example, states: 'The parable serves as an allegory of Jewish refusal and Gentile acceptance of the banquet of salvation'; Allan W. Martens, 'Salvation Today: Reading Luke's Message for a Gentile Audience', in *Reading the Gospels Today*, ed. Stanley Porter (Grand Rapids, MI: Eerdmans, 2004), 119. Meyer likewise states: 'The parable clearly intended to explain the inclusion of Gentiles in the present kingdom of God as God's response to Israel's refusal to "enter"'; Paul D. Meyer, 'The Gentile Mission in Q', *Journal of Biblical Literature* 89 (1970): 414. Other proponents who interpret the parable allegorically as being representative of God's outworking of salvation history include: Benjamin Keach, *Exposition of the Parables in the Bible* (Grand Rapids, MI: Kregel Publications, 1978), 544; Herbert Lockyer, *All the Parables of the Bible* (Grand Rapids, MI: Zondervan, 1963), 276; Reinier Schippers, *Gelijkenissen van Jezus* (Kampen: Kok, 1962), 41; Willard M. Swartley, 'Unexpected Banquet People (Luke 14:16–24)', in *Jesus and His Parables: Interpreting the Parables of Jesus Today*, ed. V. George Shillington (Edinburgh: T&T Clark, 1997), 177; John Timmer, *The Kingdom Equation: A Fresh Look at the Parables of Jesus* (Grand Rapids, MI: CRC Publications, 1990), 57; Arland J. Hultgren, *The Parables of Jesus: A Commentary* (Grand Rapids, MI: Eerdmans, 2000), 336–7.

follows a long Jewish tradition of using a messianic meal as metaphor for the entire messianic age to come.³ The gospel writer's particular emphasis, then, is on affirming that in Christ the realization of this banquet will mean the inclusion of those previously deemed ineligible to partake of the meal – an act we see appropriated numerous times throughout the Lukan narrative as Jesus celebrated meals in the presence of the disenfranchised, including tax collectors and sinners, among others.⁴

In this sense, the traditional interpretation of the parable lies in understanding those who were originally invited to the banquet as Israel itself, and in particular the Jewish hierarchy, who according to the writer of Luke, as well as the Old Testament prophetic tradition, are the ones seen as being most culpable for the nation's disobedience and sinfulness. According to this interpretation, those who were initially invited use a series of inane and ludicrous excuses in order to decline the banquet host's offer of hospitality.⁵ However, in an interesting twist, the banquet will still go ahead with the invitations now being extended to the most unexpected of recipients: those the Lukan Jesus refers to as 'the poor, the crippled, the lame and the blind'.⁶ According to many proponents of this view, this reference to the disenfranchised of the Jewish community is not one to be taken literally, but rather is representative of those the Jews considered most unclean and unworthy – the Gentiles.⁷ The parable, then, is to be interpreted eschatologically, to say that due to Israel's sinfulness and disobedience, God has rescinded his original invitation, instead emphasizing that the kingdom of God is reserved for a new community – a reconstituted Israel composed of a faithful remnant, but now also including the faithful members of the Gentile community.

However, by interpreting the outcasts as Gentiles, the Christian community has traditionally interpreted the parable as the work that God has already completed in inviting the Gentiles into the community of God. Christians have

---

3 Isa 25:5–6; 2 Baruch 29:4; 1QSa 2.17–21.
4 Luke 5:29–30; 15:1–2; 19:7.
5 Kenneth E. Bailey states that they are 'ridiculous excuses': *Through Peasant's Eyes: More Lucan Parables, Their Culture and Style* (Grand Rapids, MI: Eerdmans, 1980), 111; Michael D. Goulder says that the excuses are 'transparent lies': *Luke: A New Paradigm*, 2 vols, JSNTSS 20 (Sheffield: Sheffield Academic Press, 1989), 591. Other scholars who suggest that the excuses are implausible include: James Montgomery Boice, *The Parables of Jesus* (Chicago, IL: Moody, 1983), 89; Hultgren, *Parables of Jesus*, 336; Joachim Jeremias, *The Parables of Jesus*, rev. edn (New York: Charles Scribner's Sons, 1963), 179; John J. Kilgallen, *Twenty Parables of Jesus in the Gospel of Luke*, Subsidia Biblica 32 (Rome: Editrice Pontificio Instituto Biblico, 2008), 84–5; Simon J. Kistemaker, *The Parables: Understanding the Stories Jesus Told* (Grand Rapids, MI: Baker Books, 1980), 163; Bernard Brandon Scott, *Hear Then the Parable: A Commentary on the Parables of Jesus* (Minneapolis, MN: Fortress Press, 1989), 169; Klyne R. Snodgrass, *Stories with Intent: A Comprehensive Guide to the Parables of Jesus* (Grand Rapids, MI: Eerdmans, 2008), 687; David Wenham, *The Parables of Jesus: Pictures of a Revolution* (London: Hodder & Stoughton, 1989), 136.
6 Luke 14:21: τοὺς πτωχοὺς καὶ ἀναπείρους καὶ χωλοὺς καὶ τυφλοὺς.
7 See footnote 2.

thus come to understand themselves as the outsiders, the disenfranchised, and those who were separated from God, but who have now been brought in. This interpretation therefore negates any further obligation to seek out those who are still truly marginalized within our own communities.

This chapter proposes that along with the depth of Jewish imagery connecting the eschatological banquet with the inclusion of the Gentiles, the writer of Luke's gospel is also addressing an equally detailed wealth of pagan banqueting imagery from various Greek and Roman literary and iconographical sources. Particularly relevant to this study are the numerous depictions of people with various physical impairments shown in the context of banqueting.

It has long been understood by biblical scholars that the New Testament, and the gospel of Luke in particular, reveal a reliance on Greco-Roman banqueting imagery.[8] In his 2003 publication *From Symposium to Eucharist: The Banquet in the Early Christian World* Dennis E. Smith assesses the place of the formal banquet as a social institution in the Greco-Roman world.[9] The social institution of banqueting was not limited to the Greeks and Romans, but likewise enjoyed by Jews as well as the earliest converts to the Jesus movement. Smith concludes that this is reflected in the canonical gospels, whereby 'The Jesus tradition is permeated with rich usages of the banquet motif, from its metaphorical use in the parables to stories about meals in which Jesus took part.'[10]

In addition to his monograph on banqueting and the symposium is Smith's 1987 *Journal of Biblical Literature* article that specifically addresses the banqueting tradition in the Lukan gospel account. Entitled 'Table Fellowship as a Literary Motif in the Gospel of Luke',[11] it suggests that while the writer of Luke had received much of the imagery of table fellowship as part of the oral tradition passed down to him, in addition he chose to build upon this imagery, making

---

8 In particular, see Xavier de Meeûs, 'Composition de Lc. XIV et genre symposiaque', *Ephemerides Theologicae Lovanienses* 37 (1961): 847–70, and Joël Delobel, 'L'onction par la pécheresse: La Composition littéraire de Lc. VII., 36–50', *Ephemerides Theologicae Lovanienses* 42 (1966): 415–75; cf. S. Scott Bartchy, 'The Historical Jesus and Honor Reversal at the Table', in *The Social Setting of Jesus and the Gospels*, ed. Wolfgang Stegemann, Bruce J. Malina, and Gerd Theissen (Minneapolis, MN: Fortress Press, 2002), 180; Joel B. Green, *The Gospel of Luke* (Grand Rapids, MI: Eerdmans, 1997), 244; Jonathan Brumberg-Kraus, 'Memorable Meals: Symposia in Luke's Gospel, the Rabbinic Seder, and the Greco-Roman Literary Tradition' (PhD diss., Wheaton College, 2007); E. Springs Steele, 'Luke 11:37–54 – a Modified Hellenistic Symposium?', *Journal of Biblical Literature* 103 (1984): 379–94; Robert J. Karris, *Luke: Artist and Theologian: Luke's Passion Account as Literature* (New York: Paulist Press, 1985), 47–78; Arthur A. Just, Jr, *The Ongoing Feast: Table Fellowship and Eschatology at Emmaus* (Collegeville, MN: Liturgical Press, 1993); Michael Patella, *The Gospel According to Luke*, New Century Bible Commentary Series, vol. 3 (Collegeville, MN: Liturgical Press, 2005), 40.
9 Dennis E. Smith, *From Symposium to Eucharist: The Banquet in the Early Christian World* (Minneapolis, MN: Fortress Press, 2003).
10 Ibid., 21; cf. Patella, *The Gospel According to Luke*, 40.
11 Dennis E. Smith, 'Table Fellowship as a Literary Motif in the Gospel of Luke', *Journal of Biblical Literature* 106 (1987): 613–38.

the most of Greco-Roman traditions of banqueting and symposia in order to employ a literary genre familiar to his Gentile audience.[12]

One of the key observations Smith makes is that throughout the Lukan gospel Jesus is shown as participating in 'table talk' – using the setting of a meal as the basis for didactics.[13] While Smith determines that banqueting imagery is a pervasive motif throughout Luke's gospel, he does not specifically grapple with the banqueting parable in Luke 14:15–24 in any great detail in *From Symposium to Eucharist*.[14] In his earlier journal article 'Table Fellowship as a Literary Motif in the Gospel of Luke' Smith does delve into the banquet parables of Luke 14 in more detail; however, he only briefly addresses the references to the poor and those with physical impairments mentioned in it.[15]

Banqueting and symposia were, for a time, such an indelible part of the ancient world that the traditions are clearly displayed in archaeological evidence from the ancient world. Rooms designed specifically for reclining while eating, called *andrones*, have been unearthed in the remains of domestic dwellings in Pompeii and Herculaneum,[16] for example, as well as among the sanctuaries of the Greek healing God Asclepius in Corinth.[17]

Fragmentary remains of ancient epistles also attest to the convention of sending out invitations, as described in Luke 14:1–24.[18] There are numerous depictions of banqueting and symposia throughout the art of ancient world, which will be discussed in more detail below, and in addition to this, the social institution of the banquet and symposia was so pervasive in the ancient world that there developed a corpus of literature solely on this issue.[19] The significance of this is described by Plutarch:

> to consign to utter oblivion all that occurs at a drinking-party . . . has the most famous of the philosophers to bear witness against it – Plato,

---

12 Smith, *From Symposium to Eucharist*, 220, 256–57; cf. Steele, 'Luke 11:37–54', 394.
13 Smith, *From Symposium to Eucharist*, 253. This is seen most notably in 7:36–50 and 11:37–54, as well as Luke 14:1–24. For detailed descriptions of the comparison between Luke's gospel and other sympotic literature see Smith, *From Symposium to Eucharist*, 253–72.
14 That is because the section on Luke's gospel in *From Symposium to Eucharist* is just a rewrite of Smith's earlier article 'Table Fellowship as a Literary Motif in the Gospel of Luke'.
15 Smith states that Luke's use of 'the poor' is part of a literary motif that uses 'the poor' as a 'symbolic reference to . . . social outcasts in general'; Smith, 'Table Fellowship as a Literary Motif in the Gospel of Luke', 636. Smith also determines that 'in Luke Jesus' entire ministry is characterized as one to the poor, the captives, the blind, the oppressed' (ibid.), but he does not address this issue in any more detail.
16 Penelope M. Allison, 'Domestic Spaces and Activities', in *The World of Pompeii*, ed. John J. Dobbins and Pedar W. Foss (New York: Routledge, 2007), 269–78.
17 Smith, *From Symposium to Eucharist*, 15–18.
18 Ibid., 23.
19 For example, Plutarch, *Table Talk* and *Dinner of the Seven Wise Men*; Plato, *Symposium*; Xenophon, *Symposium*; Lucian, *The Carousel or the Lapiths* and *Saturnalia*; Athenaeus, *Deipnosophistae*. See Jason König, *Saints and Symposiasts: The Literature of Food and the Symposium in Greco-Roman and Early Christian Culture. Greek Culture in the Roman World* (Cambridge: Cambridge University Press, 2012).

Xenophon, Aristotle, Speusippus, Epicurus, Prytanis, Hieronymus, and Dio of the Academy, who all considered the recording of conversations held at table a task worth some effort.[20]

The imagery of banqueting is prolific from the Archaic period onwards, and often this imagery includes not only references to banqueting itself, but also to the symposium, which was the second course of the traditional banquet, or rather the drinking party that followed the meal proper:[21] 'During the Archaic period, symposia became a central, definitive part of Greek culture. These were not just drinking parties, but fundamental institutions for education, social definition, testing boundaries of acceptability and instituting cultural norms'.[22]

Luigi Enrico Rossi, in his work on the symposium, wrote:

> Through the symposium the Athenian elite shaped their group identity and social values. The symposium became in many respects a place apart from the normal rules of society, with its own strict code of honor . . . and its own willingness to establish conventions fundamentally opposed to those within the polis as a whole.[23]

Despite quite significant changes that took place between Greek and Roman meals, as well as changes that took place over the Archaic into the Hellenistic period, one of the common features of formal meals in both the Greek and Roman traditions was the practice of guests reclining throughout the meal and following on into the symposium. The most common seating arrangement was with the guests reclining upon *kline* (κλίνη), which were low-lying couches often arranged in the shape of the Greek letter Π set around a central table, thus called a triclinium (τρικλίνιον). Associated with the triclinium was a ranking system so that each position was assigned a place and each person present knew their rank and position in relation to each of the guests who were present.[24] The issue of rank was of such importance that it features often in the sympotic literature. Philosophers recall conversations from either real or imagined banquets regarding the issue of seating allocation. Plutarch in his *Table Talk* includes

---

20 *Table Talk*, 612d–e.
21 Smith, 'Table Fellowship as a Literary Motif in the Gospel of Luke', 614. 'The symposium, is properly, the post-eating stage of a banquet during which drinking for pleasure took place, accompanied by entertainment in the form of recitation, music, dancing, conversation, sex. In its heyday in early Greece, the symposium had social and political as well as cultural significance, so that it can be called by its historian, Oswyn Murray, "the organising principle of Greek life"'; Peter Garnsey, *Food and Society in Classical Antiquity* (Cambridge: Cambridge University Press, 1999), 129–30.
22 Tim Whitmarsh, *Ancient Greek Literature* (Cambridge: Polity Press, 2004), 53.
23 Luigi Enrico Rossi, 'Il simposio greco arcaico e classico come spettacolo a se stesso', in *Spettacoli conviviali dall'antichità classica alle corti italiane del '400*, 41–50, Atti del VII Convegno di Studio (Viterbo, 1983), as cited in Oswyn Murray, 'Sympotic History', in *Sympotica: A Symposium on the Symposion*, ed. Oswyn Murray (Oxford: Oxford University Press, 1990), 7.
24 Smith, *From Symposium to Eucharist*, 33–4.

a discussion that took place at one particular banquet about whether guests should be free to choose their own places at table.[25] The discussion is introduced by an anecdotal account of a banquet host who decided to break with tradition and allow guests to recline wherever they chose: 'Unfortunately, whenever an especially distinguished guest arrived late and discovered that no place worthy of his honor remained at the table, he was insulted and left angrily.'[26]

And yet, in spite of the ranking system, the triclinium seating arrangement was actually meant to promote a kind of equality amongst the symposiasts. François Lissarrague suggests that:

> everyone (was) positioned so as to see all the others and to be on the same level as his companions, within range of sight and speech, so that conversation may flow easily. The couches (were) set up along the walls (so that) nothing ... (took) place behind the drinkers; the whole visual space (was) constructed to make sightlines converge and to ensure reciprocity.[27]

This equality was manifested in the fact that the symposiasts each drank from a communal wine krater that resided in the middle of the room.[28] The krater therefore, as a vessel shared by all the drinkers, became an emblematic symbol of the symposium as well as encapsulating all that the symposium meant to Greek and Roman culture.[29] This idea of equality was such that Plutarch maintained that this practice was not limited solely to the wealthy and elite, but 'after the meal even ordinary and uneducated people permit their thoughts to wander to those other pleasures which are far removed from the concerns of the body'.[30]

So it was the banquet that was focused around eating and the symposium that was centred around the drinking party, and this drinking party was accompanied by various kinds of entertainment. This entertainment, according to the literature and artwork of this period, may have included musicians playing

---

25 Plutarch, *Table Talk*, 1.3.
26 Ibid., 1.2.
27 François Lissarrague, *The Aesthetics of the Greek Banquet: Images of Wine and Ritual*, trans. Andrew Szegedy-Maszak (Princeton, NJ: Princeton University Press, 1990), 19; cf. 'The symposion is often actually and metaphorically a political occasion; in the *Banquet of the Seven Sages* (*Septem Sapientium Convivium*) Mnesiphilos of Athens, friend and admirer of Solon, observes: "In my opinion, Periander, conversation, like wine, should not follow the rules of plutocracy or aristocracy; rather, like democracy, it should be equally shared among all and belong to them in common"'; ibid., 46.
28 A krater is an earthen vessel designed for the mixing of wine and water.
29 Lissarrague, *Aesthetics*, 46. 'The krater, therefore, is imbued with symbolic significance. It is the symbol of hospitality; it is linked with music and dance'; ibid., 36. It is worth noting that equality was not genuine. Lucian's *Saturnalia* is a satire of the festival of the same name, and focuses on turning upside normal sympotic conventions. For example, at this banquet 'everyone slave and free man, is held as good as his neighbour' (*Saturnalia* 7) and each man is directed to 'take the couch where he happens to be. Rank, family, or wealth shall have little influence on privilege' (ibid. 17).
30 Plutarch, *Table Talk*, 673a.

stringed instruments such as an aulos,[31] as well as dancers and comedic acts, and it was also the setting of philosophical discussion.[32] What is significant in terms of this chapter is how often people with various physical impairments or deformities are referred to in the context of ancient banqueting and symposia.

The recent interest in disability and deformity in the ancient world has highlighted that in the Greco-Roman world there was a general interest in people, as well as animals, with unusual physical characteristics.[33] As a result, many people with physical anomalies were placed on display in order to satisfy the curiosity of eager onlookers. Both Greek and Roman philosophers include examples of people with unusual physical characteristics being displayed in both private and public settings. There are examples of people with physical anomalies being kept as slaves and pets within the imperial court[34] as well as being publicly displayed at banquets[35] and public events such as the theatre and at gladiatorial battles.[36] The Roman historian Suetonius, for example, writes that the Emperor Augustus (63 BCE–14 CE) 'abhorred dwarfs, cripples and everything of that sort, as freaks of nature and of ill omen',[37] but at the same time had an interest in displaying such human and animal oddities as a form of entertainment. Suetonius writes that after being publicly criticized for organizing certain public entertainment events such as chariot and foot races between wild beasts and young officers of high rank, Augustus instead limited his public displays to those featuring humans or animals that might 'gratify curiosity',[38] and this included people with various kinds of physical deformity.[39] The Roman philosopher Pliny the Elder also tells us of Augustus' granddaughter Julia, who was in possession of the smallest person then known in the empire, a man named Conopas she kept as a pet.[40]

---

31 A woodwind instrument with a double-reed mouthpiece.
32 Smith, *From Symposium to Eucharist*, 12–13.
33 Robert Garland, *The Eye of the Beholder: Deformity and Disability in the Graeco-Roman World*, 2nd edn (London: Duckworth, 1995, 2010); Martha L. Rose, *The Staff of Oedipus: Transforming Disability in Ancient Greece* (Ann Arbor, MI: University of Michigan Press, 2003); Christian Laes, C.F. Goodey, and M. Lynn Rose, eds., *Disabilities in Roman Antiquity: Disparate Bodies*: A Capite ad Calcem (Leiden: Brill, 2013).
34 For example, Pliny, *Natural History*, 7.16.75.
35 For example, Historia Augusta, *Commodos*, 11.1.
36 For example, Suetonius, *Lives of the Caesars*, Domitian, 4.2.
37 Suetonius, *Lives of the Caesars: Augustus*, 82.
38 Ibid., 43.3.
39 Ibid. Suetonius also informs us that if anything rare or noteworthy was brought into Rome, Augustus was in the habit of making it available for public display; moreover, he is even said to have decorated the rooms of his villas with such objects, especially those noteworthy for their age and rarity; ibid., 43.4 and 72.3.
40 Pliny, *Natural History*, 7.16.75: 'The tallest man that has been seen in our times, was one Gabbaras by name, who was brought from Arabia by the Emperor Claudius; his height was nine feet and as many inches. In the reign of Augustus, there were two persons, Posio and Secundilla by name, who were half a foot taller than him; their bodies have been preserved as objects of curiosity in the museum of the Sallustian family.'

But whatever interest Augustus may have had in keeping oddities, it paled in comparison to that of Emperor Elagabalus (c. 203–222 CE). Elagabalus' penchant for human oddities was apparently such that he kept an enormous collection amongst those who resided in his court. The *Historia Augusta*[41] states that when Alexander Severus (208–235 CE) came to power he inherited an extensive collection of human oddities from Elagabalus, such as:

> dwarfs, both male and female, fools, catamites who had good voices, all kinds of entertainers at table and actors of pantomimes he made public property; those, however, who were not of any use were assigned, each to a different town ... in order that no one town might be burdened by a new kind of beggar.[42]

Other Roman emperors were also inclined to keep company with people considered to be out of the ordinary. According to the Roman historian Tacitus (56–c. 117 CE), the Emperor Claudius (10 BCE–54 CE) liked to pass time in conversation with a certain buffoon named Julius Pelignus who Tacitus describes as being renowned for his 'feebleness of mind and his grotesque personal appearance'.[43]

Suetonius also writes about the Emperor Domitian (51–96 CE) who at public events such as gladiatorial battles was often seen in the company of a boy with an 'abnormally small head'.[44] Tacitus also informs us about a certain Vatinius during the reign of Nero, about whom he states: 'Vatinius ranked among the foulest prodigies of that court; the product of a shoemaker's shop, endowed with a misshapen body and a scurrile wit, he had been adopted at the outset as a target for buffoonery.'[45]

This interest in the human oddities is described in detail by Roman rhetorician Quintilian (35–100 CE). In his 12-volume work *Institutes*, which outlines the art of oratory and rhetoric, Quintilian states:

> It will even at times be of value to read speeches which are corrupt and faulty in style, but still meet with general admiration thanks to the perversity of modern tastes, and to point out how many expressions in them

---

41 On the historical unreliability of the *Historia Augusta*, see Ronald Syme, *Emperors and Biography: Studies in the Historia Augusta* (Oxford: Oxford University Press, 1971); Dennis Pausch, 'Unreliable Narration in the *Historia Augusta*', *Ancient Narrative* 8 (2010): 115–36.
42 Historia Augusta, *Alexander Severus*, 34.2. In its ancient usage, a catamite was a pubescent boy who acted as the companion and sexual partner of an older man.
43 Tacitus, *Annals*, 12.49.1.
44 'During the whole of every gladiatorial show there always stood at his feet a small boy clad in scarlet, with an abnormally small head, with whom he used to talk a great deal, and sometimes seriously'; Suetonius, *Lives of the Caesars*, Domitian, 4.2.
45 Tacitus, Annals, 15.34; cf. Plutarch, *Lives: Cicero*, 9.3, Quintilian, *Institutes*, 6.3.77, Seneca, *On the Firmness of the Wise Man*, 17.3.

are inappropriate, obscure, high-flown, grovelling, mean, extravagant or effeminate, although they are not merely praised by the majority of critics, but, worse still, praised just because they are bad. For we have come to regard direct and natural speech as incompatible with genius, while all that is in any way abnormal is admired as exquisite. Similarly we see that some people place a higher value on figures which are in any way monstrous or distorted than they do on those who have not lost any of the advantages of the normal form of man.[46]

This view is likewise confirmed by the Greek historian Plutarch, who mentions a 'monster-market' in Rome which specialized in the sale of slaves with various physical abnormalities. Plutarch writes:

> there are some who take no account of . . . the beauty of the boys and women for sale, but haunt the monster-market (τεράτων ἀγορὰν), examining those who have no calves, or are weasel-armed, or have three eyes, or ostrich-heads, and searching to learn whether there has been born some commingled shape and misformed prodigy.[47]

While it is possible that Plutarch's speech contains some degree of hyperbole, there are other examples from the ancient sources of people purchasing physically and intellectually deformed slaves.[48] Indeed, the Greek rhetorician Longinus writes that the desire to have a deformed slave was such that some children were deliberately deformed by being bound and confined in boxes.[49]

In addition to a generalized interest in human deformity there are also numerous references to people with physical impairments specifically in relation to banqueting and symposia. The best-known image is that of the court jester.[50]

---

46 Quintilian, *Institutes*, 2.5.10–12.
47 Plutarch, *On Being a Busybody*, 10 [520c].
48 Martial states that he bought a slave: 'He was said to be a *morio* (idiot/jester). I paid twenty thousand for him. Give me my money back, Gargilianus – he has his wits' (*Epigrams*, 8.13); 'A muleteer was lately sold for twenty thousand sesterces, Aulus. Are you astonished at so large a price? He was deaf' (ibid., 34.6). This worth of the slave is increased because he is unable to eavesdrop on his master's conversations; cf. Pliny (*Natural History*, 34.6) relates the story of Gegania, who receives a free hunchback slave with her purchase of a chandelier. Garmaise refers to a household dwarf named Zerkon in the 430s CE who provided amusement 'because of his bodily deformity, and because he provoked merriment at his stammering speech and at his very appearance (for he was short, hunchbacked, with misshapen feet, and surprisingly flat-nosed . . .'; Michael Garmaise, 'Studies in the Representation of Dwarfs in Hellenistic and Roman Art' (PhD diss., McMaster University, 1996), 44–5.
49 *On the Sublime*, 44.5. This idea of deliberate mutilation seems to be confirmed by the account related by the Elder Seneca entitled 'The Crippled Beggars', which features a story about a man who would pick up exposed children and deliberately cripple them in order to use them as beggars to promote sympathy (10.4.1–25).
50 There are numerous Greek and Roman terms used to describe the jester, such as *balatro* (a professional jester) and παράσιτος ('parasite'; someone wheedling a dinner from some wealthy person).

This image of the jester being ugly and/or deformed and exchanging insults with banquet guests for entertainment seems to have been commonplace in the Greco-Roman world, and there are numerous literary references to such spectacles.[51] Lucian, in his satirical work on the symposium entitled *The Carousel or the Lapiths*, relates the account of a misshapen dwarf entertaining the banquet guests:

> In came an ugly fellow with his head shaven except for a few hairs that stood up straight on his crown. First he danced doubling himself up and twisting himself about to cut a more ridiculous figure; then he beat time and recited scurrilous verses in an Egyptian brogue, and finally he began to poke fun at the guests. The rest laughed when they were made fun of, but when he took a fling at Alcidamas in the same way, calling him a Maltese lapdog, Alcidamas got angry . . . .[52]

Both the Roman rhetoricians Cicero and Quintilian allude to the philosophy belying such behaviour: those with deformity were the ideal subjects for ridicule and derision. Cicero, although advocating a belief that such humour can be taken too far and end up only in jokes of 'bad taste', still endorses the view that 'there is good matter enough for jesting' in deformity (*deformitas*) and bodily disfigurement (*corporis vitia*).[53] Quintilian agrees, stating that 'laughter has its basis in deformity'.[54]

It seems, therefore, that there was a ready supply of slaves or jesters or others with physical deformities who would make themselves available to be insulted and ridiculed as the entertainment for the guests of the symposia. This mockery may have taken place simply in the form of lively discussions and insult-hurling between jesters and symposiasts, or it could have taken on a much more sinister guise. An example of the former is from Horace's *Satires*, where he recalls the repartee between a former slave called Sarmentus and a certain Messius Cicirrus which takes place in the context of a symposium: 'Cicirrus mocks Sarmentus for his servile origin and puny stature, while Sarmentus in turn mocks the disfiguring scar on Cicirrus' bristly forehead, claiming that the latter could play the part of the Cyclops without the aid of a mask.'[55] Although Horace's poetry may be based on imagined rather than historical events, it is not difficult to imagine such banter taking place in the context of banquets.

---

51 Lucian (*True History*, 2.18) refers to an imaginary banquet in Elysium where (the ugly and deformed) Aesop is present as a jester.
52 Lucian, *The Carousel or the Lapiths*, 18.
53 Cicero, *De Oratore*, 2.58.238–9.
54 Quintilian, *Institutes*, 6.3. 'That laughter has its origin in the contemplation of the ugly or defective is a fundamental and frequently recurring definition in Greek and Roman theories of the laughable, and it is equally significant that usually only the defects of the weak are represented as truly ridiculous'; Mary A. Grant, *Ancient Rhetorical Theories of the Laughable: The Greek Rhetoricians and Cicero* (Madison, WI: University of Wisconsin, 1924), 19.
55 Horace, *Saturnalia*, 1.5.50–70.

On the other hand there are also numerous accounts of people with various deformities being used as entertainment at banquets without such a light-hearted feel. Another story of the Emperor Elagabalus states that he was in the habit of inviting to his banquets 'eight bald men, eight one-eyed men, eight men with gout, eight deaf men, eight black men, eight tall men or eight fat men' simply 'to provoke laughter at them all'.[56]

The Emperor Commodus also used people with deformity in the context of banquets for the sake of entertainment. In one very shocking story the *Historia Augusta* recalls Commodus' general fascination with the monstrous, including the fact that at a private banquet, along with the evening's meal, he also served up on a silver platter two live misshapen hunchbacks covered in mustard.[57] Whether Commodus' intention was to entice people to touch them or not is unclear,[58] but at the very least the whole elaborate display seems to be for comedic effect.

Throughout his work *Table Talk* Plutarch directs that a symposium must have a director or symposiarch to co-ordinate the evening's events. He must, Plutarch says, also 'caution the guests, lest scoffing and affronts creep in (and) lest in their questions or commands they grow scurrilous and abusive'.[59] Plutarch states that such attitudes may entice guests to make requests that are inappropriate. Such requests might have been to petition 'stutterers to sing or bald men to comb their hair, or the lame to dance on a greased wine skin'.[60] Such things, he suggests, are prone to occur with the absence of proper instruction from the symposiarch. He then goes on to give the example of one Agapestor the Academic who was thus abused in the context of a symposium. Plutarch states:

> Thus, by way of rudely mocking Agapestor the Academic, who had a weak and withered leg, his fellow-banqueters proposed that each man of them all drain off his cup while standing on his right foot, or pay a penalty. But when it came the turn of Agapestor to give the order, he commanded them all to drink as they saw him drink. Then he had a narrow jar brought to him, put his defective foot inside it, and drained off his cup; but for all the others, since it was manifestly impossible for them to do so, though they

---

56 Historia Augusta, *Heliogabalus*, 29.3.
57 Historia Augusta, *Commodos*, 11.1.
58 '[T]he fact that these hunchbacks were covered in mustard perhaps also played upon an ancient superstition that rubbing the hump of a hunchback was considered good luck'; Lisa D. Trentin, 'Deformity in the Roman Imperial Court', *Greece & Rome* 58(2) (1993): 205. In general, it was believed that hunchbacks were lucky, and there are examples of figurines and mosaics of hunchbacks, along with dwarfs, that clearly had an apotropaic function; see Doro Levi, 'The Evil Eye and the Lucky Hunchback', in *Antioch-on-the-Orontes* 3, ed. Richard Stillwell (Princeton, NJ: Princeton University Press, 1941), 224–9; William Edward Stevenson, 'The Pathological Grotesque Representation in Greek and Roman Art' (PhD diss., University of Pennsylvania, 1975).
59 *Symposium*, 621E.
60 Ibid.

tried, (they) paid the penalty. Thus, Agapestor showed himself an urbane gentleman; and, following his example, one should make his ripostes good-natured and merry.[61]

Plutarch, in this particular case, seems to commend Agapestor for his good-natured attitude, and indeed his wit, yet we can only imagine the shame and embarrassment Agapestor might have experienced had he not been so quick-witted.

But where did all these people with deformity come from? What were their origins? It seems clear from some of the examples we have already seen that a number of them were professional jesters who lived in the court of the emperors or suchlike. However, Fehr, in an enormously influential chapter entitled 'Entertainers at the Symposion: The *Akletoi* in the Archaic Period', makes the suggestion that at least a portion of these entertainers in the symposium were what he labels *akletoi*, uninvited participants in the banquet.[62] Fehr suggests that due to the economic changes that occurred during the Archaic period[63] many people were forced into difficult financial circumstances. The most vulnerable members of the community, however, would have been those unable to continue in employment, which would have included many people with chronic illness and physical deformity. Fehr therefore suggests that some people who were willing to stand the degradation and derision took on the role of the *akletoi*, the uninvited member of the banquet who would entertain the invited guests. This entertainment may have taken the form of music, such as singing or playing stringed instruments, or perhaps dancing, acrobatics, acting, and mime, or even comedic acts, which included the kind of repartee we have already heard about it.

While it is not at all to be suggested that every person considered to be an *akletos* was someone with a physical anomaly, Fehr certainly notes that those with physical deformity made up a significant portion of this group. He suggests that *akletoi* were a distinct social group that existed in association with the practice of banqueting and symposia. Their role as marginal, as 'other', their social inferiority to the real recipients of banquet invitations, is understood by all present at the banquet. But despite their marginal status their place within the symposium is not only accepted, but deemed important as a means of entertaining the guests. Fehr states the following about the *akletoi*:

> driven by a hungry stomach or by a feeling or personal threat, the *akletoi* perform themselves as physically and morally imperfect. This makes the

---

61 Ibid.
62 Burkhard Fehr, 'Entertainers at the Symposion: The *Akletoi* in the Archaic Period', in *Sympotica: A Symposium on the Symposion*, ed. Oswyn Murray (Oxford: Clarendon Press, 1990), 185–95.
63 Ibid., 188 cf. Michel Mervyn Austin and Pierre Vidal-Naquet, *Economic and Social History of Ancient Greece: An Introduction* (London: Batsford, 1977), 53ff.

invited guests laugh and assures them of their superiority. The *akletoi* characterize themselves as unqualified in the broadest sense, as men who lack every basis for an accepted achievement and a respectable social existence. When they try to act like athletes, cup-bearers, dancers or other similarly strong, beautiful, or skilful men, they do so with the intention of failing in a ridiculous way.[64]

Fehr goes on to say that in addition to the literary sources,[65] the proof of the existence of *akletoi* can be seen in the artwork of the ancient world. Fehr makes the suggestion that the large body of ancient pottery that features the images of the *komast*, or padded dancer, is reflective of the prevalence of the *akletoi* as a social group.[66]

The Greek word *komos* is the root of the verb *komazein*, 'to stage a feast', and of the noun *komastes*, 'a reveller'.[67] There is understood to be such a long-standing connection between the *komasts* of Greco-Roman iconography and the beginnings of comedic drama that the English word 'comedy' has its etymological roots in the Greek term *komos*.[68]

Remarkably little is known about the *komoi* in terms of their function or purpose. Axel Seeberg, in his exhaustive work on Corinthian komos vases, states that the:

> typical padded dancer ... is a male profile figure of squat proportions dressed in a belted sleeveless chiton .... A big swelling fold of stuff overhang(ing) the belt in front. Th(e) dance ... is not (necessarily) obscene or particularly boisterous, but in conjunction with (the rest of his) appearance it gives him a grotesque and incongruous air .... He may carry a horn, and a wine-bowl may be at hand; occasionally, too, the accompanying music is shown (for example) flutes played by a comrade.[69]

The padded dancer is thus named due to the unusual shape of the body, which usually features an enlarged stomach and perhaps also buttocks. Figure 11.1 shows a *kantharos*, a drinking vessel with large handles on each side. This image features the typical padded dancer with enlarged belly and buttocks, and the *komast* on the left is clearly depicted as having twisted feet, which is a feature

---

64 Fehr, 'Entertainers at the Symposion', 187.
65 Fehr states that the very first *akletos* in Greek literature was Odysseus: 'As an ugly old beggar Odysseus asks the suitors at their banquet for food and drink'; *Od.*, 13.430ff.; Fehr, 'Entertainers at the Symposion', 185; cf. Xen. *Symp.*, 2.22; Plato, *Symp.*, 212c4–214b8.
66 Fehr, 'Entertainers at the Symposion', 187.
67 Lissarrague, *Aesthetics*, 31.
68 Ibid.
69 Axel Seeberg, Corinthian Komos Vases, *Institute of Classical Studies Bulletin* supplement 27 (London: University of London, 1971): 1.

Figure 11.1 Black-figure Laconian *kantharos* with *komast*, fifth century BCE, from the Louvre, Paris

Source: Photo by Louise Gosbell.

commonly represented on *komast*s.[70] The context of the symposia is apparent by the imagery used in artwork. In many of the representations of padded dancers the symposium context is implied through the use of symposia-related paraphernalia – the presence of a *kline*, a wine krater, drinking-horns, or a combination of the above. In this case, the depiction of a wine krater next to the dancers firmly sets this image in the context of a symposium.

Fehr suggests that the enlarged stomach of the padded dancers makes sense if these characters are to be understood as the *akletoi* of the literary sources because they were renowned for being present at the banquet in order to indulge in the food.[71] Naturally, if it is poverty that has led them to become part of this social group, then in the context of their marginal role they would surely want to make the most of the food at the banquet. So the *akletoi* had a reputation for being gluttonous as well as consuming large amounts of alcohol.

In addition to this, the padded dancers are also represented as flagrantly casting off social decorum by their base behaviour. They are shown with enlarged phalluses; in undignified positions, such as spread-eagled; they are shown urinating, vomiting, and involved in all manner of sexual activity.[72] The behaviour of the *komast*s marks them as being different from invited guests of the banquet; they are representatives of the lower-class, and therefore it is understandable that they do not know how to behave appropriately in the context of a civilized symposium.

70 Tyler Jo Smith, "Komastai or 'Hephaistoi'? Visions of Comic Parody in Archaic Greece," *Bulletin of the Institute of Classical Studies* 52 (2009): 69–92.
71 Fehr, 'Entertainers at the Symposion', 189.
72 Ibid.

Fehr comments generally about the representation of deformity common to the images of padded dancers, stating: 'It is not always easy to decide whether they twist their feet on purpose to imitate a limp or whether they are actually physically disabled. The deformed feet have sometimes been interpreted – like the padded bellies – as an artificial prop.'[73] He suggests that it is not particularly important whether it is a genuine deformity or otherwise, but rather what is important is simply that it has been made visible in the artwork and is a vital part of the overall imagery of the padded dancers.[74]

In this brief summary we have seen that included in the enormous breadth of literature and iconography that features the Greco-Roman banquet and symposium is a tradition that associates it to some extent with people with various physical anomalies. Not only are there numerous examples of people with physical deformities being shown to be part of the entertainment in the symposium among different kinds of ancient literary sources, but this is also supported by the images of symposia on Greco-Roman pottery. The question is: Does the writer of Luke's gospel have any of this imagery in mind when he records the parable of the great banquet in Chapter 14 of his gospel?

As stated at the beginning, Dennis Smith and other New Testament scholars have already addressed the parallels between Luke's use of table imagery and that which we see in the sympotic literature of the Greek and Roman philosophers. The issue of ranking at table, Smith suggests, is one clear example. The discussion of rank was quite a popular topic of conversation among the symposiasts, and it is one that also appears within Chapter 14 of Luke's gospel. In this account the Lukan Jesus is seen to criticize the established mode of guests vying for higher-ranked positions. Smith suggests that the 'parable functions to symbolize how rankings will be assigned in the kingdom by reference to a recognized custom in the culture. The custom is obviously well understood and taken for granted; otherwise the parable would not work.'[75] Smith also outlines numerous other parallels between the Greco-Roman sympotic literature and the gospel of Luke, which can be seen in his aforementioned article.[76]

Therefore, assuming that this sympotic literature permeated the rationale of the ancient world to such an extent that the writer of Luke can build upon, and subvert it, in such a manner, does it not raises the question of whether the writer of Luke is also making an association with the sympotic literature in making reference to 'the poor, the crippled, the blind and the lame' being the recipients of banquet invitations. If this indeed is the case, what would the implications be for interpreting the passage?

In addition, as stated earlier, the symposium was a place that was believed to represent all that was good about the culture. The Greek idea of symposium

---

73 Ibid., 189–90.
74 Ibid.
75 Smith, 'Table Fellowship as a Literary Motif in the Gospel of Luke', 619.
76 See footnote 14.

was one of mutual enjoyment and egalitarianism; all those present had access to the feast and wine and entertainment the evening provided. And yet, of course, this was a forged equality. It was not an equality that was shared with women, outsiders, or non-citizens; they were not equal. And it was certainly not an equality that was shared with the servants bringing the food to the symposiasts or the *komasts* bringing joviality and entertainment to the symposiasts. In the Lukan parable of the banquet those who would not normally have been recipients of banquet invitations are now being specifically invited. Those who in the Greco-Roman culture were only the servants, only the entertainment, are now being invited as equals to partake of the joys of the symposium.

In light of this Greco-Roman imagery, then, the Lukan parable of the great banquet is making a social statement about the marginalized members of the community. The first, in an eschatological context, is that in the future kingdom equality will be experienced not only by the wealthy and elite of this world, but by all those who are invited, and choose to attend, the eschatological banquet. But secondly, perhaps it is in a pragmatic sense also that this equality is not one that should be sought only in the future kingdom, but should be lived out as part of the experience of seeking to follow Christ. The references to the poor, the crippled, the blind, and the lame are not random or incidental categories of people, but clearly set Luke 14 in the context of the inequality of the banqueting culture of the ancient world, setting a standard of what is expected for those who belong to the new community being created in Christ.

Interpreting this parable in the light of the imagery of the *akletoi* means we no longer interpret the outsiders solely as the Gentiles and see ourselves, as the Christian, as those outsiders who have been brought into God's house. Instead, it forces us to think beyond a work that God has already completed, rather focusing on a work that is still in progress – a work of seeking out and inviting in, indeed imploring, the disenfranchised in our communities to accept God's invitation. We are indeed the ones then who must heed the banquet host and go out quickly into the streets and lanes and compel them to come in so that God's house may be full.

12 Mephibosheth at the Table

A High Point in Davidic Kingship – 2 Samuel 9:1–13

Rod Thompson

> And I will appoint a place for my people Israel and will plant them, so that they may live in their own place, and be disturbed no more; and evildoers shall afflict them no more, as formerly, from the time that I appointed judges over my people Israel; and I will give you rest from all your enemies. (2 Sam 7:10–11, NRSV)

Two events particularly characterize Israel at rest under Davidic kingship in the book of Samuel. Perhaps in these two events we see David at his most admirable. It is certainly the case that much of the time the reader of Samuel cannot be confident of the integrity of David's character, the trustworthiness of his words, or the purity of his motives. Throughout he is portrayed as double-minded and shifting at best, and violent, deceitful, and power-hungry at worst. However, in these two events, both initiated by David, it seems we have a glimpse of what Davidic rule could have looked like and should have been in the longer term – an all too brief glance at David's kingdom at its best, and a significant indication of the character of God's kingdom as it will unfold and be established in its fullness in the person and work of Jesus Christ and the coming new creation.

These two events are found in 2 Sam 9:1–13 (David brings Mephibosheth to Jerusalem and to his table) and 2 Sam 10:1–5 (David seeks to console Hanun, King of the Ammonites, after the death of his father Nahash). In this chapter our main focus is on 2 Sam 9:1–13. However, the Mephibosheth passage initially needs to be seen in relationship with 2 Sam 10:1–5. And as we commence, it is important that both passages be held in relationship with the surrounding context.

The two events are framed by summaries of military victories as the kingdom is established and then expanded. 2 Sam 8:1–14 lists David's attack, defeat, and subduing of the Philistines (8:1), defeat and subjugation of the Moabites (8:2), defeat of the Arameans (8:3–12), and victory over the Edomites (8:13–14). At the end of the chapter a summary statement (8:15–18) indicates that the kingdom is settled. David reigns over all Israel. His officials are in place, and he administers justice and equity to all his people. 2 Sam 10:6–19 then summarizes another set of significant military campaigns. David attacks and defeats the Ammonites (10:6–14). This is followed by a comprehensive victory over the Arameans (10:15–19). Summaries of military campaigns and victory over Israel's enemies frame these two events that characterize David's kingdom at rest. The sequence of chapters in Samuel may be set out as shown in Table 12.1.

In the chapters *prior* to 2 Sam 8 David had secured the kingdom. Jerusalem was conquered, Philistines defeated, and the ark brought up (2:1–7:29). Immediately *after* 2 Sam 10 David's failures dominate the narrative. Adultery occurs. Deception and treachery are explicit. The narrative becomes preoccupied with the problems of Davidic succession, made complex by his tangled personal life. In 2 Sam 9:1–10:5 we have these two events that portray the recently secured kingdom at peace. We have only two events that display, albeit briefly, David's new administration of justice and equity. These are the events to which our attention now turns.

The narratives of David and Mephibosheth (9:1–13) and David and Hanun (10:1–5) have much in common. Both commence with David speaking. The king is taking initiatives, declaring intentions. War, for the time being, has ceased, and David reigns over a kingdom at rest. His speaking reveals something of his desire for the kingdom and the character of his intended reign. In both passages, David uses the word *ḥesed* ('kindness' in 9:1 and 'loyally' in 10:2) to describe these intentions: 'David asked, "Is there still anyone left of the house of Saul to whom I may show *kindness* for Jonathan's sake?"' (9:1; italics mine) and 'David said, "I will deal loyally with Hanun son of Nahash, just as his father dealt *loyally* with me"' (10:2; italics mine).

Ḥesed comes from the vocabulary of covenant. The rendering 'keep faith' (NJPS) helpfully captures the meaning of the original.[1] *Ḥesed* denotes devotion

Table 12.1 Sequence of chapters in 2 Samuel 8–10

Military campaigns 2 Sam 8:1–18	David's kingdom at peace 2 Sam 9:1–10:5	Military campaigns 2 Sam 10:6–19
8:1 – Philistines	9:1–13 – David and Mephibosheth	10:6–14 – Ammonites
8:2 – Moabites	10:1–5 – David and Hanun	10:15–19 – Arameans
8:3–12 – Arameans		
8:13–14 – Edomites		
8:15–18 – David reigns over all Israel		

Source: Author.

---

1 James E. Smith, *1 and 2 Samuel*, *College Press NIV Commentary* (Joplin, MO: College Press, 2000), 410.

to a covenant, and so, when used of God, his covenant-love (Ps 89:28).[2] When used of God's covenant partners, or of humans in covenant with one another, it conveys a reciprocal commitment to faithful love. David's expressed commitment to covenantal faithfulness shapes the initiatives in 2 Sam 9 and 10. He seeks to honour covenantal commitments to Mephibosheth's father Jonathan and Hanun's father Nahash. David, God's servant (7:5), seeks to act out of steadfast love to Mephibosheth, and also to Hanun, just as God has promised to forever act out of steadfast love (*ḥesed*) to David's house (7:14–15). Covenantal faithfulness is at the heart of God's kingdom, and it characterizes David's royal initiatives in these passages.

On both of these occasions the recipients of covenantal love are not those one might have expected. Mephibosheth is from the house of Saul. Much of the history recounted in Samuel tells of war between the house of Saul and the house of David (see 3:1, 6). And the Ammonites are traditional enemies of Israel. They will be enemies again. However, David seeks to act out of covenantal commitment forged by his love for Jonathan and friendship with Nahash. Such devotion, such friendship, covenantal in character, disrupts anticipated lines of enmity or exclusion. However, David's offer of covenantal kindness to Hanun comes under suspicion. His servants, sent to console, are treated shamefully and humiliated. David is dishonoured, the offer of kindness rejected. The Ammonites become 'odious' to David (10:6). War erupts. The initiative of 2 Sam 10:1–5 does not give rise to further friendship, and the attempt to 'keep faith' fails. Nonetheless, David's offer of kindness to Mephibosheth does bear fruit. We see in 9:1–13, and subsequently, the consequences of this kindness largely being realized. It is to this event that we now turn our attention.

In 2 Sam 9:1–13, on three occasions, David uses *ḥesed* to describe his intentions towards Mephibosheth (9:1, 3, 7). Each time it is set in covenantal terms: 'kindness for Jonathan's sake' (9:1), 'the kindness of God' (9:3), and 'kindness for the sake of your father Jonathan' (9:7). David intends to honour his covenant with Jonathan. His kindness is for Jonathan's sake. David seeks to show Mephibosheth the love of God which he himself has been granted (7:4–17). However, Mephibosheth is not confident that David is to be trusted. After David has 'sent' for and 'brought' (9:5) him from Lo-debar to Jerusalem, Mephibosheth's only spoken words in this passage are 'I am your servant' (3:6) and 'What is your servant, that you should look upon a dead dog such as I?' (3:8). Schipper points out that 'dead dog' occurs on only three other occasions in the Bible, and all within the Deuteronomic history (1 Sam 24:14, 2 Sam 16:9, 2 Kgs 8:13): 'In all three cases, it is used in reference to someone who is a political enemy of the king . . . . Mephibosheth's seemingly obsequious response places him in the

---

2 J.W.L. Hoad, 'Mercy, Merciful', in *New Bible Dictionary*, 3rd edn, ed. D.R.W. Wood et al. (Leicester: InterVarsity Press, 1996), 751.

company of usurpers and political enemies.'[3] Mephibosheth is from the house of Saul, David's enemy. He is completely at the mercy of the king.

It is significant that David addresses Mephibosheth by name (9:6). This is particularly noticeable in contrast with Ziba's depersonalized naming in response to David's initial enquiry. To David's question 'Is there anyone remaining of the house of Saul to whom I may show the kindness of God?' Ziba replies: 'There remains a son of Jonathan; he is crippled in his feet' (9:3). David addresses this crippled son of Jonathan by his personal name, Mephibosheth. Peterson comments:

> David's first word to Mephibosheth is the speaking of his name (v. 6). Mephibosheth is recognized as a person. He is not a nameless exile; he is not a subcategory of victim. He has a name, and David goes to the trouble to learn it: Mephibosheth. If there was any shame or dishonor associated with this name through the years, as some conjecture – a name that he was called rather than a name by which he was addressed – it is wiped clean of ignominy as David addresses him in loyal-love. The name is used seven times in this story of their meeting, without a hint of denigration in the usage.[4]

David's response to Mephibosheth's fearful posture is 'Do not be afraid' (9:7). It is in keeping with his stated intentions. His actions then bear this out. The narrator concludes this passage by summarizing the consequences of David's kindness:

> Mephibosheth ate at David's table, like one of the king's sons. Mephibosheth had a young son whose name was Mica. And all who lived in Ziba's house became Mephibosheth's servants. Mephibosheth lived in Jerusalem, for he always ate at the king's table. Now he was lame in both his feet. (9:11–13)

The social makeup of the king's household has changed. The grandson of his enemy, the son of his covenanted friend, now sits at table as one of the sons of David. Mephibosheth is served and provided for. He has a young son named Mica. The future of his family is secured and will continue.[5] It is important,

---

3 Jeremy Schipper, 'Why Do You Still Speak of Your Affairs? Polyphony in Mephibosheth's Exchanges with David in 2 Samuel', *Vetus Testamentum* 54 (2004): 347–8.
4 Eugene H. Peterson, *First and Second Samuel*, *Westminster Bible Companion* (Louisville, KY: Westminster John Knox Press, 1999), 174.
5 David spares Mephibosheth's life in 2 Sam 21:7. The family line continues through Mica, and according to 1 Chr 8:34, 35, and 9:40, 41, Mica had four sons named Pithon, Melech, Tarea, and Ahaz.

however, to note that not all commentators agree with a generous interpretation of David's motives and behaviour. Rouse comments:

> Mephibosheth is seemingly remembered and redeemed in the context of covenant ('the Jonathan and David covenant'). However, not everyone is convinced of the inherent purity in David's motivations. David keeps the grandson of Saul under careful watch, by means of reinstatement, so that any plan of being restored to the throne is made impossible from the start. Though David's generous offer towards Mephibosheth does appear pure in its intentions, the text allows for ambiguity in David's actions.[6]

Although David's character is flawed and his actions often ambiguous, his behaviour in this passage is admirable. As previously noted, there is reason to argue that this is David at his best. This is an all too brief glimpse at David's kingdom as it should have been in the longer term.

As 2 Sam 9:1–13 closes, Mephibosheth's name is used four times by the narrator (9:11–13). His identity has been established and his future secured. Nevertheless, the passage closes with what has been a repeated identity marker: 'Now he was lame in both feet' (9:13). Schipper notes that in referring to Mephibosheth the Hebrew Bible 'drives home the point that he had a disability by mentioning "lameness" almost every time his character appears in 2 Samuel (once in 4:4 and 19:27 and twice in ch. 9 in v. 3 and v. 13)'.[7] What do we make of this emphasis?

Saul and his family have come under God's judgment. After Saul's disobedience in dealing with the Amalekites (1 Sam 15:1–9) the LORD turned against him. Saul was rejected as king (1 Sam 15:23). The LORD did not answer his prayers, 'not by dreams, or by Urim, or by prophets' (1 Sam 28:6). From the grave Samuel proclaimed that the LORD had become Saul's enemy (1 Sam 28:16). In battle with the Philistines Saul and Israel's armies were overwhelmed. Saul was killed. So were his sons Jonathan, Abinadab, and Malchishua (1 Sam 31:2). Death and affliction continue to attend Saul's family after his death. Ishbaal (Ishbosheth), Saul's son and successor, is betrayed, murdered, and beheaded (2 Sam 4:7). Michal, Saul's daughter, is cursed with barrenness (2 Sam 6:21). Seven more of Saul's male descendants are vengefully murdered – impaled before the LORD – by the Gibeonites (2 Sam 21:4). We are struck by the horror of this family's demise, and yet it is fully in keeping with Deuteronomic covenantal curses promised by God against those who, like Saul, disobey God's

---

6 Christopher D. Rouse, 'Scripture and the Disabled: Redeeming Mephibosheth's Identity', *Journal of Pentecostal Theology* 17 (2008): 190.
7 Jeremy Schipper, *Disability Studies and the Hebrew Bible: Figuring Mephibosheth in the David Story* (New York: T & T Clark, 2006), 60.

word and rebel against the covenant. In the words of Deuteronomy 28:25–8, the consequences would include the following:

> The LORD will cause you to be defeated before your enemies; you shall go out against them one way and flee before them seven ways. You shall become an object of horror to all the kingdoms of the earth. Your corpses shall be food for every bird of the air and animal of the earth, and there shall be no one to frighten them away. The LORD will afflict you with the boils of Egypt, with ulcers, scurvy, and itch, of which you cannot be healed. The LORD will afflict you with madness, blindness, and confusion of mind . . . .

Deuteronomic curses include death, sickness, blindness, and various afflictions. Mephibosheth is crippled, lame in both feet. This emphasis throughout the Samuel texts is in keeping with the narrative of God's rejection and affliction of Saul and his family. The repeated reminder of Mephibosheth's lameness is to be understood in terms of Deuteronomic covenant cursing. His lameness must also be understood in light of another important passage in Samuel. In 2 Sam 5 David comes to conquer Jerusalem. The Jebusites, David's despised enemies, assert: 'You will not come in here, even the blind and the lame will turn you back' (5:6). The passage continues: 'David had said on that day, "Whoever would strike down the Jebusites, let him get up the water shaft to attack the lame and the blind, those whom David hates." Therefore it is said, "The blind and the lame shall not come into the house"' (5:8).

Ceresko remarks: 'Commentators in general agree that v. 6 contains a claim about Jerusalem's impregnability. J. Mauchline notes, for example, that ". . . its meaning as a whole is quite clear. It is to the effect that even the blind and the lame men could successfully defend Jerusalem against any enemy."'[8] The Jebusites are defiant, they mock David, and his response is hateful. He names them as 'the lame and the blind' – the afflicted, weak, and helpless, those unfit to be warriors, those easily defeated. Henceforth, it becomes a saying that 'the blind and the lame shall not come into the house' (5:8) – that is, the Jebusites will be cast out of Jerusalem and will not return. They will never again be welcome in David's city or palace. They will be excluded from the king's house.

In 2 Sam Mephibosheth is repeatedly identified as lame. The emphasis on this fact serves to remind the reader that first, he is from the family of Saul against which God has turned. Saul has been rejected and his family afflicted by covenant curses. Some are killed, Michal has become barren, and Mephibosheth is lame. He will never be Israel's king, and God will not establish his house. The family of Saul will never again rule from Jerusalem.

---

8 Anthony R. Ceresko, 'The Identity of "the Blind and the Lame" ('iwwēr ûpissûaḥ) in 2 Samuel 5:8b', *Catholic Biblical Quarterly* 63 (2001): 26.

In the light of 2 Sam 5:6–8, Mephibosheth is like the enemy Jebusites that David hates. Since the capture of Jerusalem, there had been a saying, the word had gone around that 'the blind and the lame shall not come into the house' (5:8). It would seem that, like the Jebusites, there was no place for a person such as Mephibosheth in Jerusalem or in David's house. He was not only from the family of Saul. He was also weak and unfit, and he was to be excluded. But 2 Sam 9 provides us with a significant disruption, Mephibosheth *is* in Jerusalem; he *is* in the king's house and at the king's table. He is treated as one of the king's own sons. David's embrace of covenantal kindness has overcome covenantal cursing, offering hospitality to one who would otherwise have been excluded, one who could have been dealt with as the enemy, the cursed, the unfit, the unwelcome. In 2 Sam 9 we have a significant disruption to the expected sequence of failure, judgment, and exclusion. It is in this sense that the story of Mephibosheth acts as a counter-narrative, not only within the books of Samuel and the stories of David, but also in the larger scope of the Old Testament.

As we commenced, we asserted that in 2 Sam 9:1–13 we have a glimpse of what Davidic rule could have looked like and should have been in the longer term – an all too brief glance at David's kingdom at its best and a significant indication of the character of God's kingdom as it will unfold and be established in its fullness in the person and work of Jesus Christ and the coming new creation. It is a kingdom shaped by faithful covenantal kindness, a kingdom of radical hospitality and welcome. The story of David and Mephibosheth ought to be well known and celebrated. It is a significant story of hope, hospitality, and friendship in Samuel's account of Davidic kingship.

13 Welcoming and Including People with Intellectual Disability

A Report on a Study of Five Churches

Carol Fearon

> It is not only to open one's door and one's home to someone. It is to give space to someone in one's heart, space for that person to be and to grow; space where the person knows that he or she is accepted just as they are, with their wounds and their gifts.
>
> *Jean Vanier*[1]

My daughter has an intellectual disability. We have been fortunate that she has been welcomed as part of our family in the churches we have belonged to and is now accepted, as an adult, in our current church. Without welcome and acceptance as an adult my daughter would not be happy to attend church, and church is important to her as she has a personal faith and wants to be involved in the ministry of the church. It is this age group, young adults, that is the focus of this chapter.

In 2014 I completed a master's thesis which examined how some churches were able to welcome people with intellectual disabilities.[2] The results showed that welcome and inclusion requires significant input from pastors and leaders, but also brings benefits to the whole church. This chapter is a report on that thesis, covering how the research was undertaken and the results obtained.

The church, with its message of God's unconditional love and grace towards humanity, would be expected to lead the way in including people who are on the margins of society. Most people assume that this is the case in their church, as Jeff McNair found in his 2007 study: 85 per cent of respondents felt

---

1 Jean Vanier, *Community and Growth*, rev. edn (Homebush, New South Wales: St Paul Publications, 1989), 265.
2 Carol Fearon, 'Welcoming and Including People with Intellectual Disability: A Study of Five Churches', (MAppTheol. diss., Carey Graduate School, 2014).

that people having disabilities would be welcome at their church.³ Research demonstrates a different reality, as Jason Forbes and Lindsey Gale found that only 22 per cent of the churches in their Australian study had a 'welcoming culture' towards people with disabilities.⁴ Brett Webb-Mitchell lamented that many parents of children with intellectual disabilities have experienced the gentle recommendation to 'find another more suitable church'.⁵ Ault, Collins, and Carter found that only half of parents having children with intellectual disabilities felt supported in their church, a third had changed church to find a welcome, and the likelihood of a welcome declined for children who were behaviourally challenging. Over half of parents in their study were expected to provide support to enable their child to participate in activities; furthermore, support declined as the child became an adult.⁶

There are two major reasons for a lack of welcome by the church. First, people with intellectual disabilities can be disruptive. McNair contends we have come to expect an experience on Sunday morning that is uplifting and undisturbed.⁷ He says that the church has 'embraced the culture' and rejects those people who are not capable of participating in the 'normal' way. Second, do people with intellectual disabilities understand about faith, and if not, how will they benefit from being in church?⁸ The Enlightenment bias towards rational thought has led to a popular understanding that belief and spirituality are primarily about comprehension and mental assent. This has made it difficult to talk about people with intellectual disabilities having 'knowledge of God'. However, Bill Gaventa has pointed out, 'How do we know anyone understands?'⁹ He says we have a responsibility to teach and demonstrate our faith so that all can understand at their level. Furthermore, it is important not to underestimate people's understanding, since studies by John Swinton¹⁰ and Susannah Turner

---

3 Jeff McNair, 'Christian Social Constructions of Disability: Church Attendees', *Journal of Religion, Disability and Health* 11 (2007): 51–64.
4 See Chapter 9 in this volume.
5 Brett Webb-Mitchell, *Beyond Accessibility: Towards Full Inclusion of People with Disabilities in Faith Communities* (New York: Church Publishing, 2010), 78; Charlene Y. Schultz, 'The Church and Other Body Parts: Closing the Gap Between the Church and People with Disabilities', *Journal of Religion, Disability and Health* 16 (2012): 195.
6 Melinda Jones Ault, Belva C. Collins, and Erik W. Carter, 'Congregational Participation and Supports for Children and Adults with Disabilities: Parent Perceptions', *Journal of Intellectual and Developmental Disability* 51 (2013): 48–61.
7 Jeff McNair, 'Knowledge, Faith Development, and Religious Education that Includes All', *Journal of Religion, Disability and Health* 14 (2010): 186–203.
8 Reverend Craig Modahl, 'Finding a Place at the Table', *Journal of Religion, Disability and Health* 13 (2009): 320–22. Sarah R. Nettleton, 'Come to the Table', *Journal of Religion, Disability and Health* 13 (2009): 314–15.
9 William Gaventa, 'How Do We Know Any of Us Understands? Communion as Community Building', *Journal of Religion, Disability and Health* 13 (2009): 317.
10 John Swinton, 'Restoring the Image: Spirituality, Faith, and Cognitive Disability', *Journal of Religion, Disability and Health* 36 (1997): 21.

and her colleagues[11] have revealed the importance of spirituality in the lives of people with intellectual disabilities.[12]

My aim in this study was to be encouraging to the church. I wanted a positive focus, so the emphasis was on churches that were already welcoming and including people with intellectual disability. I wanted to learn how and why this was happening, and to learn about the benefits and difficulties churches experienced. I also wanted to demonstrate to other churches that welcome and inclusion is neither a recipe for disaster, nor is it a special ministry for special places, but that this can and should be done in every church.

Methodology

Defining 'welcome' and 'inclusion' is difficult, and even contentious. To be 'included' can imply a choice made by the church to include people with intellectual disabilities; this opens the door to the option *not* to include, and for people with disabilities this is contentious.[13] There is no accepted definition of 'welcome' in the literature, despite 'a welcoming attitude' being the most important feature of a church for the parents of children with disabilities. For the purpose of this study, 'welcome' and 'inclusion' mean that people are not only accepted as a presence on the margins of the church, but that they are brought into the mainstream life of the church, both worship and ministry.

Intellectual disability is also frequently misunderstood and confused with mental illness. This study used a broad definition, including developmental delay, Down syndrome, people affected cognitively by brain damage, and those on the autism spectrum when this involves cognitive impairment.

Confidentiality was important to safeguard the participants in the study.[14] Churches were identified only by broad interdenominational terms, such as 'Evangelical', 'Pentecostal', and 'mainline'.[15] Details of the churches' services and ministries were altered to preserve anonymity. In order to ensure that future relationships between pastor and congregants were not prejudiced, parents' comments were reported with no reference to the church concerned.

The study was concerned with analysing the reasons behind situations in order to understand *how* churches are able to welcome and include people with

---

11 Susannah Turner et al., 'Religious Expression Amongst Adults with Intellectual Disabilities', *Journal of Applied Research in Intellectual Disabilities* 17 (2004): 161–71.
12 People trusted God to protect them, and had a relationship to God through prayer, often describing God as a friend.
13 Webb-Mitchell, *Beyond Accessibility*; Herman P. Meininger, 'The Order of Disturbance: Theological Reflections on Strangeness and Strangers, and the Inclusion of Persons with Intellectual Disabilities in Faith Communities', *Journal of Religion, Disability and Health* 12 (2008): 347–64.
14 Pranee Liamputtong, *Qualitative Research Methods*, 4th edn (Melbourne: Oxford University Press, 2013), 41.
15 'Mainline' is an American term referring to Presbyterian, Anglican, Methodist, and Congregational churches.

intellectual disability, not simply that they do. In-depth qualitative interviewing allowed me to do more than collect data on how many people with intellectual disabilities are in the church and how they participate, but also to encourage pastors to reflect on why some things work and others do not. By enabling participants to tell stories freely about their congregations, their children, and actual incidents, they reveal the contradictions, challenges, and benefits of involving people with intellectual disabilities in church life.

Since the focus of the study was young adults, each church had to have two or more people aged 16–30 with mild to moderate intellectual disabilities in the congregation and involved in church life. Contact with potential churches was by recommendation from people in the disability community. Interviewing the parents of people with intellectual disabilities from each church gave a perspective on how people were experiencing what the leaders perceived to be welcome and inclusion.

Results and Discussion

The five churches involved in the study came from four different denominations. They varied in size from large, with over 600 people in the congregation and multiple services on a Sunday, to the smallest church, which had approximately 100 people in the congregation and one service on Sunday. I interviewed two pastors, one senior pastor, and two pastoral leaders who were part of the leadership team of their church.

In addition to the required two or more young people with intellectual disabilities, churches in the study also had significant numbers of people with a variety of disabilities that appeared to be around the level of disability in the general population. However, the numbers are hard to evaluate.[16] Forbes and Gale (Australia) report that levels of attendance by people with disability vary with denomination from under 1 per cent in Pentecostal churches, 7 per cent in Evangelical churches to 8–10 per cent in mainline churches.[17] The Pentecostal church in my study was noticeably different from this denominational norm since the pastor reported that 20 per cent of the congregation had some disability.

The churches also had a wide age range of people with intellectual disabilities, from children to older adults with dementia. In two churches larger numbers of people with intellectual disability formed a sub-group within the congregation. Each group had an age range from young adults to middle-aged, and a variety

---

16 In the 15–44 age range in which my participants fitted, 9 per cent of the population has some level of disability. The overall rate for all types of disability in the population is 17 per cent. No direct figures exist for the proportion of people with intellectual disability in the 15–44 age range, but extrapolation produces a rough figure of 4 per cent with intellectual disability, with approximately a third of those disabled from birth and two-thirds caused by accidents; 'Disability Survey 2006' [accessed 9 September 2013]. Online: http://www.stats.govt.nz/browse_for_stats/health/disabilities/DisabilitySurvey2006_HOTP06/Commentary.aspx.
17 There are no figures available for New Zealand. For Australian figures, see Chapter 9 in this volume.

of intellectual disabilities from mild developmental delay to behaviourally challenging, such as autism.[18]

How Young People Participate in the Church

All of the churches in the study had activities that were open to people with intellectual disabilities, though this did not extend to all the programmes the churches ran. Three churches had special services for people with intellectual disabilities (Elevate Christian Disability Trust meetings in two churches and a weekday service in another), but these meetings were in addition to regular meetings, and people with intellectual disabilities were encouraged to attend regular services and activities. However, despite all the pastors saying that participation in the life of the church was encouraged, three of the eight parents said their child did not participate in any activities except the Sunday meetings.

All the churches provided support to enable participation in some activities; there were both formal and informal supports in place. One church had a well-organized buddy system to enable participation in youth groups and other activities, including support for volunteer work in the ministries of the church. Two churches had a roster system for everyone, including people with intellectual disabilities, and tasks included helping in the kitchen, welcoming on the door, and being on the band roster. Parents in Ault and colleagues' study commended the buddy type of formal support since it enabled participation without parents having to accompany their child.[19] They noted, however, that support declined as children reached adolescence, so churches in my study were doing well in continuing to provide support. All three churches with formal supports encouraged involvement, and the young people with intellectual disabilities were engaged in a wide variety of activities and roles.

The other two churches were less structured; involvement by those who wanted to participate was facilitated by informal congregational support. This flexibility is a potential strength of smaller congregations, and was also noted in Ault and colleagues' study, where 'one parent indicated that [while] small congregations often did not have specialised programs or personnel, their family was well known there, people loved and cared for their child, and they were willing to adapt and provide programs'.[20]

Access to youth groups was a problem for three parents. Only two out of the five churches had suitable youth groups.[21] However, two churches did have

---

18 One group had approximately eight people, the other group had approximately 12 people.
19 Melinda Jones Ault, Belva C. Collins, and Erik W. Carter, 'Factors Associated with Participation in Faith Communities for Individuals with Developmental Disabilities and Their Families', *Journal of Religion, Disability and Health* 17 (2013): 194.
20 Ault et al., 'Congregational Participation and Supports for Children and Adults with Disabilities', 201.
21 If the youth group is for young teens, it is often not appropriate to have older men in the group. Groups aimed at an older age range were sometimes focused on students or young married couples, again not suitable for people with intellectual disabilities.

flexible criteria and an inclusive attitude, and two parents mentioned that their adult children had been welcomed at the youth groups of other churches. Because social activities for people with intellectual disabilities are limited and these young people are often unable to socialize without support from family or support workers, opportunities like youth groups are important.[22]

On the positive side, three of the young people had jobs at their church. These included working in the cafe, taking responsibility for signage, cleaning at the church, and helping in the crèche. These roles provided a sense of self-worth. The young people who were proactive in offering to help seemed to get more involved than others, though in some cases the leadership was proactive. Their desire to serve and willingness to volunteer could be a positive challenge to other young adults in the church, and because people with intellectual disabilities often do not have paid employment, they are available to volunteer during the week.[23]

Parents also have differing desires for their children. One pastor commented that parents 'don't want to meet lots of other Down syndrome children at church, they want their kids to be accepted by other children'.[24] However, another said, 'We have met all their parents [the group of people with intellectual disabilities] and they are just delighted that they have this little community within the community.'[25] There is still debate around inclusion in education and how best to support people with intellectual disabilities. Inclusion has been shown to improve the performance of some students with intellectual disabilities.[26] However, there is a counter-view that full inclusion can overlook the value of 'disability culture' for fostering friendships between people with similar disabilities and life experiences, so it is understandable that parents also have differing views.[27] McVilly's study, which talked to groups of young adults with intellectual disabilities, found that 'sharing the experience and identity of intellectual disability appeared to enhance the sense of equality that was important to the formation and maintenance of what expert group participants perceived to be "true friendship"' (the 'expert group' were young people with intellectual disabilities who belonged to People First, a self-advocacy group).[28] This demonstrates that it is important not to dictate the type of inclusion available on the

---

22 Keith R. McVilly et al., 'Self-advocates Have the Last Say on Friendship', *Disability & Society* 21 (2006): 704.
23 Jeff McNair, 'The Indispensable Nature of Persons with Intellectual Disabilities to the Church', *Journal of Religion, Disability and Health* 12 (2008): 322.
24 Fearon, 'Welcoming and Including People with Intellectual Disability', 78.
25 Ibid.
26 David Mitchell, 'Education that Fits: Review of International Trends in the Education of Students with Special Educational Needs' [accessed 30 September 2013] Online: http://www.education counts.govt.nz/publications/special_education/education-that-fits-review-of-international-trends-in-the-education-of-students-with-special-educational-needs/chapter-eleven-inclusive-education.
27 Ibid.
28 McVilly et al., 'Self-advocates Have the Last Say on Friendship', 703.

basis of a particular philosophy, and that people with intellectual disabilities are allowed to have their say.

The Response of the Congregations

All the parents felt their children experienced positive and accepting interaction from most members of the congregation. However, pastors noted that some members of the congregation found interaction with people who had intellectual disabilities challenging, and avoided it.[29] But in every church there were members of the congregation who did actively engage with the young people. The proportion of people currently interacting confidently varied from a small percentage to most of the congregation. One pastor said that their congregation were becoming more accepting, and some even comfortable, with the presence of people who were different. This suggests that those people who did make the effort to relate came to appreciate the presence of people with intellectual disabilities.[30]

Congregations were not necessarily negative towards people with intellectual disabilities, but pastors were aware that the congregation had to adapt in order to be welcoming towards people with intellectual disabilities. Pastors saw a gulf between their own ability to relate easily to people who were different and that of the congregation, and most actively modelled good interaction. Meininger points out: 'Making our communities accessible means primarily that we have to make our hearts accessible too.'[31] The simple phrase 'make our hearts accessible' hides a complex process of facing fears, overcoming personal discomfort, and granting people the right to be in *our* space. Parents mentioned their appreciation of the effort pastors put in. One parent commented that 'if the leader is introducing you to this person ... then you take the lead from that. You know who they are, valued and respected, so you treat them that way.'[32] Six parents confirmed that leaders were proactive in interaction with people with intellectual disabilities.

There were a few complaints about the presence of people with intellectual disabilities in the church. However, complaints to pastors mostly related to the

---

29 This is also noted in studies by Meininger, 'The Order of Disturbance'; Thomas E. Reynolds, 'Theology and Disability: Changing the Conversation', *Journal of Religion, Disability and Health* 16 (2012): 33–48, and Brian Brock, 'Praise: The Prophetic Public Presence of the Mentally Disabled', in *Blackwell Companion to Christian Ethics*, 2nd edn (Oxford: Wiley-Blackwell, 2011), 139–51.

30 This is endorsed by John Swinton, *From Bedlam to Shalom: Towards a Practical Theology of Human Nature, Interpersonal Relationships, and Mental Health Care* (New York: Peter Lang, 2000), 157. And the following study found that 49 per cent of pastors noted benefits in having people with intellectual disability in the congregation: Angela Novak Amado et al., 'Accessible Congregations Campaign: Follow-up Survey of Impact on Individuals with Intellectual/Developmental Disabilities (ID/DD)', *Journal of Religion, Disability and Health* 16 (2012): 411, 413.

31 Meininger, 'The Order of Disturbance', 348.

32 Fearon, 'Welcoming and Including People with Intellectual Disability', 85.

presence of individuals who have little concept of personal space. It appears that acceptance can depend on how different one's behaviour is from accepted social norms.[33] One pastor had responded by teaching one-to-one how to establish boundaries and relate to people who have no concept of personal space, but it had not been easy. There appears to be a need to train the congregation not only in how to relate to people who are challenging behaviourally, but also in how to maintain reasonable personal boundaries. Parents confirmed that the most significant factor in congregational interaction was the level of intelligibility and social competence of their child. Parents who attended the same church as their child noticed how people might appear rather uncomfortable to begin with in relating to their children. In response to this, most parents had actively educated members of the congregation on how to listen to and interact with their child. Behavioural modelling is also needed for people with intellectual disabilities who may have little social awareness.[34] Pastors had worked hard to teach their people with intellectual disabilities how to behave appropriately. However, it is difficult to change the behaviour of people with disabilities such as those on the autism spectrum, and minor change may be all that is possible.

The presence of people with intellectual disability in the churches shows there was a welcoming culture in the churches I surveyed. Most pastors promoted this culture by personally relating to the people with disability and modelling this relationship to the congregation. Parents were also active in helping the congregation to relate to their child. Despite difficulties around challenging behaviours and complaints about some individuals, none of the pastors had contemplated changing their policy of welcome to people with all forms of intellectual disability.

The Reasons for the Presence of People with Intellectual Disabilities in the Churches

A welcoming attitude was the reason pastors felt their church included people with intellectual disabilities. Comments from pastors related to leadership – 'because of our attitude; reaching out and welcoming in ... and all the leadership is clearly comfortable with rag tags or people who are different'[35] – and being intentional: 'you have to be intentional. It does not just happen, and you have to create that space'.[36] A common feature of the five churches was initial welcoming that translated into long-term acceptance.

Three churches had adults with intellectual disabilities who had grown up in the church. Two of these churches had seen an increase in numbers due to leadership who encouraged participation, and people with intellectual disabilities

---

33 Ault et al., 'Congregational Participation and Supports for Children and Adults with Disabilities', 56.
34 Gaventa, 'How Do We Know Any of Us Understands?', 318.
35 Fearon, 'Welcoming and Including People with Intellectual Disability', 87.
36 Ibid.

had invited their friends. The other two churches in the study had proactively sought and welcomed people.

In three churches the pastor appeared to be largely responsible for the number of people with disability in the church. This involved personally inviting people, developing an outward focus for the church, and the ability to relate easily to people with intellectual disability because of previous experience. Three of the pastors were described as 'wonderful' by parents.[37] This is both encouraging, because the pastors considered people with intellectual disabilities to be an important part of the church, and also of concern, since overseas studies have noted that when leaders leave, programmes can flounder.[38] This is not inevitable, however; the church culture can transform the pastor, as demonstrated in one church where the pastor had gone from fear of people with intellectual disabilities to appreciating the gifts they brought to the church. In another church the leadership had built welcome into the long-term vision of the church, thus protecting it from individual agendas. This is recommended by Forbes and Gale, who noted: 'If there is a commitment in the mission statement, this is something that can be talked about with each new minister, and the statement will help to keep people committed to the work of inclusion.'[39]

Parents gave a variety of reasons why they attended a particular church. Several parents had been personally invited to the church and found a welcome for their child that had kept them coming back.[40] One parent said: 'suddenly Jake was a welcomed person and we were welcomed . . . we loved the people here and we loved [the pastor]'.[41] Three parents had moved from another church to find a place that would welcome or suit their child.[42] Another parent mentioned that the more traditional nature of the services at her son's church suited him, and that one of the reasons he liked the church was that it had more traditional music. People with intellectual disabilities are very different from each other; it is a mistake to think 'they' need a particular type of service any more than non-disabled people. While people with Down syndrome can enjoy informality and socializing, people on the autism spectrum may appreciate a more structured traditional service.

Participation by their child was important to parents. Parents agreed that if people do not get involved 'they become pew warmers and it is not good

---

37 Ibid., 88.
38 Ault et al., 'Factors Associated with Participation in Faith Communities for Individuals with Developmental Disabilities and Their Families', 197.
39 See Chapter 9 in this volume.
40 Over 90 per cent of parents considered a 'welcoming attitude' important; Ault et al., 'Congregational Participation and Supports for Children and Adults with Disabilities', 58.
41 Fearon, 'Welcoming and Including People with Intellectual Disability', 89.
42 Almost one-third of parents in their study reported having changed church because of non-acceptance of their child. Ault et al., 'Congregational Participation and Supports for Children and Adults with Disabilities', 55.

for them'.⁴³ Four parents said that greater expectations of their child led to improved behaviour.⁴⁴ Recognizing people's abilities was also important to parents. For example, one parent said her son loved to talk to new people; she said that if it was recognized as a ministry, he could be trained to help with greeting at the door.

Three young people had chosen the church themselves. This is reflected in other studies in both the USA and the UK.⁴⁵ All the young people attended church because it was what they wanted to do. This was demonstrated by four of them travelling to church on their own, either all the time or when their parents were unable to take them, and the fact that five of the young people, either now or in the past, had attended different churches than their parents. It is remarkable that for a group of people often assumed to be incapable of looking after themselves, in the five churches pastors reported that 11 of the young people attended without their families, having chosen the church for themselves.

Only one family I interviewed had come to their current church simply by having moved into the area. However, pastors mentioned location as a factor, as several people had started attending because they lived locally. Being within walking distance can be important for people with intellectual disabilities since most are dependent on others for transport.⁴⁶ This emphasizes the need for all churches to be welcoming.

Difficulties

All the pastors said that people with intellectual disabilities required more input of time and resources than the average church member. The larger churches were coping well with the additional demands on personnel in the form of buddies and sponsors. Some pastors struggled with the amount of work involved. One pastor commented: 'from the outside looking in, it all looks great and wonderful, but there are lots of issues'.⁴⁷ The sociability of people with intellectual disability can be draining, and they also require more pastoral work: 'There is always relational stuff going on, and I have to deal with all that.'⁴⁸ Another pastor said that even one person with few social skills who was enthusiastic and attended everything added a level of stress to activities. People with intellectual

---

43 Fearon, 'Welcoming and Including People with Intellectual Disability', 92.
44 This is also noted by Mary Beth Walsh, Alice F. Walsh, and William C. Gaventa, eds, *Autism and Faith: A Journey into Community* (New Brunswick, NJ: UMDNJ-Robert Wood Johnson Medical School, 2008), 27.
45 Ault et al., 'Factors Associated with Participation in Faith Communities for Individuals with Developmental Disabilities and Their Families', 199. Turner et al., 'Religious Expression Amongst Adults with Intellectual Disabilities'.
46 Ibid., 168.
47 Fearon, 'Welcoming and Including People with Intellectual Disability', 92.
48 Ibid.

disabilities who attended without their families added to the workload, as pastoral staff might need to get involved in advocacy with support organizations.

A major difficulty in one church was the perception of visitors that the church had an overwhelming number of people with disabilities. This was not actually true: at 21 per cent of the congregation it was above the overall rate for the general population of 17 per cent, but not hugely so. This could reflect the continuing relatively low visibility of people with disabilities in society.[49]

Benefits

All the pastors mentioned the enthusiasm, reliability, and regularity of attendance of their people with intellectual disabilities. In this respect, people with intellectual disabilities are a stark contrast to the growing transitory nature of church attendance generally. Pastors mentioned that when properly organized they were reliable and competent in their areas of strength, such as setting out chairs, though lack of flexibility could be an issue. Parents echoed the pastors' experience that people with intellectual disabilities work well and are reliable. In two churches the group of people with intellectual disabilities added something to the worship through their freedom and lack of inhibition. Pastors said a major benefit was seeing people with intellectual disabilities grow and take on new roles.

Two pastors mentioned that the challenge of people who are different is good for the congregation: 'you need difficult people . . . . White, middle-class people need to be confronted and moved out of their complacency.'[50] Swinton would concur: 'In encountering people with profound developmental disabilities in friendship, people's lives are changed, their priorities are reshaped and their vision of God and humanness are altered at their very core.'[51]

Despite the significant cost of welcome in four of the churches, they all reported benefits that more than outweighed the problems.

Parents' Perceptions

The dominant benefit reported by the parents was the acceptance and support of their children. One parent reported that for her son, being accepted as 'one of the kids [had] been an incredibly normalising process for him'.[52] Another said

---

49 This low visibility is recognized by the government: 'In particular, we need to increase the visibility of disabled people across society'; Office of Disability Issues, 'Progress in Implementing the NZ Disability Strategy 2004–2005. Chapter One: Upholding Citizenship' [accessed 12 November 2013] Online: http://www.odi.govt.nz/nzds/progress-reports/july04-june05/chapter-one-upholding-citizenship.html.
50 Fearon, 'Welcoming and Including People with Intellectual Disability', 94.
51 John Swinton, 'The Body of Christ Has Down's Syndrome: Theological Reflections on Vulnerability, Disability, and Graceful Communities', *Journal of Pastoral Theology* 13 (2003): 66–78.
52 Fearon, 'Welcoming and Including People with Intellectual Disability', 96.

her daughter had been consistently invited to help, and supported in helping, and 'she has become less disabled and more abled because they have shown her that she is fearfully and wonderfully made'.[53] One parent expressed appreciation of the support offered to her when she was feeling low, and felt that the approach of the church to people with disability, of welcoming and accepting and valuing them, really worked well. The consistency of welcome and inclusion over time was noticed and praised by five parents.

Parents were not very demanding of the church in relation to their children. Only one parent reported asking for additional support or activities. Two parents reported the pastor proactively inviting their child to participate and offering support to enable the participation, and this was really appreciated. Studies by Collins and Ault, Turner and colleagues, and Treloar have noted that parents often do not ask for support, and they emphasized the need for a church to be proactive.[54]

However, there is no reason for complacency: despite the welcome extended by the churches and the gratitude of parents there are major shortcomings. One parent in particular had been challenged by the questions raised, and realized that in spite of support for them as a family and acceptance of their son, 'it is not inclusion'.[55] His participation had declined over time, leading to his finding another church. Three parents also mentioned a lack of social activities for their children.

Andy Calder's Australian study has the title 'To Belong, I Need to be Missed'.[56] This is a challenging statement for me, as I am not sure that my daughter would be missed in a positive sense if she stopped coming to church, though her absence would be noticed and commented on. Acceptance is not quite the same as being missed. Several parents commented that their child was not approached with a view to pursuing relationships outside the meetings. One parent's somewhat bitter comment is realistic: 'so I guess it is paid people for life for him'.[57] Verdonschot notes a study showing that the average number of people in the social network of people with intellectual disability was 3.1, and one of those was usually a paid staff member.[58] Loneliness is a common experience for people with intellectual disability. Only one parent said that people in the

---

53 Ibid.
54 Belva C. Collins and Melinda Jones Ault, 'Including Persons with Disabilities in the Religious Community: Program Models Implemented by Two Churches', *Journal of Religion, Disability and Health* 14 (2010): 113–31. See also Turner et al., 'Religious Expression Amongst Adults with Intellectual Disabilities', and Linda L. Treloar, 'Disability, Spiritual Beliefs and the Church: The Experiences of Adults with Disabilities and Family Members', *Journal of Advanced Nursing* 40 (2002): 594–603.
55 Fearon, 'Welcoming and Including People with Intellectual Disability', 96.
56 Andy Calder, 'To Belong, I Need to be Missed', *Journal of Religion, Disability and Health* 16 (2012): 262–86.
57 Fearon, 'Welcoming and Including People with Intellectual Disability', 97.
58 M.M.L. Verdonschot et al., 'Community Participation of People with an Intellectual Disability: A Review of Empirical Findings', *Journal of Intellectual Disability Research* 53 (2009): 303–18.

congregation had asked for assurance that her daughter would still be attending church when she moved into a group home. For parents, the provision of a circle of friends for their child can be an ongoing challenge and a source of frustration and grief, as they witness the loneliness of their child.[59] Where the church could be of great benefit, too often what is forthcoming is acceptance of the person's presence, but this does not translate into personal friendships.

Ideas from Participants for Improving Inclusion

All pastors recognized that opportunities for interaction within the congregation were vital. The need for interaction is borne out by studies showing that familiarity is a major determining factor in attitudes towards people with disabilities. Interaction with the congregation could be improved by greater integration in the activities of the church.

Parents' suggestions for improvement echoed the difficulties they experienced with church. Social activities such as youth groups needed to be accessible to young people with intellectual disability.[60] This accessibility requires some training for helpers in understanding disability and providing extra help in the form of buddies or mentoring. Two parents noted spiritual and character growth in their child associated with a mentoring style of friendship, so this method seemed to be working. Parents wanted more opportunities for their children to participate in the activities of the church, and to help with the running and ministry of the church.

Only one pastor had considered changing the way 'we do church' in order to be more inclusive. To some extent this reflects the stage that integration has reached in New Zealand society. Programmes run specifically for people with intellectual disabilities are being discouraged; and people with intellectual disabilities are encouraged to join existing community programmes. However, without individualized support community programmes may not achieve the goals of gaining life skills or forming friendships for many people with intellectual disabilities.

In relation to teaching on disability, pastors felt that they either had done teaching on disability or that there was no need for such teaching. However, many parents of children with disabilities had never heard any teaching on issues around disability in church.[61] One pastor implied that teaching about disability would not be relevant to most of the congregation. But my experience, and that of three parents, had been that members of the congregation, rather

---

59 This is also observed in every study that asked parents about their experiences; for example: Treloar, 'Disability, Spiritual Beliefs and the Church', 599. Ault et al., 'Factors Associated with Participation in Faith Communities for Individuals with Developmental Disabilities and Their Families', 200.
60 Amy Elizabeth Jacober, 'Youth Ministry, Religious Education, and Adolescents with Disabilities: Insights from Parents and Guardians', *Journal of Religion, Disability and Health* 14 (2010): 167–81.
61 Treloar, 'Disability, Spiritual Beliefs and the Church', 599–600.

than the pastor, offered unhelpful theological advice.[62] Thus, teaching the whole congregation is important.[63] Several parents volunteered that they could teach the congregation about disability since they were somewhat experts in the field.

Concluding Reflections

Pastors Need Experience

The attitude of leadership is vital. It is important for pastors to model good interaction so that people with intellectual disabilities become seen firstly as *people*. A major hurdle for pastors to overcome is unfamiliarity with people having intellectual disability. One pastor demonstrated that becoming familiar with people does not take long, and that it transforms one's attitude. Pastors sometimes found their people with intellectual disabilities annoying, incomprehensible, time-consuming, and a nuisance. However, they also found them adorable, encouraging, loyal, and reliable. They recognized that people with intellectual disabilities have gifts to offer, and were encouraging them to serve in the church. Behaviour management is important, since there were examples of the escalation of unchecked behaviour.[64] This is not in the best interest of the congregation or the person with intellectual disability. The more experienced pastors in the study coped better both with people having intellectual disabilities and with the congregation's reactions to their presence.

Congregations Need Education

Every congregation has people with fears around disability. While Forbes and Gale discovered that nearly 50 per cent of people in the church have some contact with persons with disability,[65] generally it appears that as a community we are losing the ability to relate to different sorts of people. One parent said that people were afraid that relating to a person with intellectual disability

---

62 For example: 'What have you done in your past that would make God give you a child with a disability?'; ibid., 598.
63 McNair's study demonstrates the prevalence of faulty theological assumptions about disability: 38 per cent agreed that 'Parents of a child with mental retardation were selected by God to have a disabled child because he knew they could handle it'; 14 per cent agreed that 'If a person with a disability had sufficient faith, he/she would be healed of the disability'; 35 per cent agreed that 'People with disabilities have disabilities in order to teach those around them lessons about life', and 54 per cent agreed that 'Children with mental retardation are God's special angels unaware'; McNair, 'Christian Social Constructions of Disability'.
64 One church in the study had experienced congregation members who had involved the police to prevent unwelcome intrusion into their lives by people with intellectual disabilities who also attended the church.
65 Although much of this may be superficial and related to physical disability, there should be some people in a congregation who know how to relate to people with intellectual disability; see Chapter 9 in this volume.

would lead to becoming a caregiver. Pastors need to teach people about setting boundaries around interaction, and the pastors in my study often used complaints about behaviour as teaching opportunities.

However, teaching people how to relate to people with disabilities does not have to come only from the pastor. In all five churches parents had actively educated members of the congregation on how to relate to their child. Parents also noted that new people to the church tended to imitate the rest of the congregation when faced with disruptive behaviour. Smaller churches seemed to cope better with disturbances during services, some pastors interacting positively with the person causing the disturbance. In larger churches where disturbances were not appropriate, facilities were available, for example having the cafe area available and serving coffee, with a closed-circuit television screen showing the meeting.[66] The study produced stories of congregation members becoming comfortable around people with intellectual disabilities and spontaneously providing appropriate support.

Integration is Dependent on Flexibility and Support

The experience of welcome was not dependent upon *how* the church supported people with intellectual disabilities to participate; it was actually doing it that was important.[67] This means that resources and facilities are not vital; the community of a smaller church can have a flexibility that makes up for its lack of facilities. It is also important not to rely on parents to provide support for their young adults' activities, though studies show this is often the case. None of the churches in this study expected parents to do this; support was provided for people with intellectual disabilities to participate independently. This is encouraging.

People with intellectual disabilities are not all the same. This study found people who drove themselves to church and people who worked in the crèche. However, there were also people who needed multiple supports in order to participate. It is important to individualize support. Some people with intellectual disabilities just want to attend on Sunday; others want to be involved in helping in many areas during the week. Youth groups were one area where flexibility made the difference between integration and exclusion. Consultation with parents and people with intellectual disabilities is important, and something that pastors need to work on.[68] People with intellectual disabilities have desires and goals that need to be heard. One pastor detailed an example of co-operation between the church and family which produced a business opportunity and

---

66 It is important not to send parents with older children and adults to 'the cry room' – there are examples of the mothers being the ones who cry there. Walsh et al., *Autism and Faith*, 12.
67 This was also found in other studies: Ault et al., 'Congregational Participation and Supports for Children and Adults with Disabilities', 193–94; Schultz, 'The Church and Other Body Parts', 195.
68 Collins and Ault, 'Including Persons with Disabilities in the Religious Community', 55.

personal growth for one young man. When supported, people with intellectual disabilities are committed members and enthusiastic participants in churches full of busy, stressed people. Many of them volunteered for roles in the church, rather than waiting to be asked, and were reliable within their limitations. This shows that people with intellectual disabilities are not simply passive receivers of whatever support is provided, but contribute to the life of the church.

Leaders and Congregations Need Training to Support People

When the leaders of youth groups and home groups are trained in strategies to involve people with intellectual disabilities, then integration is more effective. Some leaders will require a support person present whereas others may cope well on their own. Simply allowing a person with intellectual disability to turn up and sit in the corner is not enough. The buddy system implemented to improve integration in two churches had the additional benefit of increasing the number of people in the congregation who were able to relate well to people with intellectual disabilities.

While the congregation may never be entirely supportive of the inclusion of people with intellectual disabilities, they will become more supportive over time. Familiarity alone will overcome fears, even with little motivation by the people.[69] It is important that the congregation understands that the stance of welcome is non-negotiable and that they are a part of that welcome. Leadership must be intentional; if the church as a whole is not taught the importance of welcome, then people will not be prepared to put in the work needed to fully integrate people with intellectual disabilities.[70] This study shows that people do adapt over time to the presence of people with intellectual disability.

Implications of the Study

The implications of this study are encouraging, as they highlight the benefits of inclusion. However, they also demonstrate that the church needs teaching about disability.

It was the conviction of pastors in the study that the role of the church was to welcome all who came, and further, to extend a welcome by reaching out to serve the community and to invite people in. In doing this they had found that welcoming people with intellectual disabilities had benefited the church.

---

69 Swinton, *From Bedlam to Shalom*, 157.
70 Brian Brock, 'Theologizing Inclusion: 1 Corinthians 12 and the Politics of the Body of Christ', *Journal of Religion, Disability and Health* 15 (2011): 351–76; McNair, 'The Indispensable Nature of Persons with Intellectual Disabilities to the Church'; John Swinton, 'From Inclusion to Belonging: A Practical Theology of Community, Disability and Humanness', *Journal of Religion, Disability and Health* 16 (2012): 172–90.

Meininger argues that for people with intellectual disabilities to be included in a local church, people have to develop the capacity to cope with difference. As well as practical supports being available, mental and theological barriers must be dismantled. This will require personal growth and openness of heart.[71] Pastors felt that this imperative to growth was one of the main benefits of the presence of people with intellectual disabilities. Congregations can become comfortable in their communities and their theology, and people with intellectual disabilities challenge this by 'disturbing the peace', often literally. Pastors have found for themselves, and for others in the congregation, that encounter with people who have intellectual disabilities has been radically transforming, changing priorities, worldviews, and even their vision of God.[72]

McNair says we have a lot to learn about love and acceptance from people with intellectual disabilities.[73] Social conventions keep us from sharing who we really are, whereas people with intellectual disabilities cannot hide who they are, and often speak the truth as they see it, appropriate or not. In New Zealand self-reliance is an important virtue, but people with intellectual disabilities are continually dependent on others and learn ask for help when they need it, thus they find it easier to depend on God. Pastors appreciated these characteristics as modelling how we should relate to each other in church, being more 'real'. One parent's experience of people with intellectual disabilities was: 'They are socially very accepting of people, and if you are nice to them you've got a friend for life. So a very positive influence, I think.'[74] Gaventa emphasizes the need to 'look for the shared interests, passions, and gifts that can build bonds between people with and without disabilities, rather than inviting people into roles of volunteer and consumer'.[75] Pastors mentioned the enthusiasm of people with intellectual disabilities and their eagerness to help practically. All mentioned their reliability and enthusiasm for jobs within their capabilities. Spiritual gifts were also recognized in people with intellectual disabilities. They can benefit the church with their time and their gifts, provided they are recognized.

One church cannot do everything; this especially applies to smaller churches. There needs to be co-operation between churches. Johnstone's study on Generations X and Y in New Zealand churches looked at young people who attended two churches at the same time as a strategy to access the support and activities they wanted. He said: 'Church two-timing offers potential encouragement to smaller churches with very few young adults who do not wish to lose their valued members of the congregation.'[76] People with intellectual disability

---

71 Meininger, 'The Order of Disturbance'.
72 Swinton, 'The Body of Christ Has Down's Syndrome', 67.
73 McNair, 'The Indispensable Nature of Persons with Intellectual Disabilities to the Church'.
74 Fearon, 'Welcoming and Including People with Intellectual Disability', 120.
75 Bill Gaventa, 'From Strangers to Friends: A New Testament Call to Community', *Journal of Religion, Disability and Health* 16 (2012): 212.
76 Carlton Graeme Johnstone, 'The Embedded Faith Journeys of Generation X and Y within New Zealand Church Communities' (PhD diss., University of Auckland, 2008), 243.

at a church need to be recognized as 'valued members of the congregation', and attending more than one church has the potential to extend their social life considerably.[77]

This study found that people with different disabilities preferred different types of churches. A helpful strategy for both the church and people with intellectual disabilities would be for pastors to share their experiences with other pastors about who fits into their church. Webb-Mitchell suggests that the following approach could be helpful: 'We would love to have you as part of our congregation, but if you find it too noisy/unstructured/formal, in the past people with autism/Down's syndrome have found it more peaceful/structured/relaxed at . . . church. Would you like me to arrange an introduction?'[78]

Lastly, parents and people with intellectual disabilities need to understand how God accepts them, how they reflect God's image, and what their value is to the church. While it is vital to realize that people with intellectual disabilities can know God, it is also necessary to recognize that they can grow in faith, learn more about God, and learn how to minister the gospel to others. Discipleship is just as important for people with intellectual disabilities as for anyone else in the church.[79] Parents also need support and resources to work through the issues involved in having a child with a disability, as they often have to fight for resources from government agencies that assume this person is primarily a burden rather than an asset to the country, despite the Disability Strategy.[80]

Postscript

McNair reported a modification of campus pavements in his college in response to a request from the disability community. Most people thought it was for bikes, and many found it useful. Perhaps the people who might benefit from a truly inclusive church are not simply people with intellectual disability, but the whole congregation.[81]

One parent articulated clearly what many parents hinted at:

> If you want this person to be here . . . nothing is too hard, we will make this work, and if you do it in a way that everyone is comfortable, then you will

---

77 Verdonschot et al., 'Community Participation of People with an Intellectual Disability'.
78 Webb-Mitchell, *Beyond Accessibility*, 78.
79 Hubert Allier, 'A Place for Human Growth', in *The Challenge of L'Arche* (London: Darton, Longman and Todd, 1982), 51.
80 Reinders points out that in an age of genetic testing the perception is that 'society is therefore entitled to hold people personally responsible for having a disabled child'; Hans Reinders, *The Future of the Disabled in a Liberal Society: An Ethical Analysis* (Notre Dame, IL: University of Notre Dame Press, 2000), 14.
81 McNair, 'Knowledge, Faith Development, and Religious Education that Includes All', 187.

[make inclusion work]. After all, families don't have options . . . they can't say 'Oh, sorry Jake, we can't cope today – go away.'[82]

However, the church does not have the option to send people away either: 'We know love by this, that He laid down his life for us – and we ought to lay down our lives for one another . . . . Little children, let us love, not in word or speech, but in truth and action' (1 John 3:16, 18).

The primary aim of this study was to find out how different churches were actually welcoming people with intellectual disabilities. The study's findings suggest that neither denomination nor the size of a church significantly impacted a church's ability to welcome people with intellectual disabilities; commitment to inclusion was the determining factor for success.

Although this study was conducted in New Zealand, it found the same issues as studies done in the USA and the UK. The recommendations are thus applicable beyond the local context.

---

82 Fearon, 'Welcoming and Including People with Intellectual Disability', 114.

14 From Inclusion to Belonging

Why 'Disabled' Bodies are Necessary for the Faithfulness of the Church

John Swinton

A few years ago I and some colleagues at the Centre for Spirituality, Health, and Disability at the University of Aberdeen[1] carried out a piece of research looking into the spiritual lives of people with intellectual disabilities.[2] We were curious about what kinds of spiritual needs people with intellectual disabilities were articulating and the ways in which religious communities were responding. The findings were most interesting. Many people we talked with had active church lives and had encountered deep spiritual experiences. The responses of religious communities, however, were mixed. Some communities were fully engaged, creating welcoming spaces where people were offered meaningful hospitality and were genuinely integrated. Others were not so welcoming. Sometimes the problem was the theological beliefs of that community, which framed disability in particularly negative ways. If disability is considered to be a product of sin or the demonic, it is unlikely that people with disabilities will find much of a welcome. Sometimes the lack of welcome stemmed from the particular ways in which the church's message was communicated and the intellectual requirements for participation. If one's presence within a community, or indeed one's salvation, is perceived to be dependent on one's ability to understand and articulate complex statements of faith, then it will be difficult for a person with an intellectual disability to find a safe space. If a community assumes that God only speaks in words and that salvation requires certain oratory abilities and skills, it can be confusing to know how to frame those who can neither orate nor cognate in the ways demanded by the assumptions of that community.

But there was a third group of churches. These churches *seemed* to be welcoming places. However, deeper reflection revealed that they were not quite what they seemed to be. June's story will help to draw out this point.

June was an elderly woman with a significant intellectual disability. She could not read nor write, but she really enjoyed going to chapel. Every week she

---

1 University of Aberdeen, Centre for Spirituality, Health, and Disability: http://www.abdn.ac.uk/sdhp/centre-for-spirituality-health-and-disability-182.php.
2 John Swinton and Elaine Powry, *Why are We Here? Understanding the Spiritual Lives of People with Learning Disabilities* (London: Mental Health Foundation, 2004).

would go along, participate in the service, and then stay around for coffee and a chat after the service. So far, so good! Once coffee had finished, she went home. She did not see anyone from the church again until the following Sunday, when she once again enjoyed the service, had coffee, and went home. June was lonely. In effect, she had a series of friendships that lasted for around an hour and a half on a Sunday morning (or half an hour of personal face-to-face time). The rest of the time the body of Christ was missing from her life. She was *included* in the congregation, but she did not really *belong*. No one was truly committed to her; no one really missed her. The church thought that it was doing well in including and integrating her. And on one level, of course, it was – at the level of *inclusion*. At another level it certainly was not – the level of *belonging*. June needed to belong to that community, and she simply did not.

I imagine that June's story may well be typical of many people with and without disabilities. June's story raises quite sharply the way in which the body of Christ can be broken and fragmented even though on the surface it can look quite whole. It also highlights the problems of including people with disabilities. To include someone, you just need to get them in the door. Inclusion simply means being in the room. To create a space within which people truly belong requires another dimension of community. In this chapter I want to explore some of the dynamics of belonging and offer a perspective that suggests that the fullness of the body of Christ is dependent on the fullness of its welcome to those perceived as different. In what follows, we will explore something of this tension between inclusion and belonging and lay out some possibilities for the church as the body of Jesus to become a place of radical hospitality, not just for people with disabilities, but for all of Jesus' disciples.

Disability Theology

This chapter is an exercise in what has come to be known as disability theology: 'Disability theology is the attempt by disabled and non-disabled Christians to understand and interpret the gospel of Jesus Christ, God and humanity against the backdrop of the historical and contemporary experiences of people with disabilities.'[3]

Disability theology seeks to open up new theological space by allowing fresh questions that emerge from the human experience of disability to address Christian tradition and practice with a view to challenging false beliefs and assumptions, thus allowing for the development of fresh new perspectives that help the whole people of God to see Jesus more clearly. In this chapter we will wrestle with the theological complexities of inclusion and, through a critical exploration of the body of Christ and the nature of human bodies, begin to show some of the ways in which disciples (disabled and able-bodied) and

---

3 John Swinton, 'Disability Theology', in *Cambridge Dictionary of Christian Theology*, ed. Ian McFarland et al. (London: Cambridge University Press, 2010), 140–41.

churches can live into their identity as a whole people who require the diversity of human bodies in order to be what they are. That requires that we begin to recognize the importance of belonging.

The Communal Nature of Christian Bodies

In beginning to unpack the issues, it will be helpful to start with a very simple observation: *The body of Christ is a place of unity and diversity*. In 1 Cor 3:16 Paul says: 'Don't you realize that all of you together are the temple of God and that the Spirit of God lives in you?'

'All of you *together*' – radical interdependency in the midst of human diversity is the way of the coming Kingdom. We are only who we are when we are together. We cannot be who we are without the other members who form the body of Jesus. Within such a body, Elizabeth Kent observes:

> Our bodies should not be an autonomous project of self actualization. The radical disruption of Scripture calls us to understand the individual bodies as primarily part of the body of Christ. In sharp contrast to the secular culture which enshrines the autonomous individual body, and at variance with evangelicals who have appropriated that same concept, the challenge to view our own bodies through the lens of participation in the body of Christ subverts what we have been led to believe the body is for.[4]

As we are baptized into the Body, so we lose ownership of our own bodies and become one body. It is not that our bodies cease to matter. As we lose ownership of our own bodies, so we begin to discover what the bodies that we inhabit are actually for. Our bodies are in Jesus and for Jesus. Paul thus tears away the veneer of individualism and challenges us to think corporately and christologically about who we are and what we should be doing with our bodies.

More than that, it is in the *diversity* of bodies within the Body that we find unity. The toe is no more important than the eye, the eye is no more important than the leg, and the ear is no more important than the brain. Each dimension of the body of Christ is necessary for the body to be the body (1 Cor 12). We are not talking here about equality and normalization. We are talking about a radical interdependence that requires difference and within which the exclusion of difference and those who are different breaks the body. Importantly within such a context, our brains do not trump other parts of our bodies. Those who can think quickly and sharply do so for Jesus. Those who take more time to think or whose gifts are not primarily intellectual use those things that they have been given for Jesus. Neither has priority or superiority over the other. We are not our

---

[4] Elizabeth Kent, 'Embodied Evangelicalism: The Body of Christ and the Christian Body', in *New Perspectives for Evangelical Theology: Engaging with God, Scripture and the World*, ed. Tom Greggs (London: Routledge, 2010), 116.

brains or our bodies. We are who we are in Jesus and for Jesus. Each member of the body is necessary, just as they are. It is the diversity of the body that gives it its wholeness in Christ.[5] In the light of Paul's imagery, disability begins to take on a rather different form and meaning. If diversity is the essence of the body of Christ, then the contribution to diversity that is brought by the incorporation of disabled bodies is both good and necessary if the body is truly to be whole. The body of Christ is a place where disabled bodies should feel at home.

The Strange New World within the Bible

In his insightful essay titled 'The Strange New World within the Bible', Karl Barth[6] offered an important insight into the ways in which the Bible shapes and forms our imagination. He suggests that the Bible is not simply a place that we go to in order to find rules, regulations, and guidelines for good living. Rather, the Bible is the doorway into a strange new world. The world of the Bible is 'not our world', and yet, at the same time, it is very much our world. The stories, the images, the rituals, and practices that are revealed in Scripture are actually invitations to enter into a strange new world. This 'new world' is of course already here; we just need to learn to see it. As we read the stories of Abraham, Moses, Jesus, and Paul, as we allow them to re-fund and expand our imagination,[7] we come to recognize that their stories are in fact our stories. As we recognize our place within these stories and as they begin to form the lens through which we re-examine the world we thought we knew, so our understanding of that which we previously assumed to be normal is transformed. In this way our imagination is re-funded, and the possibilities for being in the world in creative and faithful ways are expanded.

The Question of Healing

If we adopt this way of thinking as a beginning point for understanding fresh ways in which the Bible might help us to understand the role of people with disabilities in God's coming Kingdom, interesting things begin to come to light.

---

5 It is important to note that the unity that is held within the diversity of the body of the Christ I found only in Christ. It is not a unity that is bound by a quest for equality or justice. It is a unity that is found as we encounter our true identity as being 'in Christ'. Col 3:10–14: 'and have put on the new self, which is being renewed in knowledge in the image of its Creator. Here there is no Gentile or Jew, circumcised or uncircumcised, barbarian, Scythian, slave or free, but Christ is all, and is in all. Therefore, as God's chosen people, holy and dearly loved, clothe yourselves with compassion, kindness, humility, gentleness and patience. Bear with each other and forgive one another if any of you has a grievance against someone. Forgive as the Lord forgave you. And over all these virtues put on love, which binds them all together in perfect unity.'
6 Karl Barth, 'The Strange New World within the Bible', in *The Word of God and the Word of Man*, trans. Douglas Horton (New York: Harper & Row, 1957), 28–50.
7 Walter Brueggemann, *The Prophetic Imagination*, 2nd edn (Minneapolis, MN: Fortress Press, 2001).

Take, for example, the issue of healing. In highly medicalized cultures such as those found in the Western world, the temptation to begin conversations around disability with discussions of healing seems irresistible. In cultures where ideas about health have become restricted to striving to eliminate that which we think is undesirable, the eradication of difference has become strangely normalized.[8] Within a medical model approach to disability, the idea of healing is certainly alluring. But is it theologically the best place to begin? What do disability and healing look like when perceived from the viewpoint of the strange new world within the Bible?

At one level one might note that Jesus clearly had a healing ministry.[9] That being so, does this not indicate that God's response to disability and illness is healing and transformation? Whilst we cannot go into great detail on this point here, a brief observation might help to change the frame a little.[10] It is not a coincidence that it is almost impossible for Westerners to think about illness and disability without firstly thinking about medicine. This is despite the fact that the vast majority of healing and therapeutic activities occur outside the medical sector.[11] Medicine has great interpretive power. It is therefore tempting to infuse Jesus' healings with medical rather than theological significance. It is 'obvious' that Jesus heals in the same way as a doctor heals. People are 'clearly' moved from a state of sickness or disability into a state where these things are no more. However, the healing miracles, like the whole of the gospels, are not intended to be read as medical texts. They are *theological* expressions designed to provide *theological* meaning. If we read Jesus' healings theologically, or more accurately, christologically, as statements about who Jesus was, and in particular his Divinity, then we can begin to move away from the temptation to suggest that God's purpose is simply to eradicate disabilities. Take, for example, the story of the paralysed man in Matt 9:1–8:

> Jesus stepped into a boat, crossed over and came to his own town. Some men brought to him a paralyzed man, lying on a mat. When Jesus saw their

---

8   This normalization is made apparent, for example, within the commonly accepted practice of pre-natal testing for children with Down syndrome. Why would we assume that the world would be a better place without folks with Down syndrome, and why would it feel natural that people should have the choice to abort such people?

9   The theological dynamics of Jesus' healing are worth mentioning, if only briefly. It is tempting for those of us who reside in a highly medicalized culture to attribute Jesus' healings with medical significance. However, it should be borne in mind that Jesus' healings should be read theologically, or more accurately christologically as statements about who Jesus was and in particular his Divinity. 'Your sins are forgiven' (Luke 7:48). Who can forgive sins? Only God can forgive sins. Jesus forgives sins, therefore Jesus is God. If we take a christological rather than a medical approach to the miracles, then some (but not all) of the problems that the miracles raise for folks with disabilities begin to ease.

10 For a fuller development of the issues around healing and disability, see Amos Yong, *The Bible, Disability, and the Church: A New Vision of the People of God* (Grand Rapids, MI: Eerdmans, 2011).

11 Arthur Kleinmann offers a very interesting discussion on the variety of healthcare systems within any given culture in *Patients and Healers in the Context of Culture: An Exploration of the Borderland between Anthropology, Medicine, and Psychiatry* (Oakland, CA: University of California Press, 1980).

faith, he said to the man, 'Take heart, son; your sins are forgiven.' At this, some of the teachers of the law said to themselves, 'This fellow is blaspheming!' Knowing their thoughts, Jesus said, 'Why do you entertain evil thoughts in your hearts? Which is easier: to say, "Your sins are forgiven," or to say, "Get up and walk"? But I want you to know that the Son of Man has authority on earth to forgive sins.' So he said to the paralysed man, 'Get up, take your mat and go home.' Then the man got up and went home. When the crowd saw this, they were filled with awe; and they praised God, who had given such authority to man.

A medical reading focuses on the man's disability. A christological reading recognizes the miracle as a statement about Jesus' divinity and authority. The miracle provides an empirically verifiable sign that states very strongly who Jesus is. Who can forgive sins? Only God can forgive sins. Jesus forgives sins, therefore Jesus is God! If we take a christological rather than a biomedical approach to the miracles, then some (but clearly not all) of the problems that the miracles raise for folks with disabilities begin to ease.[12]

God can, of course, heal whomsoever God desires to heal. That is God's prerogative. Nevertheless, at a human level these observations, combined with the fact that the Bible has, as we will see in a moment, a variety of responses to disability, would indicate that moving too quickly to healing is not necessarily a wise thing to do. This is so theologically, but it is also the case in terms of the practices that emerge from misunderstandings of healing.

Looking at One Another Properly

The problem with beginning our conversations around disability with a focus on healing is that the basic dynamic revolves around looking past and through the person with a disability towards someone whom the healer has never met. Those who choose healing as their first port of call exhibit a desire to get rid of disabilities (eradicate what was) in order to create a 'new person' (what is) in anticipation of that time when we will all be transformed (what will be) (1 Cor 15). From this perspective, healing provides the person with a disability with a new history, a new identity, and a different place in time (a new beginning). The general assumption tends to be that what was before – that time when the disability was with us – was meaningless, and has been overpowered and eradicated in order that a new era can come upon us. We can now act as if the 'then person' never existed, and assume and live as if a person's previous life as a person with a disability had absolutely no meaning. Such a perspective, whether

---

12 For a deeper discussion on the christological focus of Jesus' miracles, see Colleen C. Grant, 'Reinterpreting the Healing Narratives', in *Human Disability and the Service of God: Reassessing Religious Practice*, ed. Nancy Eiesland and Don Saliers (Nashville, TN: Abingdon Press, 1998).

it is laid out implicitly or explicitly, omits the crucial fact that living with a disability is a meaningful and formative aspect of who a person is. It is not just something that can be discarded in the way we might throw out an old pair of shoes and slip on a new pair. Our disabilities have been formative of who we are and who and what we have become. Disabilities are identity-forming. Frances Young, talking about her son Arthur, who has a profound and complex intellectual disability, comments on such ahistorical assumptions about disability and healing in this way:

> There is no 'ideal Arthur' somehow trapped in his damaged physical casing. He is a psychosomatic whole . . . . What sense would it make to hope for 'healing' in cases like this? . . . There are twenty-two years of learning process that he has missed out on. In what sense could we expect normality, even if the physical problems were sorted out? . . . Arthur has personality at his own limited level . . . . Healed he would be a different person.[13]

Arthur is Arthur. Taking away his disability and implanting a whole new set of abilities would make him someone else – a person with no meaningful memories, no past, and a very difficult future. Arthur is not best understood as someone who could have been something, or someone who will be something if we pray a little harder. Likewise, he is not what he may or may not become in the eschaton. He would not somehow become Arthur if he was to be healed. He *is* Arthur. Looking backwards or looking forwards, looking past or looking around him only serves to turn our attention away from who he is in the now and how we can love him. Arthur's body has been baptized into Jesus' body; his difference is now a vital aspect of that body. The primary question is not 'How can he be healed?' but 'How can we learn to live together in the midst of our diversity; what is Arthur's vocation?'[14]

Disability, Vocation, and the Bible

Reflecting on disability in these ways draws attention to another important observation: *At key points in God's plan of salvation he uses disabled people as key players*. God does not heal people in order to bring them into God's service. God does not try to overcome diversity by homogenizing human beings. The people whom God calls are blessed and used precisely as they are. A good example is Moses and his stutter. It seems clear that Moses had a significant

---

13 Frances Young, *Face to Face: A Narrative Essay in the Theology of Suffering* (Edinburgh: T&T Clark, 1990), 22.
14 Young expands on the idea of Arthur's vocation in her most recent book: *Arthur's Call: A Journey of Faith in the Face of Severe Learning Disability* (London: SPCK, 2014).

speech impediment.[15] So significant was it that when God asked him to lead the people of Israel, Moses declined and asked God to send someone else (Exod 4:10–17). Moses felt his disability was a barrier to his calling from God, but God had other ideas. God did not respond by healing Moses and then sending him out. Rather, God simply told him to do what he was told! More mysteriously, God seems to indicate that it was God who caused Moses's stutter (Exod 4:11). Even more mysteriously, God seems to indicate that God is behind other forms of disability: 'The LORD said to him, "Who gave human beings their mouths? Who makes them deaf or mute? Who gives them sight or makes them blind? Is it not I, the LORD?'

We cannot explore all of the implications of such a startling statement in detail here. It is, however, worth noting that if God is good and if, for whatever reason, God decides to create disability, then disability cannot be perceived as evil. There is no indication in this text that God creates disability as a punishment. God just says that God does. It may not be desirable for some, and it may make for very difficult lives, but it is not bad or evil, because God is not bad or evil. The suggestion, for example, that disability is the product of evil or the demonic is significantly challenged by this passage. My point is not, of course, that we should become fatalistic. Some forms of disability are very difficult to live with, requiring therapy and medical intervention. That is not a problem. My point is that a theology of disability must wrestle with texts such as this and not rush to find the 'causes' of disability in sin and demon possession. There may be much to learn about God and human beings by simply dwelling in the nuances of a text such as this.

Again, in 2 Cor 12:7–10 the apostle Paul prays three times for the thorn in his flesh to be removed. But God does not choose healing as the appropriate course of action. As there is no indication in Scripture that Paul suffered from doubts or a lack of faithfulness, it seems safe to presume that the reason he was not healed was not due to a lack of faith. Instead, God assures Paul that: 'My grace is sufficient for you, for my power is made perfect in weakness.' In other words, you do not need to change or be changed to be called into God's service. God's grace is the point, not our ability or inability as humanly perceived. Paul responds by recognizing that God's grace is revealed in Paul's weakness; in his weakness Paul finds God's strength. So neither Paul's thorn in the flesh nor Moses's speech impediment were barriers to vocation and service. It was not necessary for them to be changed in order to have a calling and to fulfil their vocation. Indeed, their so called 'disability' was the power of their vocation.

Perhaps the most powerful example of God's tendency to use bodies that society perceives to be broken and of little worth for God's glory is in the broken body of Jesus. It is as we look upon the disabled body of Jesus on the cross that we come to realize that God saves precisely through those things that

---

15 Jeffry H. Tigay, '"Heavy of Mouth" and "Heavy of Tongue" on Moses' Speech Difficulty', *Bulletin of the American Schools of Oriental Research* 231 (1978): 57–67.

society assumes to represent brokenness. It is in the blood and the incapacitation of Jesus' body that we encounter our redemption. One of the surprises of the resurrection is that Jesus' wounds remain a part of his resurrected body (John 20:24–7). This indicates many things, but at a minimum it suggests that standard perceptions of beauty and perfection are open to challenge. God is present in brokenness, suffering, and pain as well as in joy, happiness, and hope. If the risen body of Jesus continues to bear scars, maybe our current ideas about perfection and beauty and what needs to happen before we can proceed with our calling need to be rethought. It seems that it is possible to be whole, diverse, and beautiful and to live with or experience profound disability. *There is no incompatibility between disabled bodies and Christian vocation. There is no incompatibility between diversity and the wholeness of the body of Christ.*

From Inclusion to Belonging

We can now return to June's situation of being included, but not belonging. June is a member of the body of Christ with gifts, talents, and a vocation. Her place within the body is not the outcome of charity, pity, or a desire to help 'the weak'. She is a disciple; someone called by God for a particular purpose. To include her without offering her a place of belonging is to miss something vital: *If June is not missed, the body is not whole.* If June is not a part of the community in all of the fullness of the community's life, then the community is not really functioning as a community at all. If June is included without her belonging, then the body remains broken. It is June as she is in the now that the community is called to love, and vice versa. This way of thinking about disability and belonging draws us into the heart of a Christian understanding of *hospitality*. Our experience of working with religious communities is that there is a tendency to think that our communities are places that host people with disabilities. Inclusion is all about hosting people: 'come into my house and be my guest'. Belonging, however, is something quite different. To belong one needs to be both a guest *and* a host. In closing this chapter, I want us to think about what it might mean for churches to move from being hosts to being guests in the lives of people with disabilities.

The Rhythm of Guesting and Hosting

I recently came across a wonderful painting of Pope Francis when he was Cardinal Jorge Mario Bergoglio of Buenos Aires. It is a realist picture which looks remarkably like a photograph. At the centre of the painting is a young boy in a wheelchair. The young boy is weak and frail; he is in the later stages of AIDS. He is dying. His left foot is stretched out, and the cardinal is on his knees, holding the boy's foot. Cardinal Bergoglio is stooping down and kissing the boy's foot. The picture is powerful. Here we see one of the world's most powerful religious representatives kneeling at the feet of one of the world's weakest and most vulnerable people. Now, had Cardinal Bergoglio been standing, towering over the boy, he would have seen him in a very different perspective. Had he reached down, patted him on the head, and offered some friendly words of comfort, he would have seen a very different boy. But on his knees before the boy he has to look up; he has to look closely at his body, at his face, look into his eyes and take seriously his pain and distress. Cardinal Bergoglio has to place his own body in a position of deep intimacy, and in doing so he reaches out to the boy from a position of mutuality rather than power. It is not a coincidence that Cardinal Bergoglio has to adopt the postures of worship – to bow down, and reach out and upwards – in order to engage with the boy. In shaping his body in this way, Cardinal Bergoglio models belonging.

One of the things that we sometimes miss within Jesus' ministry is the odd shape of his hospitality. Sometimes he was a guest in people's houses, and sometimes he was a host. This constant movement from guest to host is a primary mark of the incarnation. When Jesus was a guest in people's lives he did not try to change them. He sat with tax collectors and sinners, not reformed tax collectors and sinners, hence the accusation of gluttony and drunkenness (Matt 11:19). He simply sat, offered friendship, and waited to learn. He did not try to impose a norm. It is true that sometimes he offered healing, and we have discussed that in some detail previously. But even then he had a tendency to ask folks whether that was what they wanted (Mark 10:51). In other words, healing was not a necessary prerequisite for hospitality, friendship, and belonging.

Imagine for a moment that we chose to move with the divine rhythm of guesting and hosting. What would it be like to be a guest in June's life, to spend time in her life, in her house, to come to know what her vocation is and what God looks like as God is encountered in the midst of her different experience? Imagine what it might look like if we were to become guests in the lives of people with advanced dementia. What might it actually be like to encounter God without memory? Imagine being a guest in the life of a person who has a hearing impairment. What might it be like to encounter God without hearing the word of God? Or what would it be like to come to know the Word without ever being able to see the Scriptures? What could we learn about encountering God with the whole of our bodies? Understanding what it means to be human requires a community of diversity and hospitality. The body of Christ is just such a place.

But there is one final dimension of Jesus' friendships that we must reflect upon. Often we think of Jesus' ministry as being with and for the marginalized. Jesus sat with the tax collectors, the sinners, and the outcast (Mark 2:13–17). It is true that Jesus did act in such ways. However, the suggestion that he sat with the marginalized is not quite accurate. Think of it this way. Jesus who is God enters into relationships of friendship with those whom society has marginalized. However, in doing so Jesus *shifts the margins*. The religious community continue to carry out the rituals and practices they think bring them closer to God, but God is somewhere else – with those whom they have marginalized: with Jesus. So it turns out that it is the religious folks who are marginalized because they could not understand the significance of those they chose to reject. My fear is that precisely the same thing happens today. When churches fail to see the significance of seeking to include those with different needs and experiences, so it finds itself marginalized from Jesus. Working to create communities of belonging is not simply a good thing to do. It is vital for the faithfulness of the church. If the church truly wants to be the body of Jesus, perhaps it needs to recognize its own alienation and embrace the fullness of Jesus' body in ways that are hospitable, faithful, and friendly. If belonging relates to missing, then perhaps religious communities need to recognize their alienation and return to that place where God waits for and misses them – that place of belonging.

Part III

Theology, Disability, and Becoming

15 Unseen Disability in the Australian Pentecostal Church

Australian Christian Churches, the Four-fold Gospel, and Challenges for the Mentally Ill

Greta E. C. Wells

In the Australian context there is a significant lack of peer-reviewed research regarding Christian attitudes towards mental illness – an issue of disability that impacts a significant percentage of Australians. Yet the diversity of Christianity in Australia means that research needs to avoid falling into the trap of generalization, recognizing the nuanced theological dynamics that ultimately impact upon different attitudes and responses between Christian denominations. In assessing where we might begin with this task, it is necessary to consider which Australian denominations are currently growing, as well as considering those denominations whose theological frameworks may lead to an understanding of mental illness that eschews broader medical or psychological explanations and interventions. This chapter will begin with a preliminary consideration of some of the key issues impacting upon Australian Christian attitudes and responses to mental illness as a whole. After this, it will turn to consider the Australian Christian Churches (ACC) movement – a growing Australian Pentecostal denomination that provides a fascinating case study of shifting theological dynamics that inevitably affect pastoral care practices. In exploring these dynamics and their potential implications for the mentally ill, the dynamics of the Pentecostal four-fold gospel will be analysed. In providing a well-rounded conclusion that brings together theological dynamics and pastoral care practice, this chapter will suggest ways in which the ACC may strengthen their care for the mentally ill.

An Echo of Silence: Mental Illness and Australian Christians

According to the Australian Bureau of Statistics (ABS), in 2011–12 13.6 per cent of Australians identified as having a long-term mental or behavioural condition – a stark comparison to the 9.6 per cent recorded in 2001.[1] More

---

1 Commonwealth of Australia, Australian Bureau of Statistics, 'Mental and Behavioural Conditions' [accessed 4 December 2012]. Online: http://www.abs.gov.au/ausstats/abs@.nsf/Lookup/4D709A4 E0614C546CA257AA30014BD06?opendocument.

recently, Australian research institute Beyondblue highlighted that three million Australians are currently 'living with depression or anxiety'.[2] It is not surprising, then, to learn that over the course of a lifetime 45 per cent of the Australian population will personally experience some form of mental illness.[3]

Disability surely comes in many forms, but many find it difficult to perceive mental illness – particularly more common forms such as depression and anxiety. Often this is because individuals coping with these conditions do not display overt signs of being incapacitated, making it seem quite nebulous to the general population. Furthermore, it can be hard to know what to do when someone has a panic attack, displays unhealthy obsessive-compulsive behaviour, experiences things that are not real, or loses a previous zest for life for no apparent reason. However, taking a step back, the impact upon Australian society is apparent. When considering non-fatal forms of disability, the Australian Institute of Health and Welfare states that 'mental disorders constitute the leading cause of disability burden in Australia, accounting for an estimated 24% of the total years lost due to disability'.[4]

In the light of these statistics, the role of the Christian community is of significant importance. While the multicultural, pluralistic context of Australia may lead us to believe that explicit Christian adherence is less evident than, say, in the United States, it has been suggested that two-thirds of mentally ill Australians use religious coping mechanisms,[5] many of which can be found within Christian communities. Beyond those who are unwell, such tools are also used by the large proportion of church-goers who struggle with mental illness in their families and have to cope with the rippling financial and social effects.[6] In terms of the church's role, there is also evidence suggesting that it is 'clergy, not psychologists or other mental health professionals, [who] are the most common source of help sought in times of psychological distress'.[7] Yet, given the nebu-

---

2 'Beyondblue – Home' [accessed 18 April 2013]. Online: http://www.beyondblue.org.au/.
3 Commonwealth of Australia, Australian Bureau of Statistics, 'Feature Article 2: Mental Health' [accessed 21 January 2013]. Online: http://www.abs.gov.au/AUSSTATS/abs@.nsf/Lookup/1301.0 Chapter11082009%E2%80%9310.
4 Commonwealth of Australia, Australian Institute of Health and Welfare, 'Mental Health' [accessed 28 March 2013]. Online: http://www.aihw.gov.au/mental-health/.
5 Harold Koenig, Dana King, and Verna B. Carson, *Handbook of Religion and Health*, 2nd edn (New York: Oxford University Press, 2012), 91.
6 Edward B. Rogers, Matthew S. Stanford, and Diana R. Garland, 'The Effects of Mental Illness on Families Within Faith Communities', *Mental Health, Religion and Culture* 15 (2012): 1–2. Mental illness not only impacts upon one's day-to-day activities, such as the ability to work, but may also materially and relationally cripple the functionality of families – particularly if the individual affected is the main financial or care provider. In addition, friends and family may find themselves not only dealing with added stressors, but also with their own feelings in having someone close to them experiencing something that is largely misunderstood – and thereby often stigmatized – by the local community.
7 Matthew S. Stanford and Kandace R. McAllister, 'Perceptions of Serious Mental Illness in the Local Church', *Journal of Religion, Disability and Health* 12 (2008): 144; Christopher G. Ellison et al., 'The Clergy as a Source of Mental Health Assistance: What Americans Believe', *Review of Religious Research* 48 (2006): 190–211.

lous nature of mental illness, there is often an uncertainty as to how this support role of the Christian minister and community should be carried out. What is the responsibility of the church in caring for the mentally ill?

Several factors contribute to this uncertainty within the Australian context. First, a 7 per cent drop in nominal Christian affiliation between 2001 and 2011[8] may lead some to believe that the Australian church's responsibility should logically decrease in regards to community issues such as mental health. Secondly, a largely state-based tertiary education system that has left theological faculties mostly in the hands of private providers with little to no funding has resulted in minimal research exploring the connections between Australian Christians and their responses to mental illness.[9] Thirdly, the nebulous role of the church in the face of mental illness is impacted by the sheer diversity of the Australian Christian context. With denominational breadth comes theological and doctrinal diversity, which ultimately shapes a number of attitudes and responses. Differing Christian perceptions of illness, healing, personhood, salvation, and eschatology – among other things – will directly and indirectly impact upon the manner in which we perceive and respond to mental illness.

If we look to broader literature from the Western context, we find suggestions that Christian attitudes towards mental illness are generally strung between two polar opposites: being viewed as either a personal or spiritual problem that can only be healed through faith, or part of our life on earth in which the church becomes a refuge of safety and support that minimizes environments where such illnesses are triggered.[10] Denominational and ethnic factors also significantly influence where one sits on this continuum. While mainline Protestant congregations have been found more likely to view depression as biological, and thus refer to appropriate external services, Charismatic and Pentecostal pastors are more likely to believe that depression is purely situational and strongly influenced by spiritual causes. This view results in treatment being kept 'in-house'.[11] Obviously, both approaches have weaknesses as well as strengths. Yet the key issue here is that both responses lack comprehensiveness. In polarizing

---

8 Commonwealth of Australia, Australian Bureau of Statistics, 'Cultural Diversity in Australia – Reflecting a Nation: Stories from the 2011 Census' [accessed 10 May 2013]. Online: http://www.abs.gov.au/ausstats/abs@.nsf/Lookup/2071.0main+features902012–2013. This has decreased from 68 per cent to 61 per cent. This statistic obviously does not reflect the lower percentage of Australian church-goers.
9 Kristine Hartog and Kathryn M. Gow, 'Religious Attributions Pertaining to the Causes and Cures of Mental Illness', *Mental Health, Religion and Culture* 8 (2005): 274. This is best highlighted by the notion that while a variety of relevant literature is available in the American and British contexts, one multi-denominational study undertaken by Hartog and Gow stands as the only recent piece of peer-reviewed research in the Australian context.
10 Alison Gray, 'Attitudes of the Public to Mental Health: A Church Congregation', *Mental Health, Religion and Culture* 4 (2001): 73.
11 Jennifer Shepard Payne, 'Variations in Pastors' Perceptions of the Etiology of Depression by Race and Religious Affiliation', *Community Mental Health* 45 (2009): 363; Stanford and McAllister, 'Perceptions of Serious Mental Illness in the Local Church', 151.

responses to mental illness, there is the danger of truncating care. This happens either by minimizing the much-needed support of the Christian community once a referral occurs, or preventing a referral to professional services being made altogether.[12] Underpinning this key issue is the ultimate failure to construe a consistent biblical and psychological understanding of anthropology and well-being that could lead to a position of strong advocacy and broader collaboration for those experiencing mental health difficulties.[13]

Indeed, there is a dire need to recognize that responding to mental illness in a single-faceted manner is, in the words of the American Psychiatric Association, 'a reductionistic anachronism of mind/body dualism'.[14] Such dualisms, while often assumed in the Christian community, do not reflect the scriptural portrayal of people as integrated beings whose mental, physical, and spiritual capacities are inextricably interdependent. N.T. Wright reminds us that while contemporary readers often use biblical terms such as 'flesh', 'soul', 'spirit', 'mind', and 'heart' to compartmentalize the person, these terms are actually intended to '*denote* . . . the entire human being, while *connoting* some angle of vision on who that human is and what he or she is called to be'.[15] Such thoughts are congruent with the earlier works of Rudolf Bultmann,[16] F.F. Bruce,[17] and Robert Jewett[18] in articulating a holistic, integrated understanding of the person.[19]

Yet negative responses to mental illness, either through lack of support or an incorrect attribution of the cause of and intervention needed, are evident in broader literature. With regards to a lack of church support, Matthew Stanford notes that while 30 per cent of mentally ill people seeking assistance from churches found 'interactions counterproductive to successful treatment', 60 per cent of these were a result of 'abandonment or lack of involvement by the

---

12 Gerard Leavy and Gloria Dura-Vila, 'Finding Common Ground: The Boundaries and Interconnections Between Faith-based Organisations and Mental Health Services', *Mental Health, Religion and Culture* 15 (2011): 5.
13 Shepard Payne, 'Variations in Pastors' Perceptions of the Etiology of Depression by Race and Religious Affiliation', 364.
14 American Psychiatric Association, *Diagnostic and Statistical Manual of Mental Disorders, Fourth Edition: DSM-IV-TR* (Arlington, VA: American Psychiatric Pub, 2000), xxx.
15 N.T. Wright, 'Mind, Spirit, Soul and Body: All for One and One for All – Reflections on Paul's Anthropology in His Complex Contexts', paper presented at the Society of Christian Philosophers: Regional Meeting, Fordham University, 2011 [accessed 12 November 2015]. Online: http://ntwrightpage.com/Wright_SCP_MindSpiritSoulBody.htm.
16 Rudolf Bultmann, *Theology of the New Testament* (Waco, TX: Baylor University Press, 1951), 209: '[Humans do] not consist of two parts, much less of three . . . [r]ather, [humans are] living unit[ies].'
17 F.F. Bruce, *The Epistle to the Hebrews* (Grand Rapids, MI: Eerdmans, 1964), 378.
18 Robert Jewett, *Paul's Anthropological Terms: A Study of Their Use in Conflict Settings* (Leiden: Brill, 1971).
19 Joel B. Green, *Body, Soul, and Human Life: The Nature of Humanity in the Bible* (Grand Rapids, MI: Baker, 2008), 53–8.

church'.[20] In another study among Christian congregants it was found that a desire for church support was the second priority for those in the context of mental illness, but forty-second for those who were not.[21] In terms of misunderstanding mental illness, multiple studies suggest that a significant proportion of Protestant Christians connect the cause of mental illness to sin and the spiritual realm, somewhat negating the role of possible genetic and psychological predispositions. Stanford and McAllister found in one study that 60 per cent of their participants had their mental illness diagnosis 'dismissed' by their church. Within this dismissed group 60 per cent and 62.9 per cent had their condition attributed to 'personal sin' or 'demonic involvement'.[22] Interestingly, they noted that spiritualizing mental illness occurred most amongst Charismatic or 'Spirit-filled' participants. In another study Jennifer Shepard Payne found that compared to other Protestants, Pentecostal Christians were significantly 'more likely to believe that depression was caused by spiritual . . . or moral problems rather than biological reasons', often viewing the condition as situational.[23]

While local research has been lacking, Hartog and Gow's Australian study found that, 'as many as one third of participants . . . sanctioned belief in a demonic aetiology' of mental illness.[24] As a prominent theme within this piece of research, such findings provide an opportunity to explore the justification of such beliefs within the Australian context. This is particularly the case within the Charismatic-Pentecostal context, which is more likely to view the demonic and personal morality as substantial contributors to mental illness.[25] As such, in moving forward to consider one Australian Pentecostal denomination it is necessary to briefly consider the place of the Pentecostal church within the Australian Christian landscape. There is also a need to examine the broader Pentecostal framework of the four-fold gospel, as this has a significant influence on shaping attitudes and responses to mental illness. A careful study of these assumptions is necessary in order to ensure a relevant analysis of the ACC.

Pentecostalism, the Four-fold Gospel, and Mental Illness

Despite a decrease in overall Christian affiliation, census data surprisingly indicate that the number of Australians identifying as Pentecostal actually increased

---

20 Matthew S. Stanford, 'Demon or Disorder: A Survey of Attitudes Toward Mental Illness in the Christian Church', *Mental Health, Religion and Culture* 10 (2007): 448.
21 Rogers et al., 'The Effects of Mental Illness on Families Within Faith Communities', 8.
22 Matthew S Stanford & Kandace R McAllister, 'Perceptions of Serious Mental Illness in the Local Church', *Journal of Religion, Disability and Health* 12 (2008): 9.
23 Jennifer Shepherd Payne, 'Variations in Pastors' Perceptions of the Etiology of Depression by Race and Religious Affiliation', *Community Mental Health* 45, (2009): 363.
24 Hartog and Gow, 'Religious Attributions Pertaining to the Causes and Cures of Mental Illness', 274.
25 Donald F. Calbreath, 'Seratonin and the Spirit: Can There be a Holistic Pentecostal Approach to Mental Illness?', in *Science and the Spirit: A Pentecostal Engagement with the Sciences*, ed. James K.A. Smith and Amos Yong (Bloomington, IN: Indiana University Press, 2010), 134.

numerically 'by one fifth' between 2001 and 2011.[26] While Pentecostals still only make up 1.1 per cent of the total Australian population, such growth over the course of a decade is indicative of the globally successful movement that, according to David Barrett, could hit almost 812 million adherents worldwide by 2025.[27]

In reflecting upon such statistics it is clear that the theological dynamics of Australian Pentecostalism have been informed significantly by the broader Pentecostal movement in the twentieth century. Yet, in saying this, Pentecostalism is in some ways a difficult movement to define. Ideally, the movement has been described as occurring in three waves throughout the last century: that of 'classical Pentecostalism' in the early twentieth century, 'the charismatic-renewal movement' of the 1960s, and the 'neo-charismatic' movement that accounts for other 'non-denominational' movements.[28]

However, such descriptions may be overly simplistic, and it is important to note the limitations of such categorizations. In much the same way, presumptions about the beginning of classical Pentecostalism can also be simplistic. While the much-presumed key events occurring in Azusa Street in 1906 are exemplary of the earliest Pentecostal revivals – with tongue-speaking, miraculous healing, and exuberant expressions of 'Spirit possession, dance, ecstatic worship, shouting, [and] celebration'[29] occurring in a radically egalitarian setting[30] – it is unwise to regard them as the sole catalyst for global Pentecostalism. A strong orientation for mission and evangelism arising out of Azusa Street may have led those impacted to be 'commissioned to Africa and Asia as early as 1907'[31] and operating in South Africa and Northern Russia by 1908[32] – but such themes were also evident in other similar revivals occurring in multiple locations globally.

Consequently, while 'defined internally . . . as a singular movement of the Christian Spirit', Pentecostalism is better described as 'multi-centred from the beginning, never defining itself in centre/periphery terms'.[33]

---

26 Commonwealth of Australia, Australian Bureau of Statistics, 'Cultural Diversity in Australia – Reflecting a Nation: Stories from the 2011 Census, 2012–2013'.
27 Brett Knowles, 'Is the Future of Western Christianity a Pentecostal One? A Conversation with Harvey Cox', in *The Future of Christianity: Historical, Sociological, Political And Theological Perspectives from New Zealand*, ed. John Stenhouse, Brett Knowles, and G.A. Wood (Hindmarsh, South Australia: ATF Press, 2004), 39.
28 Amos Yong, *The Spirit Poured Out On All Flesh: Pentecostalism and the Possibility of Global Theology* (Grand Rapids, MI: Baker Books, 2005), 3. For the purpose of the rest of this chapter, the discourse will focus on the dynamics of the earliest wave, classical Pentecostalism.
29 Michael Wilkinson, *The Spirit Said Go: Pentecostal Immigrants in Canada* (New York: Peter Lang, 2006), 10.
30 Cecil Robeck, *The Azusa Street Mission and Revival* (Nashville, TN: Thomas Nelson, 2006), 1. Obviously, racial segregation was still very much the norm – even within churches – in this context.
31 Michael Wilkinson, *Global Pentecostal Movements: Migration, Mission, and Public Religion* (Leiden: Brill, 2012), 8.
32 Robeck, *The Azusa Street Mission and Revival*, 8.
33 Peter Beyer, *Religions in Global Society* (Abingdon: Routledge, 2006), 149.

Anderson in particular is careful to emphasize that:

> Pentecostalism is neither a movement with distinct beginnings in the US or anywhere else, nor a movement based on a particular theology; it is rather a series of movements that have taken several years and several different formative ideas and events to emerge. Pentecostalism ... is best seen as historically related, revivalist movements where the emphasis is on the experience of the Spirit and the exercise of spiritual gifts.[34]

Primarily, this has meant that Pentecostalism has been well placed to be adapted to local cultures, leading it to be described repeatedly as a prime example of 'glocalization'.[35] The ultimate consequence of this is that unique Pentecostal phenomena occurring within different cultural norms are framed mostly by notions of orthopraxy rather than orthodoxy, and shared through '"testimonies" of God's great work'.[36] Noting the 'emotion and experience theology' of Pentecostalism,[37] Simon Chan particularly emphasizes that doctrinal explanation and theological exploration are *not* strengths of the movement,[38] with Theron further stipulating an 'original anti-intellectual stance' that avoided interaction with 'scientific research'[39] – including fields such as medicine and psychology. However, this is not to say that early Pentecostalism is completely devoid of theological frameworks. It seems that early, and subsequent, Pentecostal belief and action is very much undergirded by a schema of the Christ-centred four-fold gospel, which, as suggested by name, contains four doctrinal elements: Jesus as 'personal' saviour, Spirit baptizer, 'divine' healer, and soon-coming king.[40]

While the first element of Christ as saviour is virtually undisputed in the broader church, and divine healing and the imminent, often pre-millennial, return of Christ[41] have been adopted in varying levels of adherence in other

---

34 Allan Heaton Anderson, *To the Ends of the Earth: Pentecostalism and the Transformation of World Christianity* (New York: Oxford University Press, 2013), 47.
35 Claudia Wahrisch-Obalu, *The Missionary Self-perception of Pentecostal/Charismatic Church Leaders from the Global South in Europe: Bringing Back the Gospel* (Leiden: Brill, 2009), 43; Wilma Wells Davies, *Embattled but Empowered Community: Comparing Understandings of Spiritual Power in Argentine Popular and Pentecostal Cosmologies* (Leiden: Brill, 2010), 3.
36 Simon Chan, *Pentecostal Theology and the Christian Spiritual Tradition* (New York: Continuum, 2000), 20–21.
37 R.H. Gause, 'Issues in Pentecostalism', in *Perspectives on the New Pentecostalism*, ed. Russell P. Spittler (Grand Rapids, MI: Baker, 1976), 14.
38 Chan, *Pentecostal Theology and the Christian Spiritual Tradition*, 20–21.
39 Jacques P.J. Theron, 'Towards a Practical Theory for the Healing Ministry in Pentecostal Churches', *Journal of Pentecostal Theology* 14 (1999): 50.
40 Teresa Berger and Bryan D. Spinks, *The Spirit in Worship: Worship in the Spirit* (Collegeville, MN: Liturgical Press, 2009), 226.
41 Peter Althouse, *Spirit of the Last Days: Pentecostal Eschatology In Conversation with Jürgen Moltmann* (London: Continuum, 2003), 17; Allan Anderson, *An Introduction to Pentecostalism: Global Charismatic Christianity* (Cambridge: Cambridge University Press, 2004), 217.

denominations, this specific interpretation of Spirit baptism is of unique importance for Pentecostals. Understood as an experience subsequent and separate to conversion, evidenced initially by speaking in tongues, this rendering of Spirit baptism initially demarcated Pentecostals clearly from other mainline denominations.[42] To this end, early Pentecostals viewed Spirit baptism as an empowerment for witness; initially in the provision of other languages (*xenolalia*) to speed up the evangelizing of nations.[43] In speeding up evangelism, a hastening of Christ's return was understood as a primary motivation, fulfilling Matt 24:14: 'And this gospel of the kingdom will be proclaimed throughout the whole world as a testimony to all nations, and then the end will come.'[44] Evidently, this initial view of tongues as *xenolalia* was quickly discredited, but the adjusted understanding of *glossolalia*, or Spirit-fuelled language, has enabled Pentecostals to maintain their interpretation of the phenomena as evidence of democratized empowerment for ministry and leadership, regardless of gender, ethnicity, education, or mental well-being.[45]

Following this point is the closely related issue of eschatology. As seen from an understanding of Matt 24:14, Spirit baptism within Pentecostalism cannot be understood apart from the fourth element of the four-fold gospel: an imminent, often pre-millennial, understanding of eschatology. However, unlike Spirit baptism, which might be viewed by the mentally ill as an assurance of their inclusion in this egalitarian community, perceptions of related eschatology may result in mixed perceptions.

Pre-millennialism views the impending end of all things with the entropy of the created earthly order prior to Christ's return, ultimately creating a dualism that reorients one's priorities to non-tangible, spiritual realities.[46] Positively, it could be argued that a future, non-physical heavenly eschatology may provide the mentally ill with the hope that while present circumstances are crippling, ultimately one will be liberated from entropy. Yet the very notion of separating, polarizing, and prioritizing spiritual over earthly realities is the biggest issue that needs to be addressed, given that such dualisms are more reflective of neo-Platonism and modernistic thought than the holistic, integrated portrayal of the person in Scripture.[47]

---

42 Stanley Grenz, *Theology for the Community of God* (Grand Rapids, MI: Eerdmans, 2000), 416.
43 Amos Yong, *Discerning the Spirit(s): A Pentecostal-Charismatic Contribution to Christian Theology of Religions* (Sheffield: Continuum, 2000), 152; Anderson, *An Introduction to Pentecostalism*, 217.
44 Ibid., 218.
45 Eric Nelson Newberg, 'The Pentecostal Mission in Palestine, 1906–1948: A Postcolonial Assessment of Pentecostal Zionism' (PhD diss., Regent University, 2008), 167–8; Veli-Matti Kärkkainen, 'Pneumatologies in Systematic Theology', in *Studying Global Pentecostalism: Theories and Methods*, ed. Michael Bergunder et al. (Berkeley, CA: University of California Press, 2010), 228.
46 L. William Oliverio, Jr and L. William Oliverio, *Theological Hermeneutics in the Classical Pentecostal Tradition: A Typological Account* (Leiden: Brill, 2012), 28.
47 Green, *Body, Soul, and Human Life*, 52–3.

These dualisms have the potential to deepen feelings of hopelessness for the mentally ill with regard to being trapped in a perceived worsening reality until death, or Christ's return. While it is possible that the four-fold framework of classical Pentecostalism may provide a 'structured and ordered' worldview for the mentally ill, it could also catalyse excessive worry and stress with regard to the futility of the current order.[48] These dualisms are often manifested in the urgency of 'saving the souls' of non-believing family and friends. Similarly, in relation to healing, potentially holistic perspectives may give way to these evangelistic motivations. A focus on the supernatural healing of one's intangible condition in order to witness may lead to perceptions that mental illness has an intangible, spiritual cause. While Theron is quick to note that 'most [Pentecostals] have moved away from extremist positions of forgoing medical assistance in times of illness',[49] such dynamics can still lead to simplistic attitudes about mental illness which do not address biological and psychological vulnerabilities alongside spiritual issues. At worst, there is a danger that simplistic attitudes may result in prayer and scriptural encouragement that exacerbates feelings of guilt, shame, and isolation when the hoped-for healing does not come. At best, prayer for miraculous healing may actually be oriented in such a way as to provide the mentally ill with a sense of peace, comfort, hope, and belonging. However, the failure to understand mental illness beyond such spiritual measures truncates the multi-faceted care required in such situations.

Since early Pentecostals viewed themselves as Spirit-empowered for ministry to a world soon bound to end, the role of higher-level education has also traditionally been viewed as a lesser priority.[50] Consequently, there should be little surprise of a purported 'reluctance . . . to embrace modern psychiatric thinking'.[51] However, given that the multi-centred nature of the movement has not been 'restricted by ancient traditions and hierarchical structures', allowing for adaptation where needed,[52] it should be clarified at this point that this suspicion may or may not still exist. Consequently, if we are to analyse how Pentecostalism shapes attitudes and responses to mental illness within Australia, it is best to now turn and consider the doctrinal dynamics of the largest and oldest Australian Pentecostal denomination.

---

48 Harold G. Koenig et al., 'Religion and Anxiety Disorder: An Examination and Comparison of Associations in Young, Middle-Aged, and Elderly Adults', *Journal of Anxiety Disorders* 7 (1993): 338.
49 Theron, 'Towards a Practical Theory for the Healing Ministry in Pentecostal Churches', 56.
50 Pamela D. Trice and Jeffrey P. Bjorck, 'Pentecostal Perspectives on Causes and Cures of Depression', *Professional Psychology: Research and Practice* 37 (2006): 284.
51 Calbreath, 'Seratonin and the Spirit', 134.
52 Neil J. Ormerod and Shane Clifton, *Globalization and the Mission of the Church* (London: Continuum, 2009), 17.

A Case Study in Australian Pentecostalism: Australian Christian Churches

Nationally, Australian Christian Churches has 'over 1,000 churches with over 280,000 constituents'.[53] The ACC movement formed officially in 1937 as the Assemblies of God in Australia, out of an amalgamation of the Pentecostal Churches of Australia and the Assemblies of God in Queensland. However, the movement can trace its roots back to the establishment of the first Pentecostal mission in North Melbourne, pioneered in 1909 by ex-Methodist Sarah Jane Lancaster and her contemporaries.[54] Prior to her exposure to Pentecostal ideas via a pamphlet she ordered from Britain in 1906, Lancaster developed a belief in supernatural healing in 1902, when 'an ailing older gentleman ... read to her James 5:13–15 and demanded she find the elders and pray for his healing'.[55] In forming her ministry of healing, which would be integrated into her Pentecostal faith, she was significantly influenced by the ministry of restorationist Alexander John Dowie, who espoused a 'dualist' framework that clearly preferred miraculous supernatural interventions over secular interventions.[56] Thus, it is not surprising to find the earliest Australian Pentecostals engaged in hastened missionary activity, reflecting an imminent and pre-millennial eschatology.[57]

As such, the four-fold gospel heritage of early Pentecostalism is evident in the doctrinal statements of the ACC. In their national constitution 'divine healing', 'the premillennial, imminent and personal return of our Lord Jesus Christ', and empowerment for 'effective witness' through Spirit baptism are articulated.[58] However, contextualized forms of Pentecostalism should take into account not just the location of outworking, but also *when* they are outworked.[59] In considering contemporary doctrinal statements of the ACC and their implications regarding mental illness it is essential to set them in the context of particular shifts within the movement in recent decades. One subtle shift that has occurred is with regard to the place of tongues as initial evidence of Spirit baptism. While clearly outlined in the constitution,[60] it has been suggested that the language used can often be perceived as 'divisive' by non-Pentecostal

---

53 Australian Christian Churches, 'Who We Are' [accessed 24 November 2015]. Online: http://www.acc.org.au/about-us.aspx.
54 Barry Chant, *Heart of Fire: The Story of Australian Pentecostalism*, rev. edn (Ascot Park, South Australia: Endage Print, 1984), 34–5.
55 Shane Clifton, *Pentecostal Churches in Transition: Analysing the Developing Ecclesiology of the Assemblies of God in Australia* (Leiden: Brill, 2009), 53.
56 Ibid.
57 Michael Bergunder et al., *Studying Global Pentecostalism: Theories and Methods* (Berkeley, CA: University of California Press, 2010), 181; Chant, *Heart of Fire*, 34–6.
58 Australian Christian Churches (Assemblies of God in Australia), 'United Constitution (Incorporating National By-Laws)' (May 2011), Articles 4.13, 4.15, 4.13.
59 Wilkinson, *Global Pentecostal Movements*, 8.
60 Australian Christian Churches (Assemblies of God in Australia), 'United Constitution (Incorporating National By-Laws)' (Australian Christian Churches, May 2011), Article 4.13.

denominations. Over time this has led to a decreased mention of this phenomenon within ACC publications.⁶¹ Such reasoning may explain why the ACC's largest church has reworded its statement of beliefs to note tongues as *one of many* spiritual gifts, rather than *the* initial evidence of Spirit baptism.⁶² No doubt, while adjustments to doctrine are anomalies in the wider ACC landscape, such occurrences may be indicative of a movement that has become more established and less concerned with dismissing the current created order. This is also seen in a more nuanced understanding of eschatology than the pre-millennial and immanentist positions officially articulated in ACC doctrine.⁶³

The ACC's understanding of eschatology has become more nuanced in the last several decades. As Shane Clifton suggests, there are several factors that may have contributed to earlier views on eschatology becoming untenable: namely, the increasing presence of megachurches within the ACC movement, as well as the influence of prosperity theologies that focus on current blessings in all areas of life.⁶⁴ Consequently, at the ACC 1999 biennale conference it was officially decided that while the imminent return of Christ would remain as an official doctrinal position, pastors did not have to agree with this to be ordained.⁶⁵ More recently, this broadening of eschatological beliefs has become evident on the ACC's national website, where the language of imminent pre-millennialism has been replaced with a generalized statement of belief: 'We believe that the Lord Jesus Christ is coming back again as He promised.'⁶⁶ Given that Spirit baptism and imminent eschatology are closely linked in the four-fold gospel schema, the decreasing stress upon these within ACC has certainly shifted the manner in which temporal matters are viewed.⁶⁷ Certainly, the continuing growth of ACC megachurches and their stress upon temporal blessings are physical evidence of this notion. But it is another statement of belief on ACC's website that demonstrates this best: 'We believe that God wants to heal and transform us so that we can live healthy and prosperous lives in order to help others more effectively.'⁶⁸ While such a statement has its bearings in notions of evangelism and healing, reticent of the four-fold gospel of early Pentecostalism, aspects of prosperity teachings are also present, 'which intuitively recognise that the gospel has implications for human existence in both its natural and spiritual

---

61 Clifton, *Pentecostal Churches in Transition*, 167.
62 Hillsong Church, 'What We Believe' [accessed 12 November 2015]. Online: http://hillsong.com/what-we-believe/. Hillsong's website notes: 'We believe that in order to live the holy and fruitful lives that God intends for us, we need to be baptised in water and be filled with the power of the Holy Spirit. The Holy Spirit enables us to use spiritual gifts, including speaking in tongues.'
63 Australian Christian Churches (Assemblies of God in Australia), 'United Constitution (Incorporating National By-Laws)', Article 4.16.
64 Clifton, *Pentecostal Churches in Transition*, 165–166.
65 Ibid.
66 Australian Christian Churches, 'Our Beliefs' [accessed 24 November 2015]. Online: http://www.acc.org.au/about-us/.
67 Clifton, *Pentecostal Churches in Transition*, 165–66.
68 Australian Christian Churches, 'Our Beliefs'.

dimensions'.[69] Furthermore, this more inclusive statement allows for a variety of avenues through which healing may come, such as via medical or psychological services, as compared to the original constitutional statements, which focus on '*divine* healing for the body'.[70]

In addition to a broadened understanding of the cause and purpose of healing, a shift away from immanentist views of the parousia is arguably linked to a decrease of previous anti-intellectual attitudes towards education and training. This is reflected in the 23 per cent of ACC congregants who currently hold a tertiary degree or higher, compared to 18 per cent of the general Australian population.[71] However, while requirements for ordination have risen from a minimum of no education to some sort of vocational ministry training in recent years,[72] this is still significantly lower than other denominations[73] and may impact upon assistance given to the mental ill.[74] Also, while there have been clear nuances in perceptions of doctrine as it relates to the four-fold gospel, the integration of prosperity ideas that bring a more holistic perspective may also perpetuate the notion that those who are faithful do not experience mental illness. The result is that seeking assistance for such things could be viewed as a sign of 'weak faith'.[75] As such, while a focus on ministering in divine healing may be less explicit, the underpinning frameworks of these practices are still very much present in the movement. These continuing patterns of belief may unconsciously (or even consciously) shape dualistic, spiritually focused frameworks and practices with regard to mental illness. Going forward, the developing nuance in belief may continue to shift further over time.

---

69 Clifton, *Pentecostal Churches in Transition*, 199.
70 Australian Christian Churches (Assemblies of God in Australia), 'United Constitution (Incorporating National By-Laws)', Article 4.15; emphasis added.
71 Ruth Powell et al., *Enriching Church Life: A Guide to Results from the National Church Life Surveys for Local Churches*, 2nd edn (St Marys, South Australia: Mirrabooka Press, 2012), 131. However, it does need to be noted that the ACC is still below the 27 per cent of Australian Christians who have completed a tertiary award.
72 Australian Christian Churches (Assemblies of God in Australia), 'United Constitution (Incorporating National By-Laws)', Article 11.2.3.
73 Moore Theological College, 'Anglican Ordination in the Diocese of Sydney', in *Moore College Student Handbook 2013*, Version 1.1 (Sydney: Moore Theological College, 2013), 11. One pertinent example is the Sydney diocese of the Anglican Church, where '[t]he normal academic requirement for ordination/commissioning in the Diocese of Sydney is the award of the [four year, full-time] Bachelor of Divinity'.
74 Harold G. Koenig, *Faith and Mental Health: Religious Resources for Healing* (West Conshohocken, PA: Templeton Foundation Press, 2009), 268–9. Harold Koenig suggests that those with greater training – particularly in the area of mental health – will equip pastors to recognize specific signs of mental illness. This is especially important in 'minority and other underserved populations with limited access to professional mental health services'.
75 Anderson, *To the Ends of the Earth*, 222; R.D. Dobbins, 'Psychotherapy with Pentecostal Protestants', in *Handbook of Psychotherapy and Religious Diversity*, ed. P. Scott Richards and Allen E Bergin (Washington, DC: American Psychological Association, 2000), 168.

In creating a more holistic, multi-faceted approach within the ACC, several courses of action need to take place for better engagement with the mentally ill. First of all, further efforts must be made to reorient an understanding of the person as an integrated being. Classical four-fold gospel frameworks, while positively emphasizing an inclusive empowerment of all through Spirit baptism, also tend to lead to unhealthy dichotomies that truncate our understanding of human well-being. While the autonomous structure of the ACC movement provides pastors with the relative freedom to shape their congregational vision and mission,[76] the nature of pastoral ministry does not often allow time and space for critical reflection upon the relationship between ministry practices, doctrinal dynamics, and contextual factors. Australian Pentecostal academics in various tertiary institutions are able to assist ACC leadership and pastors in developing appropriate theological norms for the movement as society continues to shift. As such, opportunities should be made to strengthen ties between Pentecostal academics operating within Australian tertiary institutions and different levels of leadership within ACC.

Secondly, related to this, it has been found that most clergy consider themselves ill-equipped to assist a congregant with mental illness.[77] As such, there is a need to further educate and train congregants and pastors within this movement in how to appropriately care for the mentally ill within their congregations. Within a constituency of 250,000, who are more likely to hold a tertiary award than their average fellow Australians, there are numerous opportunities to utilize experienced psychologists, doctors, and social workers who understand the movement to put together a variety of resources appropriate for such a task.

Thirdly, pastors with lower educational levels and conservative theologies are less likely to refer congregants to further support.[78] Therefore, the ACC needs to facilitate further collaboration with local community health services. Working with the current structure of the movement, appropriate individuals within each ACC local region (such as doctors, psychologists, or social workers) could work with regional leaders to build up inventories of local resources (such as reputable counsellors, psychologists, and support groups) that could be made readily available to all congregations in the region. In addition, resource selection criteria could be developed and set by appropriately qualified individuals for the national office, to ensure benchmarking across all regions and states.

Along with creating a clear network of verified referral sources for each region, qualified professionals within local services could prove to be helpful resources in running regional-level workshops for pastors, leaders, and

---

76 Australian Christian Churches (Assemblies of God in Australia), 'United Constitution (Incorporating National By-Laws)', article 2.2.2.
77 Robert Joseph Taylor et al., 'Mental Health Services in Faith Communities: The Role of Clergy in Black Churches', *Social Work* 45 (2000): 76; Stanford and McAllister, 'Perceptions of Serious Mental Illness in the Local Church', 151.
78 Taylor et al., 'Mental Health Services in Faith Communities', 76; Stanford and McAllister, 'Perceptions of Serious Mental Illness in the Local Church', 151.

congregants on locally relevant issues related to anxiety, depression, and other mental disorders. Such partnerships, as well as communicating an integrated understanding of well-being, would also hopefully break down the 'historically embraced antipathy between religion and psychology' that may be held by some pastors and congregants.[79] Likewise, such processes would help health services 'to respect and learn from ... communities of faith[,] ... enter[ing] into these communities with humility, and to recognize that the psychological skills ... offer[ed] must be viewed in the context of religious, cultural and historical factors'.[80] Practically, such relationships may serve to further expose counsellors and psychologists to the benefit of integrating spiritual coping tools, such as prayer and meditation, into their sessions with clients.[81]

Ultimately, there is much that the Australian Pentecostal community has to offer the mentally ill. First, the theological framework of the four-fold gospel has the amazing potential to create a community of inclusiveness where all are invited to experience God tangibly, regardless of background. Secondly, when conducted in a manner that minimizes feelings of shame, guilt, and isolation, spiritual practices (such as prayer, meditation, and sacraments) have the ability to contribute to the well-being of someone facing mental illness by providing avenues to externalize associated stress and worry. Thirdly, the faith communities in which these practices originate have the potential to provide friendship, support, and understanding that not only bring comfort, but also pre-emptively safeguard others against the development of conditions such as anxiety and depression.[82] It is unfortunate that these same frameworks and practices may also create a dualistic understanding of the world and self that may truncate the fullness of assistance required. As argued through an exploration of the ACC movement, attitudes and responses may be shifting, but there is still a long way to go. Hopefully, by engaging in further education and collaboration, the Australian Pentecostal church will become a place where the integrated nature of well-being, regardless of condition, will flourish.

---

79 Trice and Bjorck, 'Pentecostal Perspectives on Causes and Cures of Depression', 284; Jennifer L. Farrell and Deborah A. Goebert, 'Collaboration Between Psychiatrists and Clergy in Recognising and Treating Serious Mental Illness', *Psychiatric Services* 59 (2008): 437–40.
80 Mark R. Minn et al., 'Training Psychologists to Work with Religious Organizations: The Center for Church–Psychology Collaboration', *Professional Psychology: Research and Practice* 32 (2001): 326.
81 Leavy and Dura-Vila, 'Finding Common Ground: The Boundaries and Interconnections Between Faith-based Organisations and Mental Health Services', 8; Andrea K. Shrieve-Neiger and Barry A Edelstein, 'Religion and Anxiety: A Critical Review of the Literature', *Clinical Psychology Review* 24 (2004): 394.
82 Rogers et al., 'The Effects of Mental Illness on Families Within Faith Communities', 8–10.

16 Beyond Charity

How can Society have a High Value of Disabled People?

Evan Clulee

Am I Not Valued?

As a disabled person living in Aotearoa New Zealand it is my belief that people with disabilities are afforded a very low place in society. This is seen in a variety of ways, impressions, and practices. While I make a case for this belief, it is also my belief that societal attitudes are changing for the better, with an increase in 'power shift' towards disabled people, and this offers some hope for the future. However, for real progress to be made, society as a whole needs to be convinced that a high view of people with disabilities is a good thing, and that is the task I have set myself in this chapter.

I am a disabled person. I live my life in a wheelchair, three feet below the majority of the adult population. From this vantage point my perspective is different! I wish you could all journey with me once on a trip to my local mall. Here you would witness me being treated differently, as 'the other'. In this space I am more than occasionally not served, not spoken to, stared at, objectivized, or worse, ignored. I am therefore not valued as an equal, and not treated with dignity and respect. In large and small ways New Zealand society does not value difference.

How do we know disabled people are not valued in New Zealand society? One recent example was the media's reporting of the alleged abuses of disabled people at Parklands Residential Home.[1] Despite serious allegations of abuse and neglect against the disabled residents, including one young boy being left to eat grass, this story seemed to come and then go just as quickly. What other stories were deemed as 'more important', and what does that say about the value of disabled people? Why did this story disappear from the media so quickly? If it was important to society, then the story would have remained in the news.

---

1 Kate Shuttleworth, 'Minister to Review Parklands Historic Abuse Claims' [accessed 25 February 2014]. Online: http://www.nzherald.co.nz/nz/news/article.cfm?c_id=1&objectid=10884896; Ashlee Tulloch, 'Alleged Abuse at Parklands Home for Mentally Disabled' [accessed 25 February 2014]: Online: http://www.3news.co.nz/nznews/alleged-abuse-at-parklands-home-for-mentally-disabled-2013050517#axzz3Xe8xTRSy; Kirsty Johnston, 'Boy Left to Eat Grass at Horror Home' [accessed 25 February 2014]. Online: http://www.stuff.co.nz/national/health/8633676/Boy-left-to-eat-grass-at-horror-home.

This raised for me a number of questions about value, and why people were not advocating for justice. Where were the voices speaking up and supporting the individuals with disabilities who were affected? More to the point, why was society (including the church) fairly silent on the issues raised? Do we not feel strongly enough about justice, or the marginalized, to speak up?

Disabled commentators were vocal and outspoken. In his article 'Lack of Outrage . . . but They're Only Disabled and Vulnerable' Philip Patston writes: 'I care about the victims, without wanting to blame the alleged perpetrators. Hurt people hurt people.'[2] Patston's point is that this example demonstrates that society does not seem to care enough about disabled people. I agree with him.

How did New Zealand society get to a place where it seems to be acceptable that disabled people are not treated with dignity and respect? To begin to understand, we need to take a look back through history. Some readers will remember well the days of psychiatric institutions in New Zealand, where many disabled people were set apart from society and put in 'special' places. Names such as Kingseat, Carrington, Mangere Hospital, Cherry Farm, and Templeton[3] are familiar on our landscape and collective history, evoking varied memories. Going further back, we have other names, Seacliff Mental Asylum, Whau Lunatic Asylum, and more places that evoke memories, and perhaps thoughts of large, dark places.[4]

Why were disabled people kept in these places? The reasons are many and varied: because society did not accept people who were different, for the 'safe treatment' of the individual with a disability, and for the 'safety' of society, people who were deemed to be dangerous or a risk were kept away.[5] As Hunt says: 'A sharp dividing line is drawn between the social lives and interests of 'able-bodied' and disabled people. The latter are set apart from the ordinary because they pose a direct challenge to commonly held societal values: As unfortunate, useless, different, oppressed and sick.'[6]

Institutions were seen as a 'better place', with 'experts' available to give people the 'treatment' they needed.[7] The sad fact is that although touted as 'safe' places to be, the statistics eventually said otherwise: rates of abuse were higher

---

2   Philip Patston, 'Lack of Outrage . . . but They're Only Disabled and Vulnerable' [accessed 25 February 2015]. Online: http://www.philippatston.com/blog/lack-of-outrage-but-they-re-only-disabled-and-vulnerable/.
3   Archives New Zealand, 'Mental Health' [accessed 25 February 2015]. Online: http://archives.govt.nz/research/guides/mental-health.
4   Erin Kavanagh-Hall, 'Spotlight on Hospital Cruelty' [accessed 25 February 2015]. Online: http://www.stuff.co.nz/dominion-post/news/local-papers/the-wellingtonian/8392805/Spotlight-on-hospital-cruelty.
5   Cheryl Caldwell, 'Truby King and the Seacliff Asylum 1889–1907', in *Unfortunate Folk: Essays on Mental Health Treatment 1863–1992*, ed. Barbara Brookes and Jane Thomson (Dunedin: University of Otago Press, 2001), 47.
6   Paul Hunt, 'A Critical Condition', in *Stigma: The Experience of Disability*, ed. Paul Hunt (London: Geoffrey Chapman, 1966), 146.
7   Barbara Brookes and Jane Thompson, eds, *Unfortunate Folk: Essays on Mental Health Treatment 1863–1992* (Dunedin: University of Otago Press, 2001), 15.

in these places of 'care' than they were in the community.⁸ Yet, importantly, as a society we continued to justify these places of 'care' right up until the early 1990s.⁹ There have been some moves to bring about justice for people with disabilities abused and mistreated in these institutions.¹⁰

I am inspired by the life of Janet Frame (1924–2004),¹¹ a person of difference, known to us as a gifted New Zealand author. Frame spent much of the eight years from 1947 to 1955 in institutional care, including time in Seacliff Mental Hospital, wrongly diagnosed as being schizophrenic.¹² Frame was scheduled for a lobotomy that was cancelled when, just days before the procedure, her debut publication of short stories was unexpectedly awarded a national literary prize. As part of her treatment Frame was given shock treatments to 'help' her. In her fictional book *Faces in the Water* Frame writes about Istina Marvet and describes her experiences of life in a psychiatric unit:

> Every morning I woke in dread, waiting for the day nurse to go on her rounds and announce from the list of names in her hand whether or not I was for shock treatment, the new and fashionable means of quieting people and of making them realize that orders are to be obeyed and floors are to be polished without anyone protesting and faces are to be made to be fixed into smiles and weeping is a crime.¹³

Faces in the Water is about recognizing how misunderstood mental illness was in the 1950s, and misuse and abuse of power in places of care, and while not an autobiography, it clearly draws upon Frame's own experiences.¹⁴

I long to know more of the hidden histories of these psychiatric institutions, and the stories of people who lived and died there. There exists a sobering statistic: that if you had epilepsy and were committed to Seacliff Asylum, there was a high chance you would die there: 'Out of 102 patients admitted for some

---

8   Linda Teplin et al., 'Crime Victimization in Adults with Severe Mental Illness: Comparison with the National Crime Victimization Survey', *Archives of General Psychiatry* 8 (2005): 911–21; Joan R. Petersilia, 'Crime Victims with Developmental Disabilities: A Review Essay', *Criminal Justice and Behavior* 6 (2001): 655–94.
9   Te Ara, 'Mental Health Services: Page 5 – Closing the hospitals, 1960s to 1990s' [accessed 25 February 2015]. Online: http://www.teara.govt.nz/en/mental-health-services/page-5; Jeff Kavanagh, 'Cherry Farm, 1952–1992: Social and Economic Forces in the Evolution of Mental Health Care in New Zealand', in *Unfortunate Folk: Essays on Mental Health Treatment 1863–1992*, ed. Barbara Brookes and Jane Thomson (Dunedin: University of Otago Press, 2001), 168, 182.
10 *Te Āiotanga: Report of the Confidential Forum for Former In-patients of Psychiatric Hospitals* (Wellington: Department of Internal Affairs, 2007); Te Ara, 'Mental Health Services: Page 5 – Closing the hospitals'; Kavanagh-Hall, 'Spotlight on Hospital Cruelty'.
11 Te Ara, 'Frame, Janet Paterson' [accessed 25 February 2015]. Online: http://www.teara.govt.nz/en/biographies/6f1/frame-janet-paterson.
12 Ibid.
13 Janet Frame, *Faces in the Water* (London: Virago Press, 1991), ch. 1.
14 Brookes and Thomson, eds, *Unfortunate Folk*, 240.

sort of epilepsy during this period, 71 percent never left the asylum.'[15] Other sources state that if you were initially in Seacliff Mental Asylum for more than six months, you were very unlikely to make it out again. Speaking of Truby King, Chapman says: 'He recognised early in his career that "unless a patient was discharged within six months he (sic) was there for life".'[16] Long stays in psychiatric hospitals continued to be an issue right up until the 1980s, when discussions were under way and plans were being made to close these places, and shift the 'patients' into community care.[17]

Bringing to life the stories of the people who lived in these large places of 'care' would honour those disabled people who are currently nameless and unknown. A recent example of a story brought to life is that of Ada Green, who was committed to Seacliff Mental Asylum as a 22-year-old, and died there at 74 years old. Fifty-two years in Seacliff, her medical files made clear, was a life of sadness and abuse. More stories like Ada's need to be brought to life and told in order to honour individuals who lived in these places.[18] The alternative, which I find unacceptable, is that disabled individuals will continue to be nameless, faceless, and therefore of no value. We need to acknowledge the past, and honour those who were not treated with the dignity and respect due to them in their own lifetime.

My own family has strong personal connections with both Cherry Farm Psychiatric Hospital and Seacliff Mental Hospital. My paternal grandmother was admitted to Seacliff for a short time. I believe she may have had post-natal depression. I don't believe the time she spent in Seacliff helped her. My maternal grandfather worked at Cherry Farm Hospital as a psychiatric nurse for some years in the 1970s. My mother worked there as an occupational therapist for a short time, and my father was a maintenance carpenter at Cherry Farm Hospital for 26 years. As a family we are acquainted with these 'places of care', some people who lived in them, and some people who worked in them.

My mother recounted a story that a former staff member at Seacliff Mental Hospital had told her: that, on occasions, in order to subdue 'out of control' patients, soap was put in a stocking then swung around, and the offending patient was hit in the head, knocking them out. I am disturbed and saddened hearing stories like this of obvious mistreatment. Is that really the best we could do at the time to change behaviour? I wonder what made those 'patients' so out of control or angry? Was it perhaps because they felt so devalued, so mistreated, they had no other way of communicating this clearly, or that they simply were

15 Ibid., 62.
16 Lloyd Chapman, *In a Strange Garden: The life and Times of Truby King* (Auckland: Penguin Books, 2003), 60.
17 Brookes and Thomson, eds, *Unfortunate Folk*, 177.
18 TV 3, 'Family Secret' [accessed 25 February 2015]. Online: http://www.tv3.co.nz/Shows/FamilySecret/About.aspx; 'Four Seasons in One Kiwi: The Story of Ada Green' [accessed 25 February 2015]. Online: http://fourseasonsinonekiwi.blogspot.co.nz/2013/12/the-story-of-ada-green.html.

not heard? Who was listening to these individuals and their concerns? Who cared for their welfare? Who were the people who loved these individuals?

Another life that inspires me is that of Sir Truby King (1858–1938).[19] Dr King recognized injustices at the time in the treatment of people, and set about making reforms to these large places of care that would give disabled people more dignity and respect, and therefore a higher value.[20] In his lifetime as director of Seacliff Mental Hospital, King challenged the societal norms of the time and the way the community perceived people of difference. He is recorded, after a move to Wellington, as saying that he missed the residents of Seacliff.[21]

Here we see King recognizing the humanity of people, and the fine line – if there is one – between 'normality' and 'difference': 'Having now spent many years in daily and hourly contact with the insane, the one fact about them which continually impresses me with more and more conviction is [the] wonderfully little difference that there is between them and other people.'[22]

In this King quotes from 'Night Walks', Chapter 13 of Charles Dickens's *The Uncommercial Traveller*, which says: 'Are not the sane and the insane equal at night as the sane lie a dreaming? Are not all of us outside this hospital, who dream, more or less in the condition of those inside it, every night of our lives?'[23]

It is unknown whether Dr King may have been on the autistic spectrum. What we do know is that he was a man who was academically different, had radical ideas, but did not easily cope with life, and not without the support of his wife to get him organized. He was different himself. I wonder if this is possibly why he identified so strongly with the 'patients' he served and worked tirelessly for? In terms of speaking up for the marginalized, I ask: 'Where are the Truby Kings of today?'

What About Me?

As a disabled person, have I felt valued as a person in our modern, developed, civilized, 'inclusive', and tolerant society? Many times I have not. Following are two brief personal stories.

In 1998 I travelled with a friend to the top of the North Island of New Zealand to visit Cape Reinga. The trip up was fairly uneventful, and we walked to the lighthouse. Shortly before leaving I heard boys behind me laughing. I turned around, and there were two boys standing close to me, pointing at me and laughing, saying things like 'What is that ... a dwarf?' 'Look at his short legs!' and laughing louder. I was completely shocked, and stunned – so shocked that

---

19 Te Ara, 'King, Frederic Truby' [accessed 25 February 2015]. Online: http://www.teara.govt.nz/en/biographies/2k8/king-frederic-truby.
20 Chapman, *In a Strange Garden*, 61, 79.
21 Te Ara, 'King, Frederic Truby'.
22 Truby King, cited in Donald A. Laird, 'Psychopathic Nursing', *American Journal of Nursing* 20 (1920): 687.
23 Ibid.

I could not, and did not, respond at all. After some time their mother came and whisked them away quickly – no words, no apologies.

Here's another story. I was at my home church, the only difference was that on this occasion I was at a night service that I did not normally attend. As the service was coming to an end a person went up the front and said that they felt someone in the church had a 'spirit of infirmity'. All of a sudden I felt multiple sets of eyes looking in my direction. I wanted to disappear, people were looking at me like I was an evil object that needed to be fixed. I eyeballed many of them, shaking my head, 'NO.' I do not believe I have a spirit of infirmity or anything like it. I felt deeply hurt by my 'friends'. Why would we do this to our friends? Why would we bother speaking about love, and God, and action, then turn to our friend and treat them as the 'evil one'? Why, in a church, of all places, did I feel like I was less than human? I did not, and still do not, understand. I did not feel like going back to my church the following Sunday.

The boys laughing at me at Cape Reinga really hurt. Their mocking went to my core, to the deepest inner parts of self-value. I do not understand why the boys saw me as non-human, as 'other', and that it was OK to laugh and mock a person of difference.

At many other times in my life I have felt invisible, people have ignored me, and often people have disrespected me. I am different, and many times society and individuals seem to be at pains to communicate this message.

Why I am Not Valued

A helpful tool to look at the valuing of disabled people over time is to look at the predominant model of disability in each age and see how each respective model perceives disabled people. There are many models of disability, and we will look at three. It is important to understand how individuals with disabilities perceive themselves under each model.

The Charity Model of Disability

The charity model looks at disabled people as those in need of help. Unable to do things for ourselves, others would need to look after us, protect us, and make decisions on our behalf. As much of this 'care' was not state-funded, charities needed to raise money, and traditionally this was done by emphasizing the helplessness of disabled people. Whilst charities offer vital services, the danger is that this takes any autonomy, independence, and even rights away from disabled individuals. Control and power rests with well-meaning non-disabled people who strive to bring about change for the benefit of the 'afflicted'. The language used is similar to that used in the medical model. People are 'crippled' with polio, 'afflicted' with arthritis, 'suffering' from a stroke, and so forth. Disabled people are ultimately expected to be grateful for what they receive and to be submissive.[24]

---

24 Handicap International, 'The Four Models' [accessed 25 February 2015]. Online: http://www.making-prsp-inclusive.org/en/6-disability/61-what-is-disability/611-the-four-models.html.

The Medical Model of Disability

The medical model focuses on the impairment – on what is 'wrong' with the person.[25] It looks at the ways in which the person deviates from the norm, and tries to narrow that gap. The assumption here is that 'normal' is automatically desirable and to be aspired to. The 'problem' lies with the individual and what they can or cannot do. This model is presented as viewing disability as a problem of the person, directly caused by disease, trauma, or other health conditions which therefore requires 'fixing' by sustained medical care provided in the form of treatment by professionals. Management of the disability is aimed at a 'cure', or the individual's adjustment and behavioural change that would lead to an 'almost-cure', or effective cure.[26]

The Social Model of Disability

Brought about by disability activists, this model suggests that the person is disabled by society's inability to adapt to their needs. So, for example, the wheelchair is not the problem, the stairs are. The social model removes the focus and 'blame' from the disabled person to society in general. The social model has encompassed not just people with physical impairments, but also people with sensory impairments, learning disabilities, and mental health issues. The barriers that society puts in the way of those with disabilities include both physical (the built environment) and attitudinal factors. The social model of disability sees the issue of 'disability' as a socially created problem and a matter of the full integration of individuals into society. In this model, disability is not an attribute of an individual, but rather a complex collection of conditions, many of which are created by the social environment. Hence, the management of the problem requires social action, and it is the collective responsibility of society at large to make the environmental modifications necessary for the full participation of people with disabilities in all areas of social life.[27]

An example of the valuing, or not, of disabled people is clearly seen through yet another model of disability: the economic model. This model:

> [d]efines disability by a person's inability to participate in work. It also assesses the degree to which impairment affects an individual's productivity and the economic consequences for the individual, employer, and the state. Such consequences include loss of earnings for and payment for assistance by the individual; lower profit margins for the employer; and state welfare payments. This model is directly related to the charity/tragedy model.[28]

---

25 Evenbreak, 'The "Models" of Disability' [accessed 25 February 2015]. Online: http://www.evenbreak.co.uk/blog/models-of-disability/.
26 Handicap International, 'The Four Models'.
27 Ibid.
28 Disabled World, 'Definitions of the Models of Disability' [accessed 25 February 2015]. Online: http://www.disabled-world.com/definitions/disability-models.php.

I have a growing interest in seeing disabled people being freed financially. I am saddened by economic statistics of disabled people here in New Zealand. Statistics New Zealand states: 'Disabled people are not only much less likely than non-disabled people to participate in the labour force, but those who do are also considerably more likely to be unemployed.'[29] The overseas statistics are no better.[30] This must change if the value of disabled people in modern societies is to be raised. Disabled people I engage with want to make a contribution to society. I think it is about finding creative ways together for people to have greater financial freedom. For example, why are we not looking at a more flexible government support system that allows disabled people to earn a living without basic and necessary government support being considerably reduced when you start earning more than NZ$100 a week?[31]

I agree with Martin Luther King when he says: 'more and more, we've got to begin to ask questions about the whole society. We are called upon to help the discouraged beggars in life's marketplace. But one day we must come to see that an edifice which produces beggars needs restructuring. It means that questions must be raised.'[32]

A fundamental question to be raised is: Do disabled people have the right to be economically free? I believe the answer is yes! Why would we not support a change when you have people that wish to work, are able to work, yet currently a social support system that actively discourages this.

How Do Disabled People Perceive Themselves Under Each of These Models?

There are individual perceptions, but we can draw some conclusions from the underlying assumptions of the value of the disabled individual. Under the charity model a person with a disability may well see themselves as not feeling important, as they 'need help'. They may have low self-worth, being far from equal with able-bodied people and in need of help or assistance from them, while always being the recipient of care or attention. There is the perception that 'others know best what I need'. The charity model by its very nature creates ongoing dependence.

---

29 Statistics New Zealand, 'Disability and the Labour Market: Findings from the 2013 Disability Study' [accessed 25 February 2015]. Online: http://www.stats.govt.nz/browse_for_stats/health/disabilities/disability-and-labour-market/labour-force-partic.aspx.
30 United Nations Enable, 'Factsheet on Persons with Disabilities' [accessed 25 February 2015]. Online: http://www.un.org/disabilities/default.asp?id=18.
31 Work and Income New Zealand, 'What Happens to My Payments if I Work?' [accessed 25 February 2015]. Online: http://www.workandincome.govt.nz/individuals/a-z-benefits/supported-living-payment.html#Whathappenstomypaymentsiflwork6.
32 Martin L. King, Jr, 'Martin Luther King Speech: Where Do We Go from Here?' [accessed 12 November 2015]. Online: http://www.famous-speeches-and-speech-topics.info/martin-luther-king-speeches/martin-luther-king-speech-where-do-we-go-from-here.htm.

Under the medical model a disabled person may feel they are inadequate as they are, it is often pointed out, not 'normal', and not the same as everyone else. Therefore, we are not OK as we are, and we need to be fixed to be made closer to the norm. A high value is placed on doctors, nurses, therapists, and the medical system – on the people and systems who can 'fix' us. The system is powerful, and it is not OK to challenge the system and its views. (Have you ever had to attempt to receive better care in a hospital and spoken up about something you were not happy about?) Disabled people may view themselves as 'needing to be fixed', taking on board an external viewpoint. Again, the disabled individual's self-image can be very low.

With the social model, an individual's self-perception may include the viewpoint: 'I know best about myself. I am a valuable and unique person, with something of value to contribute to my community.' In this model disabled people are recognized as having the same dreams and goals as any other person. Disabled people have a growing respect of self and their own ideas. There is sometimes a significant power shift – 'I have the power to make the changes in my life that I want to make.' Disabled people, as well as every other individual member of society, have inherent value.

I am not advocating for one particular model. There are strengths and weaknesses in each model. Personally, I have benefited from each one: first, by being the recipient of benevolent charity (in the beginning this amounted to a hand-pedalled tricycle from a local Rotary group! I was most grateful). Secondly, where would I be without the medical model? To be blunt, six feet under! I am grateful for many successful operations and treatment from skilled medical personnel that have resulted in improved health.

The social model of disability seems to be the 'best' model, but it is not perfect. Tom Shakespeare makes this clear in saying that there is no 'right' model, and the social model is imperfect.[33] What the social model of disability does is place a much higher value on disabled people. On the down side, it could be perceived as blaming society for the barriers put before us, and creating a disabling society in the first place. However, the big picture under the social model is an increasing value of disabled people, and society intentionally heading towards a place where all people are valued.

There are many people and places offering support disabled people. It makes a huge difference what the underlying philosophy of practice is, and the disability model that underpins it. These relate directly to the dignity, respect, and value afforded to disabled people. I am saddened by many places and people still operating only under the charity and medical models of disability, and the resulting low level of value given to many of my disabled brothers and sisters. This is the litmus test for me: As we look at different organizations, services, or places where disabled people live, ask the question 'Where does the power lie

---

33 Tom Shakespeare and Nicholas Watson, 'The Social Model of Disability: An Outdated Ideology?', *Research in Social Science and Disability* 2 (2002): 9–28.

here?' The honest answer to this question will ascertain how disabled people are valued in this place. For example, in one place where my friends live, adults with disabilities go to bed at 7 p.m. Why so early? Is there no choice? On further investigation I found out that the 'evening shift' staff came on at 7.30 p.m. and wanted things all nice and tidy on their arrival. A further empowering question could be asked: 'Whose needs are being met?'

In relation to the aforementioned Parklands Residential care facility, what does the lack of quality of care say about the values of the organization? Where does the power lie? It was obviously *not* with the people with disabilities living there. Why was there no further investigation, and what does this say about the value of the disabled people living there?[34] Where is the justice in this?

On this same property at Parklands it was reported that there were also 35 dogs on-site.[35] Barry, a disabled brother, said that if it had been the dogs that had been mistreated there would have been an investigation by the RSPCA, and such a public uproar that the place would have been closed down immediately. I am sad to say I think Barry is correct.

Do we as a society really have such a low value of disabled people that we just do not care enough, and somehow by default we justify abuse? Where is the justice for the individuals concerned if there is to be no investigation? I humbly suggest this will not be the last occurrence of disabled people being shown to have a low value by support services in New Zealand.

How I Might be Valued

New Zealand society is changing, and the power is shifting – maybe not fast enough for me, but we are moving towards where we need to be. There is meaningful conversation and a growing understanding of what it means to be in partnership with, and to walk alongside, a disabled person, to support, where the power – the choice and control over one's own life – rightly sits with the disabled individual.

Do we have good historical examples of social change where people spoke up and as a result society was transformed for the better? Yes, we do. The Civil Rights movement in the USA is a good example. Significant numbers of people supported a just cause, and positive change was created. I think it may require a similar kind of social movement worldwide to shift the value system with regard to people with disabilities. If we want significant social change to continue, the first step is sending a very clear message that the current situation is not OK.

Internationally, we see an increase in the value of disabled people through powerful legislation such as the United Nations Convention on the Rights of

---

34 Kirsty Johnston, 'No Further Parklands Investigations' [accessed 25 February 2015]. Online: http://www.stuff.co.nz/national/health/8651354/No-further-Parklands-investigations.
35 Ibid.

Persons with Disabilities.³⁶ Ratified in 2008, as of June 2013 it had 114 countries as full signatories.³⁷ This document clearly outlines the rights of disabled people and has resulted in increased value of disabled people in many countries. There is huge potential for this legislation to create global change. It will be up to organizations and individuals following up on this good legislation to create positive change.³⁸

As a society we need to ask, and engage with, the bigger questions of value. How do we as a society get from where we are now in valuing disabled people to where we need to be? The answer depends on where we as a society want to go. If it is about heading to a place where disabled people are highly valued, and are equal members of society, then we need to fully understand the transition we all need to make. I suggest we have two very good road maps of how to get to that place in New Zealand. In one hand we would hold God's Word, our primary source of wisdom, guidance, and influence, and in the other hand we would hold the New Zealand Disability Strategy (2001).³⁹ The New Zealand Disability Strategy clearly outlines 15 key objectives that would move us towards a non-disabling society.⁴⁰ A fundamental question to be raised, and discussed together is: Do we want to be a community, city, or country where disabled people can say, 'We live in "[a] society that highly values our lives and continually enhances our full participation"?'⁴¹

How Jesus Values Me

One story from Mark 10:46–52 illustrates how Jesus valued people with disabilities. Bartimaeus was rejected by society and placed on the margins, literally on the outskirts of town. He was visually impaired, and therefore unable to work in this society, forced into begging to sustain himself. He had heard of Jesus, so when Jesus came by he called out to him. Jesus stopped and spoke: 'Tell him to come here' – An invitation to come and speak with him. 'What do you want me to do for you?' Jesus spoke to Bartimaeus directly, thereby honouring him as a person. Jesus asked *his* opinion, no one else's. By doing this Jesus is giving Bartimaeus power and control: he asked a question and awaited his response. *Seeing* – Jesus noticed Bartimaeus. *Stopping* – Jesus chose to be with

---

36 United Nations, 'Convention on the Rights of Persons with Disabilities' [accessed 25 February 2015]. Online: http://www.un.org/disabilities/convention/conventionfull.shtml.
37 United Nations Enable, 'Convention and Optional Protocol Signatures and Ratifications' [accessed 25 February 2015]. Online: http://www.un.org/disabilities/countries.asp?navid=17&pid=166.
38 Ministry of Social Development, Office for Disability Issues, 'United Nations Convention on Rights of Persons with Disabilities' [accessed 25 February 2015]. Online: http://www.odi.govt.nz/what-we-do/un-convention/.
39 Ministry of Social Development, Office for Disability Issues, 'New Zealand Disability Strategy' [accessed 25 February 2015]. Online: http://www.odi.govt.nz/nzds/index.html.
40 Ibid.
41 Ibid.

Bartimaeus. *Speaking* – Jesus valued Bartimaeus. *Asking* – Jesus respected Bartimaeus. *Inviting* – Jesus honoured Bartimaeus.

What did the restoration of sight mean for Bartimaeus the disabled person, what did it accomplish, and what difference would this change make for him? With sight in this context, Bartimaeus was able to see, was able to live in the town again and be accepted by his peers. He could go back and live with his family, gain a job, and earn a living for his family. As he would no longer be declared 'unclean', he had free entry to the temple, and this would enhance his ability to connect with God. In summary, with restored sight Bartimaeus was restored to community, restored to his family, restored to work, restored to temple worship, and restored to relationship with God. Ultimately, he could now be accepted by society – his 'societal' value increased greatly, and he now had greater choices and control over his life.

I would suggest that in this day and age we do not need physical healing to make some of the same positive changes towards a disabled person. It is about accepting a person as they are now, shifting power towards a disabled individual in such a way that their life choices are enhanced. It is about ensuring our places of worship are welcoming and fully inclusive – places of belonging. It is about actively working towards eliminating barriers that prevent full and equal participation in our communities. We would do well to follow Jesus' example in working towards a society that values disabled people.

Conclusion

We have looked at some of the reasons why disabled people have historically not been highly valued in New Zealand. By using the predominant models of disability we saw an increase over time of the value that society places on disabled people, with the outcome now that we have the social model of disability. This is a model that values difference, and paints a picture of what a non-disabling society looks like, and as such, it is a valuable addition to our approach to and understanding of people with disabilities.

We looked at the economics of disability – disabled people are not equal in an economic context. I have a dream to be part of a society where disabled people are economically free – free to live and work towards the lives individuals want to build for themselves.

There are positive discussions around inclusion and belonging now, and sectors of society are actively working towards a non-disabling society. We also have maps to get us there: first, the Bible, God's Word to us, and helpful documents such as the New Zealand Disability Strategy (2001).[42] We would do well to go back to these maps and follow the journey they would lead us on.

Society is heading towards a place of full inclusion for people with disabilities, both in legislation and practice. Auckland Council has a clear mandate to become

---

42 Ibid.

'the world's most liveable city'.[43] Part of this is the aspiration to be the world's most 'liveable, accessible, and inclusive city'.[44] This is a great direction to head in, and I am excited about the journey. Many people are already involved in removing barriers to full participation, and in initiatives that value disabled people.

How will we know when we have arrived at a place where we highly value all people? I would join with Erik W. Carter in saying we have arrived when we no longer talk about 'them' and 'us', disabled and non-disabled, but 'we' – in life together.[45]

Let us dream together, and be possibility thinkers. Here are a few initiatives I would love to see:

- disabled people being business owners, employing other people in their successful businesses;
- disabled people as educators, respected academics, in our educational institutions;
- disabled people as members of parliament[46] – the movers and shakers of our nation;
- disabled individuals as models, and in major advertising campaigns;
- disabled people in influential positions in churches;
- aid agencies that are serious about disability, and not only putting inclusion into policy, but practice, where millions of disabled people worldwide are fully included in their communities;
- accessible housing – making economic sense and future-proofing the houses by incorporating principles of universal design;
- disabled people living in places they choose to live in, with people they wish to live with, and choosing the people they wish to support them.[47]

God is actively increasing the value of disabled people in New Zealand society. I humbly suggest that believers could play a greater role in transforming their communities into truly being places of belonging. There are many and great opportunities to speak up and be a positive voice for change. My challenge to the reader is: How could you help shift the communities you live in to value disabled people more highly? How will *you* be the change you wish to see?

---

43 Auckland Council, 'The Auckland Plan' [accessed 24 November 2015]. Online: http://www.aucklandcouncil.govt.nz/EN/planspoliciesprojects/plansstrategies/theaucklandplan/Pages/theaucklandplan.aspx.
44 Auckland Council, 'Aspirations for the World's Most Liveable, Accessible, and Inclusive City' [accessed 24 November 2015]. Online: http://www.aucklandcouncil.govt.nz/SiteCollectionDocuments/aboutcouncil/advisorypanels/disabilitystrategicadvisorygroup/dsagaspirations.pdf.
45 Erik Carter, *Including People with Disabilities in Faith Communities: A Guide for Service Providers, Families, and Congregations* (Baltimore, MD: Paul H. Brooks, 2007), 168.
46 'Mojo Mathers MP' [accessed 25 February 2015]. Online: https://www.greens.org.nz/ourpeople/mojo-mathers-mp.
47 Chris Grantham, *The Chocolate Seller on Broadway – and His Kids* (Auckland: Cocoa Bean Press, 2009).

17 Disability and Divinization

Eschatological Parables and Allegations

Myk Habets

Introduction

We are all interested in the resurrection, for various reasons, and we all have questions concerning our glorified state. Will we be married? What will we look like? How might we act? The gospel invites us to ask such questions, and the human condition demands we find answers.

Matthew tells the story of the time when some Sadducees sought to put Jesus to the test and asked him:

> Teacher ... there were seven brothers with us; and the first married and died, and having no children left his wife to his brother; so also the second, and the third, down to the seventh. Last of all, the woman died. In the resurrection, therefore, whose wife of the seven will she be? For they all had married her. (Matt 22:23–8)

Jesus replied, saying they had no idea of what the Scriptures teach, nor of the power of God; if they did, they would know that in the resurrection 'they neither marry nor are given in marriage ...' (vv. 29–31), and that the God of Abraham, Isaac, and Jacob is the God of the living not of the dead (vv. 32–3).

We might rephrase this dialogue between Christ and the Sadducees with a modern twist, minus the intent to trap, and say: 'Teacher, in the resurrection, will amputees have all their limbs? Will those with severe mental disabilities flourish cognitively, emotionally, spiritually, and physically? Will my depression be cured? Will my OCD be healed? Teacher, what will we be like in glory?' In fact, questions such as these were asked in the early centuries of the faith, amidst intense persecution.

I am particularly interested in those with profound and severe intellectual disabilities for the precise reason that their presence with us questions and tests our dogmatic formulations and the existential viability of the message and reality of the Good News Jesus himself embodied and passed on to his church. I would like to present one very small contribution to a larger perspective on theology and disability by bringing several conversations together in order to see how each formally explains and enriches the other. As such, this is a work in constructive Christian dogmatics. This builds on earlier work of mine where I endeavoured to prove, if such can ever be done, the salvation of the severely intellectually disabled by means of a version of a Reformed doctrine of election.[1] In this chapter I wish to start at the other end from protology and election, that of eschatology and theosis, in order to join the dots, as it were. In my prior work I argue for the salvation of all people with profound intellectual disabilities, and in this chapter I want to further argue that in the eschaton all such persons will be deified, as will all others found savingly in Christ. What such deification might entail is the specific subject of this chapter. In order to achieve this I will briefly define my understanding of theosis; this will then allow me to suggest and expose forms of ecclesial communion which act as parables of eschatological hope, before concluding with a few eschatological allegations whereby I respectfully disagree with several recent accounts of human glorification.

Theosis and the Transcendental Determinism of Human Persons

The Christian tradition, both East and West, has developed various models and theories of the atonement as explanations of what it means to speak of the reconciling activity of God in Christ. Central to these has been the claim that God has reconciled the world to himself in Christ. One way of testifying to the reconciling love of God has been the adoption of the metaphor theosis ('divinization', 'deification') as an explanation of salvation. While central to Eastern Orthodoxy, a doctrine of theosis also has a rich tradition within Western, especially Reformed, theology. We are reminded by one patristic scholar that:

> *Theosis* was the term the Fathers used to emphasize the fact that through the Spirit we have to do with God in his utter sublimity, his sheer Godness or holiness; creatures though we are, men on earth, in the Spirit we are made to participate in saving acts that are abruptly and absolutely divine, election, adoption, regeneration or sanctification and we participate in them by grace alone. *Theosis* describes man's involvement in such a mighty act of God upon him that he is raised up to find the true centre of his existence not in himself but in Holy God, where he lives and moves and has his being in the uncreated but creative energy of the Holy Spirit. By *theosis*

---

1 See Myk Habets, '"Suffer the Little Children to Come to Me, for Theirs is the Kingdom of Heaven": Infant Salvation and the Destiny of the Severely Mentally Disabled', in *Evangelical Calvinism: Essays Resourcing the Continuing Reformation of the Church*, ed. Myk Habets and Robert Grow (Eugene, OR: Pickwick Publications, 2012), 287–328.

the Greek fathers wished to express the fact that in the new coming of the Holy Spirit we are up against *God* in the most absolute sense, God in his ultimate holiness or Godness.[2]

As the true Man and the last Adam, Christ represents the *archē* and *telos* of human existence, the one in whose image all humanity has been created and into whose likeness all humanity is destined to be transformed from glory to glory. Through the Incarnation the Son becomes human without ceasing to be divine, to unite humanity and divinity together and effect a 'deification' of human nature, mediated to men and women who are said to be 'in Christ' by the work of the Holy Spirit. By means of a 'wonderful exchange' Christ takes what is ours and gives us what is his.

The goal of humanity is worship, something we might helpfully define, after James Torrance, as the gift of participating through the Spirit in the incarnate Son's communion with the Father, and in his mission from the Father to the world. It follows that the *locus* of worship, and thus of theosis, is the church, the communion of saints created by the fellowship of the Holy Spirit.[3] In brief, and in the words of Thomas Torrance:

> *Theosis* is an attempt to express the staggering significance of Pentecost as the coming from on high, from outside of us and beyond us, of divine power, or rather as the coming of Almighty God, the Maker of heaven and earth, to dwell with sinful mortal man, and therefore as the emancipation of man from imprisonment in himself and the lifting of him up to partake of the living presence and saving acts of God the Creator and Redeemer.[4]

Theosis dogmatically explains salvation more in *relational* than *rational* terms. Salvation is the literal reunion of men and women in God through Christ. Salvation is the restoration of divine–human intimacy, the joy and love of interpersonal communion, and the healing of all creation. God's redemptive love goes far beyond giving payment for broken *laws*; it restores *relationships*; for salvation is, foremost, communion with God and one's fellow humanity. God's *chief*

---

2 Thomas F. Torrance, 'Come, Creator Spirit, for the Renewal of Worship and Witness', in *Theology in Reconstruction* (Grand Rapids, MI: Eerdmans, 1965), 243.
3 Archimandrite George writes: 'So, being baptised, chrismated, confessing, we commune through the Body and Blood of the Lord, and we too become gods by Grace; we unite with God; we are no longer strangers, for we have become familiar with God. Inside the Church in which we unite with God, we live this new reality which Christ brought to the world: the new creation. This is the life of the Church, of Christ, which becomes ours as a gift from the Holy Spirit. Everything in the Church leads to Theosis; the Holy Liturgy, the Mysteries, divine Worship, the Gospel sermon, the fasting; all of these lead to this one thing. The Church alone is the place of Theosis'; *Theosis: The True Purpose of Human Life* (Mount Athos, Athens: Holy Monastery of St Gregorios, 2006), 36.
4 Torrance, *Theology in Reconstruction*, 244.

motive in redemption was to restore our *communion* with Him. Communion with God thus forms the central image or model for theosis. It is *union, communion*, or *participation* in God that is central to such a theology. One Orthodox writer is adamant about this when he writes:

> Christ did not save us just by going to the cross and dying for us. His *whole* life was redemptive. Without the incarnation, He could not have had a ministry. Without His ministry we would be unprepared for the meaning and significance of His death. Without His resurrection, His death would hold no meaning. Without His ascension, the Spirit would not have been sent, and we could not have been adopted as sons of God.[5]

This is an important point for us to note. While the West has tended to look to the cross exclusively for what it means to be saved, Eastern Orthodoxy looks also to the life or incarnation of Christ to see what salvation means. And in this I think they are quite correct. This becomes especially apparent when we tend to the doctrine of the resurrection, where the goal of salvation is to be in communion with the triune God by means of our resurrection into the likeness of Christ.

While the legal dimension has dominated Western thinking about salvation, we do learn from Scripture that there are other motifs or images of salvation we would do well to draw from. In justification we have been forgiven: what a wonderful truth. But, and this is the important point, we need to start thinking more about what we have been saved *for* rather than simply what we have been saved *from*. Christian experience is more than just a feeling of relief at having evaded divine judgment. Justification points forward to a transformation and union with God. God is not only an angry judge needing satisfaction. He is also a passionate lover seeking at-one-ment with men and women. According to Paul, believers are incorporated into the perfect life, death, and resurrection of Jesus Christ. As such, we participate in his perfect human nature and so we are being transformed from glory to glory, as Paul expresses it. The key thing about salvation is transformation![6]

Theosis is a comprehensive doctrine of the Christian life which encompasses all the facets of salvation from election through to glorification. Implicated in a doctrine of theosis are commitments around one's theological anthropology, theology proper, ecclesiology, and eschatology. All these points are relevant to our topic, but I would like to deal briefly with theological anthropology, specifically the idea that there is a transcendental determinism built into every image bearer of Christ, and later tackle the issue of the eschaton.

---

5 Jordan Bajis, *Common Ground: An Introduction to Eastern Christianity for the American Christian* (Minneapolis, MN: Light & Life, 1991), 232–3.
6 Although it appeared after I wrote this chapter, see David A. deSilva, *Transformation: The Heart of Paul's Gospel* (Bellingham, WA: Lexham Press, 2014).

Theological Anthropology: Transcendental Determinism

In rejecting a naïve anthropology that posits a trichotomy of body, soul, and spirit, we may, after Athanasius, Karl Barth, and Thomas Torrance, utilize the language that a human person is a 'body of her soul and soul of her body'.[7] Human persons are an anthropological duality of body and soul, related to God 'through the power and presence of God's Spirit, and thereby endowed with the capacity to think and act in accordance with the nature (*kataphysin*) of what is other than himself'.[8] The human spirit is actually an essential and dynamic correlate of the divine 'Spirit' – not a third object distinct from body and soul. The presence of the Holy Spirit in the human results in a 'transcendental determination' implanted within each of us. The human person is created with a goal (*telos*) in view, to participate in the triune relationship of the Father for the Son in or by the Holy Spirit. This transcendental determination of the Spirit impels the human towards God, and this movement may be characterized as theosis.[9]

What drives the human being to personality and relatedness is the Holy Spirit who is the Spirit of sonship and Spirit of fatherhood and the bond of unity between Creator and creature in space-time. The S/spirit of men and women is not some 'spark of the divine' (Origen),[10] but the 'ontological qualification of her soul' brought about and maintained by the Holy Spirit.[11] In this way the human person is capable of thinking objectively of what is other than them – it is the very essence of their human rationality and relationality. As Torrance clarifies:

> It is not through any alleged participation in the essence of God, as Hellenic religion and philosophy maintained, but through the objective

---

7 See Thomas F. Torrance, *The Christian Frame of Mind* (Edinburgh: Handsel Press, 1985), 29. Cf. Thomas F. Torrance, *The Trinitarian Faith: The Evangelical Theology of the Ancient Catholic Church* (Edinburgh: T&T Clark, 1995, first published in 1988), 150, and Thomas F. Torrance, *The Soul and Person of the Unborn Child* (Edinburgh: Handsel Press for the Scottish Order of Christian Unity, 1999), 7; Athanasius, *De Incarnationis* 15; *Contra Arianos* 2.53–4; 3.20, 30–35, and Karl Barth, *Church Dogmatics*, ed. and trans. G.W. Bromiley and T.F. Torrance, 2nd rev. edn (Edinburgh: T&T Clark, 1975 and 1977), vol. III/2, 325.

8 Thomas F. Torrance, 'The Soul and Person in Theological Perspective', in *Religion, Reason, and the Self: Essays in Honour of Hywel D. Lewis*, ed. S.R. Sutherland and T.A. Roberts (Cardiff: University of Wales Press, 1989), 110.

9 Wolfhart Pannenberg, *Toward a Theology of Nature: Essays on Science and Faith*, ed. Ted Peters (Louisville, KY: Westminster John Knox Press, 1993), 133, speaks of an 'ecological self-transcendence' inherent to living organisms which corresponds to the biblical idea of a spiritual origin of life. This is wedded to a field of energy which in turn is wedded to a concept of spirit. While Pannenberg's idea of 'self-transcendence' sounds similar to Torrance's 'transcendental determination', the fundamental difference lies in the identity of the S/spirit. For Torrance 'spirit' in this context is always the Holy Spirit, while for Pannenberg 'spirit', as with much philosophy, identifies an anthropological predicate as much as it does a divine Person.

10 David Cairns, *The Image of God in Man*, 2nd edn (London: Collins, 1973), 66–78.

11 Torrance, 'The Soul and Person in Theological Perspective', 110.

orientation of man in soul and body to God, the Source and Ground of all creaturely rationality and freedom, that man is constituted a rational subject and agent, i.e. a person.[12]

What makes men and women so distinctive is that as unitary beings – body of their soul and soul of their body – they span two 'worlds' – the physical and spiritual – and are thereby able to reach knowledge of the created contingent order and divulge the secrets of its vast intelligibility.[13] As a result, a correspondence between God and humanity is spanned by human persons created in the *imago Dei*. Like the rest of creation, the soul and body are created *ex nihilo* and are contingent rather than immortal.[14] The soul and body of human beings are 'continuously sustained by the creative presence of God and are given immortality through the grace of a relation with God who only has immortality'.[15]

This graced relation to God is initiated in space-time, but extends to the eschaton, in which the resurrection of the whole being of the person as body and soul is realized. Resurrection is to a creaturely participation in the uncreated eternal Life of God, a kind of theosis.[16] Resurrection must be seen not only as deliverance from corruption, but also as an ontological act in which true creaturehood is restored through the intimate relation with the creative triune God.[17]

Theosis is the goal of all human existence. At the resurrection of body and soul, human beings can fully participate in the eternal life of God. This participation always has one qualifier, however: it is a participation in the eternal life of God *embodied in the incarnate Son*.[18] There is no life without the Source of Life, no resurrection without the resurrected One, and no theosis outside of the incarnate Son of God. Thus theosis is not, strictly speaking, the 'divinization'

---

12 Ibid., 113.
13 Torrance, *The Christian Frame of Mind*, 33. For this reason Torrance terms humanity the 'mediator of order'. For more on Torrance's conception of the body–soul relation, see Eric G. Flett, 'Priests of Creation, Mediators of Order: The Human Person as a Cultural Being in Thomas F. Torrance's Theological Anthropology', *Scottish Journal of Theology* 58 (2005): 164–8, and sympathetic to Torrance's anthropology, see Ray S. Anderson, 'On Being Human: The Spiritual Saga of a Creaturely Soul', in *Whatever Happened to the Soul? Scientific and Theological Portraits of Human Nature*, ed. Warren S. Brown, Nancey Murphey, and H. Newton Malony (Minneapolis, MN: Fortress, 1998), 175–94.
14 See Thomas F. Torrance, *Transformation and Convergence in the Frame of Knowledge: Explorations in the Interrelations of Scientific and Theological Enterprise* (Grand Rapids, MI: Eerdmans, 1984), 333–49.
15 Torrance, 'The Soul and Person in Theological Perspective', 105.
16 It is noteworthy that Torrance refers to the 'illuminating essays' of Georges Florovsky, the prominent Eastern Orthodox theologian who advocated a doctrine of theosis throughout his works. The two essays noted are: 'Creation and Creaturehood' and 'The Immortality of the Soul', in *Creation and Redemption, Collected Works*, vol. 3 (Belmont, MA.: Norland Publishing, 1976), 43–78 and 213–40.
17 Torrance, 'The Soul and Person in Theological Perspective', 106.
18 Ibid.

of the human person as such, but the 'personalizing' of the human being in *the* Person of the incarnate Son. This is the meaning behind the words of Torrance, 'for man to live in union with God is to become fully and perfectly human'.[19] Jesus alone is the *personalizing Person*, while we are *personalized persons*.[20] It is from Christ alone, the one through whom creation came and the one for whom humanity was created, that men and women are radically made persons in the divine image.[21]

Evident in the discussion so far is the deliberate distinction between *being* and *person*, a distinction that applies both theologically and anthropologically. Theologically, the being of God refers to *ousia*, while person, when applied to God, is described by *hypostasis*. We may apply a similar distinction to anthropology. The human creature is created in a special sense, as Gen 1:27 makes clear, but because the *imago Dei* is ultimately christological, soteriological, and eschatological, the relational aspect of the *imago* is what makes human beings human persons, true men and women. Because Jesus Christ is the only true human, he is the true image of God, so only in Christ can the human creature be fully a *person*.[22] The movement within the salvation of men and women is from human *being*, a biological fact, to human *person*, a moral, theological fact. Anything outside of Christ falls short of true personhood. This is important for an articulation of theosis.

Theosis begins now as we participate in the new creation through the Spirit; it is also 'not yet' as we wait for the *Parousia* of the Lord when God in Christ will make all things new. The goal of theosis is not to become 'God', or even, technically speaking, to become 'gods'. It is not the process of transcending the confines of human nature, but the process and means by which the human can achieve true personhood. Theosis does not do away with our creatureliness; it fulfils it. In a similar vein, Staniloae suggests that theosis cannot be taken *literally*. One cannot *literally* become God since that would be as absurd as if we were to state that God is a creature.[23] The 'transcendental determination' inherent within each human person and realized by those united to Christ Jesus means that men and women will be able to be and do what they were created to be and do – mirror God back to God, through Christ by the Holy Spirit. This is the goal of humanity summarized by the term 'theosis'.

What, then, does a doctrine of theosis have to say to the people with severe mental disabilities? That question will occupy the remainder of the chapter.

---

19 Thomas F. Torrance, 'The Goodness and Dignity of Man in the Christian Tradition', *Modern Theology* 4 (1988): 315.
20 Torrance, 'The Soul and Person in Theological Perspective', 116.
21 Torrance, *The Christian Frame of Mind*, 31.
22 Torrance is reliant upon the seminal work of Barth, who argued that in the strict sense it is God who is properly Person, and humans are persons in derivation from him; Barth, *CD* II/1, 272. See Thomas F. Torrance, *God and Rationality* (Eugene, OR: Wipf & Stock, 1997), 141–2.
23 See Emil Bartos, *Deification in Eastern Orthodoxy: An Evaluation and Critique of the Theology of Dumitru Stăniloae*, Paternoster Biblical and Theological Monographs (Carlisle: Paternoster Press, 1999), 145.

Inaugurated Parables of Eschatological Hope

Severe mental disability, or cognitive disability as it is often called, may be defined as those human persons whose IQ may be measured as 25 and below.[24] Social factors must also be taken into consideration: for instance, those whose mental age is considered to be equivalent to a two-year-old or younger, lacking the kind of abstract thinking that can make connections, follow out consequences of their actions, or learn from past mistakes. Thus the severely mentally disabled persons of whom this chapter speaks are unable to make rational decisions, and are unable to account for moral right and wrong. They live in a world of their own, seemingly affected only by external physical stimuli, and often not even those.[25]

To further define the severely mentally disabled, we may appeal to the definition of such given by the World Health Organization.[26] According to this report, mental disability involves four levels: mild, moderate, severe, and profound. Furthermore, the definition includes two essential components: intellectual functioning and adaptive behaviour. Of these four levels, only 1.5 to 5 per cent of all individuals classed as 'retarded'[27] are found in the category of the profoundly mentally disabled.

Scripture, Disability, and Resurrection

Scripture is largely silent on the presence or destiny of the mentally disabled: 'In fact, researchers who set out looking for a biblical theology of disability will be quickly disappointed because our contemporary notions of disability are for the most part foreign to the worldview of the biblical authors,'[28] writes Amos Yong. He continues by adding that 'the Bible does not say anything about what

---

24 Standard IQ tests are divided into various sections: 140 or higher – genius; 120–40 – very superior; 100–110 – superior; 90–100 – normal/average; 80–90 – dull/feeble-minded; 50–70 – moron; 20/25–50 – imbecile; below 20/25 – idiot. It is the last category of 'idiot' alone that I am calling the severely mentally disabled. On the emergence of the IQ test and its various adaptations, see Amos Yong, *Theology and Down Syndrome: Reimagining Disability in Late Modernity* (Waco, TX: Baylor University Press, 2007), 57–60.

25 This definition approximately corresponds to the definition of 'idiot' given by Alfred Binet and Theodore Simon, authors of the modern (Binet-Simon) IQ test. Henry H. Goddard further refined this test, which became the standard in the field of mental retardation: 'idiots' were those with a mental age of less than two years; 'imbeciles' ranged from two to seven years; 'proximates'/'morons' were ages 8–12. See Scheeringberger, *A History of Mental Retardation* (Baltimore, MD: P.H. Brookes, 1983), 144.

26 *Mental Retardation: Meeting the Challenge*. Prepared in collaboration with the Joint Commission on International Aspects of Mental Retardation (Geneva: Albany, NY: World Health Organization; WHO Publications Centre USA, 1985).

27 Ibid., 9. The profoundly mentally retarded according to World Health Organization are those with IQ scores less than 20, thus corresponding to the earlier category of 'idiot' according to the Binet-Simon test.

28 Yong, *Theology and Down Syndrome*, 20.

we today call intellectual disability'.²⁹ This is not to say that Scripture is of no use to us in formulating a theological account of and response to disability. Scripture does speak of people with physical deformities and disabilities; notably, it speaks of the deaf, the blind, the lame, and the mute. While a biblical theology of disability is not my goal here, we may simply say that in Scripture human disability is abnormal, even though those with disabilities come from the Creator God (Exod 4:11). Such severe disability is often portrayed as a result of the fall and corruption of the world. In the Old Testament it is linked to uncleanness (although even here, see the later reversal of the eunuch in Isa 56:3–5), or being unfit to serve in priestly service and other activities to do with the religious cult (Lev 21:16–23).

Given these restrictions, however, Scripture does make it clear that all people, even those with disabilities, are equal image-bearers of God, and thus deserve respect and dignity, care and inclusion (Lev 19:14; Job 29:12–17; Jer 31:8; Zeph 3:19). The fact that disabilities are not God's final intention for people is implicit in the healing narratives of the New Testament. This is evident in Jesus' healing of the blind, the lame, and the deaf (cf. Luke 5:17–26; 9:37–43; 13:10–13; 18:35–43).³⁰ One-fifth of all the material in the four gospels is concerned with the healing of physical disease. Jesus is a healer. His healings present or reveal him as the Messiah, and the healings are presented as a sign of 'the End', the eschatological incarnation of the promised One who would redeem Israel and the entire world. Healings in the gospels act as Messianic *kairoi*, revelatory windows into Jesus' true identity as the Dominical man, but they also serve as a foretaste of the Kingdom of God and God's purposes for his creatures.

As Holmes writes, with reference to the man healed in John 5:1–18:

> That Jesus heals . . . is a very concrete sign that bespeaks God's present and anticipates God's advent rule wherein the power of evil which manifests itself in sickness is vanquished, and that all things be rendered transparent to God's Sabbath rest. Evil as manifested in this man's illness has indeed met its end: Jesus Christ abolishes what distorts, disfigures and corrupts the creatures whom he and his father love.³¹

Throughout the gospels Jesus heals sickness and disease, disability and disfigurement, exorcises demons, rules over creation, and forgives sin. In each of these Messianic moments Jesus is exercising his divine prerogative to judge sin. Jesus

---

29 Ibid., 21. For a survey of Scripture and disability, see further ibid., 21–7, and Amos Yong, *The Bible, Disability, and the Church: A New Vision of the People of God* (Grand Rapids, MI: Eerdmans, 2011).
30 Yong's helpful survey of Scripture concludes: 'Clearly, then, "disability" in the New Testament functions rhetorically to call attention to negative realities such as sin, evil spirits, spiritual degeneration, and moral reprobation'; Yong, *Theology and Down Syndrome*, 27.
31 Christopher R.J. Holmes, *Ethics in the Presence of Christ* (London: T&T Clark, 2012), 28.

is 'Judging sickness, announcing it as incommensurate with his Father's eschatological rule of life'.[32]

The text with which I began this chapter comes to mind again and again in Jesus' healing ministry – his healings display the power of God at work in Jesus the son of the Father. And such power as the Son has, given by the Father, is fully on display in the resurrection, the event which brings to fulfilment the eschatological foretastes provided by the healings. Resurrection is the end of healing, for it is its fulfilment. The resurrection exhibits the 'new "normal" of which the church is the herald',[33] as Holmes helpfully phrases it.

We see a clear example of this link between healing and resurrection in the healing of the paralytic who was let down through the roof to be put in touch with Jesus which we read about in Mark 2:1–12. Jesus' command for the man to 'rise up' utilizes the most typical word for resurrection in the New Testament – *egeiro*. For the early church, the forgiveness and healing offered meant nothing less than the manifestation of the 'full reality in the healing and creative work of God upon the whole man' effected as a result of the resurrection.[34] As Kärkkainen says:

> It is highly significant that in Acts this linkage between forgiveness and physical healing remained intact – linked with the resurrection and ascension of Christ and the pouring out of the Holy Spirit (Acts 3:12–16, 4:8–12). In the raising of Jesus the Spirit of God who is the spirit of life is working in a mighty way overcoming death and decay.[35]

Ecclesial Membership

Seeing people with disabilities as fellow human beings, equal in status and dignity to the rest of humanity, made as we are in the image of God, is basic to any theological anthropology, and the point has been made repeatedly across many works. Indeed, to say anything else is both unethical and un-Christian. Given this, I don't want to transverse theological anthropology in detail in this chapter, merely to assume it and draw some implications from that. Here I want to make the suggestion – not unique to me, of course, but nonetheless worth repeating – that people with severe disabilities act, in God's redemptive plan, as parables of eschatological hope and grace. In a world in which God has, for whatever reason, allowed disabilities to exist, lessons of hospitality, service, grace,

---

32 Ibid., 30.
33 Ibid., 32.
34 This argument is made by Thomas F. Torrance, *Space, Time and Resurrection* (Edinburgh: T&T Clark, 1996), 62.
35 Veli-Matti Kärkkainen, *A Constructive Christian Theology for the Pluralistic World, Volume 1: Christ and Reconciliation* (Grand Rapids, MI: Eerdmans, 2013), 355.

love, acceptance, and friendship are embodied in faith communities which are made up of people from the 'centre' and those of the 'margins'. And of course, we are each both at the centre and at the margins, depending on who is drawing the lines.

But first we have to address the issue of ecclesial inclusion. The severely mentally disabled are part of our lives, our families, and our communities of faith. A fundamental issue thus arises: if we are to consider the severely mentally disabled as 'saved' by the gracious election of God – as I have argued elsewhere – then what status should we accord them within the church? More specifically, should the severely mentally disabled be baptized and take communion? This question has not been asked before in the literature, at least not to my knowledge. Amos Yong has addressed these issues in relation to the mentally disabled in general, but not to the severely mentally disabled. Thus he approvingly cites Joseph Bernardin, who seeks to find signs that would indicate the readiness of a developmentally delayed person to receive the sacraments. Included in his helpful list are desire, relationships, and a sense of the sacred, however that may be made manifest.[36] In short, cues are taken from the disabled person of an interrelation, interpersonal, and intersubjective kind.

Such indicative signs as are noted above are all well and good in general, but do not apply to the *severely* mentally disabled as we have defined them here, for such persons exhibit no such signs of the sacred or of any outward response to God. At this point I can accept the position of Beach, who argued that 'the sign of salvation may not be separated from the thing signified, which is to say, if one participates in the reality of salvation he or she must receive the sign of that salvation – the mark of baptism'[37] – and, I would add, the ongoing sacrament of inclusion: Eucharist.

In the ecclesial contexts which practise paedobaptism, the issue of baptizing the severely mentally disabled is a non-issue. But in Free Church and especially Baptist ecclesial contexts, of which I am involved, where believer's baptism is the norm, the issue of baptizing the severely mentally disabled is as acute as the issue common to all ecclesial traditions of whether or not to serve the Eucharist to the severely mentally disabled.

If the arguments proffered so far are accepted, then we must insist on the acceptability of baptism for all those considered part of the family of faith – young and old, men and women, and the severely mentally disabled. Baptismal regeneration has never been acceptable to Reformed or Baptist theology, thus it is not valid to appeal to this in the case of the severely mentally disabled. The only legitimate consequence of the theology developed so far is to baptize, if their parents or guardians are willing (normally believing parents), the severely

---

36 Joseph Bernardin, *Access to the Sacraments of Initiation and Reconciliation for Developmentally Disabled Persons*, 9, cited in Yong, *Theology and Down Syndrome*, 210.

37 J. Mark Beach, 'Original Sin, Infant Salvation, and the Baptism of Infants', *Mid-America Journal of Theology* 12 (2001): 51.

mentally disabled and, also if their parents or guardians allow it, to allow them to receive the Eucharist. As means of grace, baptism and the Eucharist feed and nourish the recipient, and these acts speak powerfully to the inclusion of all God's children in the covenant of grace through faith, not of works (Eph 2:8, 9).

Faith communities are therefore on solid theological ground to offer baptism and communion to the severely mentally disabled, thus showing their inclusion in the family of God, the Body of Christ, and the fellowship of the Saints. Such acts of inclusion, grace, and fellowship would provide a powerful sign of the reality of the Kingdom of God, breaking into the structures of fallen reality, pointing powerfully to the salvific work of the triune God of grace. To exclude such persons from our central ecclesial acts is, I suggest, a violation of the very meaning of what it means to be the church – Baptist, Presbyterian, or otherwise.

This raises the related issue, however: once included within our ecclesial communions, then what? If such people are accorded full ecclesial status within our communities of faith, we must then seek to worship, minister, and serve God together. Yong reminds us that:

> People with profound disabilities are not agents of ministry in the normal senses of that notion, but they are conduits of the revelatory and transformative gifts of God's Spirit for those who will slow down enough to befriend them, to see, hear, and touch in faith, and to receive God's presence into their own lives.[38]

Here I agree with Amos Yong's insistence on bringing people with disabilities, especially intellectual disabilities, not simply into the community of faith, but into its centre: 'Of course, people with intellectual disabilities shouldn't be expected to minister in the same way as people with physical disabilities,' Yong writes:

> But their contributions are no less profound once these are identified and received as the wisdom of God that reveals the saving, sanctifying, and redeeming work of the cross of Christ. How might the church begin to realize the power of the gospel in the lives of people with intellectual disabilities so that we consider not only ministry *to* such people but also ministry *with* them?[39]

And it is ministering with that makes all the difference. Yong continues:

> What would happen if the public discovered that church communities were creating inclusive educational and liturgical environments because they valued the presence of children and people with intellectual disabilities? How might the mission of the church be reinvigorated precisely

---

38 Yong, *The Bible, Disability, and the Church*, 114.
39 Ibid., 111.

through having people with disabilities and their families in its midst? In what ways would the church be seen as more rather than less relevant to the world if it were to become a more hospitable community especially for people with intellectual disabilities? . . . Wouldn't such 'weakness' manifest itself as the strength and power of the cross and as the wisdom of God?[40]

Here Yong gets to the heart of the issue I am trying to present when he writes: 'The resulting flowering of friendships, of course, is precisely what forms, transforms, and renews the people of God as present signs to the world of the salvation that is expected in the coming kingdom.'[41]

The point of ministering not simply *to* the severely mentally disabled, but *with* them is another way of stating a more general principle of theosis: that the way to deification is through incorporation into the church, participation in the means of grace, *and active engagement in* koinonia-*constituting relationships*, each of which, of course, is established and maintained in our union with Christ and his vicarious humanity. Once more I simply echo Yong's words:

> Hence the goal cannot be just to minister to such people (people with disabilities) as objects of care, concern, or charity – although such ministry is precisely what is needed in many cases; the goal must be the full inclusion of all and the reception of each contribution, resulting in the enrichment and edification of others.[42]

But such ministry will have to take on the radical cruciformity of the gospel of Jesus Christ.

Paul is an example of one afflicted in the flesh; whatever the nature of that affliction – and it is contested – it was a means to witness to the power of God in his life. 2 Cor 11:30 reads: 'If I must boast, I will boast of the things that show my weakness.' 2 Cor 12:7–10, for example, tells us in this regard: 'for power is made perfect in weakness'. One chapter later, in 2 Cor 13:4, we are told: 'for we are weak in him [Christ], but in dealing with you we will live with him by the power of God'. Here we see a theology of weakness put to work to explain, in part, the power of God. But the conditions which occasion such weakness are *temporary*, limited to this age, and not the age to come. What remain are the lessons learnt and the virtues embodied from such limitations. As the law was the means by which God discipled the people of God in the Old Testament, the Israelites, our finitude is the means by which the people of God in the present age, the church, are discipled, kept humble, taught dependency upon God, and are made fit for infinity. This applies to all humanity, of course, not simply to the intellectually disabled, but it is they above all people, I suggest, who are the most

---

40 Ibid., 112.
41 Ibid., 116.
42 Ibid., 79.

visible signs and agents of such. And it is these signs of the Kingdom which I am calling inaugurated parables of eschatological hope. And the disability literature is replete with examples of such parabolic signs.

Parabolic Signs

Hans Reinders reminds us of the words and work of Jean Vanier, founder of L'Arche:

> So he tells us about Luisito, a man with severe disabilities who was left alone when his mother died. Luisito used to live in the streets of Santo Domingo before he came to L'Arche ...Vanier explains. 'He was dirty and smelly; his body was twisted; he could not walk, nor talk. People found it difficult to look at him; he disturbed them. Yet today he is one of the founding members of L'Arche in Santo Domingo.' Vanier continues, 'That is the mystery; the secret of the Gospel of Jesus: Luisito renders Jesus present! It seems foolish to say that. Much that I say may well seem foolish because the gospel is truly a message of folly ....'.[43]

Vanier's point is that the people on whom our world has turned its back reveal the mystery of Jesus. In my words, they act as parables of eschatological hope and grace.

Henry Nouwen and his friend Adam provide a further example. God turns disability into parables of eschatological hope, of dependence, trust, humility, strength in weakness, and community. But lest I be misunderstood, in a fallen world our disability is miraculously turned into a means of God's blessing, but it is a means not an end. Nouwen writes:

> Could Adam pray? Did he know who God is and what the Name of Jesus means? Did he understand the mystery of God among us? For a long time I thought about these questions. For a long time I was curious about how much of what I knew, Adam could know, and how much of what I understood, Adam could understand. But now I see these were for me questions from 'below,' questions that reflected more about my anxiety and uncertainty than God's love. God's questions, the questions from 'above' were, 'Can you let Adam lead you in prayer? Can you believe that I am in deep communion with Adam and that his life is a prayer? Can you let Adam be a living prayer at your table? Can you see my face in the face of Adam?'
>
> And while I, a so-called 'normal' person, kept wondering how much Adam was like me, he had no ability or need to make any comparisons. He

---

43 Hans S. Reinders, 'Being with the Disabled: Jean Vanier's Theological Realism', in *Disability in the Christian Tradition: A Reader*, ed. Brian Brock and John Swinton (Grand Rapids, MI: Eerdmans, 2012), 468, citing Jean Vanier, *Befriending the Stranger* (Mahwah, NJ: Paulist Press, 2010), vii.

simply lived and by his life invited me to receive his unique gift, wrapped in weakness but given for my transformation. While I tended to worry about what I did and how much I could produce, Adam was announcing to me that 'being is more important than doing.' While I was preoccupied with the way I was talked about or written about, Adam was quietly telling me that 'God's love is more important than the praise of people.' While I was concerned about my individual accomplishments, Adam was reminding me that 'doing things together is more important than doing things alone.' Adam couldn't produce anything, had no fame to be proud of, couldn't brag of any award or trophy. But by his very life, he was the most radical witness to the truth of our lives that I have ever encountered.[44]

What I am calling 'inaugurated parables' others call sacramental presence. One such is Jennie Weiss Block, who speaks affectionately about Robert Perske's little book *Circle of Friends*, in which he narrates stories of friendships between people with disabilities and those without, showing how these relationships have enriched their lives. Citing Perskes, Block comments: 'To our surprise, these friendships became our living documents,' and continues: 'I would go so far as to call these stories "sacramental" documents for they narrate the spirituality of friendship that must characterize a theology of access with staying power.'[45]

Block also touches on something I happen to think is central to the whole discussion: her central conviction on eschatology is that human vulnerability is the source of communion in the Kingdom, and that in the present it is those with disabilities, amongst many others, who can teach us how to be vulnerable through the sharing of our joys, our tears, our pain, our limitations, and our hopes. While we might argue over whether or not vulnerability is the key virtue to be cultivated, and I don't think it is, Block's point is well taken. Such vulnerable communion serves a deeper purpose: to form the eschatological people of God for the coming Kingdom. Such formation includes moving away from self-absorption, beyond ourselves towards community, giving us the courage and the freedom to seek the other. Such friendship encourages openness, generosity, graciousness, and hospitality, and ultimately leads to ecstasy (*ekstasis*), the source of communion in the Kingdom.[46] Note how for Block people with disabilities, and all humanity living under the conditions of the fall, are drawn towards a deeper and fuller way of relating which reflects but a foretaste of Kingdom living. Disabilities will go, persons remain – but persons in the fullness of glory and in the abundance of communion.

---

44 Henry Nouwen, *Adam: God's Beloved* (Maryknoll, NY: Orbis Books, 1997), 55–6.
45 Jennie Weiss Block, *Copious Hosting: A Theology of Access for People with Disabilities* (London: Continuum, 2002), 162.
46 Weiss, in ibid., 163, speaks of vulnerability as the key virtue, not ecstasy, as I do here. But ecstasy is better, I suggest, due to its theotic implications.

A theotic vision of salvation along the lines I have drawn earlier, whereby the goal or *telos* of each human person is for participation in the triune life of God, through the Incarnate Word, and by means of the Holy Spirit, looks towards a dynamic eschatology whereby creation – human creatures included – continues to develop, grow, mature, and flourish, into eternity, from glory to glory. Hence disabilities of all kinds – physical, intellectual, and social – are redeemed and turned into signposts to a yet greater destination and way of being.

I now wish to turn to some brief eschatological allegations before concluding this chapter.

Theosis and the Eschaton: Eschatological Allegations

So far I have argued that human beings are created to be conformed to the image of Christ and by the Spirit are destined in grace to participate in the triune life of God. When worked into a full theology, this is known as a doctrine of theosis. I also argued that theosis takes place within the church and that the severely mentally disabled should rightly be considered saved, thus they should partake of the sacraments – baptism and Eucharist – and then be fellow ministers with the rest of the body of Christ. When and where this happens, ministry with the severely mentally disabled presents inaugurated parables of eschatological hope, or in simpler terms, provides opportunities to glimpse aspects of the Kingdom which would otherwise not be available to us this side of the *Parousia*. In this final section I want to simply draw some conclusions about our ongoing theosis in the new heavens and the new earth, as I argue the resurrection requires a dynamic eschatology in which we continue to be transformed into the likeness of the risen Christ.

According to the doctrine of theosis I am suggesting, and its attendant transcendental determination of human persons in the image of Christ, the resurrection will involve an embodied existence in which the human person found in Christ and animated by the Spirit will flourish. There will be growth, development, learning, work, rest, play, worship, entertainment, and relationships. Theosis is about becoming more fully human than we ever dreamed possible. Those with severe mental disabilities will be healed and will find themselves able to function like Christ, as will the rest of us. We will all be changed into Christ's likeness without being changed from who we are as distinct persons.

Yong, across various works, argues against what he calls 'ableist' or 'normate' interpretations of texts which would argue that in the eschaton all disabilities are removed precisely because 'wholeness is defined according to a normate view of what nondefective bodies are or look like'.[47] Yong then states: 'Of course, this ableist reading is consistent with the view of the eschatological body being in the image of Christ: unblemished, perfect, whole, and beautiful – at least

---

[47] Yong, *The Bible, Disability, and the Church*, 38.

as measured by conventional (normate) views of perfection, wholeness, and beauty.'[48] But Yong then goes on to draw the following conclusion:

> But this requires people with disabilities to internalize a self-understanding that rejects who they are as unacceptable to God or as less fit for participation in the Deity's eschatological blessing. If they are to fit into the 'acceptable' mold, their blemishes, defects, and disabilities will need to be removed. But what if some disabilities are identity-making in the sense that they are inextricable from who persons are in essence . . .? How might these disabilities be removed without eliminating the person entirely?[49]

It would seem that a central charge of Yong's against what he calls normate interpretations of the eschaton have to do with identity continuity, current oppression and exclusion, and a devaluing of human life in its diversity.[50] He suggests that:

> the normate perspective which expects the eschatological elimination of such disabilities essentially devalues the lives and experiences of such people in fact, even if not in rhetoric, and that the normate eschatology is generated not necessarily out of concern for alleviating the suffering of such lives but more so out of uncriticized biases and fears that project a certain existential experience into differently-abled lives in a normate world. In short, the normate prejudice creates a world that stigmatizes and oppresses people with disabilities, thus aggravating normate fears about the disability experience and alienating non-disabled people from people with disabilities.[51]

---

48 Ibid.
49 Ibid. This claim is reiterated in later chapters when Yong argues that 'some impairments are so identity-constitutive that their removal would involve the obliteration of the person as well', ibid., 121.
50 Yong's account of human identity has been challenged by Ryan T. Mullins, 'Some Difficulties for Amos Yong's Disability Theology of the Resurrection', *Ars Disputandi* 11 (2011): 24–32, to which Yong provided a reply: Amos Yong, 'Disability Theology of the Resurrection: Persisting Questions and Additional Considerations – a Response to Ryan Mullins', *Ars Disputandi* 12 (2012): 4–10.
51 Yong, *The Bible, Disability, and the Church*, 121. While arguing for continuity of personal identity, I am not arguing for the elimination of diversity in the eschaton, rather the opposite. Here I note a comment by Herman Bavinck: 'Tribes, peoples, and nations all make their own particular contribution to the enrichment of life in the new Jerusalem (Rev 5:9; 7:9; 21:24, 26). What we have sown here is harvested in eternity (Matt 25:24, 26; 1 Cor 15:42ff.; 2 Cor 9:6; Gal 6:7–9). The great diversity that exists among people in all sorts of ways is not destroyed in eternity but is cleansed from all that is sinful and made serviceable to fellowship with God and each other'; Herman Bavinck, *Reformed Dogmatics*, Volume 4: *Holy Spirit, Church, and New Creation*, ed. John Bolt, trans. John Vriend (originally published 1911; reprint Grand Rapids, MI: Baker Academic, 2008), 727.

Later, Yong manages to capture his point in a sentence: 'If we expect that the eschatological good news abolishes all disabilities, then the gospel for today does so as well.'[52] In practice, that looks like a preoccupation with miracle services, faith-healings, and the exorcising of demonic spirits which supposedly cause sickness and disability. But who is Yong's real argument with: so-called normate interpretations of the eschaton, or some forms of current Pentecostal practice? I would suggest Yong's aim is out, and he shoots the former when he should be firing at the latter.

Yong's argument seems to require a commitment to the priority of present identity rather than a priority given to eschatological fulfilment. In John 9:25 the man given sight by Jesus exclaims: 'I was blind, now I see.' The townsfolk question his identity – 'Is this the same man?' – but he keeps saying 'I am the man' (v. 9). There is no annulment of personal identity after the healing and cure, rather continuity of personal identity. A rather weak example might help. I am disabled – I have a relatively major colour defectiveness which, in the eschaton, I have no doubts, will not exist. I am also tone-deaf and can't keep a beat – things I also consider to be minor disabilities; things I also believe will be abolished in the eschaton. But I remain. Who I am in my personal identity remains, as I become more like the risen Christ. I also have other, more important, moral defects, which, in the eschaton, will no doubt be removed – at least my family and friends pray for it to be so!

Throughout Yong's eschatology I find numerous false assumptions and non sequiturs: for instance, the false move from defining atonement as salvation from non-discriminatory assumptions for the non-disabled, but no change for the disabled, as if people with disabilities need no conversion. In *The Bible, Disability and the Church* Yong writes:

> The case I have attempted to make so far is that there is nothing intrinsically wrong with the lives of people with disabilities, that it is not they who need to be cured, but we, the non-disabled, who need to be saved from our discriminatory attitudes and practices, and that people with disabilities should be accepted and honored just as they are.[53]

With what level of seriousness is this statement to be taken, however – with full force, that people with disabilities need no redemption or sanctification (or glorification!), or is it a case of overstatement to make a point, in which case, where is the overstatement and where is the point? Surely we are all in need of redemption, sanctification, and glorification, each from our own sins and our own fallen contexts, to be sure, yet saved nonetheless. And surely the resurrection speaks to the eradication of all vestiges of a fallen world and how

---

52 Yong, *The Bible, Disability, and the Church*, 121.
53 Ibid., 118.

that is translated into the human condition, be it faulty chromosomes, chemical imbalances, genetic abnormalities, moral aberrations, or the like.

Yong then critiques what he calls 'normate biases' in interpretations of the eschaton with this argument: 'If there are no disabilities in the life to come, then that implicitly suggests that our present task is to rid the world of such unfortunate and unwanted realities.'[54] Later he advances this claim and links an eschatological view of cured and healed bodies to the rise in abortion rates:

> After all, if disabilities are the cause of the suffering and evil that the normate bias says they are, and if they are not to be found in our eschatological visions of the perfect world, then shouldn't we do all we can in this life to eliminate the world of disabilities, even if it might mean preventing the births of children with disabilities as well?[55]

But such an over-realized eschatology needs to be challenged head-on. Nothing within the biblical narrative demands such assumptions. Rather, we are to work towards the elimination of human suffering, injustice, oppression, and exclusion – not the elimination of human persons. In the time-between-the-times which we find ourselves in, the 'last times' or 'end times' as Paul calls it, we exist in the state of the already-not yet, or the existence of Romans 7 *and* 8, the state of being saved and re-created, yet still carrying around with us these bodies of death.

That people are not healed immediately upon salvation simply means they will be in the eschaton. In the time in-between, such unhealings become a means of God's teaching, presence, and blessing. As Yong rightly argues:

> Yet from a disability perspective, it is crucial to underscore that these healings are representative of a more fundamental reality: the saving work of God in Christ. In this framework, the Gospel accounts are less about the curing of bodies than they are about the saving power and authority of Christ and his name. The saving work of God can occur even if the curing of bodies doesn't happen, and we would do well to assure people with disabilities that cures are not the norm by which to measure the reality of divine salvation.[56]

I agree with Yong if these comments are related to the present. However, Yong extends such conclusions into the eschaton; I clearly do not.

In the fifth and final chapter of Yong's short work *The Bible, Disability, and the Church* he finally comes to the most central and defining aspect of his study as far as I am concerned when he suggests that 'Jesus Christ's body should be

---

54 Ibid.
55 Ibid., 120.
56 Ibid., 66.

the theological norm for our understanding of the image of God, and that this has normative implications for a more inclusive vision of the people of God not only in the present (ecclesially) but also in the afterlife (eschatologically)'.[57] That Christ's resurrected body bore the marks of the resurrection (deformities) is uncontested; why it did so and for what duration *are* contested, however. According to Yong's thesis, Jesus is the firstfruits (1 Cor 15:20–23) of the resurrection, thus his marked body becomes paradigmatic for our understanding of eschatological life.[58]

But what Yong gives on the one hand throughout the book is seemingly taken back with the other hand when he slips in the following comment: 'My argument is that there will be no more tears in the eschaton not because our impairments will be eliminated but because they will be redeemed. By this I am not insisting that people with disabilities will exist literally as such eschatologically.'[59] Yong explains that he means disabled bodies will be *transvalued* and *transfigured* in the resurrection.[60] But what does this mean, other than that disabilities are merely symbolic in the eschaton, not literal, the point I am making following a more traditional interpretation? Yong realizes the difficulty of his reading when he states: 'The mystery, of course, pertains to how the marks of our impairments can be present but perhaps not "felt", at least not in the same manner as they are now.'[61] Yong's only solution is that the shame 'felt' in the present by people with disabilities is removed. But this misses the point – it is not simply shame and ostracism that requires removal, but the pain (if such exists), and the limitations such disabilities inflict upon people. Amputees, for instance, can look forward to not only full acceptance in a community of love, but fully functioning limbs. More pointedly, the severely mentally disabled can look forward to praising God with their mind, soul, body, and strength, when they shall be able to 'rest', that state of peace with God in the absence of the enemy or anything which might hinder human flourishing in the presence of Christ.

Yong becomes an ally for my own project of viewing people with disabilities as signposts of eschatological hope and grace when he speaks of the 'marks of impairment' as 'signs that herald the coming reign of God',[62] and later, and with

---

57   Ibid., 125.
58   Ibid., 130.
59   Ibid., 135.
60   The term 'transvaluation' has been used in disability studies by John Swinton to refer to 'the way in which people's lives and worldviews have been radically transformed through their encounters with people who have profound developmental disabilities. [Their] lives are changed, their priorities are reshaped and their vision of God and humanness are altered at their very core.' Following Frances Young, he names this 'a process of transvaluation within which personal encounter with people with profound developmental disabilities initiates a movement towards a radically new system of valuing'; John Swinton, 'The Body of Christ Has Down Syndrome', *The Journal of Pastoral Theology* 13 (2003): 67.
61   Yong, *The Bible, Disability, and the Church*, 135.
62   Ibid., 135–36.

more detail, he comments: 'Seen in this way, people with disabilities become sacraments – conduits for the presence and activity of Christ – to an unsuspecting world, confronting the powerful, the rich, and the wise with the weakness that God has chosen to embrace and identify with.'[63] The theme of sacramental presence is a good one, one I too wish to embrace; however, Yong seems to make sacramental presence exclusive to people with disabilities when he writes '"the least of these" are the standard and sacramental media of God's grace, apart from whom there may be no opportunity to encounter and experience the redemption of Christ',[64] or again in his conclusion: 'I have attempted to show . . . that the people of God are to be marked by their weaknesses in such a way that people with disabilities become the most tangible and honoured expression of God's mode of operation in a world wherein they are otherwise despised.'[65] This, I argue, is far too strong and far too exclusive. It repeats all the problems made earlier by liberation theology and repeated by all subsets of that enterprise: black theology, feminist theology, LGBTQ theology, and now disability theology: it allocates God's preferential option to a small sub-set of the human race on the basis of an anthropological criteria: colour, race, sexuality, physical or mental ability.[66]

Theotic views of the eschaton all trade, in one way or another, on the view put forward so powerfully by Gregory of Nyssa, that of *epectasis* – or everlasting process (even if they don't follow all his universalist tendencies). For instance, 'Having been created in the image of the infinite God,' says Nellas, man 'is called by his own nature . . . to transcend the limited boundaries of creation and to become infinite.'[67] By 'infinite' Nellas and the Orthodox do not mean to equate humanity with God, but rather to say that because God is infinite and we participate in him through Christ, then our progress in him is inexhaustible. 'God is the source of power and light who draws us always higher up into knowledge and perfection of life,' says Staniloae. 'He is not a ceiling that puts an end to our ascent.'[68]

Now Yong himself is aware of Gregory of Nyssa's theology of *epectasis* and discusses it briefly in his work on Down syndrome and other articles.[69] He notes that for Gregory of Nyssa, 'what for human beings is closure in terms of satisfaction and perfection is for God a further invitation to creatures through

---

63 Ibid., 139. The theme of sacramental presence is repeated in ibid., pp. 140 and 141.
64 Ibid., 141.
65 Ibid., 145.
66 The link with liberation theology is made explicit in Yong, *The Bible, Disability, and the Church*, 141. Of course, Yong is not the first to make this link; see the influential work of Nancy Eisland, *The Disabled God: Toward a Liberatory Theology of Disability* (Nashville, TN: Abingdon Press, 1994).
67 Panayiotis Nellas, *Deification in Christ*, trans. Norman Russell (Crestwood, NY: St. Vladimir's Seminary Press, 1987), 28.
68 Dumitru Staniloae, *The Experience of God, Volume 1: Revelation and Knowledge of the Triune God*, trans. Ioana Ionita and Robert Barringer (Brookline, MA.: Holy Cross Orthodox Press, 1994), 107.
69 Yong, *Theology and Down Syndrome*, 274–8.

deifying grace to "travel" the continually receding horizons of the eschatological *epectasis* into the divine life'. Yong then rightly links such a dynamic view of the eschaton to a robust pneumatology to further explain and apply the concept. He writes: 'I suggest, Gregory's dynamic eschatology illumines how disability will be transformed even if its particular scars and marks will be redeemed, not eliminated.'[70]

On this basis, Yong offers some justified (perhaps we might even say sanctified) speculation when he suggests that those who die in infancy enter heaven as infants, but grow and develop and mature in an unending transformation along with other members of the eschatological community in and towards the triune God.[71] Further, people with disabilities retain their phenotypical features in their resurrection bodies such that they will be recognizable. Yong then favourably cites Christian philosopher Jerry Walls when he suggests: 'Those who negotiated this life with the additional struggles of mental or physical deformities will retain the memories of doing so as well as the positive character traits they formed as a result.'[72] But this final citation from Walls seems to run contrary to what Yong's actual thesis is, and thus supports my own project. Yong's argument is not simply that memories and character traits remain, but that the physical effects of disabilities remain as well. But again Yong is not as clear as he means to be when, in reference to those texts which speak of the blind, the lame, and others with physical impairment being present at the eschatological banquet (Luke 14:12–23), he concludes:

> This is not to imply, however, that people with disabilities will stay merely blind, lame, and crippled in the eschatological long run. Eschatological salvation means not only that there will be no more oppression, marginalization, or discrimination because of physical or mental impairments but also that there will be unexpected transformations – both suddenly and eternally – now inconceivable to us.[73]

Now to a piece of sanctified speculation of my own. The Transfiguration tells us, amongst other things, that Christ can change his physical constitution to some degree. Theophanies of the Old Testament teach us the same thing. The same argument is one I want to take up with the post-resurrection but pre-ascension body of Jesus. It is at least possible that this was what I am calling an intermediate body for an intermediate state. Thus the marked hands and feet are there, features of Christ's body, yet they may not be permanent. They are there for a purpose – for identification, authentication, historical witness – but

---

70 Ibid., 281.
71 Ibid., 282.
72 Ibid., 283–4, citing Jerry Walls, *Heaven: The Logic of Eternal Joy* (Oxford: Oxford University Press, 2002), 112.
73 Yong, *Theology and Down Syndrome*, 284–5.

they may just pass away in time. The same may be true of features of our present physical and cognitive identity.

Orthodox writers since the seventh century have associated the Transfiguration with theosis, seeing the spiritual life as the climbing of a mountain through prayer and good works (faith) in order to experience at the summit a transformative vision of God. Here in the Transfiguration we have a proleptic vision of the resurrected and ascended Jesus Christ – a vision without blemish, deformity, or wounds. Instead Jesus' face shines like the sun and the apostles are filled with awe (Matt 17:1–8); he is 'transfigured/transformed' (*metamorphothe*, Mark 9:2), 'altered', and he appeared in 'glory' (Luke 9:29, 31). But before glory comes suffering and the cross – both for Christ and for those who would follow him. I greatly value the vision of our future life offered by Amos Yong, especially as it pertains to those with disabilities, and I see the present chapter as an appreciative engagement with his work rather than a critique.

18 Hope in the 'Mountain Manifesto'

The Beatitudes' Alternative to the Social Model's Hope

Immanuel Koks

The development of the social model of disability is often set against the medical model. Nevertheless, these two ways of understanding disability hold two beliefs in common: life with a disability is difficult, and therefore life for people with disabilities could be better. Thus hope is implied within both models of disability. Over recent decades Jürgen Moltmann and other theologians have constructed theologies of hope. They recognize that the fundamental movement of Scripture is God's saving work, in Christ, to take us from the pain and difficulties of our broken lives to the restoration and renewal of the promised new creation. Matthew's beatitudes outline this restoring work. In this chapter, therefore, I want to ask how Moltmann's understanding of hope sheds new light on Jesus' ministry-defining statement. This new perspective clarifies our hope for those with disabilities, and therefore invites us to reconsider the way we conceptualize disability.

I appreciate the theology of Moltmann, one of the key architects of a theology of hope, because he does not write from a vantage point that is disconnected from the realities of life. Rather, who he is and what he has experienced dramatically shape his theology. My own search for hope also arises out of my experiences. I need hope as one with a physical disability (moderate athetoid cerebral palsy) who knows the unrelenting stress of dealing with infuriating bureaucracy and social barriers, as highlighted by the social model of disability. But I also need hope as I deal with the frustrations which invariably arise from my impaired embodiment, as identified by the medical model.

These two understandings of disability will shape this chapter, in which I examine the way hope can transform the lives of those with disabilities in the present. Using the 'Mountain Manifesto' – Matthew's version of the beatitudes – I will argue that our lives can be transformed by the promise that God is working in the here and now. This work, I argue, is not just transformation of the world around us, but perhaps most importantly, the transformation of the way we respond to the world. Before proceeding, however, some context is required.

Disability Power Play

The disabling effect of societal oppression has been highlighted by the disability rights movement, and its academic variant – disability studies.[1] For those with diverse embodiment, barriers are profoundly limiting. These oppressive barriers must be dismantled for those with disabilities to experience a better life. Carolyn Thompson's work borrows Young's understanding of oppression to convincingly demonstrate the five ways in which society oppresses those who experience disability. The first is cultural imperialism, whereby those with disabilities are rendered invisible by dominant non-disabled society. The second is marginalization, whereby those with disabilities are excluded from the centre of society and forced to depend on welfare systems. The third is powerlessness, whereby those with disabilities are unable to change the circumstances in major domains of life such as employment and education. The fourth is exploitation, whereby those with disabilities are taken advantage of in a multitude of different ways. And finally, there is every conceivable form of violence.[2]

In its least nuanced form, this view of disability as societal oppression – called the social model – argues that the diversity of embodiment which people experience is not disabling in and of itself. Rather, it is society and the barriers it creates which disable individuals with diverse bodies. Barriers exist in all aspects of society: from architecture to the language we use, from education to employment, from philosophy to theology.

Exposing the reality of oppression is vital. By doing so, we are naming the existence of a power imbalance. We exclaim that there is a powerful, dominating majority who overtly and covertly suppress and control the disempowered, subjugated minority. This naming empowers the minority by identifying what is wrong, and exposing a path beyond it.

For emancipation to occur, the minority must intrinsically have the wherewithal to move beyond its oppression. However, naming the oppression associated with disabilities has two liabilities. First, we have seen those who have this ability make great strides towards overcoming oppression in the civil rights movements of the last century. However, Hans Reinders recognizes that the ability to name and push against societal oppression in the disability sector belongs to a 'disability bourgeoisie' who possess the intellectual and social skills

---

1 Tom Shakespeare, 'What is a Disabled Person?', in *Disability, Divers-ability and Legal Change*, ed. Melinda Jones and Lee Ann Basser Marks (The Hague: Martinus Nijhoff, 1999), 29–30. Shakespeare distinguishes this from the minority model, which construes disability in terms of a social minority. For my purposes this distinction is not essential, as one often informs the other. What is important is that language of minority often draws in the concept of oppression; ibid., 31.
2 Carolyn Thompson, 'Ableism: The Face of Oppression as Experienced by People with Disabilities', in *Injustice and the Care of Souls: Taking Oppression Seriously in Pastoral Care*, ed. Sheryl A. Kujawa-Holbrook and Karen Brown Montagno (Minneapolis, MN: Fortress Press, 2009), 214–19.

to argue our case.³ Those with disabilities who cannot engage in this dialogue are inadvertently marginalized again.

The second liability is a hidden shift in the power game which impacts all of those who – like myself – identify themselves as disabled by social barriers. Intrinsic in this self-identification as a person with a disability is the acknowledgement that, for some reason, we are either unable, or at least it is much harder for us, to do what we would like to do. By identifying oppression as the cause, we highlight the fact that we need others around us to change themselves or our environment in order to mitigate that disability. Whereas the medical model overtly takes power from us and hands it to medical 'professionals', the social model hands power to the oppressing other, because it says the other must change in order for our disability to be removed.

Consider architectural barriers. When I use my wheelchair, I need ramps or lifts to be able to access any space that does not have level access. I cannot build these structures, but must rely on others to do so. When I identify the need for structural modification, I hand the power to mitigate my disability to those who can fund and build the ramp.

The State of Hope for Those with Disabilities Today

Understanding the locus of hope, and the locus of power to achieve this hope, is crucial. Hope in the social model is achieved by changing society, not by changing individuals or their impairments. The latter is interpreted as a failure to accept them as they are. It is seen as an imposition of oppressive power to change them to comply with a socially constructed norm, much like powerful medical professionals – under the medical model – used their power (as experts) to change what they perceived as impairments. Under the social model, the way to work towards hope is to become involved in disability rights movements which lobby powerbrokers to make the necessary changes. Yet, as I have demonstrated, by doing this we cede power, while in other ways we are empowered.

As the social model has become the conceptually dominant way of understanding disability, it has had a dramatic effect on some streams of disability theology. Historically, disability has been interpreted by ableist theology (theology done for and by those who do not identify themselves as disabled) as something intrinsic to the individuals who need God's healing touch. In the last decade or two some theologians have begun to engage disability studies, identifying ways traditionally held beliefs can be construed as disabling. Therefore, they argue that ableist theology legitimizes marginalization of those with disabilities by

---

3 My term; see Hans S. Reinders, *Receiving the Gift of Friendship: Profound Disability, Theological Anthropology, and Ethics* (Grand Rapids, MI: Eerdmans, 2008), 80.

upholding the assumed normalcy.[4] This is especially prevalent in the claim that God must change – that is, heal – those with disabilities. The covert message, however, is that those who do not identify as disabled do not need healing, and consequently these disability theologians seek to de-construct and reconstruct theology in a 'disability-friendly' manner.[5] This reconstructed theology both highlights the marginalization of older constructs and minimizes the notion that God will change those with disabilities. Such a hope, it is argued, confirms the desired trajectory towards normalcy which dominates ableist theology. Nevertheless, for all the valuable ways it has helped us identify the barriers facing those with disabilities within our churches, and in our theology, I will argue that the social model carries within it a problem which may inhibit the articulation of Christian hope.

The Way Hope Works

Before investigating hope for those with disabilities, I will turn to Moltmann's understanding of hope. To begin his discussion of the way hope works, he highlights a key difference between ancient Israel and its surrounding neighbours. When Israel's neighbours encountered their gods, Moltmann reports that they did one of two things: either they settled, setting up their settlements and farms near that particular spot, or they became nomads so that they could periodically return to those places of visitation.[6] But Israel was different. After its people had their defining encounter with God at Mount Sinai, they were nomads for the next forty years before making the unique transition of settling *in another place* – the Land of Israel.[7]

Moltmann argues the difference was that Israel's encounter with Yahweh was filled with promise.[8] 'Go,' God said, 'Go to the land I will give you.' The transportable tabernacle was a sign of God's promise, 'I will go with you.' The ongoing manna was a continual sign of God's promise: 'As you go, I will provide for you.' To finish it off, God's promise to Israel was: 'When you arrive at the Promised Land, I will help you conquer it.' What made Israel so different, then, was that the promises of Yahweh gave the hope of a different future.

Moltmann uses the concept of a 'horizon' developed by twentieth-century German Philosopher Hans Gadamer to explain the way promises work to create hope. According to Gadamer, a horizon is 'a thing towards which we are

---

4 Two examples of such theological constructions are Sharon V. Betcher, *Spirit and the Politics of Disablement* (Minneapolis, MN: Fortress Press, 2007), 5, and Thomas E. Reynolds, *Vulnerable Communion: A Theology of Disability and Hospitality* (Grand Rapids, MI: Brazos Press, 2008), 25–34.
5 A justification for such an approach can be found in Amos Yong, *The Bible, Disability, and the Church: A New Vision of the People of God* (Grand Rapids, MI: Eerdmans, 2011), 11–13.
6 Jürgen Moltmann, *Theology of Hope: On the Ground and the Implications of a Christian Eschatology*, trans. James W. Leitch (Minneapolis, MN: Fortress Press, 1993), 96–7 (hereafter *TH*).
7 Ibid., 96.
8 Ibid., 99.

moving, and which moves along with us'.⁹ We can never reach a horizon by moving towards it because it always moves ahead of us as we move. Therefore, when a promise is given, God sets up a 'horizon' ahead of Israel. He tells them about a future that is different to the present, and invites them to move towards that future.¹⁰ Thus what is on the horizon engenders our hope. The fact that the future horizon of promise is different to the present means that it stands at odds with our experience now. *Promise* sets up a contradiction, or critique, of the present by proclaiming that the future will be better than the present.¹¹ As we walk towards the horizon of promise, therefore, we are invited to walk away from the things which the promise critiques.

Because our hope is looking towards the fulfilment of God's promises for us, hope itself is critical. While hope prophetically paints a picture in our imagination of a future better than today, it also points out the problems of today and invites us to move beyond them.¹² I am drawing on the ideas of Walter Brueggemann, who – like Moltmann – argues that the prophet's role was to create an alternative consciousness in the minds of the hearers. This new way of thinking would critique the experience of the present while creating in the minds of the hearers a picture of a different reality.¹³

Unpacking the 'Mountain Manifesto'

Turning to Jesus' first proclamation, as recorded by Matthew, we now ask how Jesus excited prophetic imagination in the hearts of his listeners. By way of comparison, Luke's record of Jesus' first public address will be consulted first. After recounting Jesus' early life, baptism, and temptation in the wilderness, Luke has Jesus stand up in a synagogue in Nazareth to read Isa 61:1–2:

> The Spirit of the Lord is on me,
> because he has anointed me
> to proclaim good news to the poor.
> He has sent me to proclaim freedom for the prisoners
> and recovery of sight for the blind,
> to set the oppressed free,
> to proclaim the year of the Lord's favour.¹⁴

---

9   Hans-Georg Gadamer, *Wahrheit und Methode; Grundzüge einer Philosophischen Hermeneutik* (Tübingen: Mohr, 1960), 231, 286, quoted and translated in Moltmann, *TH*, 106.
10 Moltmann, *TH*, 103–4.
11 Ibid., 103.
12 Here my use of 'imagination' refers to the process of creating a *mental image* of something that cannot be experienced through the senses, just as an architect may 'imagine' the house they are designing a long time before it is built. 'Imagination' in the way I am using it does not imply 'fanciful'.
13 Walter Brueggemann, *The Prophetic Imagination*, 2nd edn (Minneapolis, MN: Fortress Press, 2001), 5–6.
14 As recorded in Luke 4:18–19.

Bock argues that this passage summarizes Jesus' mission.[15] Therefore, this passage is often called the 'Nazareth Manifesto'. It can be argued that the beatitudes function in a similar way.

Looking at the book of Matthew as a whole, we have a repeated pattern of actions of Jesus, followed by extended sections of teaching; action then teaching: what Jesus did, then what he taught, throughout the book. While teaching and action are crucial in all four gospels, the rhythmic nature of the way Matthew returns to recording in detail Jesus' teaching demonstrates a special importance of what Jesus said for Matthew. Thus what Jesus says first, on the mountainside, sets the stage for the whole book.

Stassen recognized that Isa 61:1–2 also forms a backdrop to the beatitudes.[16] I suggest that, like Luke, Matthew wanted to set 'high on a hill' the fact that Jesus came to bring God's liberation and good news to the downtrodden. While, like Luke, Matthew does this by drawing the reader's minds to Isa 61's gospel proclamation, he does it in a very Matthean way. He couches it in the context of Jesus' teaching. From this point on, the themes of liberation and release permeate Matthew's record of Jesus' teaching, inasmuch as they infuse Luke's accounts of Jesus' actions. Thus, in the same way that Luke's record of Jesus' recital of Isaiah's gospel proclamation is called the 'Nazareth Manifesto' I am referring to the beatitudes as Matthew's 'Mountain Manifesto'.

Re-reading the 'Mountain Manifesto'

A number of underlying frameworks shape the way commentators read the Sermon on the Mount, particularly the beatitudes. On the one hand there are those who, like Carson, tend to interpret the text as moral ideals which we are called to live up to.[17] They give less importance to the idea that these words promise that God will overcome the tangible experience of oppression which the first listeners were facing. Thus, for them, those who receive blessing demonstrate certain *moral* characteristics. On the other hand, commentators like Gundry and Stassen want to focus more on the reality of tangible oppression and God's desire to overcome that oppression.[18] Rather than presupposing that one approach is better than the other, both are surprisingly at play in this message of hope, but only when we give credence to the oppression faced by the first audiences.

---

15 Darrell L. Bock, *Luke, Volume 1: 1:1–9:50* (Grand Rapids, MI: Baker Academic 1994), 404.
16 Glen H. Stassen, *Living the Sermon on the Mount: A Practical Hope for Grace and Deliverance*, 1st edn (San Francisco, CA: Jossey-Bass, 2006), 41. In ibid., p. 42, there is an informative table listing the ways Stassen believes Matthew drew on Isa 61.
17 Donald A. Carson, *Jesus' Sermon on the Mount and His Confrontation with the World: An Exposition of Matthew 5–10* (Grand Rapids, MI: Baker, 2004), 16–30.
18 Robert H. Gundry, *Matthew: A Commentary on His Handbook for a Mixed Church under Persecution*, 2nd edn (Grand Rapids, MI: Eerdmans, 1994), 67–73.

Patte argues for a diversity of 'legitimate' interpretations.[19] While bounds may need to be set in order to define what is 'legitimate', there is merit in this proposal insofar as Scripture speaks to those with many different experiences.[20] This fact is self-evident in a Christian faith which has spread into, but (at its best) has not destroyed, a myriad of cultures, and is believed by those with a huge diversity of experiences. Against this background we shall investigate what the 'Mountain Manifesto' says to those of us with disabilities in a Western culture. And, given the fact that hope and promise drip from every line of the manifesto, Moltmann's framework of hope will be brought to bear on the topic as well.

Audiences

While the question of original audience can seem like a technical exegetical issue, it is crucial for our context as it becomes the backdrop from which we make connections with our audience and with disabilities today. There are two audiences to be considered: the audience that first heard Jesus speak, and the one that received Matthew's gospel.

The few verses prior to the beatitudes give us a clue to the location and audience of the original proclamation:

> Jesus went throughout Galilee, teaching in their synagogues, proclaiming the good news of the kingdom, and healing every disease and sickness among the people. News about him spread all over Syria, and people brought to him all who were ill with various diseases, those suffering severe pain, the demon-possessed, those having seizures, and the paralysed; and he healed them. Large crowds from Galilee, the Decapolis, Jerusalem, Judea and the region across the Jordan followed him. Now when Jesus saw the crowds, he went up on a mountainside and sat down. His disciples came to him, and he began to teach them . . . . (Matt 4:23–5:2)

Matthew situates the sermon in Galilee – away from the centres of power in Rome and Jerusalem. His audience comes from all over the surrounding regions which were controlled by the oppressive Roman Empire. While some of those in the audience do come from Jerusalem, and therefore may be part of the privileged religious aristocracy, it is likely that many feel the weight of this oppression in very tangible ways. This is borne out by the fact that the beatitudes speak about those who are poor in spirit, those who mourn, those who hunger for justice, and those who are persecuted. This is not a message intended

---

19 Daniel Patte, *The Challenge of Discipleship: A Critical Study of the Sermon on the Mount as Scripture* (Harrisburg, PA: Trinity Press International, 1999), 16–17.
20 It is beyond the scope of this chapter to argue these bounds.

first and foremost for those sitting comfortably in a life of ease. On the contrary, the first audience lived life with the reality that things are not as they should be.

People who had experienced, or were experiencing, both disability and Jesus' healing were also among the crowd. While the topic of healing is beyond the scope of this chapter, we must recognize that the context Matthew creates in which Jesus gives his manifesto is the outworking of healing hope, and a recognition that some of the audience needed it. Proponents of the social model, as I have indicated, will want to minimize this because allowing that some needed healing would be to overly critique the individual. But because our investigation is looking at where hope's critique lies, for the moment we must let it be as it is.

The other way of looking at the question of the audience is to consider the audience that received the whole book of Matthew. Blomberg argues that the book of Matthew was written to a predominantly Jewish church that had recently split from the synagogue where it had met until this time.[21] As such, its members were seen as outsiders who had become 'apostate' and were thus sharply criticized by their Jewish kin.[22] The weight of oppression also came to bear on this audience from two angles: they were Jews in a Roman society *and* they were ostracized by their Jewish brethren.

Both audiences share the experience of oppression with our current audience. Even though the way these minority groups are marginalized is radically different, we all know the reality of living on the margins of a society which oppresses them by erecting a myriad of subtle and not so subtle barriers for them. Realizing this is important for readers with disabilities today.

Before leaving the question of audience, there is one more vital point to recall for any contemporary audience, including those with disabilities. Matthew is retelling the words Jesus spoke before the cross, resurrection, ascension, and Pentecost to an audience that lived after these events. It is anachronistic (out of chronological order) to read the sermon as if the first audience on the mountainside knew of the Spirit's empowering presence. Nevertheless, it is equally anachronistic to read the sermon as if the original readers of Matthew's gospel did not know of the empowering presence of the Spirit in their lives – as do we! This means that when we hear the call to live differently on Jesus' lips, we neither hear it as an otherworldly call that cannot be practically lived out now nor as a call to live an impossible life by our own strength. It is an earthy life, immensely connected to the realities we face now, which we can seek to live out now only because we have the empowering of the Spirit who was sent by the Father and the Son.[23]

---

21 This does not exclude the possibility that Gentiles were part of the church community, but it is unlikely that they were the majority; Craig Blomberg, *Matthew*, vol. 22 (Nashville, TN: Broadman & Holman, 1992), 35.
22 Ibid.
23 Michael J. Wilkins, *Matthew: From Biblical Text to Contemporary Life, the NIV Application Commentary* (Grand Rapids, MI: Zondervan, 2004), 223.

Patterns in the 'Mountain Manifesto'

Using Moltmann's framework of hope, my objective is not to give a detailed exegesis, but to probe the *patterns of hope* within the manifesto. In this section I want to probe the way Matthew frames the hope Jesus proclaimed. First, I suggest my own paraphrase of the beatitudes:[24]

> Blessings now and blessings to come for the poor in spirit, for theirs is the Kingdom of Heaven.
>
> Blessings now and blessings to come for those who mourn, for they shall be comforted.
>
> Blessings now and blessings to come for those who face life's problems with gentle strength, for they will inherit the earth.
>
> Blessings now and blessings to come for those who crave for when God brings his righteousness, for they will be satisfied.
>
> Blessings now and blessings to come for the compassionate, for God will show them compassion.
>
> Blessings now and blessings to come for the authentic and sincere, for they shall see God.
>
> Blessings now and blessings to come for those who make peace with their enemies, for they shall receive the dignity of being 'Sons of God'.
>
> Blessings now and blessings to come for those who are persecuted because they live righteously (according to what I've just said), for theirs is the Kingdom of Heaven.

I translate the first Greek word (*makarios*) in each beatitude with the phrase 'Blessings now and blessings to come'. *Makarios* is often translated with one word, for example 'blessed'. Hauck notes the paradoxical nature of the beatitudes.[25] A paradox is where we hold two seemingly opposing truths together, insisting that one *does not contradict* the other. Therefore, I am unconvinced by Green's translation of *makarios* as 'happy'.[26] Some are not 'happy', but mourn because life is not as it should be. Nor are those who crave God's righteousness 'happy' in a world of injustice and pain. Blessings, however, need not contradict any of the experiences of those named in the beatitudes. God can still richly bless even in the midst of deep sorrow and struggle.[27]

---

24 I recognize that this paraphrase, while attempting to be faithful to the text, is significantly different to a word-for-word, literal translation. However, I believe it does convey the meaning.
25 Friedrich Hauck, 'Μακάριος', in *Theological Dictionary of the New Testament*, vol. 4, ed. Gerhard Kittel, Geoffrey W. Bromiley, and Gerhard Friedrich (Grand Rapids, MI: Eerdmans, 1964), 367–70.
26 Michael Green, *The Message of Matthew: The Kingdom of Heaven*, rev. edn (Leicester: InterVarsity Press, 2000), 89.
27 This point is illustrated in Carolyn Kelshaw and Rod Thompson, *Shocked by Blessing: Stories of the Awful Grace of God* (Sydney: Christian Parent Controlled Schools, 2007), 6.

Another issue is the timing of blessings. The grammar in the first clauses of each beatitude is interesting. A word-for-word translation of the first clause of the second beatitude, for example, would be 'blessed those who mourn'. Notice there is a 'missing verb'. In English a clause must contain a verb from which we gain a sense of timing, so translators insert the verb 'are', though the equivalent verb (*este*) is not provided in the Greek. The absence of such a verb in Greek leaves some ambiguity as to the timing of the blessing. Blomberg argues that the blessings in the first and last beatitude are for the present experience of God's reign, while the remaining blessings are for 'future consolation'.[28] While grammatically correct, I think this dichotomy should not be overstated. While the Kingdom of Heaven is a promise for the present, the fullness of it is still in the future. Conversely, God will ultimately wipe away all tears, but nevertheless he brings comfort to those who mourn now. Because of this 'now-but-not yet' theology which runs the length of the manifesto, I have chosen to make explicit the grammatical ambiguity created by the 'missing verb'. Therefore, I translate μακαριος as 'Blessings now and blessings to come'.

Horizon of hope

According to Moltmann's framework of promise, Jesus explicitly identifies what is on the horizon of hope. The hope of the 'Kingdom of Heaven' bookends – that is, defines and surrounds – all the other promises.[29] This eschatological blessing is one which is to come at the end. Yet Jesus pulls it into the present by proclaiming to the poor in Spirit and the persecuted that 'theirs *is* the Kingdom of Heaven'. This is not an otherworldly hope, but an opportunity to live within the reign of God in the here and now.[30] Jesus is saying that there is hope because God's people can dwell within the sovereign reign of God now, even as they look forward to its full expression in the future. For a people who use gentle strength to counter the constant barrage of problems associated with living in 'theological exile' – in their own land – the horizon of promise is for the whole earth.[31] In a world of hurt and suffering, Jesus puts God's compassionate response on the horizon.[32]

---

28 Blomberg, *Matthew*, vol. 2, 97.
29 Kingdom of Heaven is Matthew's cypher for the Kingdom of God, because he tends to avoid using 'God'. See Donald A. Hagner, *Matthew 1–13*, Word Biblical Commentary (Dallas, TX: Nelson/Word, 1993), 92. Gundry notes the way the repetition of the promise of the Kingdom of Heaven in the first and last beatitudes forms an 'inclusio'; Gundry, *Matthew*, 73.
30 Hagner, *Matthew 1–13*, 47–8.
31 N.T. Wright, *The Challenge of Jesus: Rediscovering Who Jesus Was and Is* (Downers Grove, IL: InterVarsity Press, 1999), 36.
32 Often 'mercy' and 'merciful' are used in the fifth beatitude. I have opted for 'compassion', because mercy is often understood as a synonym of grace, but the Greek words *eleēmōn* and *eleeō* ('merciful' and 'mercy') relate more to compassion. They refer to the deliverance from all manner of difficult situations, not only setting people free from the consequences of poor ethics. See Stassen, *Living the Sermon on the Mount: A Practical Hope for Grace and Deliverance*, 54. Carson describes the concept as

Double-edged critique

As Moltmann's model predicts, there is also critique. The first hearers would have heard a resounding critique of Roman oppression. Mathew's first blessing is not, as Carson suggests, a blessing to those with a pious poverty of spirit such as repentance.[33] Matthew cuts to the heart of socio-economic inequality. He recognizes the broad-ranging, nagging sense of emotional insufficiency that is endemic in being oppressed. Along with withdrawing the necessities of life, oppression strips one's inner sense of living well, leaving one in a semi-depressed trudge through life's challenges.

We crave – intently hunger and thirst – when we cannot have what we desire. The fact that Christ pronounced blessing on those who crave God's righteousness highlights its absence in their society.[34] Authenticity and sincerity are a resounding critique of an oppressive culture which lays a thin veneer of purity over the top of lies and deceit. You only need to read Matthew's woes in Matt 23 to realize just how effective double-mindedness is for oppressing the masses. The presence of enemies is only too clear in Christ's call to make peace with them.[35]

In some ways, if the critique contained in the promises of the manifesto were aimed solely at the oppressor, then the beatitudes would have simply confirmed the feelings of angst the oppressed hearers felt against their oppressors, but would not have offered a path forward. Now I turn to those at the sharpest point of Jesus' critique – the hearers. For Jesus, countering evil with evil will not bring blessing, rather his hearers are called to a righteous response.[36] Jesus is not backward in pointing his finger at those too calloused to mourn over their own suffering, or too cold to grieve with others. To receive God's comfort, they must mourn. In this world of constant battles Jesus condemns our violent rage, and insists that his listeners respond to life's challenges with

---

follows: 'Mercy is a loving response prompted by the misery and helplessness of the one on whom the love is to be showered'; Carson, *Jesus' Sermon on the Mount*, 25.

33 Carson over-spiritualizes this beatitude by restricting 'poor in Spirit' to 'the personal acknowledgement of spiritual bankruptcy'; ibid., 18. But given the fact that Luke only refers to the 'poor', and the reality of oppression that the audiences faced, I think such an interpretation is unlikely.

34 Burner makes clear that the righteousness that people were to hunger and thirst for was God's righteousness. See Frederick Dale Bruner, *The Christbook: A Historical/Theological Commentary: Matthew 1–12* (Waco, TX: Word Books, 1987), 170. Gundry adds that this desire was fuelled by the presence of evil; Gundry, *Matthew*, 70.

35 If, as Gundry suggests, Matthew is following Proverbs 10:10, then the call is not simply to make peace between disputing parties, but to make peace with *your* enemies; ibid., 72.

36 Volf begins *Exclusion and Embrace* by telling of the destructiveness of counter-violence, such as the rioting in Los Angeles following the Rodney King murder, or the brutal civil war in which Croatia regained its national independence from Yugoslavia. See Miroslav Volf, *Exclusion and Embrace: A Theological Exploration of Identity, Otherness, and Reconciliation* (Nashville, TN: Abingdon Press, 1996), 13–16.

gentle strength.[37] Like proud William Dorrit in Dickens's *Little Dorrit*, even the poorest of the poor can live inauthentic lives displaying complete disregard for their lot.[38] Those stuck in their own little world cannot see reality for what it is. Jesus cuts through the sham, insisting that only the authentic and sincere will see God.[39]

Matthew's Jesus ends on a provocative step. Whereas Luke says, 'Blessed are you when people hate you, when they exclude you and insult you and reject your name as evil, because of the Son of Man' (Luke 6:22), Matthew leaves persecution on account of Jesus for the next section. He ends the manifesto by blessing those who are persecuted because *they live righteously*. The critique is pointed at all who will not follow this difficult life in the way that is called for by the paradoxical blessing of God: even though this life invites misunderstanding and persecution.

The way forward

I have identified the manifesto's horizon of promise before considering the double-edged critique within the beatitudes. Jesus calls to account both the oppressive society and the individuals who heard him speak. There is one final part of Moltmann's framework of hope which we must identify: the path from the troubled present to the future horizon of promise.

While the promise looks to the end of oppression in the future, and offers some relief from its effects now, Jesus is unambiguous about the narrow path (Matt 7:13–14) towards the horizon of promise. *They must change.* Or – as would have been quite apparent to the readers of Matthew's first letter – they must allow God's Spirit to change them. *Those who heard* the sermon must acknowledge the multi-dimensional nature of the poverty they faced. *They* were to trust God's reign over all rulers. *They* must mourn their own losses and losses of others. *They* were to face life's challenges, battles and hurdles with gentle, calm strength, not with violent rage. *They* were to crave the time when God would bring his righteousness. *They* were to be humble

---

37 Meekness is seen most clearly in the humility and gentleness of Christ's call to the 'weary and burdened' (Matt 11:28–30). He calls them to cast their burdens on him so that he can come alongside those who are burdened and carry their load for them, and give them a lighter load. Here is a picture of strength: Jesus is saying that he is strong enough to carry whatever burdens them, but gentle (meek) enough that they need not fear him as he comes alongside them.
38 William Dorrit is a prisoner in Marshalsea debtors' prison whose unwavering pretence that he is better than his fate renders him incapable of changing it.
39 Matthew has Jesus echo Ps 24:3–6, where those with a pure heart come into God's presence. Stott interprets this purity as sincerity and an absence of hypocrisy; John R.W. Stott, *The Message of the Sermon on the Mount: Christian Counter-Culture*, 2nd edn (Downers Grove, IL: InterVarsity Press, 1992), 49.

and sincere. *They* were to make peace with their enemies and trust God's way, and his rule, even when they were persecuted because *they chose* to live righteously.

There is no doubt that the world around the various audiences of the manifesto, including ourselves, will be entirely different when God fulfils all his promises. However, given the fact we are talking about a context of oppression, the question arises: Who has the power to make the world better? While the beatitudes do not preclude political action that seeks to influence those in power to improve the lot of the oppressed, it also does not cede more power to those already in power by insisting the powerful must choose to change so that the oppressed can experience a better life. Rather, the power is ascribed to God, who can change reality, and to the listeners, who can be/become the people who are blessed. Even though there is an unequivocal sense that God will faithfully fulfil his promises, it is equally clear that the catalyst for experiencing a changed life lies with the hearers themselves. They must be open to becoming the sort of people God desires them to be. Thus, if we are to consider any other power in the human realm, the beatitudes offer hope because the people themselves are empowered to change.

Letting the Manifesto Speak to Us

Earlier, the achievements of the social model in highlighting the many ways society limits and oppresses people with disabilities were pointed out. It was also shown that there is an aversion to critiquing those with disabilities, as this only serves to confirm the oppressive normalcy. But when this line of thought is the starting point for developing a disability theology, it may prove to be an Achilles heel; especially when an aversion to the idea that people with disabilities need to change means we are unable to tolerate a theology which prioritizes God's change in us, so in its place we construct a theology where God must change the other.

I have shown that the 'Mountain Manifesto' was spoken in a context of oppression. It is in that context which the beatitudes stand in opposition to this fundamental claim of the social model. Whereas the social model prioritizes changes in the world around a person with a disability for them to realize their hope, conversely the beatitudes prioritize God's change in us through his Spirit. Only then will we experience God's change in the world around us.

Since healing is a part of the context in which Matthew frames the hope of Jesus' ministry, and since that hope prioritizes God's transformation of us, we must now briefly return to the topic of cure of impairment. Instead of an a priori aversion to the notion – as the social model would urge upon us – perhaps we must accept that God has placed transformed embodiment on the horizon of promise.[40] The beatitudes highlight four things which may help us process this. First, Matthew sees healing as a part of a much larger holistic work of God. Second, we must be willing to allow God and His word to critique us wherever it does. Thus, third, God's reign breaks into each person's life where they need it in a myriad of different ways. Therefore, it is equally problematic to isolate healing of impairment as *the* most important thing that God will do for a person with a disability, or, conversely as *the least* important, or least desirable, thing that God will do for a person with a disability. And fourth, all this happens within a 'now-but-not yet' context. Therefore, even if we believe God will heal, it is for him to decide his own timing.

If I, as one who hopes and as one with a disability, am going to realize the hope of Christ, I must be willing to reflect on myself.

Has my drive for independence left me unwilling to acknowledge the depth of my need for God in the many dimensions of my being? Instead, I must acknowledge my need, assured that as I do, God will reign now and in the future.

Am I so calloused by the relentless disappointments and frustrations of disability that I've ceased to constructively lament them? Instead, I must lament, assured of the blessing of God's comfort.

Do I get so riled by the barriers of society that I can't deal with them productively? Instead, I must push the barriers with gentle strength, knowing that God's blessed inheritance is assured when I do so.

In a society where resources and support are rationed, do I become preoccupied with having my own needs met? Instead, I must seek a just dispersal of support for all in need, trusting that as I do so, God will bring my satisfaction.

Am I so preoccupied with the constancy of my own battles and suffering that I do not reach out to others in need? Instead, I must reach out in compassion to them, trusting in God's blessing of compassion for me.

Are my dealings with bureaucracy and the 'system' marked by a desire to 'stretch the truth'? Instead, my dealings should be transparent and clear, trusting that I will see God.

Do I seek to make war with those who administer governmental systems? Instead, I must seek to make peace with them, trusting that as I do so, I will have the blessing of the dignity of being one of God's children.

Finally, am I going to be the person who lives life God's way, even as society continues to oppress and find new ways of marginalizing those with disabilities? I must trust that as I do so, God will continue to bring his kingdom.

---

40 Christ's resurrected body shows us this hope. It has both radical continuity – affirming the goodness of being shaped by embodied *human* experience in the here and now – and radical discontinuity – affirming something different is on the horizon, when we consider our *human* embodiment. That discontinuity/continuity tension is a thoroughly human tension, and should not be contorted into one which people with disabilities face uniquely, as ableist theology might implicitly be inclined to do. Rather, 'we will *all* be changed . . . in a twinkling of an eye' (2 Cor 15:51–2).

This way of reading Christian hope does not leave those of us with disabilities powerless. It does not render us explicitly powerless, as the medical model does when it insists that only medical and allied health professionals have the skills to change our impairments. Nor does it render us implicitly powerless while purporting to offer empowering hope, as the social model does. For all the rhetoric of those with disabilities finding their voice to speak out against the oppressive barriers of society, we are powerless to change the oppressive other unless they choose to change themselves.

What the 'Mountain Manifesto' says is that we may be oppressed, but we are not powerless to change our experience. Rather, our world will change when *we* turn our sails to catch the wind of the Spirit. We neither need to look to experts to change us, nor society to change for us. Rather, we turn to God, and let him change what is in us. Then we can have true hope.

Trust God's Hope

Biblical hope strikes at the heart of a narrative of oppression which dominates the social model. Oppression's story is that the other's power and control is at the heart of our problems. Therefore, the other must change for us to have hope. Through the lens of Moltmann's understanding of hope, the message of hope in the 'Mountain Manifesto', which is Matthew's summary statement of the gospel, critiques the oppressor. Nevertheless, the sharpest critique falls on oppressed individuals. Matthew's Jesus invites them to allow God to change them now, and not yet. If this is true, then Christians with disabilities face a choice: we can trust the social model's weak hope and join its refusal to critique the individual with a disability, or we can accept God's hope, knowing it will painfully critique our hearts. But when we allow that critique, God will then lead us into his promises.

19 Disability and the Renewal of Theological Education
Beyond Ableism

Amos Yong

Ableism, unlike its more widely recognized 'cousins' *racism* and *sexism*, might well be dismissed by some as no more than another political identity ideology that these same critics insist the others reduce to. However, for those who find at least some value in how the hermeneutics of suspicion retrieves marginalized and neglected perspectives amidst a dominant culture,[1] ableism names the unconscious elevation of non-disabled experiences as normative for all human beings, as well as the resulting marginalization of those who are unable to live up to its expectations. Understood in this way, ableist biases have proven to be no respecters of people or institutions, as they happen also in churches and in institutions of theological education. What is unfortunate is that there are authoritative (scriptural) sources in the latter contexts which have long named and rejected this ableist attitude, but yet have been subjugated by the ableist regime.[2]

Others have addressed the ableist reality in the church and are attempting to develop alternative ways forward.[3] The focus of this chapter will be on theological education. In particular, we will be looking at the theological curriculum and asking, first, how ableist perspectives have traditionally structured theological teaching and learning, and second, how disability perspectives can chart new approaches to theological studies as a whole. The four sections of this chapter explore how this shift is emerging at the conceptual and theoretical

---

1 For more on the hermeneutics of suspicion, see Anthony C. Thiselton, 'The Hermeneutics of Suspicion and Retrieval: Paul Ricoeur's Hermeneutical Theory', in *New Horizons in Hermeneutics* (Grand Rapids, MI: Zondervan, 1992), 344–78.
2 I have identified and elaborated on these elements in two books: *Theology and Down Syndrome: Reimagining Disability in Late Modernity* (Waco, TX.: Baylor University Press, 2007), and *The Bible, Disability, and the Church: A New Vision of the People of God* (Grand Rapids, MI: Eerdmans, 2011); this chapter builds on this work in order to address the opportunities and challenges that disability opens up for contemporary theological education.
3 There are many, from conservative evangelicals like Joni Eareckson Tada on the one side to mainline Protestants like Brett Webb-Mitchell on the other, as well as Roman Catholics and many others in between. I present some of my own ideas in this regard in my article 'Disability from the Margins to the Center: Hospitality and Inclusion in the Church', *Journal of Religion, Disability, and Health* 15 (2011): 339–50.

levels – hermeneutically in the field of biblical studies, historiographically in the field of Christian history, methodologically in Christian theology, and practically in ministry and practical theology courses. I will show that far from being an esoteric development driven by the ideological politics of disability, the registration of disability perspectives in the theological curriculum has the potential to revitalize theological studies as a whole, and also to renew theological education. In other words, the appearance of disability in the theological guild is neither just to assuage the guilty feelings of non-disabled people nor a token of inclusion; instead, disability insights are essential to the church's self-understanding and to an invigorated programme of theological study.

Beyond the Hermeneutics of Charity and Suspicion: Disability Studies and Biblical Studies

The Bible has long been read *vis-à-vis* disability experiences and realities. Part of the challenge is that it is anachronistic to apply contemporary notions of disability to the scriptural traditions. Yet the other extreme – of thinking that the Bible does not directly address, and hence is irrelevant for, our present experience of disability – also misses the point. The question thus remains: How should the Bible be understood with regard to disability? From a disability perspective, three types of approaches can be explicated.

First, there is no doubt that the Bible has meant many different things to many different people across the spectrum of abilities.[4] This is in part because there are a whole range of texts, some quite challenging for those with disabilities, and others quite comforting. With regard to the former, there are texts that exclude people with disabilities from priestly duties for no other reason than their impairments (Lev 21:17–24), and that link impairments of various sorts with curses that befall those who are disobedient to God (Deut 28:15–68, *passim*). If these are not enough, the New Testament seems to perpetuate the link between sin and disability (for example, John 5:14) even as it connects impairing conditions with evil spirits. Yes, Jesus rejects any causal connection between sin and disability (John 9:1–3), but he also then seems to go around healing many of those around him, which raises questions, if not self-doubts, among those who are not cured about their status in his community.[5]

---

4 For overviews, see Lynn Holden, *Forms of Deformity* (Sheffield: JSOT Press, 1991), and Saul M. Olyan, *Disability in the Hebrew Bible: Interpreting Mental and Physical Differences* (Cambridge: Cambridge University Press, 2008). Jewish perspectives include: Judith Abrams, *Judaism and Disability: Portrayals in Ancient Texts from the Tanach through the Bavli* (Washington, DC: Gallaudet University Press, 1998); Marx Tzvi, *Disability in Jewish Law* (New York: Routledge, 2002), and Judith Z. Abrams and William C. Gaventa, eds, *Jewish Perspectives on Theology and the Human Experience of Disability* (New York: Haworth Pastoral Press, 2006).
5 As documented by W. Graham Monteith, *Deconstructing Miracles: From Thoughtless Indifference to Honouring Disabled People* (Glasgow: Covenanters Press; Edinburgh: Scottish Christian Press, 2005).

On the other hand, people with disabilities have always found solace in the pages of Scripture. Many have hopes for eschatological healing, if not the removal of their impairments in this life, because of Scripture's promises. Others have drawn inspiration from the biblical laments and have been emboldened to approach God despite their afflicted condition. Families, caretakers, and friends of those with disabilities, further, have been motivated by the ethic of care that the Bible enjoins. In fact, many have embraced the vocation of caring for those with disabilities because of the biblical call to compassion for others. In short, the difficult texts on disability are counter-balanced by others that have led followers of Christ to care for the sick, the weak, and the impaired, as if they were ministering to Jesus himself (cf. Matt 25:31–46).

Yet others are unable or unwilling to live within the felt tension across the biblical spectrum. While recognizing that people of faith will read the Bible redemptively (so that even texts that discuss disability negatively are to be embraced in anticipation of fuller understanding to come) and that scholars may read it for its historical value (to understand biblical statements about disability in their original social contexts), yet the negative effects following the reception of these cannot be overlooked as it is precisely such that have led some to reject the scriptures as having any authority for contemporary life.[6] For such rejectionists there are too many unanswered questions across the surface of the scriptures that remain problematic. Either they undermine faith in the God to whom such scriptures allegedly point, or they suggest that people with disabilities are condemned by the fact of their impairments. If those informed by the hermeneutics of charity are inclined to let God off the hook or to respond kindly and generously in ministering to the needs of others, those who adopt a hermeneutics of suspicion are led now even further toward dismissal of these ancient texts as having ongoing scriptural warrant. If the lingering problem of the former approach is the historically prevalent tendencies toward paternalism, that of the latter is its ultimately non-religious and even anti-religious posture.

Is there a possible *via media* or alternative way forward? Here is where I think a disability hermeneutic – an approach to Scripture that neither absolutizes disability perspectives and experiences nor ignores them – can help us. There are at least three levels of contribution for such a hermeneutical preference. First, a disability perspective, while not making more of disability references in the biblical traditions than ought to be made, also does not treat them as merely incidental to the scriptural account, as has happened for all too long and far too often in the hands of ableist interpreters.[7] Hence the emergence of disability

---

6 As suggested by Hector Avalos, 'Redemptionism, Rejectionism, and Historicism as Emerging Approaches in Disability Studies,' *Perspectives in Religious Studies* 34 (2007): 91–100, esp. 95–6.

7 See, for instance, my reading of the Zacchaeus narrative from a 'shortist' perspective: Amos Yong, 'Zacchaeus: Short and Un-seen', in *Christian Reflection: A Series in Faith and Ethics – Disability* (Waco, TX: Center for Christian Ethics at Baylor University, 2012), 11–17 [accessed 12 November 2015]. Online: http://www.baylor.edu/christianethics/index.php?id=92614.

studies in the scholarly investigation of Scripture is lifting up disability in the ancient world in ways that have been long overlooked in the background and context of scriptural interpretation.[8] Focusing the disability lens on the biblical traditions has thus not only resulted in a deeper understanding of disability realities in ancient Israel and among the first-century Christians, but is also adding to our knowledge of the biblical world as a whole.

Second, however, a disability reading of Scripture has religious and even theological benefits beyond the disability community. For some, for instance, reading St Paul in light of disability experiences and perspectives illuminates how his theology of weaknesses has much to say not only for people with disabilities, but for the church as the one body of Christ with many types of gifted members.[9] Less obviously, as another example, a reconsideration of the Davidic kingship from an angle that foregrounds the role of Mephibosheth in the text may be suggestive not only for a more than ableist understanding of this contested period of Israel's history, but also regarding the historiographic, political, and theological agendas of Israel's historians.[10] Last, but certainly not least, along these lines, a disability perspective illuminates not only the texts of ancient Israel – like that of the famous 'Suffering Servant' in Isa 53 – but also their reception history and interpretation, including how first-century Jews and perhaps other followers of Jesus as Messiah understood and interpreted such texts in ways that reflected what we might say are their ableist biases.[11] My point here is that a disability reading of the Bible is not just for people with disabilities, but for all persons across the spectrum of abilities.

This leads to my third point: that able-bodied readers of the biblical text observe things differently than those who approach the text in light of disability perspectives and experiences. The title of John Hull's book *In the Beginning There was Darkness: A Blind Person's Conversations with the Bible* is suggestive for our purposes.[12] Whereas sighted readers have long disassociated the darkness

---

8 I am thinking here, for example, of volumes like: Hector Avalos, Sarah J. Melcher, and Jeremy Schipper, eds, *This Abled Body: Rethinking Disabilities in Biblical Studies* (Atlanta, GA: Society of Biblical Literature, 2007); Rebecca Raphael, *Biblical Corpora: Representations of Disability in Hebrew Biblical Literature* (London: T&T Clark International, 2008), and Candida R. Moss and Jeremy Schipper, eds, *Disability Studies and Biblical Literature* (New York: Palgrave Macmillan, 2011).

9 See, for instance, W. Graham Monteith, *Epistles of Inclusion: St. Paul's Inspired Attitudes* (Guildford: Grosvenor House, 2010).

10 As brilliantly elaborated by Jeremy Schipper in *Disability Studies and the Hebrew Bible: Figuring Mephibosheth in the David Story* (New York: T&T Clark, 2006), Mephibosheth's presence can be seen to symbolize the brokenness of the Davidic reign even as he becomes a symbol of why, despite David's limitations and the nation's failures, God chooses to bless Israel.

11 See Jeremy Schipper, *Disability and Isaiah's Suffering Servant* (Oxford: Oxford University Press, 2011), which shows how ableist translators and readers either minimized the impairments of the suffering servant or interpreted them away.

12 John M. Hull, *In the Beginning There was Darkness: A Blind Person's Conversations with the Bible* (New York: T&T Clark, 2001).

with the divine, Hull identifies many biblical texts, not the least of which is the creation narrative, that indicate otherwise. How else might others who make their way around the world differently from the able-bodied interact with Scripture? How might the hearing-impaired 'hear', 'read', or 'feel' Scripture otherwise? What about the 'lame' or those whose are otherwise socially or developmentally impaired? How might the many tongues of the Spirit's witness declare the biblical testimony to people across the spectrum of abilities?[13] I will return to this question periodically in this chapter.

Beyond 'Us' and 'Them': Towards a Historiography of Belonging

The discipline of Christian history is undergoing similar convulsions to that in biblical studies. Most ferocious are debates regarding the shifts from the modernist historiography with its positivist and historicist features to a postmodernist approach that highlights the subjectivist position from which all historical narrative is constructed. While we ought to be cautioned against any uncritical embrace of the kind of philosophical relativism, skepticism, and nihilism that is sometimes carried along by the postmodernist zeitgeist, I would like to suggest that there are important ways in which a disability historiography can supplement, if not also correct, the dominant Christian historical account.

In order to see this, we must first note how the appearance of disability in Christian history has been registered predominantly by ableist historical projects. Think, for instance, firstly about how history, traditionally told, is recounted by its 'winners'. To the extent that 'losers', including people with disabilities, appear in such accounts, they are inevitably marginalized from the church's institutional centres. Further, people with disabilities are less agents of historical change than they are more deterministically caught up in the currents of able-bodied actors. Thus they appear in the histories of hospitals as passive recipients of the charitable agency of others who are less impaired. Last but not least, but certainly least exemplary of our considerations, is the history of disability *vis-à-vis* the freak show; this stain in the history of the Anglo-American and 'Christian' West depicts what is certainly its 'underbelly' as far as people with disabilities are concerned.[14] I mention this only to reinforce the claim that

---

13 I take up this question in ch. 3 of my *The Bible, Disability, and the Church*; see also my article 'Many Tongues, Many Senses: Pentecost, the Body Politic, and the Redemption of Dis/ability', *PNEUMA: Journal of the Society for Pentecostal Studies* 31 (2009): 167–88. See also Mikael C. Parsons, *Body and Character in Luke and Acts: The Subversion of Physiognomy in Early Christianity* (Grand Rapids, MI: Baker Academic, 2006), and Chad Hartsock, *Sight and Blindness in Luke–Acts: The Use of Physical Features in Characterization* (Leiden: Brill, 2008).

14 There has been an explosion of scholarly literature on this topic in the last decade, including: Thomas Richard Fahy, *Freak Shows and the Modern American Imagination: Constructing the Damaged Body from Willa Cather to Truman Capote* (New York: Palgrave Macmillan, 2006); Nadja Durbach, *The Spectacle of Deformity: Freak Shows and Modern British Culture* (Berkeley, CA: University of California

the ableist rendition of disability in Christian history is underdeveloped at best, and offensive and oppressive at worst.

Not surprisingly, then, correction of this ableist historiography requires disability perspectives and voices. This is now slowly beginning to emerge. One of the most comprehensive to date is Henri-Jacques Stiker's *A History of Disability*.[15] As one of the first of its kind, it attempts a sweeping account from the ancient world to the modern West (disability in the Eastern hemisphere is by and large neglected). What is admirable is the valiant effort to tell the story of disability as one of difference rather than of abnormality. Some headway is made in terms of giving voice to people with disabilities themselves. However, the historical sources are scanty, so the bulk of the discussion remains focused on the interface of those less impaired with those more so. Stiker's history is invaluable as an introductory resource, although, of course, severely incomplete.

From a historiographical perspective, Stiker's contribution, while helpful, segregates the history of disability from Christian history in general. This is not to say that histories focused on disabilities in all of their permutations should be neglected. It is to say that to tell the story of disability in this way still separates it out from the broader considerations of Christian history as a whole. Thankfully, other historical treatments are emerging that are focused more on how disability perspectives can and do illuminate wider historical research and writing. Irina Metzler's *Disability in Medieval Europe*, for instance, elucidates medieval theological anthropologies, explicates features of medieval medicine and natural philosophy, and illuminates the range of medieval views on miracles in relationship to impairments, among other achievements.[16] Edward Wheatley's more recent book, while focused on blindness, also illuminates – pun intended! – how the church's religious understanding of disability was deployed to sanction its methods of punishment, to legitimize its control over disability and its caregiving, and to undergird its authority in matters related to the interpretation and application of the Bible.[17] In the latter case, focusing on blindness shows how

---

Press, 2009); Michael M. Chemers, *Staging Stigma: A Critical Examination of the American Freak Show* (New York: Palgrave Macmillan, 2009); Lillian Craton, *The Victorian Freak Show: The Significance of Disability and Physical Differences in 19th-century Fiction* (Amherst, NY: Cambria Press, 2009), and Robert Bogdan with Martin Elks and James A. Knoll, *Picturing Disability: Beggar, Freak, Citizen, and Other Photographic Rhetoric* (Syracuse, NY: Syracuse University Press, 2012).

15 Henri-Jacques Stiker, *A History of Disability*, trans. William Sayers (Ann Arbor, MI: University of Michigan Press, 1999).

16 Irina Metzler, *Disability in Medieval Europe: Thinking About Physical Impairment in the High Middle Ages, c.1100–1400*, Routledge Studies in Medieval Religion and Culture (New York: Routledge, 2006). Building on Metzler's work are other important collections: Joshua R. Eyler, *Disability in the Middle Ages: Reconsiderations and Reverberations* (Farnham: Ashgate, 2010), and Wendy J. Turner and Tory Vandeventer Pearman, eds, *The Treatment of Disabled Persons in Medieval Europe: Examining Disability in the Historical, Legal, Literary, Medical, and Religious Discourses of the Middle Ages* (Lewiston, NY: Edwin Mellen Press, 2011).

17 Edward Wheatley, *Stumbling Blocks Before the Blind: Medieval Constructions of a Disability* (Ann Arbor, MI: University of Michigan Press, 2010).

Jews were marginalized along with the visually impaired, albeit because of their 'blindness' (denoted in the pages of the New Testament) with regard to the messianic identity of Jesus.[18]

While many more historical accounts of disability are needed to fill in the gaps, I would suggest that a disability historiography needs to emerge that can function in Christian history writing and telling similarly to how a disability hermeneutic has leavened the field of biblical studies.[19] Recall, in the previous section, that a disability reading of Scripture has implications not only for people with disabilities, but for any and all concerned with the scriptural or authoritative nature of religious and ancient texts. Similarly, as we can see from the preceding discussion, a history of disability in Christian history should not only be of value for people with disabilities; rather, it should also inform the full range of Christian historical understanding.

John Swinton and Brian Brock's *Disability in the Christian Tradition: A Reader* documents the possibilities opened up by such a disability historiography.[20] Two trajectories of ongoing research and exploration deserve mention. First, this is one of the initial volumes that produces selections from major thinkers and theologians in the Christian tradition whose writings have touched on disability themes. As such, this is in some respects a historical theology of disability, one that documents developments in the history of Christian thought on these matters. While much of this material is by non-impaired persons, the collection is nevertheless suggestive for how a disability historiography can produce new corrections, arrangements, and conceptual frameworks for the retrieval and re-reading of the dominant Christian tradition.

Second, such an anthological organization invites fresh reconsiderations of the legacies of major figures in the history of Christian theology. Ancient thinkers (the Cappadocians, Augustine, Aquinas, and Julian of Norwich), Reformers (Luther and Calvin), and moderns (Hegel, Kierkegaard, Bonhoeffer, Barth, Vanier, and Hauerwas), among other sources, need to be revisited from a disability perspective, and when this happens, the main lines of Christian reflection on theological anthropology, embodiment, suffering, salvation, freedom, and rationality are refracted and inflected in surprising ways. A disability historiography thus reveals its potential to interrogate received traditions, with benefits not just for disability self-identities, but also for Christian self-understandings as a whole. Disability perspectives thus applied to Christian history and historical theology are helpful in carving out a *via media* 'between a survey of what "people in the past" thought, which would only be of antiquarian interest, and a project which just "mines" thinkers of the past for fresh concepts for use in the

---

18 Ibid., ch. 3.
19 The rest of this section summarizes what I otherwise explore at greater length in the second part of my '*Disability in the Christian Tradition*: An Overview and Historiographical Reflection', *Journal of Religion, Disability, and Health* 17 (2013): 236–43.
20 Brian Brock and John Swinton, eds, *Disability in the Christian Tradition: A Reader* (Grand Rapids, MI: Eerdmans, 2012).

present, without letting the thought structures of these conversation partners emerge to challenge us'.[21]

My point is that theological students and seminarians ought to understand disability not just as an (unfortunate) appendage to Christian history dictated in terms of 'us' (non-disabled) and 'them' (the disabled), but as part and parcel of its central thrust. Even to see that disability has in many instances been relegated to the margins of the drama of redemption tells us much about how the ableist presumption has clouded both the agents of history and their preservation and retelling of that account. In these and other ways, disability perspectives make essential contributions to what might be called a historiography of suspicion that can correct, while also complementing and extending, our understanding of the richness of the Christian story in its many dimensions. When adjusted in this way, new possibilities emerge for a more complete account that includes the contributions of all of 'us' across the spectrum of abilities in Christian history.

'Nothing about Us without Us': Enabling Theological Method

I now turn from a disability hermeneutics and historiography to a disability theological methodology. Again, in order for us to appreciate how disability experiences can inspire fresh and creative but no less necessary rethinking in the theological domain, some perspective on how the theme of disability has been historically treated is in order. Not unexpectedly, considerations of disability usually appear under three or four major headings in the historic theological loci: in the doctrine of creation, and especially the fall of humanity, which leads to a consideration of disability as intrinsic to human sinfulness and fallenness; in the doctrine of providence, which inevitably takes up questions regarding how disability is related to divine sovereignty; relatedly, in the doctrine of God, which treats disability within the context of theodicy; and in the doctrine of salvation, which discusses the suffering and evil of disability and also its resolution in the healing power of God, both in the present life and in the eschatological resurrection body.[22] In each of these arenas disability is a problem to be resolved and the discussion is apologetically constrained. I am not saying that

---

21 Brian Brock, 'Introduction: Disability and the Quest for the Human', in Brian Brock and John Swinton, eds, *Disability in the Christian Tradition: A Reader* (Grand Rapids, MI: Eerdmans, 2012), 1–23; quotation from ibid., 7.

22 See, for example, Larry J. Waters and Roy B. Zuck, eds, *Why, O God? Suffering and Disability in the Bible and the Church* (Wheaton, IL: Crossway, 2011). I provide constructive theological perspective on many of these themes as they interface with the philosophy of religion, which is often a central domain of inquiry within the genre of systematic theology, in my 'Disability and the Love of Wisdom: De-forming, Re-forming, and Per-forming Philosophy of Religion', *Ars Disputandi: The Online Journal for Philosophy of Religion* 9 (2009): 54–71, reprinted in Darla Schumm and Michael Stoltzfus, eds, *Disability in Judaism, Christianity and Islam: Sacred Texts, Historical Traditions, and Social Analysis* (New York: Palgrave Macmillan, 2011), 205–27, and in a shorter version, in *Evangelical Review of Theology* 35 (2011): 160–76.

apologetic endeavours are never to be allowed in disability theology; but I am not convinced that the classical frameworks within which such are engaged are helpful since they perpetuate perennial impasses regarding divine sovereignty and creaturely freedom along with other irresolvable conundrums. Even when handled with requisite sensitivity,[23] the resultant theology of care seems incommensurate with the overarching theology of divine determinism.

The emergence of disability as a civil rights issue since the late 1960s in the USA has empowered people with disabilities to advocate for themselves. Rather than merely being recipients of the (welcomed) charity of able-bodied persons, people with disabilities have been saying since that the best intentions of others are nevertheless shot through with a paternalistic and ableist mentality. Hence, the way forward must be mutual dialogue among all across the spectrum of ability: 'nothing about us [people with disabilities] without us' is the constant refrain.[24] Of course, partiality of perspective is no respecter of persons, including people with disabilities, so that even in this community, even as broadly defined as possible, those with physical disabilities often ignore or even reject consideration of those with intellectual disabilities (who are unable to express themselves). In any case, the principle remains pertinent: adequate consideration of the issues related to disability, the just society, and the common good cannot proceed without the input of people of all types of abilities. For those who are unable to make a personal contribution because of severe or profound intellectual impairment, the voices of their families, caretakers, and other related interested parties is paramount.

For these reasons, Christian theologies also need the contribution of people with disabilities. Nancy Eiesland's *The Disabled God: Toward a Liberatory Theology of Disability* has been ground-breaking in precisely this regard.[25] Eiesland (1964–2009), who lived with a congenital bone defect, was trained as a sociologist of religion, but gradually developed a theological voice while teaching at Emory University's Candler School of Theology. Her book signals a quantum leap at the interface of theology and disability. It first announces that disability perspectives can complement and extend liberationist theological methods and paradigms in terms of filling out the hermeneutical option for the poor (prevalent in liberation theology discourses) with an approach that cuts across socio-economic classes. Second, Eiesland's volume is shocking precisely because the crucified and resurrected Christ is imaged with the marks of his impairments as normative for the image of God. Hence the disability perspective here suggests that *The Disabled God* is not just the God of 'normal' people, but the God of all.

---

23 As in Michael S. Beates, *Disability and the Gospel: How God Uses our Brokenness to Display His Grace* (Wheaton, IL: Crossway, 2012), which approaches the topic within a classical Augustinian and Reformed theological framework.
24 See James I. Charlton, *Nothing about Us without Us: Disability Oppression and Empowerment* (Berkeley, CA: University of California Press, 2000).
25 Nancy L. Eiesland, *The Disabled God: Toward a Liberatory Theology of Disability* (Nashville, TN: Abingdon Press, 1994).

In this way, disability perspectives both interrogate and turn upside down the dominant theological tradition that emphasizes omnipotence alongside other classically delineated divine attributes.

Eiesland's book has opened up new possibilities for constructive theological reflection. Developments in Deaf theology illustrate the continued outworking of the promise of Eiesland's theological method. On the practical front, Deaf perspectives invite a reconsideration of classical ecclesiological motifs.[26] How might Christian community, including biblical *koinonia*, be organized and facilitated among differentiated cultural and communicative groups of people? What does worship, instruction, and fellowship mean across the spectrum of hearing abilities? How can the church be a liberating space for all people? On the more theological front, Deaf perspectives also press longstanding theological questions.[27] What does it mean to preach or proclaim the gospel across the spectrum of communicative abilities? What does a theology without words sound or look like, if one is at all possible? Put alternatively, what might a thoroughgoing and robust theology of embodiment feel like? These and other questions prompted by Deaf theologians and theologians inspired by their interactions with people who are deaf are suggestive of what can happen when disability perspectives are taken seriously in the theological task.

My point is that we need to move from a theology done only by the able-bodied for people with disabilities, since such projects, while useful and important in various respects, will unavoidably promote ableist biases, and these will inevitably be internalized by people with disabilities. However, theologies dialogically constructed with those across the spectrum of abilities – including their advocates, friends, family, and caretakers, especially of those with intellectual, severe, and profound disabilities – will be relevant for all people, including people with disabilities, albeit now more carefully guarded from perpetuating ableist stereotypes. Further, and more importantly, such theological initiatives will be beneficial for the church as a whole, not to mention faith communities in general, since they will touch on themes of perennial human import, and do so in ways that register the perspectives of those more directly touched by them. We are already seeing the fruit of such theological contributions: not just theologies of disability, but new perspectives on old themes like the doctrine of creation, theological anthropology, and hospitality, among many others.[28]

---

26 As in Roger Hitching, *The Church and Deaf People: A Study of Identity, Communication and Relationships with Special Reference to the Ecclesiology of Jürgen Moltmann* (Milton Keynes: Paternoster Press, 2003), and Hannah Lewis, *Deaf Liberation Theology* (Burlington, VT: Ashgate, 2007).

27 As in Marcel Broesterhuizen, ed., *The Gospel Preached by the Deaf: Proceedings of a Conference on Deaf Liberation Theology Held at the Faculty of Theology of the Catholic University of Leuven (Belgium), May 19th, 2003* (Leuven: Peeters, 2007), and Wayne Morris, *Theology without Words: Theology in the Deaf Community* (Burlington, VT: Ashgate, 2008).

28 On the doctrine of creation, see Deborah Beth Creamer, *Disability and Christian Theology: Embodied Limits and Constructive Possibilities* (New York: Oxford University Press, 2009); on theological anthropology and friendship, see Hans S. Reinders, *Receiving the Gift of Friendship: Profound Disability,*

These developments indicate that while courses on disability in theological, divinity, and seminary curricula are a helpful and important beginning, the goal ought to be integration of disability as a central theme across the theological curriculum. Disability is, again, not just a marginal and incidental aspect of the human condition. Rather, it is inherent in the Christian drama of redemption. Hence only a theology thoroughly informed by disability perspectives can do justice to its theological potential. This means, then, that a disability theological methodology ought to be intrinsic to theological education similarly to how feminist, postcolonial, and global South approaches are increasingly woven seamlessly into the curriculum.

The Indispensability of Disability: Practical Theology and Theology of Mission for the Third Millennium

A theological education is distinct from a secular religious studies approach, particularly in asking normative religious and theological questions and then being concerned about the application of such notions. The latter are especially the prerogative of departments of practical theology or professional ministry within institutions of theological education. Even here practical theologies and theologies of mission are only gradually experiencing revision (if not revulsion) in relationship to disability matters and perspectives.

This is most clear when we examine shifts in courses in ministry and disability as these have interfaced with disability issues. One might identify three paradigms: the more classical emphases on ministry to people with disabilities, the more recent one focused also on the families of people with disability, and a more revolutionary understanding of ministry as involving people with disabilities as well. The first approach is largely ameliorative and, when theologically informed, concerned about spiritual matters. The goal is to minister to the needs of people with disabilities, although the priorities are their spiritual condition (related to an underdeveloped theology of embodiment). Further, disabling or impairing conditions are understood largely according to the medical model, which views these as individualized situations and focuses on 'fixing' the associated 'problems' through pharmaceutical, technological, therapeutic, and other medical advances. Ministerial approaches labouring under these assumptions hence also consider disability mostly in individualistic or privatized terms, ignoring the social dimensions of disability, including their identity-formative dimensions when people with disabilities internalize the dominant (ableist) prejudices.[29]

Theological Anthropology, and Ethics (Grand Rapids, MI: Eerdmans, 2008), and on hospitality and theology, see Thomas E. Reynolds, *Vulnerable Communion: A Theology of Disability and Hospitality* (Grand Rapids, MI: Brazos Press, 2008).

29 I do not cite any literature here since this is largely a type that persists in the pew rather than in official theological curricula; however, its prevalence in the popular Christian imagination means that it remains effective in many local congregations and parishes, and thus deserves mention at least in this regard.

More recent theologies of pastoral ministry are more holistic and hence sensitive not only to the embodied dimension of living with disability, but also to the family, communal, and social environments within which lives with disabilities are always negotiated. Hence there is greater awareness of and intentional engagement with families, caregivers, and service providers, and often a sensitivity to the needs of these significant others who are in relationship with people with disabilities.[30] Such approaches are certainly much healthier in terms of enabling ministers and congregations to deal more effectively with the many levels of challenges that accompany disability. Yet they still by and large lack an important and critical component: recognition of people with disabilities not just as passive recipients of the ministry of able-bodied others, but as agents of ministry in their own right.

It is thus the more radical paradigm of ministry *to* and *with* people with disabilities that ought to revolutionize contemporary theologies of ministry and mission. The point here is at least threefold: that people with disabilities are indeed deserving of ministry, but so also are others without disabilities; that people with disabilities can also be ministering agents, and that the imaginative horizons of theologies of ministry and mission ought to be expanded in order that all people can expect and benefit from (be edified with) the gifts of those across the spectrum of abilities; and that even in the cases of those with severe and profound disabilities, the Scriptures indicate that they are more indispensable, honourable, and central to the church than able-bodied folk might recognize (cf. 1 Cor 12:14–26). In fact, people with disabilities may be unique conduits of the Spirit's gifts (see also 1 Cor 12:4–13), even if those saddled with ableist assumptions are often incapable of (impaired from!) recognizing these charisms.[31] The point is that the church as the body of Christ (with many members) and the fellowship of the Holy Spirit (with many gifts given 'to each one individually just as the Spirit chooses'; 1 Cor 12:11) includes people with disabilities not just as recipients of the ministry of others, but as ministers with others to all.

More and more churches from across the evangelical and ecumenical spectrum are recognizing how people with disabilities can also be agents of the Spirit's ministering gifts.[32] Christian ministry in every venue thus has to be reconsidered in light of people with disabilities as agents of ministry and mission. The discipline of practical theology itself will need to be informed by

---

30 Pre-eminent in this regard is Erik Carter, *Including People with Disabilities in Faith Communities: A Guide for Service Providers, Families, and Congregations* (Baltimore, MD: Paul H. Brookes, 2007).

31 See here also my article 'Disability and the Gifts of the Spirit: Pentecost and the Renewal of the Church', *Journal of Pentecostal Theology* 19 (2010): 76–93.

32 See, for example: Joni Eareckson Tada and Gene Newman, *All God's Children: Ministry with Disabled Persons* (Grand Rapids, MI: Ministry Resource Library/Zondervan, 1993); Jennie Weiss Block, *Copious Hosting: A Theology of Access for People with Disabilities* (New York: Continuum International, 2002), and Arne Fritzson and Samuel Kabue, *Interpreting Disability: A Church Of All And For All* (Geneva: World Council of Churches, 2004).

disability perspectives and exemplars going forward.³³ To be sure, there will need to be continued and intentional effort devoted to how the church can be more effective in engaging distinct people groups in relevant ways, not the least of which is the disability community. Yet such will also increasingly need to be re-crafted not just as reaching out *to* such groups of people, but also *with* them, even as empowering the ministry of all to all.

What will continue to emerge is a revitalized community of faith, which can only be fully reinvigorated theologically and practically. What I mean is that if a theological, divinity, or seminary education is designed to renew the church, then such renewal has to occur at the levels of both beliefs (theology) and practices (ministry and Christian life). Engaging with disability perspectives is central to such revitalization since they challenge both the traditional self-understanding and classical models of ministry and mission. If disability hermeneutics invites new approaches to Scripture and disability historiography portrays a new 'we' as opposed to 'us/them', then a disability methodology reconstructs an inclusive Christian theology for the third millennium even as a disability theology of ministry and mission generates a new Christian praxis of belonging for the present time. If the rhetoric of 'inclusion' still suggests that the (ecclesial and institutional) centre retains some measure of authority in widening the margins, the rhetoric of 'belonging' counteracts such hierarchical and authoritarian tendencies by relocating the power and agency to define the church – the body of Christ and the fellowship of the Spirit – to the people. To belong can never be imposed by others; rather, it has to be claimed by each person and each group.³⁴ Yes, invitation can and should be extended – precisely what theologies of inclusion make possible – but responses can never be coerced, even as belonging will always ever be freely declared in whatever way, shape, and form such declarations can be made.

This is why consideration of disability perspectives is crucial for theologies of ministry in general and the discipline of practical theology in particular. It lifts up disability as more central to, rather than marginalized from, the Christian life and the community of faith in ways that can impact the broad scope of courses traditionally offered in at least the Master of Divinity curriculum: religious education, counselling, preaching, liturgy, mission, and so on. Again, the goal is not just that there will be courses on disability ministry in our seminaries and theological and divinity schools, as important and helpful as these are, but that there will be integration of disability themes and perspectives across the course of practical theology in particular, and also the theological curriculum as a whole.

---

33 See, for example, Anna Katherine Ellerman Shurley, 'Space for Vocation: Pastoral Care through Creative Collaboration with People with Intellectual Disabilities' (PhD diss., Princeton Theological Seminary, 2012).

34 See also John Swinton, 'From Inclusion to Belonging: A Practical Theology of Community, Disability and Humanness', *Journal of Religion, Disability and Health* 16 (2012): 172–90.

Concluding (for now) Reflections

Skeptics might still think that this is too much ado about what is of concern only to a few. There are not many people with disabilities in our churches, much less communities, they might protest. I wonder why. Perhaps people with disabilities feel neither welcomed nor as if they belong in churches that otherwise proclaim architecturally, practically, liturgically, and theologically: 'You are not welcome here!'

The fact is that about one-fifth of any population experiences impairment in some way. Certainly, there is some truth to the motto that we are all only temporarily able-bodied: we come into the world dependent on others, and if we are blessed to live long enough, we will exit this world in a similar state of dependence. Christian theologies of interdependence ought to inspire alternative perspectives on faith and ministry to either traditionalist construals or secular projects. Yet it must be confessed that the secular world, especially the civil rights movement, has led the way in championing the rights of people with disabilities. While the church should always maintain its critical posture towards society and even the political, I would suggest that ableist presuppositions have hamstrung its capacity to be the liberative force of good news for people across the spectrum of abilities. This needs to change, and such change can be facilitated by our institutions of theological education, beginning with the theological curriculum. This chapter represents but a preliminary set of considerations towards such ends.

Acknowledgements

Thanks to Andrew Picard and Carey Baptist College for the invitation to be one of the keynote speakers at their *Theology, Disability, and the People of God* conference, 1–3 July 2013, and to the conference attendees for their stimulating questions in response to this chapter. I also appreciate my graduate assistant Vince Le's help in proofreading it, and am grateful to Jason Forbes for critical comments that helped to clarify some issues. Its shortcomings remain my own responsibility.

20 The Trouble with Normal

What Difference Does a Theology of Disability Make?

Rhonda Swenson and Mary Caygill

Mary

This chapter is an exploration in the seeking of truth – truth and truths – which emanate from reflections of our embodied living experiences along with a creative searching and living into theological understandings of God, humanity, and the created world outside the exclusive and invalidating frame of both the terms and referent states of 'normal' and 'disability'. Our exploration, which is a work in progress, draws understanding and insight from the offerings of art and poetry, which Rhonda will bring, and theological musings, which I (Mary) will bring, as part of an ongoing intentional conversation between feminist, disability, and queer theological frameworks. These explorations seek to offer a contribution to the ongoing task of articulating a liberatory theological anthropology beyond the constricting and life-denying frame of 'normal'.

In my parish office, in my temporary church home in Christchurch, sits a significant symbol within a particular alcove on one of the bookshelves. It is a symbol which Rhonda created after an important conference we both attended in Wellington, New Zealand in 2003 entitled *Through the Whirlwind*. This was a significant gathering of people from Australia and New Zealand, many of whom live with the effects of varying physical and mental impairments, who gathered together in order to express for themselves their own theological and spiritual expressions of faith, articulated out of and through the materiality of their own embodiment.[1] In the centre stands this cross – named 'The Disproportionate Cross'. I hand over to Rhonda.

---

1 The proceedings of this conference have been published as Christine M. Newman, ed., *Through the Whirlwind: Proceedings from the Disability, Spirituality and Faith Conference Held at the Brentwood Hotel, Wellington, New Zealand, 1–4 May 2003* (Wellington: Disability, Spirituality and Faith Network, 2003). The importance of this conference was that in its planning and programming, most of the input came from individuals living with disability. The contents include the addresses delivered by the three keynote speakers and 22 reports from workshops.

Figure 20.1 The disproportionate cross
Source: Photo © author.

Rhonda

The cross expresses for me something of my emerging Christology. The two different-sized pieces of wood and the deliberate crooked angle reflect and encompass the body of difference within the whole body of Christ. It is deliberately disproportionate, not a straight up-and-down cross with seemingly perfect dimensions; it deliberately represents difference, the power imbalances, the varying disjunctions which I experience as part of my daily bodily living. Most disabled people do not have power, but they are whole, there is beauty in who they are, they do not have to be anything other than they are. Looking at this cross makes people think, makes people ask about my own embodied experience and my living journey to speak out who and what my Christ is. The small glass tiles around the side are grouted with black paint which runs onto the cross. Black is the colour normally used for framing, as it stands out against any other colour. Some of the glass tiles are missing – missing to create difference. The tile stuck on the front of the cross indicates that I am whole in Christ, but different, and I can be different in Christ. People often want to fix this cross, and feel uncomfortable around it. The following poem adds to the narrated framing of the cross:

Frames

Okay if you fit
the model of good
brain integration
your skills are useful
valued by pay
not half pie
fighting justifying.
Just to hang in
with something no one knows about
or how to fix.
no level of care fits the mould
the community things one does
falling apart from lack of funding.
expected to fix
no place for people
like me in the community
who don't fit the mould.[2]

My personal life journey is one marked by the constant need to navigate my way around the ideology of 'normal', never measuring up to people's perceived

---

2 This poem comes from a significant collection of poems written by Rhonda which to date have been edited, but await publication.

norms. Much of this navigating I do through my writing of poetry and creating different art forms. This assists my travels along the path of very black spaces and my coming out the other end embracing faith as a way of maintaining a sense of purpose and well-being. Creating art allows me to feel textures and mediums of paper, clay, and pencils, as well as tissue paper, torn paper, which allows me to express myself without definitions of right or wrong, or being compared with other people's art. My art is a statement of my own style, which is okay.

This piece of poetry, written between 1990 and 1995, questions why, and affirms who I am:

> To care for me
> The important skills of treating people as humans with dignity
> And the right to be no matter what
> To care to be one's self
> A composition of jigsaw and bits that don't quite fit
> Nevertheless an important contribution to society

The quiet voice of faith has allowed me to focus on art projects. For example, when feeling disassociated from my body I made a mosaic butterfly, starting with the process of smashing plates in a controlled way at Vincent's art workshop. This activity is good for the soul. Once the pieces are assembled, glued, and grouted, out of the mess comes a beautiful butterfly (Figure 20.2). This project helped me to change my mood and to feel more connected to my body.

Rhonda's evocative words, erupting out of the context of her narrated materiality, illustrate powerfully something of the implications of the hegemony of normalcy – of being trapped within the framing of normality. They also bring the stark challenge to derive and live out radically different ways of human corporeality, of being flesh, ways which will be more fully representative of the expansive, nomadic, multivariate body of God. The creation and fixing of a hegemonic frame of normality has been derived as part and parcel of the package of imperial colonial discourse, resulting in a colonization of those bodies considered to be marginal in any form, or in that distinctive language of colonialism, 'degenerate'.[3]

Now such a frame in the context of a post-capitalist age is further 'framed' by the latest 'redemptive' notions erupting out of the burgeoning industries and sciences of biotechnology fed by global economies, that in themselves feed into the mega industry of health. Such industries succeed in creating and marketing, as theologian Sharon Betcher states, a 'globally media/ted idealism' – a state in which the ideal becomes normative, and therefore 'normal'.[4] It is in Western culture, Betcher further states, where 'disability names the abject refus/al of

---

3 See Lennard Davis, *Enforcing Normalcy: Disability, Deafness and the Body* (London: Verso, 1995), chs 1 and 2, and Sharon Betcher, 'Monstrosities, Miracles and Mission', in *Postcolonial Theologies: Divinity and Empire*, ed. C. Keller, M. Nausner, and M. Rivera (St Louis, MO: Chalice Press, 2004), 79–100.
4 Betcher, 'Monstrosities, Miracles and Mission', 81.

Figure 20.2 Mosaic butterfly
Source: Author.

industrial capitalism (that is, disability as "unemployability," as deficit of "labor power"), which has now become aesthetic, consumer capitalism'.[5] Given the implication of Christianity in its legacy of casting the disabled subject in the role of 'religious other', it becomes critical that there is a critically engaged hermeneutic of suspicion around the particularity of those theological constructs which continue to feed this hegemony of the norm.

5 See Sharon Betcher, 'Becoming Flesh of My Flesh: Feminist and Disability Theologies on the Edge of Posthumanist Discourse', *Journal of Feminist Theology* 26 (2010): 107–139, 109.

Pivotal to the ongoing maintenance of this frame of 'normality' and its hegemonic power is that at its core, along with the term and category of 'disability', they are innately binary categories, and as such are a fixer of set boundaries. As feminist liberation body theologian Lisa Isherwood describes:

> dualism is a device lurking in the midst of an incarnational religion that has objectified us and made us aliens in our own skin . . . . That kind of split thinking allows us to distance ourselves, and our God, from all we do not feel comfortable with and to set in place systems that oppress and marginalize 'others'. This way of viewing the world creates a large number of 'others' and allows many perceived ills to be heaped upon them.[6]

And so normality continues to 'reign' and operate in 'Lordlike' hegemonic manner, establishing who in their varying corporeal form is to be considered as 'other' to the fixed binary norm. The result is, as Sharon Betcher states, that: 'Rather than blessing corporeal flourishing in all its multiple forms, even when it limps, wheels and winces, even progressive, liberal theologies focused on "Jesus as Healer" might be included under what theologian Marcella Althaus-Reid would designate as "decency theologies".'[7]

For 'decency theologies', read all those theological symbolic expressions which are binary in nature which 'succeed' in deciphering bodies into the status quo of the 'norm'. This norm extends to the norm of gender, heteronormativity, or the normativity which undergirds the construction of disability itself.

The radical shift espoused by the late queer feminist liberation theologian Marcella Althaus-Reid of engaging in the construction of 'indecent theology' whereby there is a 'lifting up of the skirts' of all symbolic theological constructions and theologians themselves is required in order to expose all undergirding binary fixed categorical assumptions of 'normality'. Constructing indecent theology is to engage critically in acts of 'queering'. These are acts of deliberately 'transgressing', 'querying', moving across fixed boundaries in the creative, passionate and embodied exercise of resignifying the body. As queer theologian Robert Goss helpfully outlines: 'Transgression destroys traditional boundaries or undermines established paradigms by revealing their fragility and instability. It challenges modes of regulating discourse: Who is canonically allowed to speak? Who is allowed entry? Who is denied access? Who can speak for me?'[8]

---

6 Lisa Isherwood, 'The Embodiment of Feminist Liberation Theology: The Spiralling of Incarnation,' *Journal of Feminist Theology* 12 (2004): 147.
7 Betcher, 'Monstrosities, Miracles and Mission', 84.
8 Robert Goss, *Queering Christ: Beyond Jesus Acted Up* (Cleveland, OH: Pilgrim Press, 2002), 229.

From a Foucauldian perspective, expressing resistance to an overgirding 'master' narrative is not simply to engage in a rebellious action of negation, but rather to engage in a process of creation – to give embodied voice and action and be 'driven by the imagination of alternative possibilities and hopes. Transgression is essential to the hermeneutical development of queer theologies and queer hybrid theologies.'[9]

The starting point for such queering constructions and the resultant transformative actions is the body – our bodies – the stuff of incarnation, in all our differing material forms. It is, as Isherwood speaks of being, 'the rebellious body, the body "as is" before theology starts to draw demonic and divine inscriptions upon it'.[10] It is the body both as primary context and at the same time as hermeneutical circle. But let me add, it is to the body as 'flesh' which becomes the focal text for a liberating hermeneutic. It is here more likely than not that a 'reading' of this focal text can be further and creatively explored by both feminist, queer and disability theologies to establish points of intersection.

Sharon Betcher, in an article celebrating the work of feminist and disability theologian Nancy Eiesland, who died in March 2009, suggests that: 'from a disability perspective, thinking from the flesh challenges the naturalization or normalization of the body and thereby the sociocultural and economic value of ability'.[11] Whereas *body* can invite the hallucinatory delusion of wholeness, and thus the temptation to believe in agential mastery and control, *flesh*, suggests Betcher, reflects our exposure, our vulnerability to one another.[12] Furthermore, flesh, and the realities of embodiment, cannot submit to transcendental metaphysics, and the logic of the one, as easily as the body: 'Flesh suggests that the capaciousness of a life resembles a teacup crackled with ten thousand veins.'[13] In the words of Isherwood and Althaus-Reid:

> Theology that has incarnation at its heart is queer indeed ... that the divine immersed itself in flesh, and that flesh is not divine is queer theology at its peak. There can be no sanitization here ... it is not the genetically modified, metaphysical Son of God that declares the divine-human conjunction, but the screaming baby amidst the cow shit and the fleas, covered in birthing blood and received into the uncertain arms of his child/mother, who declares salvation for all.[14]

---

9 Ibid., 230.
10 See Lisa Isherwood, 'Sex and Body Politics: Issues for Feminist Theologies', in *The Good News of the Body: Sexual Theology and Feminism*, ed. Lisa Isherwood (Sheffield: Sheffield Academic Press, 2004), 20–34.
11 Betcher, 'Becoming Flesh of My Flesh', 108.
12 Ibid.
13 Ibid.
14 Lisa Isherwood and Marcella Althaus-Reid, 'Introduction: Queering Theology, Thinking Theology and Queer Theory', in *The Sexual Theologian: Essays on God, Sex and Politics*, ed. L. Isherwood and M Althaus-Reid (London: T&T Clark, 2004), 7.

Taking incarnation as is, as Isherwood suggests,[15] enables us to see in the Jesus narrative our own multivariate material as transgressive and creative sites of revelation. In this way the flesh is enabled to become *Word*, not the other way around as it has been passed down to us, where 'The Word becomes flesh'.

It is such transgressive action which moves towards the disruption of those tendencies which are obsessed with the fixing of categories and assigning varying bodily forms and variants into imperialist neo-colonial 'zones of degeneracy'.[16] Thus 'Christ' is enlarged beyond all the encompassing heteronormative economies of the church, which include those of disabled subjective economies.

The piercing/transgressing of categories/frames in order to open up alternative spaces of discourse and action can be likened to what Musa Dube, a postcolonial feminist biblical scholar, refers to as *Semoya* space.[17] Such an openness and intentionality of space is indispensable for those seeking to give authority to the materiality of their own bodies, and thus 'talk back' to the colonial categorizations of 'degenerate', 'normal', 'abnormal', 'disabled', 'in need of redemption', by the latest commercial and neo-colonial biotechnological 'saviours'. Such movements of necessity are in themselves counter-hegemonic, and as such bring about an engagement of what theologian Eleazar Fernandez evocatively defines as a:

> 'conspiracy'. That is, following the word's root meaning, to 'breathe together'. So, to conspire together is to share breath: share life-affirming ways of thinking, dwelling and acting. The term 'companion' [*cum* + *panis* (bread)] compliments [*sic*] the term 'conspiracy'. The conspirators are companions sharing the life-giving breath as well as the nourishing bread of the journey.[18]

Both engaged actions of conspiracy and companionship, claims Fernandez, are epistemologically and politically necessary:

> They are necessary because it is only through frail instrumentality of another that we can be liberated from the regimes of truth that we create, and necessary because it is only through conspiracy and companionship that we gain the power to dismantle and construct alternative ways of thinking and dwelling.[19]

Let me hand back over to Rhonda so that she has the last word.

---

15 Isherwood, 'The Embodiment of Feminist Liberation Theology', 143.
16 See Betcher, 'Monstrosities, Miracles and Mission', 79–99.
17 Musa W. Dube, *Postcolonial Feminist Interpretation of the Bible* (St Louis, MO: Chalice Press, 2000), 116.
18 Eleazar S. Fernandez, *Reimagining the Human: Theological Anthropology in Response to Systemic Evil* (St Louis, MO: Chalice Press, 2004), 27.
19 Ibid.

Rhonda

Two other poems, written in 2011–12, reflect my battle with bureaucracy that wants everybody to be an economic unit earning a sustainable wage. Only as an economic unit earning a sustainable wage do they have value as a person. But even when the economy is booming, employers have great difficulty employing me because of the combination of the hidden disabilities I have. So there is still no fit through this frame of an economic unit.

One

Life hangs in the balance
To step off the bridge or not
To feel the wind or not
To sleep or not
Life hangs in the balance
The sun flickers
May be the switch to just absorb
Let osmosis take its place
To hang in the balance

My second poem was written after some of the political announcements were made about the major changes to come with welfare benefits. Along with these announcements were all the things assumed about people who did not fit and the judgements made about them. Without being able to find my own voice through my writing of poetry I would have turned in on myself.

To walk on water
Make the impossible happen
The sparkles drift
To carry the impossible
To only fall over time and time again
Until the fairies carry one through the water
Beyond the Pain of not achieving
Or fixing the defects that prevent
But create havoc at Work and Income
Who want the impossible?
The sparkling
Maybe it will be a relief
To entrap the impossible[1]

Author/Subject Index

ablebodied 200, 259
ableism/ableist 1, 3, 53, 62, 66, 69–71, 227, 236–238, 248, 250, 252–255, 257–261, 263
abnormalities 137, 230, 255
abortion 19, 26, 28, 230
Abraham 52, 174, 212
abuse/abused 36, 41, 89, 123, 139, 199–202, 208
accessibility 56, 70, 95, 106, 108–109, 113–114, 153–154, 164, 169
advocacy 118, 157, 162, 188
afterlife 15, 20, 231
ageing 19, 97
aid 79, 84, 105, 138, 211
akletoi 140–142, 144
alienation 125, 181
Althaus-Reid, Marcella 269–270
Ammonites 145–147
amputees 212, 231
Anderson, Ray 5, 16–18, 217
Anderson, Allan Heaton 191–192, 196
anthropology 1, 16, 48, 175, 188, 215–218, 221, 232, 237, 255–256, 259–260, 264, 271
anxiety 19, 93, 186, 193, 198, 225
Aotearoa 55, 71, 124, 199
Aquinas, Thomas 129, 256
Aristotle 12, 133
ascension 215, 221, 242
ASD (autism spectrum disorder) *see* 'autism'
assimilation 48, 55, 69, 71–72
asylum 55, 62, 202
atonement 213, 229

Augustine 67, 129, 256, 258
autism/autistic 1, 32–35, 37–40, 95, 154, 156, 159–161, 166, 169, 203
autonomy 9–11, 13, 19, 54, 64, 97, 204
Avalos, Hector 252–253

Balentine, Samuel 44, 49
banquet 129–135, 138–144, 233
baptism 120, 173, 177, 191–192, 194–195, 197, 222–223, 227, 239
Baptist 2, 70, 73, 80, 100, 222–223, 263
Barth, Karl 16–17, 44, 174, 216, 218, 256
Bartimaeus 209–210
Bauman, Zygmunt 53–55, 57–61, 63, 65
beatitudes 235, 240–241, 243–248
beggar 50, 61, 136–137, 141, 206
belonging 2, 5–6, 48, 53, 63, 68–70, 81–85, 87, 125, 128, 167, 171–173, 175, 177, 179–181, 193, 210–211, 254, 262
Bergoglio, Cardinal Jorge Mario 179–180
Betcher, Sharon 238, 267–271
Bjorck, Jeffrey 193, 198
Blomberg, Craig 242, 244
Bonhoeffer, Dietrich 18, 256
brain 13, 32–33, 39, 41, 74, 89, 96, 154, 173–174, 266
Brock, Brian 158, 167, 225, 256–257
brokenness 4, 74–75, 92, 179, 253, 258
Bromiley, Geoffrey W. 16, 44, 110, 216, 243
Brueggemann, Walter 174, 239
Buber, Martin 11–12
burden 11, 13, 54, 59, 92, 113, 169, 186
bureaucracy 235, 248, 272

Author/Subject Index

Calbreath, Donald 189, 193
Calvin, John 48, 103, 256
caregiver 24, 60, 85, 100, 166, 261
Carson, Donald A., 69, 240, 245
Carter, Erik 153, 156, 211, 261
Cartesian 12, 54, 57
celebrations 62–64, 68, 122, 126, 190
Census 95, 101, 187, 190
cerebral palsy 78, 80, 82–84, 96, 235
chaplain/chaplaincy 118, 120–121
Chapman, Lloyd 202–203
charity 43–44, 47, 51–52, 81, 85, 98, 114, 179, 204–207, 224, 252, 258
Cherry Farm Hospital 200–202
childhood 78–79, 118
Chow, John 106, 111
Christology 15, 17–20, 173, 175–176, 218, 266
church/churches 6, 63, 65, 69, 72, 81, 84, 90, 93, 95, 106–108, 113–115, 121, 123, 125–128, 152–157, 159–163, 166–171, 173, 179, 181, 188, 190, 194, 211, 238, 250, 261, 263
Cicero 136, 138
cognitive 13, 49, 73, 104, 114, 154, 219, 234
communication 33, 35, 40, 56, 71, 73, 78–79, 97, 105, 114, 116, 121–125, 259
communion/Eucharist 12–13, 15, 17–18, 63–65, 67, 70, 84, 128, 131–133, 135, 153, 213–215, 222–223, 225–227, 238, 260
companionship 91, 134, 136, 271
compassion 36, 40, 90–91, 100, 115, 174, 243–244, 248, 252
conflict 10, 27, 118
consumerism 53–54, 57–59, 61–63, 69, 72
courage 4, 79, 84, 226
covenant 16, 146–151, 223, 251
Creator 5, 174, 214, 216, 220
creaturehood 217–218
culture 48–50, 53–55, 57–59, 61–64, 66–67, 72, 97, 106–109, 113, 115, 117, 119–128, 130, 132–134, 143–144, 153, 157, 159–160, 173, 175, 186–189, 241, 245–246, 250, 254–255, 267
cure 22–23, 59, 92, 187, 189, 193, 198, 205, 229–230, 247
cystic fibrosis 21–23, 25, 27, 29–31

deaf/deafness 1, 97, 118–122, 267
deformity 42, 135, 137–140, 143, 234, 251, 254
dehumanization 3, 30, 65
deliverance 217, 240, 244–245
dementia 155, 180
demon 56, 89–91, 178, 220, 241
denominations 95, 99–100, 106–107, 117–118, 120, 126, 155, 170, 185, 189, 192–193, 195–196
dependency 62, 65, 85, 105, 125, 224
depression 89–90, 186–189, 193, 198, 202, 212
determinism 14, 16, 215, 258
diagnosis 2, 21, 24, 26–28, 34–35, 42, 89, 91, 189
dignity 10, 21, 81, 84, 98, 199–200, 202–203, 207, 218, 220–221, 243, 248, 267
disciples/discipleship 18, 83, 120, 169, 172, 241
discrimination 41–43, 45, 47–49, 51–52, 58, 97, 233
disease 11, 21–22, 27, 42, 205, 220, 241
disenfranchised 28, 130–131, 144
disfigurement 49, 138, 220
diversity 2–3, 53, 57, 62–63, 66, 82, 104–105, 126, 173–174, 177, 179–180, 185, 187, 228, 236, 241
Donskis, Leonidas 54, 59–60

ecclesiology 5, 64–65, 68, 70, 103, 194, 215, 259
education 35, 85, 106–108, 114–115, 117, 119, 121, 133, 157, 187, 192–193, 196, 198, 236, 250–251, 260, 262–263
egalitarianism 144, 190, 192
Eiesland, Nancy 70, 176, 258–259, 270
employment 9, 140, 157, 236
empowerment 45, 103, 192, 194, 197
encouragement 14, 74, 120, 168, 193
endurance 37–38
Enlightenment 10, 12, 153
epilepsy 201–202
equality 126, 134, 144, 157, 173–174
eschatology 6, 16, 18–19, 40, 66–69, 129–131, 144, 177, 187, 191–192, 194–195, 212–213, 215, 217–221, 225–233, 238, 244, 252, 257
euthanasia 19

Evangelical 154–155, 173, 250, 261
evangelism 190, 192, 195

faith 3, 25, 30–31, 38, 72, 81, 83, 90, 93, 103–105, 111–112, 114–116, 118, 120–121, 126, 146–147, 152–154, 156, 160–161, 164–166, 168–169, 171, 176–178, 186–189, 194, 196–198, 211–212, 216, 222–223, 229, 234, 241, 252, 259, 261–264, 267
faithfulness 70–71, 147, 178, 181
families 23, 53, 61, 91–92, 99–100, 117, 123, 125, 161–162, 170, 186, 222, 224, 258, 260–261
Fehr, Burkhard 140–143
fellowship 103, 105–106, 119–122, 125, 128, 131–133, 143, 214, 223, 228, 259, 261–262
feminist 232, 260, 264, 268–271
flesh 39, 178, 188, 224, 267, 270–271
Forbes, Jason 153, 155, 160, 165, 263
foreigners 36, 98
forgiveness 72, 221
Frame, Janet 201, 216–218
freedom 51–52, 54–55, 57–61, 63, 66–67, 162, 197, 206, 217, 226, 239, 256, 258
friendship 59, 78, 80, 83, 93, 102–103, 113–116, 147, 151, 157, 162, 164, 172, 180, 198, 222, 224, 226, 237, 259

Gadamer, Hans 238–239
Gale, Lindsey 153, 155, 160, 165
Gaventa, William 153, 159, 161, 168, 251
gender 106, 192, 269
genetic 17, 22, 24–27, 29, 169, 189, 230
Gentiles 68–69, 129–132, 144, 174, 242
giftedness 34, 112
Gillett, Grant 12, 14–16
glory 39, 110, 178, 212, 214–215, 226–227, 234
Goffman, Erving 48–49
gospel 2–6, 53, 63–64, 70–72, 75, 82, 84–85, 104–105, 110, 120, 124, 129–132, 143, 169, 172, 185, 189, 191–192, 194–198, 212, 223–225, 229, 240–242, 249, 259
government 9–10, 60–61, 114, 162, 169, 206

grace 4, 15, 19–20, 43, 53, 77, 104, 110, 122, 152, 178, 213, 217, 221, 223–225, 227, 231–233, 244
Grenz, Stanley 12, 14–15, 19, 192
Grudem, Wayne 103–105
guest/guesting 4, 134, 179–180
guilt 42, 92, 193, 198
Gundry, Robert 240, 244–245
Gunton, Colin 10, 12, 15–16, 64–68

Haddon, Mark 33–34
Hartley, John 44, 46
Hartog, Kristine 187, 189
Hauerwas, Stanley 53–54, 64, 70, 256
healing 15, 20, 28, 42, 67, 92–93, 99, 114, 116, 119, 132, 174–178, 180, 187, 190–191, 193–196, 210, 214, 220–221, 229–230, 237–238, 241–242, 247–248, 251–252, 257
heaven 16–17, 20, 39, 68, 72, 98, 214, 233
hermeneutics 192, 250–252, 257, 262
Hewlett, Charles 66, 71
Holden, Lynn 42, 251
holiness 39, 213–214
holistic 39, 188, 192–193, 196–197, 248, 261
hospitality 4, 94, 98, 108, 130, 134, 151, 171–172, 179–180, 221, 226, 259–260
host/hosting 4, 29, 94, 130, 134, 144, 179–180, 226, 261
Hughes, Bill 44–45, 55–58, 62, 65, 106
Hultgren, Arland 129–130
humanity 65–67, 112, 152, 172, 203, 214, 217–218, 221, 224, 226, 232, 257, 264
humanness 2, 17, 53, 92–93, 162, 167, 231, 262
humility 125, 128, 174, 198, 225, 246

identity 2, 12, 14–15, 48–49, 53–54, 57, 62, 64, 79–80, 111, 121, 133, 149, 157, 173–174, 176–177, 216, 220, 228–229, 234, 250, 256, 260
imago Dei 12, 217–218
impairment 1, 33, 43, 46–47, 57, 62, 65, 78, 82, 84, 96–97, 103–105, 117, 154, 180, 205, 231, 233, 247–248, 258, 263
incarnation 17–18, 180, 215, 220, 270–271

inclusion/inclusiveness 10, 53, 62–63, 69–70, 95, 96, 101, 106–109, 111, 113–114, 117, 121, 126–131, 152, 154–155, 157, 160, 163, 167, 170, 172, 192, 198, 210–211, 220, 222–224, 251, 262
independence 17, 59, 64, 97, 115, 204, 245, 248
individualism 10, 66, 173
inequality 50, 63, 144, 245
injustice 1, 53, 65, 97, 230, 243
institutions 41, 55–57, 59, 120, 133, 197, 200–201, 211, 250, 260, 263
interdependence 10, 106, 112, 173, 188, 263
Isherwood, Lisa 269–271
Israel 103, 129–130, 145–147, 149–150, 178, 220, 238–239, 253
IVF, 26, 28–30

Jew 68–69, 130–131, 174, 242, 251, 253, 256, 257
Jones, D. Gareth 21–31
justice 10–11, 13–14, 20, 43–44, 50, 70, 97, 145–146, 174, 200–201, 208, 241, 260

Kärkkäinen, Veli-Matti 192, 221
Kierkegaard 62, 65, 256
kindness 19, 45, 146–148, 151, 174
kingdom 129–130, 143–147, 149, 151, 192, 224, 241, 248
kingship 145, 151, 253
Koenig, Harold 186, 193, 196
koinonia 224, 259

Lawrence, Louise 2, 4
leadership 73–74, 115, 121, 123, 126, 155, 157, 159–160, 165, 192, 197
LGBTQ theology 232
Lissarrague, Francois 134, 141

McAllister, Kandace 186–187, 189, 197
McNair, Jeff 101, 152–153, 157, 165, 167–169
marginalization 99, 114, 233, 236–238, 250
marriage 75, 89, 212
Meininger, Herman 154, 158, 168

mercy 122, 147–148, 244–245
Messiah 15, 110, 220, 253
Mikaere, Ani 71–72
minorities 71–72
miracles 119, 175–176, 229, 251, 255, 267, 269, 271
mission 5, 68, 92, 111, 113, 118–120, 122, 124, 127, 160, 190, 194, 197, 214, 223, 240, 260–262
missionaries 80, 118–119, 121, 124, 191, 194
mobility 45, 56, 79–80, 96–97, 116
Modernity 1, 3, 53–64, 66, 219, 250
Moltmann, Jürgen 103, 191, 235, 238–239, 241, 243–246, 249, 259
Monteith, W. Graham 251, 253
Morris, Wayne 66, 259
Moses 174, 177–178
multicultural 63, 186

Newsom, Carol 43–44, 47, 49–50
normalization 173, 175, 270
Nouwen, Henry 225–226
NZSL (New Zealand Sign Language) 118, 120–124, 127–128

ontological/ontology 17, 44, 53, 62–66, 68–69, 216–217
oppression 1–2, 56, 63, 120, 123, 125–126, 228, 230, 233, 236–237, 240–242, 245–247, 249, 258
Origen 129, 216
orphans 36, 44
Orthodox 104, 215, 217, 232, 234
othering/otherness 2, 45, 48, 50, 52–53, 55–57, 62–64, 66–69, 245
outcast 46–47, 80, 130, 132, 180

pain 66, 179–180, 226, 231, 235, 241, 243
paralysed 175–176, 241
parenting 32–33, 35, 37–39
Parklands Residential Home 199, 208
Parousia 196, 218, 227
pastor 74, 76, 79, 101, 114, 122, 126–127, 152, 154–169, 187–189, 195–198
paternalism 50, 81, 252
patriarchal 46, 71
Pentecost 214, 242, 254, 261

Pentecostalism 96, 99–100, 149, 154–155, 185, 187, 189–198, 229, 254, 261
personhood 1, 4, 9–20, 53–55, 63–66, 73, 187, 218
Plato 132, 141
Pliny (the Elder), 135, 137
Plutarch 132–134, 136–137, 139–140
Polkinghorne, John 16, 18
postcolonial 192, 260, 267, 271
postmodern 45, 47, 55, 254
poverty 58, 95, 97, 142, 245–246
prayer 15, 30, 91, 97, 105, 112, 119, 121–122, 125, 128, 154, 193, 198, 225, 234
prejudice 55, 65, 102, 114, 228
Presbyterian 96, 100, 154, 223
privilege 71, 134
Protestant 68, 187, 189, 196, 250
psychiatric/psychiatry 42–43, 96–97, 116, 175, 193, 198, 200–202
Psychology 42, 48–49, 191, 193, 198
psychosis 90, 92
psychosomatic 42, 177

Quintilian 136–138

Rawles, John 10–11
reconciliation 53, 67–70, 103, 221–222, 245
redemption 40, 67, 179, 215, 229, 232, 257, 260, 271
rehabilitation 56, 58
Reinders, Hans 169, 225, 236–237, 259
restoration 42, 68, 128, 210, 214, 235
resurrection 18, 20, 39–40, 110, 179, 212, 215, 217, 221, 227, 229, 231, 233, 242, 257
Reynolds, Thomas 12, 15, 63–65, 84, 158, 238, 260
righteousness 39, 43, 50, 52, 243, 245–246
Rogers, Edward B., 186, 189, 198

sacraments 105, 114, 198, 222, 227, 232
salvation 68, 104, 129, 171, 177, 187, 213–215, 218, 222, 224, 227, 229–230, 233, 256–257, 270
sanctification 104, 213, 229
Schipper, Jeremy 147–149, 253

schizophrenia 1–2, 47, 89–91, 201
Schultz, Charlene 153, 166
Schumm, Darla 101, 257
Shakespeare, Tom 58–59, 207, 236
sight 134, 178, 210, 229, 239
sin 11, 17, 36, 40, 52, 58, 68, 90, 130, 171, 178, 189, 214, 220, 228, 251, 257
slave 48, 69, 134–135, 137–138, 174
Smith, Dennis 131–133, 135, 143
soul 12, 98, 188, 192–193, 216–218, 231, 236, 267
Spirit, of God 15–16, 18, 38, 40, 64, 66–68, 71–72, 96, 103–104, 173, 188–195, 197, 213–216, 218, 221, 223, 227–228, 238–239, 242, 244–247, 249, 254, 261–262
spirit 98, 188, 204, 216, 221, 241, 243, 245
spirituality 112, 126, 153–154, 171, 226, 264
Staniloae, Dumitru 218, 232
Stassen, Glen 240, 244
stereotypes 2, 71, 259
stigma 2, 4, 45, 48–49, 60, 90–91, 98, 102, 200, 255
stigmatization 49, 55, 58–59, 90, 186, 228
Stoltzfus, Michael 101, 257
strangeness 55–57, 62
strength 15, 19, 24–25, 39–40, 45–47, 52, 156, 162, 178, 224–225, 231, 242–244, 246, 248
suffering 10–11, 14, 16, 18–19, 21, 37, 42, 50, 59, 65, 91–93, 97–98, 112, 116, 123, 177–179, 204, 228, 230, 234, 241, 244–245, 248, 253, 256–257
Swinton, John 1–4, 53–54, 63–64, 70, 93, 112, 153, 158, 162, 167–168, 171–180, 225, 231, 256–257, 26

telos 14–15, 18–19, 67, 214, 216, 227
temptation 175, 239, 270
theosis 213–218, 224, 227, 234
Thiselton, Anthony 110–111, 250
Thomson, Jane 200–202
Torrance, Thomas F., 12, 16–17, 19, 44, 216–218, 221

tradition 42, 46, 67, 70–71, 126–127, 129–134, 143, 172, 193, 213, 222, 251–253, 256, 259
Transfiguration 233–234
transformation 18–20, 50, 175, 191, 215, 217, 226, 233, 235, 247
Treaty of Waitangi 62
Trinity 12–13, 18, 64, 66–67, 216
Turner, Susannah 153–154, 161, 163

United Nations Convention on the Rights of Persons with Disabilities 96, 208–209

values 10–11, 18, 27, 46, 133, 200, 208–210
Vanier, Jean 152, 225, 256
Verhey, Allen 28–29
violence 66, 236, 245
vocation 177–180, 252
vulnerability 4, 62, 65–66, 226, 270

Walton, John 44, 47, 50
Watson, Nicholas 44, 207
weakness 15, 17, 19, 46, 65, 77, 97, 110, 112, 178, 224–226, 232
wealth 41–42, 131, 134, 137, 144
Webb-Mitchell, Brent 153–154, 169, 250
welfare 26, 203, 205, 236, 272
Wharton, J. A. 44, 48
wholeness 14–15, 19, 92, 174, 179, 227–228, 270
widow 36, 44
Wilkinson, Michael 190, 194
Wolterstorff, Nicholas 11, 13, 17
women 54, 57, 73, 102, 119, 128, 137, 144, 214–218, 222
worship 63, 68, 71, 75, 93, 97, 120, 126–127, 154, 162, 180, 190, 210, 214, 223, 227, 259
Wright, N. T. 68–69, 188, 244

Yahweh 43, 51–52, 238
Yong, Amos 42–43, 175, 189–190, 192, 219–220, 222–224, 227–234, 238, 250–262
youth 80–82, 121–122, 126, 128, 156–157, 164, 167

Biblical References Index

Gen
1:27   218

Exod
4:10–17   178
4:11   97, 178, 220
22:21-23   36
31:3   103

Lev
19:11–16   97
21:16–23   220
21:17–24   251

Num
24:2–9   103

Deut
14:29   36
16:11   36
16:14   36
24:17   36
28:15–68   251
28:25–28   150
34:9   103

Judg
3:10   103

1 Sam
1:10   103
15:1–9   149
15:23   149
24:14   147
28:6   149
28:16   149
31:2   149

2 Sam
3:1   147
3:6   147
3:8   147
4:4   149
4:7   149
5   150
5:6–8   151
6:5   52
6:21   149
7:4–17   147
7:5   147
7:14–15   147
9   147, 151
9:1–13   147, 149, 151
10   147
10:1–5   147
10:6   147
16:9   147
19:27   149
21:4   149
21:7   148

2 Kgs
8:13   147

1 Chron
8:34, 35   148
9:40, 41   148

2 Chron
20:14–17   103
24:20–22   103

Job
7:4   42
7:5   32

280 Biblical References Index

7:14	42
14:5	16
19:20	42
29	43, 45, 47, 49
29:2–6	49
29:7–11	49
29:12–17	49, 220
29:15	43
30	42, 45, 47, 48, 49, 50
30:1	46, 51, 52
30:2	46
30:8	46
30:17	42
30:30	42
31	47, 49
39:5–8	51
39:7	52
39:18	52
39:22	52
41:29	52

Ps

2:4	52
24:3–6	246
68:5	36
89:28	147
104:24	52
139	16
139	17
146:9	36

Prov

10:10	245
15:25	36

Isa

10:1–4	36
25:5–6	130
52:7	69
53	253
56:3–5	220
57:19	69
61:1–2	239, 240

Jer

31:4	52
31:8	220

Amos

2:6	36

Zeph

3:19	220

Mal

3:5	36

Matt

4:23–5:2	241
7:13–14	246
9:1–8	175
10:51	180
11:19	180
11:28–30	246
17:1–8	234
22:23–28	212
23	245
24:14	192
25:24	228
25:26	228
25:31–46	252
25:39–46	18
28:19	120
22:1–14	129

Mark

2:1–12	36, 221
2:13–17	180
9:2	234
10:46–52	209
10:51	180

Luke

4:18	36
4:18–19	239
5:17–26	220
6:22	246
7:48	175
9:29	234
9:31	234
9:37–43	220
9:47–49	18
13:10–13	220
14:12–23	233
14:15–24	129–144
14:23	106
18:35–43	220

Biblical References Index   281

John
5:1-18	220
5:14	251
9:1–3	36, 251
9:25	229
10:10	82, 84
17:17	104
20:24–27	179

Acts
1:8	120
2:4	103
2:38	103
2:42	104
2:44–45	18, 36
3:12–16	221
4:8–12	221
4:32–37	18
4:34–35	36
6:1–7	36
20:32	104

Rom
5:3–4	38
7	230
8	230
8:18–38	19
8:28	15, 19
8:29	17, 104
10:13–14	104
11:11	104
12:6–8	103

1 Cor
3:3	110
3:16	173
4:8	110
1:27	77, 97
6:1–7	110
7:14	104
7:16	104
8	30
11:18–21	110
11:27–34	110
12	18, 82, 109, 173
12:4–13	261
12:7–11	103
12:11	261
12:14–26	261
12:15	82
12:21,	82
12:21–23	110
12:22	15, 97, 110
12:25–26	112
12:26	14
12:27	110
13:12	16
15	176
15:10	110
15:20–23	231
15:35–49	38
15:36–38	39
15:42	228
15:42–49	39

2 Cor
1:3–4	112
4:7	110
6:7	110
5:12	98
5:16–17	98
9:6	228
11:23–33	110
11:30	224
12:7–10	178, 224
12:9	15, 19, 110
12:9–10	77, 97
13:4	110, 224
13:11	112
15:51–52	248

Gal
2:10	36
6:7–9	228

Eph
1:13	104
2:8–9	223
2:10	37
2:11–3:21	68
2:14	84
3:10	84
4:25	105
4:32	105

Col
1:5–7	104
3:10–14	174

1 Thess
2:13 104

2 Tim
2:1–2 104

Heb
2:1 104
10:24 105
12:7–11 3

Jas
1:2–4 38
1:27 36
5:13–15 194

1 Pet
1:17 98
2:12 104

1 John
1:3 104, 105
1:24 104
3:16 170

Rev
5:9 228
7:9 228
21:24 228
21:26 228